MALE FEMININITIES

# Male Femininities

*Edited by*
Dana Berkowitz, Elroi J. Windsor, *and* C. Winter Han

NEW YORK UNIVERSITY PRESS
New York

NEW YORK UNIVERSITY PRESS
New York
www.nyupress.org

© 2023 by New York University
All rights reserved

References to Internet websites (URLs) were accurate at the time of writing. Neither the author nor New York University Press is responsible for URLs that may have expired or changed since the manuscript was prepared.

Library of Congress Cataloging-in-Publication Data
Names: Berkowitz, Dana, editor. | Windsor, Elroi J., editor. | Han, C. Winter, 1968– editor.
Title: Male femininities / edited by Dana Berkowitz, Elroi J. Windsor, C. Winter Han.
Description: New York : New York University Press, [2023] | Includes bibliographical references and index.
Identifiers: LCCN 2022036282 | ISBN 9781479839612 (hardback) |
ISBN 9781479808786 (paperback) | ISBN 9781479870585 (ebook other) |
ISBN 9781479899166 (ebook)
Subjects: LCSH: Sex role. | Masculinity. | Effeminacy. | Femininity. | Men—Identity.
Classification: LCC HQ1075 .M356 2023 | DDC 305.3—dc23/eng/20220729
LC record available at https://lccn.loc.gov/2022036282

New York University Press books are printed on acid-free paper, and their binding materials are chosen for strength and durability. We strive to use environmentally responsible suppliers and materials to the greatest extent possible in publishing our books.

Manufactured in the United States of America

10 9 8 7 6 5 4 3 2 1

Also available as an ebook

CONTENTS

Introduction: Defining and Deconstructing Male Femininities    1
*Dana Berkowitz, Elroi J. Windsor, C. Winter Han*

PART 1. HISTORICIZING MALE FEMININITIES    17

1. Toward a Typology and Genealogy of Effeminacies    21
*Peter Hennen*

2. The Effeminist Manifesto    35
*Steven F. Dansky, John Knoebel, and Kenneth Pitchford*

3. Three Contemplations on "The Effeminist Manifesto"    40
*Steven F. Dansky*

PART 2. CONFIGURING MALE FEMININITIES    47

4. Pushing (Gender) Hard on the Bike: Navigating Normativities as a Queer Spin Instructor    51
*Patrick R. Grzanka*

5. The Small ts and the Gender Binary Shake-up: The Girl in the Boy and the Boy in the Girl    55
*Diane Ehrensaft*

6. Trapped in the Glass Closet: Feminine Straight Men and the Politics of Coming Out    71
*Travis Beaver*

7. Two-Spirit, Not Trans: Joshua Whitehead's Erotic Sovereignty    90
*Lisa Tatonetti*

PART 3. EMBODYING MALE FEMININITIES    107

8. Dear Masculinity    112
*KC Councilor*

9. An Interview with Julia Serano   115
   *Stephanie Bonvissuto*

10. Unexpected Breasts, Unexpected Pleasures: Exploring Cisgender Men's Breast Development and Bra Wearing   125
    *Katelynn Bishop*

11. Brotox and the Retreat from Male Femininity   143
    *Dana Berkowitz*

12. Pregnant Men and Their Reconfigurations of Pregnancy   165
    *Mary Ingram-Waters*

### PART 4. PERFORMING MALE FEMININITIES   185

13. Welcome to the Stage: Power, Practice, and the Performance of Drag Queening   189
    *Ray LeBlanc*

14. "In My Dad's Gun Room, There's an 8×10 Picture of Me in Drag": Drag and Respect in the Deep South   193
    *Amy L. Stone*

15. The Fierce World of Gay Asian Drag   210
    *C. Winter Han*

16. "The Reason You Can Suck a Dick Is Because Some Fem Once Got Beaten Up, Right?" A Case Study of Gender, Race, and Sexuality for Latinx Queer Men   226
    *Jesús Gregorio Smith, Nikola C. Ostman, and Samantha L. Torres*

17. Radical Cheerbois: Genderqueer Bodies Performing Queer Femininity   249
    *Elroi J. Windsor*

### PART 5. MALE FEMININITIES AND INTIMACIES   255

18. Unloved   259
    *Lester Eugene Mayers*

19. Assume the Position: Bottom-Shaming among Black Gay Men   262
    *Terrell J. A. Winder*

20. Are Polyamorous Men Embodying Male Femininity?      279
    *Mimi Schippers*

21. Male Femininity as Spirituality among Radical Faeries    290
    *Rusty Barrett*

    PART 6. MALE FEMININITIES AND INSTITUTIONS    307

22. Funeral Rights    311
    *Joshua G. Adair*

23. When Our Boys Wished to Be Girls: A Retrospective Look at Parenting Gender-Nonconforming Young Boys    314
    *Graciela Slesaransky-Poe*

24. Negotiating Masculinity in the Fire Service: Accessing Brotherhood or Subverting Gender Norms    330
    *Roscoe C. Scarborough*

25. Resisting Femininity in Responsible Fathering: Men and the Gendering of Care in US Fatherhood Policy    346
    *Jennifer Randles*

    Conclusion: Male Femininities and Dismantling the Binaries and Boundaries of Gender    365
    *Dana Berkowitz, Elroi J. Windsor, C. Winter Han*

    *Acknowledgments*    369
    *About the Contributors*    371
    *About the Editors*    381
    *Index*    383

# Introduction

*Defining and Deconstructing Male Femininities*

DANA BERKOWITZ, ELROI J. WINDSOR, C. WINTER HAN

In 1998, J. Jack Halberstam published his groundbreaking book *Female Masculinity*. Instantly hailed as a classic in gender studies and queer theory, *Female Masculinity* turned traditional assumptions about the easy, casual connection between sexed bodies and gendered identities and behaviors on their heads. We now find ourselves twenty years later, and the ideas that once seemed so revolutionary percolate through our current cultural landscape in myriad ways. We are witnessing a critical historical juncture where, for small but notable populations, gender is now emancipated from the sexed body, and more and more young people are grinding against the rigidity of gender categories and labels, critiquing narrow and restrictive understandings of femininity and masculinity, and troubling the organization of gender into binary opposites.

Gender fluidity is enjoying quite the spotlight these days. In 2019, "they" used to refer to a single person whose gender identity is nonbinary, became an official pronoun and the word of the year in the *Merriam-Webster Dictionary*. Mattel has introduced the world's first gender-neutral doll.[1] In addition, since the District of Columbia and Oregon were the first to offer a third gender option on identification documents in 2017, fourteen states have followed suit.[2] Each of these individually indicate a gradual but promising chipping away at the gender binary. Taken together, they suggest that something of a monumental cultural transformation might be on the horizon.

What an exciting time to be a scholar and teacher of gender studies! In the early 2000s, when each of us began teaching about gender and sexuality, we could never have predicted the comfort with which many of our students now discuss the fluidity and permeability of gender. Today's college students came of age in a world where complicated ideas about sex, gender, and sexuality—ideas that scholars had been exploring for decades—are now taken for granted and rapidly disseminated through the Internet. The decades-long scholarly and activist project to untether sex from gender now provides teenagers the necessary muscle to unpack their own gender identities in ways that foreground more inclusive and fluid ideologies.

However, alongside this increasing comfort with gender malleability, we have found that our students struggle to grasp the complexities of contemporary gender inequality, likely because they came of age within a postfeminist and neoliberal landscape that accentuates individual autonomy, empowerment, and agency. However, as sociologists, we are all too aware that complicated systematic problems cannot be resolved with individual empowerment, and the ease with which our students embrace new gender practices and configurations often comes at the expense of a more nuanced analysis of structural and historical gender inequality.

In addition, our students are a product of the "stalled revolution"—a term coined by sociologist Arlie Russel Hochschild,[3] to refer to our current pattern of gender inequality whereby women's entrée into stereotypically masculine fields has not been matched by men's movement into comparably feminine roles.[4] While we pour tax dollars into programs that encourage girls to take up STEM subjects, we do little to encourage boys to become artists, teachers, or nurses. Feminine interests, hobbies, careers, and activities are commonly dismissed as trivial and frivolous, surely nothing to which any boy might ever aspire. Girls are regularly told they can be anything a boy can be, but to embolden a boy to behave more like a girl is an emasculating demotion. A Pew Research survey conducted in 2017 showed that, while 76 percent of the public supports parents' steering girls to toys and activities traditionally associated with boys, only 64 percent endorse steering boys toward toys and activities associated with girls.[5] One reason the gender revolution has fallen short—in addition to political, economic, and other social structural barriers—is because we have yet to culturally redefine masculinity. In a rather paradoxical twist, this has resulted in more masculinity, and not just for men. Since the 1970s, the rate at which both men and women reported masculine-stereotyped personality traits for themselves has increased. And this pattern is even more pronounced for women.[6]

Modern gender inequality is messy. It is not as simple as relegating individual women and girls to a subaltern status. More precisely, it is about the repudiation and devaluing of femininity, about a lingering disdain for all things girly and feminine. We place little symbolic and financial value on domestic labor and caregiving. Fashion, makeup, and cosmetic enhancements are trivialized as vain and shallow, yet, in most contexts, women are expected to look attractive. We penalize women who opt out of beauty culture while shaming men who opt in. Even among gay men, femininity is seen as a barrier to sexual citizenship; for them, contemporary gay life is marked by an investment in masculinity and a denouncing of femininity. An embrace of masculinity has bolstered claims of "normalhood," popular among gay rights groups, with openly gay celebrities routinely denouncing "gay stereotypes," which are understood to be characterized by gay men's feminine characteristics.

Moreover, in our very own discipline of sociology, a glaring imbalance exists in the theoretical and empirical scholarship on gender. Where sociologists have documented a multiplicity of masculinities, with complex histories and hierarchies, robust scholarship on femininities lags behind. Alongside the academic and cultural devaluing of femininity stands the aggressive objectification and (hetero)sexualization of feminine bodies—even those bodies assigned male at birth, as the 2015 *Rolling Stone* cover of Caitlyn Jenner so colorfully illustrates.

In a culture such as ours, with systemic gender inequality that depends on the repudiation of femininity and the objectification of feminine bodies, women doing masculinity has a very different social valence than men doing femininity. The former may result in increased status; think of Margaret Thatcher, Hillary Clinton, Nancy Pelosi, Kamala Harris, or any one of many other women politicians and corporate executives, who have to perform some version of masculinity in order to be taken seriously in their gender-coded professions. In that sense—as in the professions of the military, police, and firefighting—gender expansiveness by women is much more tolerated than by it is men. The assumption is that girls and women should want to experience the greater freedoms enjoyed by boys; as such, displays of female masculinity are read as a sign of liberation from the doldrums of traditional femininity.

If female masculinity often entails the embodiment of power, then what is to be said about male femininity? It is difficult to imagine it as the inverse of female masculinity—as a deliberate desire for less social and political power.

## What Do We Mean by Male Femininities?

In the pages of this volume, you will read about a diverse spectrum of male femininities. The articles and essays that grace the following pages reveal the insights we can glean from decoupling femininity from female bodies and the possibilities that open up when we critically examine femininity without women. And yet some of the examples in this volume reveal how male femininities can be strategic practices designed to maintain the problem of patriarchy against a crisis of masculinity, in which men experience uncertainty and anxiety about shifting gendered norms and expectations. As such, many of the accounts in this book reveal the limits of subversion for male femininities.

The essays selected for this volume highlight the extent to which male femininities are neither an imitation of femaleness nor an emptying of masculinity. As you will see, male femininity is not a case of men simply embracing characteristics normally associated with women, nor is it about men imitating behaviors traditionally or stereotypically associated with women. In fact, if practiced by women, much of what we might consider "male femininity" would not necessarily be seen as being particularly feminine. Definitely—borrowing conceptually from David Halperin—the lack of traits, characteristics, or qualities we deem "male femininities" among women would not make them any less "feminine."[7] Thus, male femininity is neither the opposite of masculinity nor the equivalent of femininity.

The impetus for this volume stemmed from a multitude of questions. First, given that so many studies about men have largely focused on the ways that men cling to masculinity, firmly defending its boundaries and borders, we wondered, What are the conditions under which men engage less with masculinity and more with femininity? Moreover, if femininity among men is seen as a "failure," then how can we explain the rejection of traditionally masculine ideals among some groups of men—particularly cisgender and heterosexual? Given the perceived limited value of femininity to men, traditional theorizing has largely focused on the ways that it must be managed by men or the ways that men attempt to perform, navigate, and negotiate masculinity. The question, then, is, What leads male-bodied individuals to engage in femininity in their everyday lives?

But, before we can begin to answer the questions above, we, as editors, first had to answer the most fundamental question: What even counts as "male femininity"? Is it simply men behaving in effeminate ways? And is there a reason we use the term "effeminate" only to describe feminine behavior in men? Is "male femininity" simply men "getting in touch with their feminine side"? Does it signal an absence of masculinity, or an enhancement of it? Is male femininity empowering or limiting for men? If either, when and why? It turns out that the answer is all of the above, and none of the above—that is, we find that male femininity is more than an absence of masculinity or a performance of "femininity" as it has normally been associated and/or assigned to women. In many ways, male femininity isn't simply a way for men to "get in touch" with their "feminine side," but, rather, a way of embodying, embracing, and identifying, femininities, or characteristics conventionally associated with womanhood, that are simultaneously neither "male" nor "female," but also both, and perhaps more.

In the process of conceptualizing and developing this volume, we decided to think not about male femininity in the singular or monolithic sense, but as male femininities. Male femininities are more than simply a different type of femininity that needs to be interrogated, examined, and made to fit existing theoretical and practical notions of gender. Instead, we imagine male femininities as being lived along multiple different deviations apart from both female femininities and male masculinities. It is not simply embracing the former and rejecting the latter, but a reconfiguring of both.

Our conceptualization of male femininities is based upon a social constructionist approach that accentuates varying definitions of masculinity, femininity, and the gender binary. This approach to gender reveals the ways individuals and institutions create, enforce, and challenge shared definitions of masculinities and femininities, the means by which social forces perpetuate and organize gender relations, and the role of power, privilege, and inequality in these dialectical processes. It also requires us to understand "male femininities" as occurring within this particular time period and its associated cultural contexts. In addition to viewing gender as socially constructed, our orientation to male femininities is shaped by a queer theoretical approach that problematizes and deconstructs the presumed stability of gender and sexual categories, identities, and bodies.

As a postmodern deconstruction lens applied to the domain of sexuality, queer theory unmasks the social practices that construct gender and sexual relations. This theoretical framework questions the values and assumptions embedded in constructions of sex and gender. Conceptualizing the world as composed of falsely bounded categories that give an impression of stability and permanence where none actually exists, queer theory turns the spotlight on the ways that masculinity, femininity, and the gender binary have been discursively constructed. The scholarship highlighted in this book interrogates assumptions about sexed bodies and gendered identities and teases out the complicated—and sometimes contradictory—relationships between them. Indeed, we generally use the terms "male," "female," and "intersex" to convey "sex" terminology, or the ways bodies are physically sexed through chromosomes, hormones, genitals, and gonads, but we acknowledge that sometimes people use them to articulate a gendered self. There are many terms that connote "gender" throughout this book. As you will notice, this slippage of language exists throughout the pages that follow.

Further, we challenge the notion of "femininity" itself when we focus on how men come to embody, perform, and identify with femininities. Starting from the assumption that femininity is not a submissive state, defined as the opposite or counter of masculine domination, allows us to ask a different set of questions. Specifically, what exactly is femininity? When is it empowering? When does it challenge masculinity as the "dominant" gender expression? When is it expressed independently of masculinity, and when is it commingled with it?

Much in the same way that masculinity cannot be fully understood unless it is decoupled from male bodies, we cannot fully understand femininity without decoupling it from female bodies. But we also go one step further. For example, studies of female masculinities have often focused on the ways that masculinity are embraced by people who self-identify as women, and who are most often "queer" women. Yet we note that male femininities are often embraced by people who not only self-identify as men, but as heterosexual men.

Specifically, in thinking about male femininities, we deliberately expanded our scope to include analyses of male femininities among heterosexual male bodies and men's gendered selves. That is, we were specifically interested in examining the implications of femininity not embodied by a female/girl/woman/feminine body or gender presentation. In so doing, we not only disentangle femininities from female sexed bodies but also from cisgender women's gender performances and embodiments. This allows us to move beyond thinking about "male femininity" as something that is only embodied or performed, but also negotiated and strategically deployed.

Exploring male femininities among self-identified cisgender heterosexual men also allows us to examine the ways that masculinity and femininity can be performed and embodied simultaneously. The essays in this volume illuminate the extent to which male femininity does not imply or necessitate the absence of masculinity. Thus, performing femininity does not mean that one will not concomitantly perform masculinity. Feminine traits and qualities are neither the opposite of masculine traits and qualities, nor are they on the "other" side of a continuum, which begs us to reconsider dominant configurations of gender. For example, if individuals can be simultaneously masculine and feminine, is it fair to still think of gender as a continuum rather than as discrete characteristics that can coexist?

In thinking about male femininities, we also examine how race and ethnicity complicate and expand how gender is expressed by men. In the same ways that "masculinity" is not the same for all men, we find that femininity is also often different for men of different races and ethnicities. We know from decades of critical scholarship the many ways that race has historically affected men's experiences with gender. Given this reality, there is no reason to believe that experiences of "male femininities" would be the same for all men.

## Deconstructing Male Femininity

In thinking through "male femininity" as an organizing concept, how then does it materialize? Here, lessons from queer theory and social constructionism are especially useful. These frameworks call into question the ways the term "male femininity" can function, revealing the limits and biases of language regarding sex and gender. For example, how does one's assigned sex (the sex given to us at birth and subsequently listed on government documents) and gender (everything that comes after sex assignment) give way to variations of expressing "male femininity"? What sex characteristics get coded as "male," and what gender attributes get coded as "feminine"? Is the penis always male, and breasts always feminine? The contents of this book challenge the ways certain sexed bodies are presumed to represent "natural" embodiments whereas others are artificially produced.

In reality, few bodies can be treated as truly natural. Even the most unrefined and stereotypically masculine man has likely modified his body by shaving, combing his hair, sculpting his muscles, and brushing his teeth. Sex designations, then, cannot presume an unmodified embodied state where "female" and "male" are automatically assumed to signify a particular type of sexed body that a person is born into.

Yet, in naming sex, the terms "male" and "female" do signify the sexed body—a body institutionalized as binary, despite the ways intersex bodies denaturalize this presumption.[8] Sex in humans is designated by physical traits: chromosomes, genitals, gonads, and hormones. None of these features are visible in interactions where people are clothed; all but genitals are always invisible unless detected through purposeful testing. Instead, we commonly assume one's sex category based on outward appearance.[9] A person wearing a dress and eyeliner is assumed to be a woman who must have a vagina and ovaries. A person with a bushy beard is expected to have an abundance of testosterone in his XY body. Of course, these assumptions are often inaccurate. So, the sex descriptor terms in "male femininities" and "female masculinities" rely on *assumptions* about bodies, not the *actual* bodies. In effect, anything deemed to represent a form of female masculinity or male femininity relies on assumptions—unless some kind of test is performed to determine physiological sex. And even those tests are contestable. In the absence of a sex test, bodies cue a reading as "male" or "female" that is not based on material knowledge or some objective truth. Diverse gendered embodiments carry an assortment of assumptions about sexed embodiments.

How, then, are we to characterize the gendered performances of drag queens, drag kings, and other gendered expressions? In the queer dichotomy of "male femininities" and "female masculinities," on which side would the cheerboi fall (as discussed in one essay in this book)? Halberstam's classic work on female masculinities allows for multiple formations that uncoupled maleness from masculinity.[10] Although Halberstam touches on "fag drag" as a possible performance type, the tomboys, butches, drag kings, and trans men in *Female Masculinity* usually embody a shared aesthetic. Halberstam's female masculinity projects reveal a gender expression built around traditional expressions of masculinity: stoicism, strength, dominance, aggression. But if a female-bodied person (indeed, a contestable term) deploys a sissyboy stance—a feminine masculinity—is it still female masculinity? Or is it male femininity?

To address these questions of sex and gender, we can consider the case of drag kings. Drag kings are typically assumed to have female sex traits underneath masculine drag. But the drag king's masculine gender expression also includes sex alterations—for example, a drag king may embody maleness by binding their chests flat, applying facial hair, and packing a dick. Indeed, these sexed body modifications are unnatural to that person's congenital form, but we need not privilege the natal form in designating "male." Instead, "male" bodies can include anybody that is sexed as male through both natural and modified means. After all, cissexual male bodies are varied in sex characteristics; some will have little to no facial hair, a range of testosterone levels, mircopenises that resemble large clitorises, and chests with round, full breasts. Even if we locate maleness through genital sex, a person who loses their penis and testicles through accident or illness does not also lose their social designation as "male." And chromosomes are rarely known without genetic testing; most people assume they match what we see on the body. The "male" body, then, is not a stable or universal form. Some people, like trans folks and progressive sex educators, have long accepted these truths. They have been using terms like "people with penises" in lieu of "males" or "men" for some time, recognizing the fraught usage of sex terminology. Thus, it can be argued that drag kings embody "male" bodies. A drag king who embodies the tropes of masculinity and maleness while also performing a feminine woman character may then qualify the performance as "male femininity," including Halberstam's "fag drag" performers.

Similarly, the cheerboi character resembles the drag king, but the performance is different. If we consider audience reception, we can guess that viewers familiar with drag may assume cheerbois perform from a congenital female-sexed body. But they would also be able to see hints of the sexed body—flat chests, bulging crotches, and facial hair—that signal a male-sexed body. They could not see actual genitals or gonads or review any hormone or chromosome test results. Indeed, the embodiments of drag kings and cheerbois perform male bodily sex features in ways that are exaggerated and more visible than any female traits that are simply assumed to exist. These practices can indeed be read as an expression of "male," and the fey boy performances of cheerbois and some queerer drag king performances can be read as "femininity." The embodied expression can then be called "male femininity." Yet the cheerboi can also be read as a version of female masculinity—the "true" sex of the performers expressing a gendered embodiment of fey masculinity. However, if we destabilize the privileging of congenital anatomy as the arbiter of sex, then performed embodiment reflects more of a male femininity than a female masculinity. The expressions, mannerisms, and stylistic choices lean more toward feminine/fey than masculine, while the body alterations lean heavily toward male. If we take the sexed body as the basis for designating "male" or "female," and if we include modified bodies in our designations for "male" and "female," then we can interpret these performances as embodying a male femininity.

Of course, queer theory allows us to destabilize binaries further. We might also theorize these expressions as a performed other-sexed and other-gendered embodiment, a version of the embodied self that queers both sex and gender. And, importantly, when we include intersex as a sex type, how does that wash with terms like "male femininity" and "female masculinity"? Surely intersex people and experiences may be included in the pages of this book. Yet the terms neglect to consider these embodiments. Is "intersex femininity" a possible construct? What might "intersex masculinity" look like?

Raising these questions illuminates the arbitrariness of sex and gender terms and troubles the already troubled binary that underlies them. Taking a queer theoretical approach to the language deconstructs the assumptions behind these categories and creates opportunities for exploring other shapes and shifts of these organizing concepts.

## Organization of the Volume

*Male Femininities* contributes new analyses of both emergent and historical configurations of gender. Through a collection of theoretically and empirically engaging scholarly chapters and personal essays, *Male Femininities* illuminates what happens when we decouple femininity from female bodies and how even the smallest cracks and fissures in the normative order can disrupt, challenge, and in some cases reaffirm our existing sex-gender regime.

Six interrelated sections comprise this volume: "Historicizing," "Configuring," "Embodying," "Performing," "Intimacies," and "Institutions." Siphoning essays and chapters into these discrete sections was no easy task, as many of these writings fit into many of them. Indeed, these sections and the writings within them are difficult to place into neat and tidy categories. Conceptual boundaries are porous; thus we have intersections, overlaps, and inconsistencies within and among our sections. The decisions we made about placements were fraught with tensions; in our conversations, we worried that we could misinterpret or distort the objectives of our authors. In the end, we hope that our organizational choices have honored our contributors' intentions.

We solicited readings for our volume by issuing a broad call for papers and by reaching out to selected authors who we knew had published or were currently doing innovative work on male femininities. We asked authors to compose a scholarly yet accessible essay or empirical study that interrogated the many ways that men can challenge, trouble, and subvert gender norms through practices and embodiments of varying femininities. We welcomed contributions from scholars and writers in all disciplines who could advance our understanding of the motives, experiences, and consequences associated with the individuals and groups that break gender rules through an intersectional lens. Admittedly, our final product does not exhaust the range of possible male femininities, and we acknowledge that the research and stories are situated in the contemporary United States and from mostly white scholars. Yet, at the same time, we also wonder what this focus on the experiences of white men might tell us—that is, how does whiteness afford some men different opportunities to navigate femininity? While many of the writings employ an intersectional lens to male femininities, we had hoped to include more readings that explore other axes of identity and experience, including race, ethnicity, nation, disability, body size, and age. We invite our readers to generate knowledge that more fully captures the range of male femininities not captured in these pages.

We decided to choose primarily ethnographic studies for our research-based chapters, as we wanted to present analyses of gender boundary crossings that drew from lived experiences. However, remaining true to the interdisciplinary spirit of gender and sexuality studies, some of the those chapters in this volume are more aligned with traditions in the humanities and look to history, literature, and film for illustrations of male femininities. We chose to embed six personal essays, a comic, and an interview in the text to capture the intimate and highly personal themes that reverberated among the scholarly studies. By including these personal narratives, we hope to offer readers a visceral perspective of what it feels like to resist dominant gender norms. In the end, the collection of writings that follow represent a patching together of ideas and narratives that draw from multiple perspectives and traditions in order to challenge and upend prevailing logics about gender, sex, and sexuality.

We begin the collection by looking back at some of the earliest works that explored the concept of male femininities. In this section, the readings reflect the historic origins of what we have now come to frame as male femininities. Peter Hennen's "Toward a Typology and Genealogy of Effeminacies" was among the first to explore the relationship between effeminacy and hegemonic masculinity and offered us a new way to theorize gender and sexuality. Originally published in 1973, "The Effeminist Manifesto" by Steven F. Dansky, John Knoebel, and Kenneth Pitchford was a powerful call to arms for men to embrace femininity as an antidote to hegemonic and toxic masculinity. We are also grateful that Steven F. Dansky revisited the manifesto by offering reflections on its original articulation.

We introduce the original essays in this volume with a section on "Configuring Male Femininities" that considers the social, cultural, and historical constructions of hegemonic masculinities and femininities. It begins with a first-person narrative by Patrick Grzanka, who takes us into the feminized world of boutique fitness, where he wrestles with the gender politics that surface with his emergent identity as a spin instructor. Next, clinical psychologist Diane Ehrensaft reflects on her experiences with gender-expansive children who refused to abide by cultural regulations and the implications of these young revolutionaries for a postbinary future. Drawing upon interviews with effeminate straight men who are misread as gay, Travis Beaver's chapter highlights that heteronormativity is as much about preserving binary gender norms as it is about policing sexuality. Lisa Tatonetti's essay closes out this section by exploring tensions between queer settler interpretations of "trans" and the Indigenous knowledge systems that treat Two-Spirit as a distinct gender position.

The section on "Embodying Femininities" explores what it means to alter and cultivate bodies in ways that produce or project male femininities. Using the nontraditional medium of a comic, KC Councilor explores his relationship with masculinity through the process of gender transition. Stephanie Bonvissuto interviews acclaimed scholar, artist, activist, and author Julia Serano about her musings on transmisogyny, the gender binary, and bodies, and how we might imagine a future with new and diverse articulations of male femininities. In the first empirical chapter in this section, Katelynn Bishop draws upon interviews with breasted men to demonstrate how they confront and reconfigure meanings of male femininity through the process of their breast development and decisions to wear bras. Where these findings emphasize the unexpected pleasures that emerged for some of these men and expose the way some cisgender male bodies can serve as a resource for reimagining bodies and gender, Dana Berkowitz's paper on Botox ads that target men tells a very different story; Berkowitz finds that the proliferation of these ads is neither pioneering new definitions of masculinities nor destabilizing existing binary gender systems and thus reveals the limits of subversion for some embodied male femininities. We close this section with Mary Ingram-Waters's exploration of both real and imagined male pregnancy and its potential to disrupt configurations of gender, science, and bodies.

The section on "Performing Femininities" examines the drama of male femininities from multiple perspectives and offers us ways of thinking about gender performance in new and interesting ways. Writing about their first foray into drag performance, Ray LeBlanc highlights the multiple contradictions that drag queens face, embrace, and confront. Amy Stone's examination of drag performances within the context of Mardi Gras demonstrates the ways that "femininity," often thought to divide men from one another, can be a source of respect and camaraderie within a specific context. C. Winter Han looks at the experiences of gay Asian drag queens to demonstrate how performing femininity can be a form of disidentification that works to counter negative racial stereotypes based on gender. In examining the erotic gendered performances of Latinx men, Jesus Gregorio Smith, Nikola C. Ostman, and Samantha L. Torres demonstrate the ways that gender roles and gender performances are influenced by contextual factors and how femininities can be empowering in unlikely situations. Finally, Elroi Windsor's essay on radical cheerleading illustrates the complicated ways that "femininity" and "masculinity" can coexist simultaneously.

The section on "Male Femininities and Intimacies" examines how male femininities influence the relationships men have with other men as well as with the larger society. Lester Mayer's essay explores the difficulties of forming relationships with other men as a feminine-identified Black man. Terrell Winder takes up the question of bottom-shaming among gay Black men and the complicated negotiation of both femininity and masculinity that being a bottom entails. Mimi Schippers explores the gendered negotiations among heterosexual polyamorous men and argues that polyamory can lead to men embracing a particular kind of male femininity. Closing out this section, Rusty Barrett examines the spiritual nature of male femininities in Radical Faeries.

In the final section, we offer a collection of writings about the way male femininities are experienced in the social institutions of family and work. In a deeply personal essay, Josh Adair writes about his experience at his partner's funeral, elucidating how public displays of nonheterosexual grief and mourning are disciplined in heteronormative spaces. Next, in a retrospective study that weaves together personal experience and interviews with parents raising gender-nonconforming boys, Graciela Slesaransky-Poe reflects on how parents traversed these once unfamiliar waters, and how many ultimately became radical translators of the gender order. In a compelling ethnographic study, Roscoe C. Scarborough interrogates the way gender-nonconforming firefighters negotiate masculinity on the fireground and around the firehouse. Jennifer Randles closes out this book with an analysis of a group of low-income fathers of color wrestling with messages about masculinity, femininity, and engaged fathering.

## Contributions and Implications

We believe this volume will stimulate new analyses of gender, specifically provoking discussion on the ways maleness joins with femininity to produce varied experiences, identities, embodiments, and social relationships. We engage with conversations around femininities to amplify scholarly attention to this underexplored field of analysis. In framing male femininities broadly, we also enrich the study of men and masculinities. Overall, we treat the examination of feminine gender expression, regardless of sex and gender, as a worthwhile political project. Importantly, we recognize that the idea of male femininity has taken limited forms in the popular imagination. We need an end to practices, institutions, and norms that privilege some ways of doing gender and marginalize all others. If the voices and experiences in this volume tell us anything, it is that we need to reduce pressure on people to conform to specific ways of doing gender—specifically the ways masculinity is too frequently heralded, in most institutional contexts, as the ideal form.

As the editors and contributing authors of this volume, we invite readers to discover the diverse and multifaceted experiences, performances, and embodiments of male femininities and explore the ways that gendered practices not subsumed by the masculine/feminine binary are experienced and organized. Where many of the stories in this volume illuminate our potential to unsettle and challenge our dominant gender classification system, exposing cracks in the binary façade, some also speak to the limits of gender and sexual autonomy and the extent to which our identities are constrained by an array of institutional forces. In the end, we hope the book gives readers a deeper understanding of the complexities of systematic gender inequality, and the power that we each have to trouble current conceptions of masculinity, femininity, and the gender binary.

NOTES

1 Eliana Dockterman, "'A Doll For Everyone': Meet Mattel's Gender-Neutral Doll," *Time*, September 25, 2019, https://time.com.
2 Hollie Silverman, "2 More States Will Offer a 3rd Gender Option on Driver's Licenses," CNN Health, August 1, 2019, www.cnn.com.
3 A. R. Hochschild, *The Second Shift: Working Parents and the Revolution at Home* (New York: Viking Penguin, 1989).
4 Claire Cain Miller, "Why Men Don't Want the Jobs Done Mostly by Women," *New York Times*, January 4, 2017, https://www.nytimes.com.
5 J. M. Horowitz, "More in US Say It's Good for Girls to Try Boy-Oriented Toys, Activities than Vice Versa," Pew Research Center, August 7, 2020, www.pewresearch.org.
6 J. M. Twenge, "Changes in Women's Assertiveness in Response to Status and Roles: A Cross-Temporal Meta-Analysis, 1931–1993," *Journal of Personality and Social Psychology*, 81 (2001): 133–45; J. M. Twenge, "Status and Gender: The Paradox of Progress in an Age of Narcissism," *Sex Roles* 61 (2009): 338–40.
7 David M. Halperin, *How to Be Gay* (Cambridge, MA: Belknap Press of Harvard University Press, 2014).
8 Georgiann Davis, *Contesting Intersex: The Dubious Diagnosis* (New York: New York University Press, 2015).
9 Candace West and Don H. Zimmerman, "Doing Gender," *Gender & Society* 1 (1987): 125–51.
10 Jack Halberstam, *Female Masculinity* (Durham, NC: Duke University Press, 1998).

PART 1

# Historicizing Male Femininities

It is tempting to believe that the concept of male femininities is an entirely new one that arose out of the rapidly changing gender landscape over the past few years. However, as with most things we believe to be "new," scholars and community activists have been writing about femininity among men well before our contemporary gender revolution. While they may have used other words to describe the patterns they were observing, it is obvious from their work that these were some of the earlier attempts to chronicle the ways that men were challenging masculinity by engaging in "male femininities."

For example, Esther Newton's 1972 book, *Mother Camp*, was one of the earliest attempts to systematically describe the life of drag queens and the various ways that men perform femininity. However, it was not welcomed by the scholarly community and received little attention from academic audiences. In fact, following its publication, the book was never reviewed in anthropology journals, and Newton would later note that she received little support from the original publisher, Prentice-Hall. This was startling, given that Laud Humphreys's book *Tearoom Trade*, published two years earlier, about gay public sex, not only sold well, but was widely discussed both within and outside of academia.

Perhaps the disparity can be attributed to the very different ways that the two authors framed what it means to be members of a "deviant" sexual community. For example, Humphreys's subjects were often closeted gay, bisexual, or heterosexually identified men who engaged in clandestine sexual acts with other men while leading allegedly "straight" lives. In some ways, his work was among the first to present men who had gay sex as being "normal," "just like everyone else," and therefore not threatening to general society—what today we might call the "good gay," deserving of public empathy and acceptance.[1]

Yet Newton's book focused on those "unconventional" queers that were—and continue to be—marginalized, even inside gay communities. In *Mother Camp*, Newton wrote wrote about the nellies, street fairies, aunties, and drag queens that populated gay night life with a brutal honesty that depicted them as complex human beings rather than caricatures. Doing so, Newton gave us a new understanding of "male femininities" in a culture that equates masculinity with normality. In 1979, the book was reissued by the University of Chicago Press and has remained in print ever since. In the meantime, Newton has garnered widespread acclaim for what has now come to be seen as a groundbreaking ethnographic study, and *Mother Camp* finally received its academic due in a special book review section published in the *American Anthropologist* in 2018.

In this section, we provide a glimpse into the ways that scholars and activists have historically theorized male femininities, using two previously published essays and a reflection on one of them. Originally published in 2001, Peter Hennen's "Toward a Typology and Genealogy of Effeminacies" examines the historical uses of effeminacy in Europe and the United States to reveal its linkages to "deficient citizenship, a general lack of sexual restraint, excessive heterosexual behavior, exclusive connection with passive homosexual activity, and finally as an incorrigible orientation regardless of sexual role."[2] In this essay, Hennen develops five typologies of effeminacies while also tracing the long-standing relationship between effeminacy and homosexuality.

After outlining the typology of effeminacy and its conceptualization, Hennen tracks when and where the dominant meaning of effeminacy was transformed to indicate homosexuality. Much like the way that "gay" as an identity was not a historic given, Hennen suggests that the link between effeminacy and homosexuality was also not axiomatic—that is, gay men did not come to be seen as effeminate because they were feminine, but because effeminacy was projected onto gay men. And, much like the ways that heterosexuality was conceived as oppositional to homosexuality, effeminacy was conceived as oppositional to the more masculine demands made on heterosexual men.

When first published in 1973, "The Effeminist Manifesto" was an attempt to address, and counter, what was seen as a root case of not just sexism but all other forms of oppression. The Effeminists, founded in New York City by Steven F. Dansky, John Knoebel, and Kenneth Pitchford, aligned themselves with the women's liberation movement and held the viewpoint that sexism produced racism, classism, ageism, economic exploitation, and ecological imbalance. In their manifesto, the three founders argued that "all women are oppressed by all men," and that "sexism itself is the product of male supremacy." And, as effeminate men, they were also oppressed by masculinist standards." At the same time, they recognized that, as men, despite being effeminate, they were still part of the patriarchal system that oppressed women and, by extension, all marginalized people. To counter such oppression, they challenged men to confront their own "misogyny and effemiphobia." In this vein, their manifesto hearkens back to Newton's work on demonstrating the way nellies, street fairies, aunties, and drag queens embraced femininity rather than shunned it and used femininity to confront misogyny. While the Effeminists saw homosexuality as a challenge to then-conventional notions of masculinity, they recognized that gay men contributed to the oppression of women in a number of different ways, including the performance of drag, which they perceived as a mockery of women. Although, as a group, the Effeminists never grew beyond their original three members, their manifesto had a lasting impact on the way that we came to see how masculinity is implicated in the oppression of all people, including "masculine" men.

When we reached out to the Effeminists, asking them permission to reprint their manifesto, one of them, Steven F. Dansky, wanted the opportunity to revisit his public declaration, after nearly five decades, to offer three new contemplations. In the only original essay in this anthology, Dansky helps us better contextualize the historic moment when "The Effeminist Manifesto" was written, the social changes that led to writing it, and the social changes that it brought about. More important, by historically situating the manifesto, Dansky returns to the moment of its origin in order to allow us to reconsider some of the "egregious assertions" common to the time that must now be addressed.

Taken together, these readings introduce us to the historical context of male femininities and provide a blueprint for the ways that effeminacy and femininity have long played a role in shaping the lives of men. The authors in this section were instrumental in documenting how men, at different historic moments and in different social settings, employed male femininities to challenge dominant narratives about what it means to be a "man." We are indebted to these authors for establishing the scholarly foundation of this text, by laying the groundwork for new ways of theorizing, analyzing, and thinking about masculinity that goes beyond considering it and femininity as polar opposites that need to be analyzed separately.

NOTES

1 C. Winter Han, *Racial Erotics: Gay Men of Color, Sexual Racism, and the Politics of Desire* (Seattle: University of Washington Press, 2021).
2 Peter Hennen, "Powder, Pomp, Power: Toward a Typology and Genealogy of Effeminacies," *Social Thought and Research* 24, nos. 1–2 (2002): 121–44.

# 1

## Toward a Typology and Genealogy of Effeminacies

PETER HENNEN

While effeminacy as a cultural concept has been a popular topic among scholars working in history and cultural studies, among sociologists it has not attracted the attention it deserves. This is unfortunate, as a given society's concept and deployment of effeminacy not only reveals a great deal about the prevailing sex/gender system but also yields some important clues as to the dynamics of gender relations within it.[1] My essay is an effort to address this gap in the literature. I begin by looking at some problems of definition with respect to effeminacy, then introduce a typology of effeminacies that reveals the widely varying historical uses of effeminacy, while also tracing its protean relationship with homosexuality. Next, I revisit a popular explanation for the "marriage" of effeminacy and homosexuality, applying my typology to enhance this explanation.

## Problems of Definition

In attempting to devise any meaningful definition of effeminacy, the first issue to be addressed is the misogyny inherent in the term itself. A typical dictionary definition makes it clear that effeminacy is a quality "of a man" who is considered "soft or delicate to an unmanly degree in traits, tastes, habits, etc.," who is "womanish, characterized by unmanly softness, delicacy" and "self-indulgence."[2]

What is startling here is how little this definition actually reveals. Each of the attributes included could easily be recast in a positive light ("soft" becomes "sensitive and understanding"; "delicacy" becomes "refinement"; "unmanly traits, tastes and habits" indicate the cultured man of good breeding; "self-indulgence" becomes something like "taking care of yourself"). The critical component seems to be "womanish," along with the fact that the term is used almost exclusively as a pejorative, and in most contemporary usage strongly suggests homosexuality. Effeminacy, far from implying that a person actually is a woman, signals that a man is "woman-like." The tension between the "reality" of biological sex and the prescribed gender performance is transformed into a personal failing. The fact that this charge is extraordinarily effective in bringing about a desired change in behavior is one more indication of what psychologist Robert Brannon terms "the relentless repudiation of the feminine."[3] As such, I believe it provides a unique perspective from which to analyze the sex/gender system of a given society. More specifically, an analysis of the historical uses of effeminacy can be seen as an indicator of a society's assumptions and attitudes toward women. My focus in this essay is on the varying relationships between effeminacy and hegemonic masculinity—in other words, how effeminacy is used to distribute power among men (rather than between men and women) with particular emphasis on its association with homosexuality.[4]

In an effort to revise the above definition, a brief review of the historical meanings of effeminacy is in order. In *The History of Sexuality, Volume 2* Michel Foucault observes that today "no one would be tempted to label as effeminate a man whose love for women leads to immoderation."[5] However, in ancient Greece men who indulged themselves "immoderately" (either in same- or in opposite-sex relations) were considered effeminate. This is because the virtue of "moderation" was understood as an inherently masculine trait. According to the ancient Greeks, "immoderation derives from a passivity that relates to femininity. To be immoderate was to be in a state of nonresistance with regard to the force of pleasures, and in a position of weakness and submission."[6] Thus, "the dividing line between a virile man and an effeminate man did not coincide with our opposition between hetero- and homosexuality; nor was it confined to the opposition between active and passive homosexuality."[7] The objects of normative sexual desire for adult male Greek citizens ranged from women to boys, slaves (male or female), and noncitizens (male or female). As long as the same-sex relations of the adult male citizen occurred with these partners, who assumed the passive role in any form of intercourse, and as long as the activity was considered "moderate," there was little stigmatization attached to the behavior, and the charge of effeminacy simply did not apply. On the other hand, for adult male citizens of ancient Greece, this equation of effeminacy with immoderation was of monumental importance with respect to their participation in the public life of the polis. The effeminate was understood as one who had allowed himself, through immoderate sexual activity of virtually any kind, to be distracted from his public duties.

In *The Wilde Century: Effeminacy, Oscar Wilde and the Queer Moment*, author Alan Sinfield provides what amounts to an extended history of effeminacy in Western Europe. His major claim is that the connection between effeminacy and homosexuality—advanced as necessary and natural by much of our contemporary culture—is in fact a fairly recent (and socially constructed) phenomenon. His research reveals that, in fact, the very meaning of the word "effeminate" has changed dramatically in the past three centuries. Originally it indicated an overabundance of feminine sentimentality and emotion. The object of the effeminate man's affection could be either male or female; this had essentially no bearing on his effeminacy. The critical feature was the fact that he was "woman-like" in his emotional attachment. Thus, during the eighteenth century men were sometimes warned to limit their contact with women lest it make them "effeminate."

According to Randolph Trumbach,[8] by the dawn of the eighteenth century in England, the fop, the dandy, and the beau were already coming to be replaced by the "molly," an effeminate male presumed to be interested exclusively in other, masculine men. Drawing on a range of cross-cultural evidence, Trumbach argues that figures such as the molly appear as a kind of "bridge" between binary sex roles in societies where those roles are moving toward similarity. Trumbach attributes the emergence of the molly in England to certain broad-based structural changes that were taking place with respect to marriage and the family, as well as to a growing recognition that these changes were in some appreciable way taking British society in the direction of gender equity. Thus, the molly served the interests of hegemonic masculinity in that he clearly demonstrated the distinction between those men who were quite literally "becoming women," and those whose masculinity remained untainted.

Sinfield takes a different approach, arguing that the sensational series of trials that put Oscar Wilde's homosexual affairs on display in England functioned as a kind of historical catalyst that forever cemented the connection between effeminacy and male homosexuality in the public's mind. Unlike Trumbach, he contends that, before these trials, the kind of "decadence" displayed by Wilde would have been more likely interpreted as evidence of heterosexual licentiousness than homosexuality. Wilde's effeminacy allowed for an understanding of homosexual behavior that left the sex/gender system unchallenged. Although it might be stigmatized and condemned, a "womanish" man's desire for another man served to bolster Victorian assumptions about the necessary and "natural" connections between sex, gender, and sexual object choice.

In "Chicano Men," Tomas Almaguer argues that although stigma accompanies homosexual practices in Latin culture, it does not equally adhere to both partners. It is primarily the anal-passive individual (*cochón orpasivo*) who is stigmatized for playing the subservient, feminine role. He cites Roger N. Lancaster, who observes that the insertive partner (the *activo* or *machista*) typically "is not stigmatized at all and, moreover, no clear category exists in the popular language to classify him. For all intents and purposes, he is just a normal male."[9] In fact, the active partner in a homosexual encounter often gains status among his peers in precisely the same way that one derives status from seducing many women.

In *Manhood in America*, Michael Kimmel remarks on the political uses of effeminacy in the days leading up to the American Revolution. The aristocratic world of Great Britain was understood as effete, impotent, and soft in comparison to the rugged individualism of the evolving American consciousness. In later years [the performance of] effeminacy was enlisted to assuage white men's anxieties around race and class, as in the "effeminate progeny of mixed races, half Indian, half Negro, sprinkled with white blood."[10] Effeminacy became something of a fashion statement during the early part of the twentieth century; in fact, it was all the rage during the 1920s "pansy craze" in New York City. Ironically, the "craze" was fueled by Prohibition (originally designed to control morally suspect forms of entertainment), which allowed for the expansion of a sexual underworld closely associated with illegal speakeasies. The upper crust flocked to Times Square to see all manner of "gay" entertainments featuring flamboyant, effeminate, and presumably homosexual men in various clubs and theaters.[11] After a subsequent crackdown on such entertainment in the early 1930s, many otherwise conventionally gendered gay men continued to advertise themselves sexually to other men by adopting an aggressively effeminate persona in public. Thus, an ascendant public perception that linked effeminacy with homosexuality was immediately exploited for practical purposes by gay men themselves.

Cold War America saw one of the most effective political deployments of effeminacy with McCarthyism's portrait of the homosexual as "security risk."[12] This equation revived the classical Greek notion of the effeminate as failed citizen, with at least one important change. Here the logic of hegemonic masculinity confidently assumed that the link between effeminacy and homosexuality was both natural and necessary, a situation that continued until the years immediately following the Stonewall rebellion of 1969.

In his study of gay masculinity, Martin P. Levine reveals that while an authentic challenge to the sex/gender system was launched by the more radical wing of the gay movement in the years immediately following Stonewall, its appeal was short lived. Hennen soon after documents a flight from effeminacy. In this excerpt from one of Levine's field interviews, an aging member of the gay community in New York casts a jaundiced glance backward as he assesses some of the changes in gay culture during the early 1970s[13]:

> Honey, when you have been around as long as I have, you get to know a lot of men. Over the last few years, I have watched many of these girls change as the times changed. A couple of years ago, they had puny bodies, lisping voices, and elegant clothes. At parties or Tea Dances, they came in dresses, swooning over Garbo and Davis. Now, they've "butched up," giving up limp wrists and mincing gaits for bulging muscles and manly handshakes, giving up fancy clothes and posh pubs for faded jeans and raunchy discos.[14]

From the preceding historical survey, we see that effeminacy has alternately been understood as 1) a passive disposition toward pleasure and self discipline that was perceived as "womanish"; 2) a moral failure resulting from a kind of "contamination" by the feminine; 3) a willingness toward objectification in sex; 4) a means of resolving tensions within a particular sex/gender narrative; and, finally, 5) a way of presenting oneself to the world, through either a style of dress or movement (or both) that is understood as "womanly." Although they do not correspond exactly, I use these observations to develop a five-point typology of effeminacy in the next section, but I conclude this one by offering the following (provisional) definition of effeminacy: "Effeminacy is a historically varying concept deployed primarily as a means of stabilizing a given society's concept of masculinity and controlling the conduct of its men, based upon a repudiation of the feminine that recognizes it as a 'present absence.'"

Thus, effeminacy can be seen as a disciplinary development within hegemonic masculinity: a mechanism that, despite its widely varying cultural and historical manifestations, provides a remarkably effective means of policing the boundaries of acceptably masculine behavior. Furthermore, I mean to suggest here that the concept of effeminacy encodes some of the central paradoxes of masculinity as it currently operates in most industrialized cultures. "Real men" are never feminine, yet they must remain ever vigilant against the feminine. Masculinity is an essential and natural consequence of biological sex, yet it must be carefully taught and learned. Authentic masculinity implies freedom and control, yet anything marked as feminine is strictly proscribed.

## A Typology of Effeminacies

The typology I present here is not meant to identify types of people, but, rather, a description of socially intelligible activities in which certain people occasionally engage. Although I have made an attempt to construct an exhaustive typology, I do not see the various forms of effeminacy as mutually exclusive. A great deal of overlap between these types should be expected when considering any specific historical case.

### Political

Here effeminacy represents a lack of fitness for citizenship and the demands of active involvement in state activities. This type predominated in ancient Greece.[15] Where this view of effeminacy prevails, it may or may not be associated with same-sex desires, or it may pertain only to specific practices, regardless of sexual object. For example, in Ancient Greece, same-sex desire and behavior was neither proscribed nor feminized; rather, any indicator of submission among male citizens (including but by no means limited to passive anal sexuality) was marked as effeminate and condemned as evidence of poor citizenship. On this reading, effeminacy represents a significant danger to the political health of the polis. As with nonsexual forms of passive behavior, the male citizen's active involvement in affairs of state is threatened by adopting a passive sexual role.

*Moral*

On this view, effeminacy is understood as a form of moral weakness—specifically, a "softness" with respect to pleasure. The effeminate man is prey to his passions, for food and creature comforts as well as sexual gratification. An inability to rein in these passions is understood as "womanlike" and provides a sharp commentary on the debased status of women with respect to morality. This form of effeminacy is decidedly not associated with exclusive homosexuality. Instead, it assumes that all men must remain vigilant against the temptations of excessive sexual activity in general. As sexual objects, this form of effeminacy makes no distinctions between women, men, animals, or the effeminate's own body. Lack of self-control (rather than sexual object choice) is the critical factor, and effeminacy assumes that all men are equally vulnerable to temptation from women and men.

*Cosmetic*

This form of effeminacy emphasizes outward appearance as an indicator of the "womanly" man. Specifically, the use of women's clothing, jewelry, and makeup is understood as signaling effeminacy. Thus, this type of effeminacy is employed in categorizing a wide range of men who alter their appearance in violation of conventional norms of masculine dress and grooming.

*Somatic*

This form reads the body itself, rather than the accoutrements of dress and makeup, as evidence of effeminacy. It can be further divided into kinesthetic effeminacy, where a man is judged by prevailing standards to be either moving or using his voice "like a woman," and anatomical effeminacy, where a man's genitals, build, or facial features are interpreted as feminine or less than masculine.

*Appended*

This is a new form of effeminacy that has emerged only recently: an ironic deployment of cosmetic effeminacy to underscore masculinity and, indirectly, heterosexuality. It is a flamboyant and playful display of what I would call "straight camp" that invokes a theatrical display of the "feminine side" of men whose masculinity is beyond question. This form is particularly interesting because it begins to address one of the paradoxes of masculinity outlined above: authentic masculinity implies freedom and control, yet all that is marked as feminine is strictly forbidden.

The Marriage of Effeminacy and Homosexuality

I turn now to an application of this typology to a specific historical puzzle. When and where was the dominant meaning of effeminacy changed to indicate homosexuality? Why did this transformation occur when and where it did? With his study of the sodomitical cultures of Enlightenment England, Randolph Trumbach provides the most comprehensive account in response to these questions.[16] While several scholars have placed the "wedding date" for effeminacy and homosexuality sometime in the middle to latter half of the nineteenth century, Trumbach traces the relationship back much further.[17] He finds evidence as early as the twelfth century: that "whenever homosexual behavior surfaced at the royal courts . . . it was accompanied by what contemporaries viewed as markedly effeminate behavior."[18]

This is the first instance in which distinctions between types of effeminacy may be of use. I would suggest that aristocratic effeminacy is best understood as a subset of what I have identified above as moral effeminacy, with one important caveat: the immorality of this form of aristocratic behavior is attributed to it from outside of elite circles and is understood as an aristocratic indulgence unto itself, quite separable in the popular imagination from the aristocratic indulgence in same-sex passion. Aristocrats themselves held a different view of their effeminate behaviors. First of all, despite the fact that both effeminacy and sodomy were associated with the aristocracy, they were not necessarily correlated with each other. Among the elite, effeminate behavior (including transvestism) may have been understood as "good clean fun," part of the privilege accorded to those with high social standing, appreciated even by those aristocrats who explicitly scorned same-sex activity.[19] From the perspective of the aristocrats engaged in it, effeminacy may perhaps be best described as a kind of carnival. In the terms I've introduced here, it was more likely understood as something closer to cosmetic, or perhaps even somatic effeminacy than moral effeminacy.

Trumbach makes it clear that the association between homosexuality and effeminacy was not completely secured in the popular imagination until the eighteenth century. He explains this as a reaction to the confluence of two distinct historical trends. The first trend is the development of a distinctly homosexual London subculture at least partially reliant upon secret meeting places, and the popular descriptions of these places that emphasized the effeminate behavior of their patrons. Beginning in 1699 and again in 1707 and 1726, London authorities began raiding "molly houses" in various parts of the city.[20] These houses provided clandestine places for men with same sex interests to meet. They were also the site of flamboyant displays of transvestism and effeminacy. An agent who visited a molly house in advance of a raid left this account as part of a court transcript: "On Wednesday the 17th November last I went to the prisoner's house in Beech Lane, and there I found a company of men fiddling and dancing and singing bawdy songs, kissing and using their hands in a very unseemly manner."[21]

The existence of the London molly houses shows that a subculture of men with same-sex interests existed as early as the late seventeenth century, and Trumbach notes that "descriptions of the sub-culture which were intended for the general public always emphasized its effeminacy."[22] However, there seems to be a wide discrepancy between the interpretations encouraged by such popular accounts and the understandings of the mollies themselves. The key to understanding may lie in an appreciation of the particular type of effeminacy celebrated in the molly houses. Trumbach notes that the London mollies were primarily drawn from the middle and lower classes, and that popular opinion held (erroneously) that molly houses were frequented primarily by aristocrats. Thus, the flamboyant displays of effeminacy in the molly houses may easily have been understood by their lower- and middle-class patrons as little more than a playful and theatrical form of social climbing, perhaps designed to assuage misgivings these men may have had about the legitimacy of their desires and the community they were forming.

It is important to remember that although public concern with the existence of the molly houses waxed and waned throughout the eighteenth century, when the crackdowns came they were swift and terrible. The raids (particularly one in 1726, involving some twenty houses) resulted in executions, imprisonment and suicides.[23]

The second trend that helped to secure the relationship between effeminacy and homosexuality, according to Trumbach, was the reaction against the "sentimental movement" that increasingly came to bear on heterosexual gender relations during the eighteenth century. According to its tenets, married men and women were encouraged to form close bonds that emphasized the intimacy of the marital relationship and introduced an egalitarian element not present in earlier conceptions of marriage. "But it is apparent," Trumbach remarks, "that a married man who went to whores did so in part because he wished to limit the degree of intimacy with his wife."[24] It seems that the gendered sexuality of many eighteenth-century men was still effectively governed by close associations between women, intimacy, and effeminacy. Furthermore, with the vitriolic reaction to effeminacy in London's molly houses, these men may have had an additional reason for patronizing prostitutes:

> The man without a wife who went to whores did so for a different but related reason. He was determined to show that his sexual interest was exclusively in women and that he was not an effeminate passive sodomite. Though it may not seem so at first, it is very likely that this fear of male passivity and the new sodomitical role that it produced in the early Enlightenment was also a consequence of the anxieties induced by the new ideal of closer, intimate, more nearly equal relations with women. . . . The sodomite and the prostitute guaranteed that ordinary men would never be transformed into women as a result of the intimacy or the passivity that might be produced by more nearly equal relations between men and women.[25]

"What changes, then," Sinfield writes, "is that male and female become polar opposites."[26] This is in line with the transition among natural scientists investigating the human body, from a one-sex model that emphasized sameness to the two-sex biological model that prevails today.[27] It also marks the beginning of a new understanding of gender, where masculinity and femininity are interpreted as the essential, natural developments of two entirely different sexes. In this new understanding, effeminacy quickly comes to be deployed as a means of policing the boundaries between effeminate men and "real" men, between men and women, and between prescribed homosocial relationships and proscribed homosexual relationships. This continues to be important, especially in the case of men who submit to the passive role in anal intercourse. The revised sex/gender system demands that he be feminized. Otherwise, a man who "takes his sex like a woman" might accidentally be treated socially as a "real" man.

In this concluding section, I would like to briefly examine what has become of effeminacy in light of gay liberation and poststructuralist challenges to gender essentialism. It would be inaccurate to say that such challenges have not had their effects. Gender today is much more likely to be understood as something people do than something people are.[28] Yet even a cursory glance at contemporary culture yields evidence that effeminacy's disciplinary power is far from exhausted. On the contrary, it may be generating anxieties in previously unimaginable domains.

In 1982, a novelty book entitled *Real Men Don't Eat Quiche* became an instant best-seller. The book provides a tongue-in-cheek guide to help heterosexual men secure their masculine identity and avoid looking like effeminate "quiche eaters." In addition to quizzes and cartoons, the book is filled with prescriptions and proscriptions, many in the form of lists (real men versus quiche-eaters). For example: "Three things you won't find in a real man's pocket: 1. lip balm 2. breath freshener 3. opera tickets."[29] That the book was enormously successful is perhaps not surprising; its publication seemed perfectly timed to exploit men's postfeminist gender anxieties. What is a bit surprising is that 1982 also saw the publication of another guide to masculinity, *The Butch Manual*, which targeted an exclusively gay male readership. The differences between the two books are not nearly as striking as their similarities. Consider this example from *The Butch Manual*: "Things tricks will not find in butch's bathroom: a soft plastic toilet seat, designer towels with a matching bath mat, a shower curtain."[30]

Twenty years later, this spirited revival of masculinity continues, with the parallels in the gay and straight male communities more apparent than ever. In 1999 *The Man Show* debuted on a cable comedy channel and has enjoyed high ratings ever since. Billed as the "anti-Oprah," the show proceeds from an unapologetic recuperation and boisterous celebration of "real" masculinity—political correctness be damned. On *The Man Show* real men are relentlessly heterosexual but denigrate and objectify women (gleefully; each episode ends with images of young buxom women jumping on trampolines). Male homosexuality is figured as inherently effeminate, and hosts Adam Carolla and Jimmy Kimmel spend much of their time defining the "real man" against the affectations and histrionics of the effeminate homosexual. Curiously, at about the same time, a website targeting gay men, StraightActing.com, debuted, billing itself as "masculinely politically incorrect" and dedicated to disparaging gay effeminacy. The emergence of the site can be seen as the crest of a wave of antieffeminacy sentiment that began in reaction to the brief period of post-Stonewall gender experimentation in the gay community. Since that time, gay men have been steadily reinvesting in masculinity.

Finally, poststructuralist challenges to the stability of sex/gender have had a curious effect on the disciplining of female bodies. A certain intolerance for the female who is "too femmy" seems to be slowly making its way into heteronormative culture. Whether or not this nascent trend develops into something more substantial is unclear at this time; what is clear is the use of effeminacy as a tool to discipline bodies sexed female, in a way that directly references history of male (somatic) effeminacy. Interestingly, there is not much evidence supporting the existence of a similar pattern among queer subjects engaged in what Jack Halberstam has dubbed "female masculinity."[31] Insofar as we may assume that female masculinity is performed on bodies that were (or are) sexed female and to some extent socialized as feminine, we may now be in a position to speak of gendered experiences of masculinity. It seems safe to say that various queer subjects have destabilized gender to the point where its performativity is becoming increasingly apparent, but the fact that effeminacy is not deployed to discipline female masculinity suggests that, as the products of distinctly different social processes, men and women may experience the performance of masculinity on their bodies in radically different ways.

NOTES

1. Gayle Rubin, "The Traffic in Women: Notes on the 'Political Economy' of Sex," in *Toward an Anthropology of Women*, ed. Rayna R. Reiter (New York: Monthly Review, 1975), 157–212.
2. *Webster's Unabridged*, 1994.
3. Robert Brannon, "The Male Sex Role: Our Culture's Blueprint of Manhood, and What It's Done for Us Lately," in *The Forty-Nine Percent Majority: The Male Sex Role*, ed. Deborah S. David and Robert Brannon (Reading, MA: Addison Wesley, 1976), 148.
4. R. W. Connell, *Gender and Power* (Stanford, CA: Stanford University Press, 1987); R. W. Connell, *Masculinities* (Berkeley: University of California Press, 1995).
5. Michel Foucault, *The History of Sexuality, Volume 2* (New York: Vintage, [1985] 1990), 85.
6. Foucault, *History of Sexuality*, 84.
7. Foucault, 85.
8. Randolph Trumbach, "The Birth of the Queen: Sodomy and the Emergence of Gender Equality in Modern Culture," in *Hidden from History: Reclaiming the Gay and Lesbian Past*, ed. Martin B. Duberman, Martha Vicinus, and George Chauncey Jr. (New York: New American Library, 1989), 1660–750.
9. Roger N. Lancaster, "Subject Honor and Object Shame: The Construction of Male Homosexuality and Stigma in Nicaragua," *Ethnology* 27, no. 2 (1987): 111–25; Tomas Almaguer, "Chicano Men: A Canography of Homosexual Identity and Behavior," *Differences* 3, no. 2 (1991): 75–100, 113.
10. Michael Kimmel, *Manhood in America: A Cultural History* (New York: Oxford University Press, 1996), 92.
11. George Chauncey, *Gay New York: Gender, Urban Culture, and the Making of the Gay Male World, 1890–1940* (New York: Basic Books, 1994), 305–6.
12. Robert Corber, *Homosexuality in Cold War America* (Durham, NC: Duke University Press, 1997).
13. Martin P. Levine, *Gay Macho: The Life and Death of the Homosexual Clone* (New York: New York University Press, 1998).
14. Levine, *Gay Macho*, 55–56.
15. K. J. Dover, *Greek Homosexuality* (Cambridge, MA: Harvard University Press, 1978).
16. Randolph Trumbach, "London's Sodomites: Homosexual Behavior and Western Culture in the 18th Century," *Journal of Social History* 11, no. 1 (1977): 1–33; Randolph Trumbach, "Sex, Gender, and Sexual Identity in Modern Culture: Male Sodomy and Female Prostitution in Enlightenment London," *Journal of the His-*

*tory of Sexuality* 2, no. 2 (1991): 186–203; Randolph Trumbach, *Sex and the Gender Revolution*, vol 1. (Chicago: University of Chicago Press, 1998).

17  Alan Sinfield, *The Wilde Century: Effeminacy, Oscar Wilde, and the Queer Moment* (New York: Columbia University Press, 1994); Linda Dowling, "Esthetes and Effeminati," *Raritan* 12, no. 3 (1993): 52–68; Nancy Erber, "The French Trials of Oscar Wilde," *Journal of the History of Sexuality* 6, no. 4 (1996): 549–88.
18  Trumbach, "London's Sodomites."
19  Sinfield, *Wilde Century*, 42.
20  Alan Bray, *Homosexuality in Renaissance England* (Boston: Gay Men's Press, 1982).
21  Trumbach, "London's Sodomites."
22  Trumbach.
23  Bray, *Homosexuality in Renaissance England*, 81–114.
24  Trumbach, "Sex, Gender, and Sexual Identity."
25  Trumbach, 203.
26  Sinfield, *Wilde Century*, 45.
27  Thomas Lacquer, *Making Sex: Body and Gender from the Greeks to Freud* (Cambridge, MA: Harvard University Press, 1990).
28  Judith Butler, *Gender Trouble* (New York: Routledge, 1990); Candace West and Don H. Zimmerman, "Doing Gender," *Gender and Society* 1 (1987): 125–51.
29  Bruce Feirstein, *Real Men Don't Eat Quiche* (New York: Pocket Books, 1982), 42.
30  Clark Henley, *The Butch Manual* (New York: Sea Horse, 1982), 76.
31  Jack Halberstam, *Female Masculinity* (Durham, NC: Duke University Press, 1998).

# 2

## The Effeminist Manifesto

STEVEN F. DANSKY, JOHN KNOEBEL, AND
KENNETH PITCHFORD

We, the undersigned Effeminists of Double-F hereby invite all like-minded men to join with us in making our declaration of independence from gay liberation and all other Male ideologies by unalterably asserting our stand of revolutionary commitment to the following thirteen principles that form the quintessential substance of our politics:

> ON THE OPPRESSION OF WOMEN
> 1. SEXISM. All women are oppressed by all men, including ourselves. This systematic oppression is called sexism.
> 2. MALE SUPREMACY. Sexism itself is the product of male supremacy, which produces all other forms of oppression that patriarchal societies exhibit: racism, classism, ageism, economic exploitation, ecological imbalance.
> 3. GYNARCHISM. Only that revolution that strikes at the root of all oppression can end any and all of its forms. That is why we are gynarchists—that is, we are among those who believe that women will seize power from the patriarchy and thereby totally change life on this planet as we know it.
> 4. WOMEN'S LEADERSHIP. Exactly how women will go about seizing power is no business of ours, being men. But, as effeminate men oppressed by masculinist standards, we ourselves have a stake in the destruction of the patriarchy, and thus we must struggle with the dilemma of being partisans (as effeminists) of a revolution opposed to us (as men). To conceal our partisanship and remain inactive for fear of women's leadership or to tamper with questions that women will decide would be no less

despicable. Therefore, we have a duty to take sides, to struggle to change ourselves, to act.

### ON THE OPPRESSION OF EFFEMINATE MEN

5. MASCULINISM. Faggots and all effeminate men are oppressed by the patriarchy's systematic enforcement of masculinist standards, whether these standards are expressed as physical, mental, emotional, or sexual stereotypes of what is desirable in a man.

6. EFFEMINISM. Our purpose is to urge all such men as ourselves (whether celibate, homosexual, or heterosexual) to become traitors to the class of men by uniting in a movement of revolutionary effeminism so that collectively we can struggle to change ourselves from nonmasculinists into antimasculinists and begin attacking those aspects of the patriarchal system that most directly oppress us.

7. PREVIOUS MALE-IDEOLOGIES. Three previous attempts by men to create a politics of fighting oppression have failed because of their incomplete analysis: the male Left, male liberation, and gay liberation. These and other formations, such as sexual libertarianism and the counterculture, are all tactics for preserving power in men's hands by pretending to struggle for change. We specifically reject hands that pretend to struggle for change. We specifically reject a carry-over from one or more of these earlier ideologies—the damaging combination of ultra-egalitarianism, anti-leadership, anti-technology, and downward mobility. All are based on a politics of guilt and a hypocritical attitude toward power that prevents us from developing skills urgently needed in our struggle and that confuses the competence needed for revolutionary work with the careerism of those who seek personal accommodation within the patriarchal system.

8. COLLABORATORS AND CAMP FOLLOWERS. Even we effeminate men are given an option by the patriarchy: to become collaborators in the task of keeping women in their place. Faggots, especially, are offered a subculture that is designed to keep us oppressed and also increase the oppression of women. This subculture includes a combination of anti-women mimicry and self-mockery known as "camp," which, to its trivializing effect,

would deny us any chance of awakening to our own suffering, the expression of which can be recognized as revolutionary sanity by the oppressed.

9. SADO-MASCULINITY: ROLE PLAYING AND OBJECTIFICATION. The Male Principle, as exhibited in the last ten thousand years, is chiefly characterized by an appetite for objectification, role-playing, and sadism. First, the masculine preference for thinking as opposed to feeling encourages men to regard other people as things and to use them accordingly. Second, inflicting pain upon people and animals has come to be deemed a mark of manhood, thereby explaining the well-known proclivity for rape and torture. Finally, a lust for power-dominance is rewarded in the playing out of that ultimate role, the man, whose rapacity is amply displayed in witch hunts, lynchings, pogroms, and episodes of genocide, not to mention the day-to-day (often lifelong) subservience that he exacts from those closest to him. Masculine bias thus appears in our behavior whenever we act out the following categories, regardless of which element in each pair we are most drawn to at any moment: subject/object, dominant/submissive, master/slave, butch/femme. All of these false dichotomies are inherently sexist, since they express the desire to be masculine or to possess the masculine in someone else. The racism of white faggots often reveals the same set of polarities, regardless of whether they choose to act out the dominant or submissive role with Black or third-world men. In all cases, only by rejecting the very terms of these categories can we become effeminists. This means explicitly rejecting, as well, the objectification of people based on such things as age; body; build; color; size or shape of facial features, eyes, hair, or genitals; ethnicity or race; physical and mental handicap; lifestyle; sex. We must therefore strive to detect and expose every embodiment of The Male Principle, no matter how and where it may be enshrined and glorified, including those arenas of faggot objectification (baths, bars, docks, parks) where power-dominance, as it operates in the selecting of roles and objects, is known as "cruising."

10. MASOCH-EONISM. Among those aspects of our oppression which the man has foisted upon us, two male heterosexual

perversions, in particular, are popularly thought of as being "acceptable" behavior for effeminate men: eonism (i.e., male transvestitism) and masochism. Just as sadism and masculinism, by merging into one identity, tend to become indistinguishable from one another, so masochism and eonism are born of an identical impulse to mock subservience in men, as a way to project intense anti-women feelings and also to pressure women into conformity by providing those degrading stereotypes most appealing to the sado-masculinist. Certainly, sado-masocheonism is in all its forms the very antithesis of effeminism. Both the masochist and the eonist are particularly an insult to women since they overtly parody female oppression and pose as object lessons in servility.

11. LIFESTYLE: APPEARANCE AND REALITY. We must learn to discover and value the female principle in men as something inherent, beyond roles or superficial decoration, and thus beyond definition by any one particular lifestyle (e.g., the recent androgeny fad, transsexuality, or other purely personal solutions). Therefore, we do not automatically support or condemn faggots or effeminists who live alone, who live together in couples, who live together in all-male collectives, who live with women, or who live in any other way—since all these modes of living in and of themselves can be sexist while also conceivably coming to function as bases for anti-sexist struggle. Even as we learn to affirm in ourselves the cooperative impulse and to admire in each other what is tender and gentle, what is aesthetic, considerate, affectionate, lyrical, sweet, we should not confuse our own time with that postrevolutionary world when our effeminist natures will be free to express themselves openly without fear or punishment or danger of oppressing others. Above all, we must remember that it is not merely a change of appearance that we seek, but a change in reality.

12. TACTICS. We mean to support, defend, and promote effeminism in all men everywhere by any means except those inherently male supremacist or those in conflict with the goals of feminists intent on seizing power. We hope to find militant ways for fighting our oppression that will meet these requirements.

Obviously, we do not seek the legalization of faggotry, quotas, or civil rights for faggots or other measures designed to reform the patriarchy. Practically, we see three phases of activity: 1) naming our enemies to start with; 2) confronting them; and 3) ultimately divesting them of their power. This means both the cock rocker and the drag rocker among countercultist heroes, both the radical therapist and the faggot-torturer among effemiphobic psychiatrists, both the creators of beefcake pornography and of eonistic travesties. It also means all branches of the patriarchy that institutionalize the persecution of faggots (schools, church, army, prison, asylum, old-age home). But whatever the immediate target, we would be wise to prepare for all forms of sabotage and rebellion that women might ask of us, since it is not as pacifists that we can expect to serve in the emerging worldwide anti-gender revolution. We must also constantly ask ourselves and each other for a greater measure of risk and commitment than we may have dreamed was possible yesterday. Above all, our joining in this struggle must discover in us a new respect for women, a new ability to love each other as effeminists, both of which have previously been denied us by our misogyny and effemiphobia, so that our bonding until now has been the traditional male solidarity that is always inimical to the interests of women and pernicious of our own sense of effeminist selfhood.

13. DRUDGERY AND CHILDCARE: REDEFINING GENDER. Our first and most important step, however, must be to take upon ourselves at least our own share of the day-to-day life-sustaining drudgery that is usually consigned to women. To be useful in this way can release them to do other work of their choosing and can also begin to redefine gender for the next generation. Of paramount concern here, we ask to be included in the time-consuming work of raising and caring for children, as a duty, right, and privilege.

> Attested to this twenty-seventh day of Teves and first day of January, in the year of our falthering Judeo-Christian Patriarchy, 5733 and 1973, by Steven F. Dansky, John Knoebel, and Kenneth Pitchford

# 3

## Three Contemplations on "The Effeminist Manifesto"

STEVEN F. DANSKY

Of course, memory is a reflection of the self. I recall the moments that meant the most to me, they are unrepresentative and historically subjective.
—Sarah Schulman, *The Gentrification of the Mind*

1.

"The Effeminist Manifesto" is mnemonic. Memory is always socially framed and constructed, and it shapes and contextualizes the way history is remembered, including discordant recollections, oral histories, personal narratives, and shared memories. From its first appearance in *Double-F: A Magazine of Effeminism* nearly fifty years ago, the manifesto was closely associated with the zeitgeist of New York City's Lower East Side—an era from the 1960s through the 1970s when the neighborhood was an epicenter of groundbreaking societal and cultural transformation. A vanguard of activists emerged: artists, dancers, experimental filmmakers, journalists, graffiti and pop-art painters, writers, and poets. It was a community undergoing a meteoric passage, crossing a time zone from tenement slums that once warehoused Eastern European immigrants to the same structures providing office spaces for underground newspapers, small presses, and mimeographed journals. It was an unequivocal cultural revolution.

Effeminism began at the cusp of epochal change in a hyperbolic era with unstoppable momentum, and it was within this eclectic milieu that John Knoebel, Kenneth Pitchford, and I co-wrote "The Effeminist Manifesto." Its imperative rhetoric and polemical bravura is inseparable from post–Stonewall rebellion activism and creativity; it was written within the continuum of antiwar protest, a civil rights struggle, the birth of the modern LGBTQ movement, and a burgeoning women's movement. Unmistakably, however, the foremost influence on the manifesto's authors was second-wave feminism, with manifestos such as the *Redstockings Manifesto*,[1] protomanifestos in *Notes from the First Year*,[2] and Robin Morgan's disruptive essay "Goodbye to All That."[3] We were acutely aware that "The Effeminist Manifesto" had the power and potential to be an antagonistic and challenging document. We intended it to be controversial—why else write a manifesto? Moreover, we wanted it to be catalytic and promote debate in the public square.

It's not incidental that "The Effeminist Manifesto" is as much about language as it is polemics. We used innovatively conceived terms such as "effemiphobia," "eonism," "gynarchism," "masoch-eonism," and "faggotry." We acknowledged the importance of terminology (all three of us studied literature, and two were poets). The movements that proceeded effeminism painstakingly chose their words: "colored" or "Negro" became "Black," "girl" and "lady" became "woman." On the West Coast, in Berkeley, California, there were parallel developments, when, in 1971, Nick Benton first used the term "effeminist," as publisher of the antisexist newspaper the *Effeminist*. We appropriated the term "effeminism" to describe a new movement and advanced as profeminists to develop our distinct critique of sexism and a repudiation of all forms of male supremacy.

Unfortunately, there is inadequate visual documentation that memorializes effeminist activism; thus, location facilitates continuity, identity, and memory. The reclamation of cultural and political space due to dislocation, erasure, and gentrification is essential to contextualizing the landscape of creativity, discourse, and political action, including writing manifestos.[4] There were discursive signposts—sites of discourse witnessed in public and shrouded in privacy—and there are physical locations of discourse, many documented, an acknowledgment of history making events, such as the Radicalesbians writing the iconic "Woman-Identified Woman"[5] at 338 East 6th Street,[6] Marsha P. Johnson and Sylvia Rivera at 213 East 2nd Street organizing Street Transvestite Action Revolutionaries (STAR), this author's essay "Hey Man,"[7] written at 41 East 1st Street, which carried "the struggle against sexism and its expression in maleness to the heart of gay liberation,"[8] and "The Effeminist Manifesto" signed at 109 Third Avenue, capturing the event with a Polaroid image that appears clandestine and subversive.[9]

2.

> We are only now beginning to reach for: connections between history and the body, memory and politics, sexuality and public space, poetry and physical science, and much else.
> —Adrienne Rich, "Muriel Rukeyser"

Manifestos are nonnegotiable. They are univocal, unilateral, and single-minded, with immutable assertions and unremitting positions that refuse dialogue or discussion.[10] "The Effeminist Manifesto" was considered seriously in public discourse, receiving both praise and derision. It was written when many believed gender, identity, and sexual orientation to be fundamental to societal transformation, but its determined take-no-prisoners profeminist viewpoint, along with a critique of gay male subculture and male-leftism was problematic even for the most supportive advocates.

The commentary "The Effeminist Manifesto" generated was sweeping, from mainstream print media including The *New York Times* and The *Village Voice*, to the underground press and the work of feminist theorists and gay male historians.[11] Some contemporaneous reactions to the manifesto include the following: "I knew when I first heard of the effeminists four months ago that here were the first authentic western male revolutionaries."[12] "Effeminists are formulating basic questions on gender."[13] "Radicalism unique in the history of lesbian and gay politics."[14] "The most imaginative, profound, and persuasive political analysis of gender developed by any men anywhere."[15] "Effeminism represents a milestone in political thought . . . unparalleled in the history of American thought."[16] "The first to think about how radical lesbians and radical feminist ideas applied to the behavior of male homosexuals."[17] "A far-reaching critique of sexism, including sexism in the gay liberation movement."[18] "The *Effeminist Manifesto* is one of the most enduring documents to emerge from the modern gay liberation movement."[19] "Ideas need to filter through personal history and personal psychology before their reality emerges."[20]

## 3.

> *Gender Trouble* sought to uncover the ways in which the very thinking of what is possible in gendered life is foreclosed by certain habitual and violent presumptions.
> —Judith Butler, *Gender Trouble*

There are principles in "The Effeminist Manifesto" that remain intractable. One is the central premise that patriarchy and its expression through masculinism is the root cause of all human suffering. Masculinism is fundamentally a system of power-dominance, a symbol of conquest and colonization, the trajectory of which leads to witch hunts, lynching, pogroms, genocide, and domestic, familial, and relational terrorism. During the first decades of the twenty-first century, the politics of masculinism have encouraged authoritarian conspiratorial theorists: an aggrieved class of white men whose anxiety about demasculinization has incited a global populism, a rebranded, fascistic, alternative-right wing (alt-right) movement.

Other principles in "The Effeminist Manifesto" demand reconsideration. Most egregious are the illogical, outdated, harmful, and misidentifying assertions about transgender people —rudimentary conclusions drawn without contributions from academia and transgender studies, social and political discourse, biomedical research, transgender diaristic accounts or narratives, or groundbreaking investigatory and theoretical writing, which were undeveloped or only just emergent at the time.[21] For example, the term "masoch-eonism" used in the manifesto conflates masochism with transvestism and intense anti-womanism and degrading stereotypes, and no distinction is made between gender fluidity and performance drag; each are "object lessons in servility." Nonetheless, an argument can be advanced that drag performance is as sexist as blackface performance is racist.

Even though I take the position that gender is largely a cultural phenomenon, at the time of this writing there is conflicting research on a genetic basis of gender with a number of definitional terms including (but not limited to) transgender, nonbinary, genderqueer, and genderfluid. As Shawna Williams writes, "For now, as is the case for many aspects of human experience, the neural mechanisms underlying gender remain largely mysterious. While researchers have documented some differences between cis- and transgender people's brains, a definitive neural signature of gender has yet to be found."[22] Significantly, however, representations of trans and gender-nonconforming people in print media have, until recently, portrayed subjects as singular, exceptional, and isolated; now there are networks of global communities and histories, providing us with a body of evidence that is compelling and persuasive and demands recognition.

While effeminism did not become a widespread social movement, its influence is incalculable. The manifesto has been cited and anthologized since it was written nearly forty years ago. There were like-minded groups and organizations in this country from New York to San Francisco and globally in Australia, England, and France. It's astonishing that the manifesto endured, having been written without late twentieth- and early twenty-first-century technologies—and yet somehow it was disseminated to all continents.

A manifesto is not a personal document. But a manifesto can have personal consequences. As a coauthor and, to some extent, the standard-bearer of "The Effeminist Manifesto," I've faced decades of public censorship and marginalization, shaming and shunning. The three of us saw irrevocable ruptures in friendships, conflict within our families, and the estrangement from political colleagues. As our lives became hyperpoliticized, we witnessed the dissolution of boundaries between interiority and exteriority. I disclose these generalities of experience not to be self-aggrandizing—rather, to recognize the inherency of risk-taking and subjective vulnerabilities when taking principled positions. "The Effeminist Manifesto" was personally definitional to me, and, while it shattered my boundless optimism in the face of pervasive homophobia, I own it. It's a schematic for transformative change, a singular document for relinquishing power, as much as is possible, appealing for the termination of patriarchal power-dominance over women, saving the planet, protecting the animal realm, and making men humane: our moral, conscionable, and justifiable obligation.

NOTES

1 "Redstockings Manifesto," Redstockings, www.redstockings.org.
2 "Notes from the First Year and Notes from the Second Year," Redstockings, www.redstockings.org.

3   Robin Morgan, "Goodbye to All That," in *The Word of a Woman: Feminist Dispatches* (Open Road Media, 2014), 44.
4   See NYC LGBT Historic Sites Project (www.nyclgbtsites.org) and National Register of Historic Places (www.nps.gov/nr).
5   Radicalesbians, "Woman-Identified Woman," https://repository.duke.edu.
6   Ellen Shumsky, "Radicalesbian Meeting," in *Portrait of a Decade: 1968–1978* (Allentown, PA: Graeae, 2009), 50.
7   Steven F. Dansky, "Hey Man," in *The Stonewall Reader*, ed. Jason Baumann (New York: Penguin, 2019), 194.
8   Jeffrey Weeks, *Coming Out: Homosexual Politics in Britain from the Nineteenth Century to the Present* (London: Quartet, 1977), 196.
9   Robin Morgan, "Signing the Effeminist Manifesto," in *On Bearing Witness: Images and Reflections of the LGBT Movement, 1969–1971*, ed. Steven F. Dansky (New York: Christopher Street, 2012), 43.
10  Janet Lyon, *Manifestoes: Provocations of the Modern* (Ithaca, NY: Cornell University Press, 1999).
11  See Jon Snodgrass, *For Men against Sexism* (New York: Times Change, 1977), 111.
12  Jill Johnston, *The Village Voice* (1972) and *Admission Accomplished: The Lesbian Nation Years, 1970–1975* (London: Serpent's Tail, 1998).
13  Martin Duberman, "Homosexual Literature," *New York Times Book Review*, December 10, 1972, https://timesmachine.nytimes.com.
14  Mark Blasius and Shande Phelan, *We Are Everywhere: A History of Gay and Lesbian Politics* (New York: Routledge, 1997), 435.
15  Susan Rennie and Kirstin Grimstad, *The New Women's Survival Sourcebook* (New York: Knopf, 1975), n.p.
16  *Gay Liberator* (Detroit), 1972, n.p.
17  Toby Marotta, *The Politics of Homosexuality* (Boston: Houghton Mifflin, 1981), 122.
18  Mary Daly, *Beyond God the Father: Toward a Philosophy of Women's Liberation* (Boston: Beacon, 1973), 218.
19  Jennifer Smith, *American Social Movements: Gay Rights Movement* (Farmington Hills, MI: Gale, 2003), 71.
20  Susan Sontag quoted in an email from Mark Berenson to the author in 2009. (Berenson, an early LGBTQ activist, was a housekeeper for Sontag at her penthouse apartment on West End Avenue.)
21  See Susan Stryker, "To Appear as We Please," *Aperture*, Winter 2017; or any issue of *TSQ: Transgender Quarterly*.
22  Shawna Williams, "The Transgender Brain," *Scientist*, March 1, 2018, https://www.the-scientist.com.

PART 2

# Configuring Male Femininities

What do male femininities look like? In this section—which explores configurations of male femininity across the categories of sex, gender, gender expression, and sexuality—four chapters offer different answers to that question. By no means exhaustive, these accounts describe some of the meanings of male femininities while also exposing the difficulty of fully capturing them. Clearly, there is no consensus on the concept of male femininity, which illustrates both the problem of outlining definitive parameters and the pleasure of accepting its inherent fluidity.

Each author contributes content that comprises the conceptual space of male femininities. Patrick Grzanka delivers a personal account of his experiences as a gay, cisgender man who works as a spin class instructor. Here, male femininity refers to a kind of athleticism that does not reap the benefits of hegemonic masculinity's jock culture; instead, Grzanka argues that leading a fitness class as a gay man uncovers the gender politics of sport in a woman-dominated field. By occupying the feminized position of the fitness instructor, Grzanka navigates tensions around his clients' perception of him and his own feelings of endurance and strength—qualities otherwise afforded to a masculinized position. And, in her chapter, Diane Ehrensaft discusses the gender-expansive experiences of children she has seen in her clinical psychology practice. By describing the diverse ways these youth identify their genders, Ehrensaft mulls over male femininities' different vectors.

Next, this section explores the experiences of a group of men one might think of as an expected version of male femininity: straight feminine men. Travis Beaver's interviews with feminine heterosexual cisgender men illustrate how their sexualities endure surveillance due to the constricting discourses of heteronormativity and hegemonic masculinity. Finally, Lisa Tatonetti explores the limitations of the English language and Western cultural understandings of gender nonconformity, illustrating how Western constructs of trans identities rely on binary categorizations of gender that do not neatly map onto the knowledge systems of Indigenous cultures.

The chapters in this section present different takes on the concept of "male femininity." Ultimately, their varying perspectives on what "counts" as male femininity provide examples from empirical research and lived experiences that illustrate the social constructionist and queer theoretical frameworks we use in this book. At its core, social constructionism contends that the meanings of our social realities are highly dependent on time and place. For example, men who lived during the Western medieval period expressed their masculinity by wearing form-fitting tights and frilly laced clothing; today a cisgender man with this gender presentation would be read quite differently—perhaps as an example of male femininity. In Saudi Arabia, men commonly display their trust and friendship by holding hands in public spaces, whereas men in the United States are discouraged from physical contact, lest they be perceived as gay. These socially constructed meanings both challenge viewing gender as somehow natural or innate and also explain why men who are feminine are presumed to be gay, as gayness has become synonymous with femininity, and femininity has become synonymous with submissiveness.

Thus, the concept of male femininities explored in this book relies on the meanings we have created in 2021 within predominantly Western cultures. In this particular time and place, femininity is often associated with a variety of aesthetic characteristics. Someone who wants to portray a feminine gender expression might choose to wear makeup and heels, keep their hair attractively coiffed, and regularly attend to their nails. They might work hard to stay toned and may favor the color pink. A variety of personality traits accompany these trappings of femininity: people who are feminine are expected to be gentle, demure, and nurturing. They are expected to be emotional, sensitive, and inclined to enjoy shopping.

The stereotypes associated with "femininity" are even more apparent when we apply an intersectional lens to the concept. Indeed, one may argue that they rely on white, middle-class, and heteronormative values. It is easy to expose these underlying assumptions when we preface the term "femininity" with an adjective that signifies a marginalized status, such as "Black," "queer," or "Southern." Thinking of femininity intersectionally is necessary to understand its conceptual richness. Acknowledging its diversity in turn helps us to appreciate the difficulty in neatly defining the boundaries of "male femininities."

As we discussed in the introduction, the category of "male" is not so simply defined either, which complicates the concept of "male femininities" as well. If we limit "male" to mean sex characteristics—penis, testes, testosterone, and XY chromosomes—then we have a cleaner starting point. But, just like the terms prefacing "femininity" in the last paragraph, "male" signals more than a single understanding. One may have some conventional male characteristics, but not others. For example, a person may have a penis and testicles, but low testosterone; a person may have a bushy beard and muscular chest, due to their testosterone level, but have XX chromosomes. We can also expand the concept to include qualities beyond the physical. Although we aimed in this book to use "male" when referring to physical sex, "male" is commonly used synonymously with "man" or "masculine." This slippage of male sex and gender broadens the ways some people may conceive of "male femininities."

Ultimately, the porousness of boundaries around the concept exemplifies the queer theoretical approach of this book. And while some may feel unsettled with this book's expansive conceptual framing, preferring more of a defined guide, we can never expect stability when it comes to sex, gender, and sexuality. On the contrary, a central goal in queer theory is to deconstruct the assumptions that reinforce the power systems that normalize some kinds of experiences while marginalizing others.

For example, in this section, Ehrensaft's reflections as a gender-affirming mental health practitioner reveal her willingness to accept children's distinct gender presentations. From a kindergartner's "rainbow kid" identity to the teenager's "gender smoothie" self, Ehrensaft espouses support for gender diversity. This affirmative lens differs starkly from the historic pathologization of trans clients by psychomedical institutions, whose experts often sought to suppress or change deviations from binary gender. Even among more supportive therapists, trans people still often encounter gatekeeping hurdles that prevent them from exerting bodily autonomy. Viewed another way, children as young as toddlers have been known to express strong cross-gender identifications, which challenge a pure constructivist narrative and instead suggest some innate sense of a gendered self. Then again, these expressions rely on language imbued with the social values of binary gender; one wonders what these children might express in a culture that easily and readily allows for multiple gender options.

As Lisa Tatonetti points out in her chapter, such configurations do indeed exist. Gender-crossing and gender-mixing in Indigenous societies carry different meanings than Western gender dichotomies. In some Indigenous cultures, the meanings of gender contrast with the "natural" versions that many Westerners take for granted. In declining a nomination for a "trans" poetry award, Joshua Whitehead—the subject of Tatonetti's chapter—asserted that his work and identity as "a 2SQ person" could not be truly captured that way. His case presents one example of the limitations of language: even the term he used to identify requires some unpacking, as "2SQ" is not readily legible in the Western "LGBTQ" abbreviation for the (Western) lesbian, gay, bisexual, transgender, and queer community. To Whitehead, "2SQ" means "Two-Spirit, queer Indigenous," which will still be unintelligible to many people, especially those outside of queer contexts. However, this shorthand hints at the robust ways that gender, sex, and sexuality are understood, decentering the authority of Western classification systems.

Queer theory allows for this kind of fluidity and uncertainty. To that end, we believe this section provides an introduction to the many ways that "male femininities" can be defined. Consider this collection of chapters an entry point to the concept—one that invites much more exploration as the meanings unfold.

4

# Pushing (Gender) Hard on the Bike

*Navigating Normativities as a Queer Spin Instructor*

PATRICK R. GRZANKA

In high school, heteronormativity taught me that boys like me would not access the social category of "athlete" regardless of how fit or skilled we were. My gender performance and the social norms around me made it very clear that I was not, in fact, a student athlete. These were the days long before Robbie Rogers, Michael Sam, and Adam Rippon. The only gay athlete I'd ever heard of was the flamboyant figure skater Rudy Galindo. As a queer teenager desperate to fit in, I didn't want anything to do with anyone like him, so I opted out of sports culture lest I be perceived as any more different than I already was.

But here's the thing: I actually (secretly) like sports. I love college football and basketball (go Terps!), I've been a runner since I was fourteen, and fitness is central to my mental and physical health. But, in my experience, my gender served as a barrier to my feeling safe and comfortable in athletic or sports-oriented social spaces—that is, until I found the world of boutique fitness and, later, became an actual spin instructor.

During the 2010s, a booming economy, health and wellness culture, and so-called athleisure fashion collided to form the American boutique fitness zeitgeist: the high-end, group-based workouts epitomized by ubiquitous barre, Pilates, bootcamp, and indoor cycling studios. With the exception of Crossfit, which is somewhat unique due to its own distinct branding and characteristic worship at the altar of heteromasculinity, boutique fitness is dominated by white, middle-class, straight heterofemininity and gay masculinity. In other words, in spin studios and barre classes, white straight women and gay men run the world.

Although I regularly attended barre, bootcamp, and spin classes for years, I still didn't conceptualize myself as a pro. Therefore, I was both flattered and nervous when, in the summer of 2016, the owner of a local cycling studio asked me to become an instructor. At least partially because of heteronormativity, I never thought that I could lead a fitness class; the people who teach these classes were *real athletes*, not people like me. It wasn't that believed myself to be physically incapable, but, when you spend your life thinking about fitness and athleticism in terms of your own failure to meet jock standards, I had trouble envisioning myself as anything but a fraud on the bike. A wannabe.

I am grateful every day that I left my comfort zone to accept her invitation to train and become an instructor at TurboSpin, where I now teach nearly every day of the week. "Spin instructor" has become a part of my identity, and teaching these classes has eroded much of my own insecurities about (not) being an athlete. When I teach, I feel empowered—in a space about physical fitness, bodies, and strength—to be myself, rather than compelled to make some feeble attempt to meet the heteronormative standards I learned in my high school locker room.

Yet my spin studio is not a progressive utopia, nor is it without its own normativities. There's a lot of money to be made off of people's insecurities, and boutique fitness is a major contributor to the body culture industry. As much as I love my side hustle, I am deeply ambivalent about my role in the violent capitalism of this industry, which disciplines many of its active participants and outside observers to believe that largely unattainable and profoundly racialized beauty standards are symbols of health and well-being. Further, my queer sexuality does matter on the bike, even if I generally don't experience my studio, or the boutique fitness world more broadly, to be any more heteronormative than anywhere else in contemporary America. Sometimes I feel tokenized by my women clients and coworkers, for many of whom I am the only out gay man they know (besides the dudes on *Queer Eye*). To them, I'm accessible, nonthreatening; I remind them of the gay best friend they've never had. And at least partially because I fit their stereotypical expectations of gay men—white, fit, able-bodied, gender conforming—we can maintain surface-level relationships without upsetting any of their core beliefs about gender and sexuality, much less race and social class.

It's their husbands and boyfriends who give me the most trouble. I live in what is colloquially referred to as the buckle of the Bible Belt: East Tennessee, where old-fashioned, explicit homophobia is still very much in vogue. For example, there's the fifty-something physician who takes a class every day but manages never to be in mine, even when I sub at his usual time. And I frequently encounter the first-time male client who's been dragged in by his girlfriend. While she loves my music, my sweatband, and my attitude, he's horrified enough to merely be in this class with a bunch of women, much less yelled at by a gay man in a muscle tee backlit by stage lights. Outside the studio, these men exercise hegemonic masculinity in ways I can only ever approximate, but, inside it, I command power in a way that subtly destabilizes the heteronormativity to which we have all become accustomed. Physical fitness is one of the primary ways through which men confirm and affirm their (hetero) masculinity. In the gym, I used to avoid contact with other men both because I didn't want to reveal how unsure I was of my own abilities ("Am I doing this right? How does this machine work?") and also because I didn't want them to think I was checking them out—even though, of course, sometimes I was! In the context of the spin studio, however, the gendered logic is inverted. As women deftly negotiate the equipment and perform their own prowess, pop music blasts from the speakers, and a gay man shouts commands from a disco-like stage, many straight men find themselves at an unfamiliar disadvantage. Indeed, I suspect that, for many of them, it's the first time they've felt uncertainty in an athletic context.

Just the other day, I helped one of these guys clip into his bike. As he averted his eyes from mine and only gave nonverbal grunts as I showed him how to use the equipment, I noted that his discomfort mirrored my own when I used to go to a hypermasculine gym. He couldn't bear to look at me, as if he might catch my queerness. Or was he afraid that if we made eye contact, I would see how nervous he was? My *queer* masculinity offered no refuge for him in a room full of femininity; I was less his ally than his greatest aversion. Though I wondered if he might push me away, he weaponized his nonverbal cues to repel me from his bike. After all, if he asked me for help, would I think he was weak? If he acted enthusiastic, would we think he was just a little too into this boutique fitness thing? This was precisely the kind of man who made me hate gym culture, fear the locker room, and think I could *never* be a fitness instructor. But here he was in my space, so uncomfortable that he can't even look at me, a gay man who's about to make him sweat more than he ever has in his life. I can't help but take a little bit of pleasure when, fifteen minutes into class, I see that bro completely drenched, huffing and puffing, barely keeping pace and looking fairly nauseated, while two dozen straight women and a few gay men bounce up and down on their bikes in synch to a Britney Spears remix. It's not revenge per se, but I won't lie: it feels good to make him really push.

# 5

## The Small ts and the Gender Binary Shake-up

*The Girl in the Boy and the Boy in the Girl*

DIANE EHRENSAFT

I wished our culture, language, and public bathroom situation allowed a person to hold elements of man and woman at the same time.
—Nick Krieger, *Nina Here Nor There*

Terms like "masculinity" and "femininity" are context sensitive, arising and taking meaning in particular life worlds.
—Adrienne Harris, *Gender as Soft Assembly*

A particular life world in point concerns the developmental unfolding of gender expansive and transgender children and youth. I would like to open this chapter with some recent musings from my experiences with young children and youth who let everyone know either that they are not gendered the way thought they were or that they will in no way abide by the culture's rules and regulations for their assumed gender. However, they are not only young people: I believe they are also our leaders in what has rapidly unfolded as a twenty-first-century gender revolution, as reflected on the front cover and in the widely read contents of the January 2017 special issue of the *National Geographic*, "Gender Revolution."

First, the experiences. After everyone keeps asking what pronouns their new kindergarten teacher should use—"she" or "he"—five-year-old Jordan, decked out in new sparkly sandals and a dress cascading over combat camouflage pants, shouts an anguished and angry response: "Just tell them to use 'rainbow kid.'" Nine-year-old Jess wishes there was a button they could push for themselves on any particular day: one for "boy" and one for "girl." Fifteen-year-old Steph announces with great exuberance, "I'm a chick with a dick. Or a dude with a vagina in the rear. Actually, take everything about gender, throw it in the blender, press the button, and you've got me—a gender smoothie." Seven-year-old Jaycee explains to me, "I'm a Gender Prius—a boy in the front [based on chosen clothes] and a girl in the back [based on long braid tied with a pink bow]. You see, I'm a hybrid." Four children, two designated as "female" on their birth certificates, two designated as "male," all delivering the same message: the binaries of male vs. female, boy vs. girl, masculine vs. feminine do not capture who they are at their core. They're just not working for them.

I start with these accounts to present the source of my musing. Perhaps I should not be writing a chapter for a book titled *Male Femininities* at all. Based on my experiences as a gender specialist working with gender-exploring or gender-expansive people of all ages, I no longer even know what "male femininities" means. When I started to diagram the vectors of all the directions the concept could take, I began to feel dizzy, disoriented, tripping over the question "Should there even be such a book in the context of the gender revolution that has exploded in Western culture in the first two decades of the twenty-first century—an eruption boldly challenging the gender binary both in theory and practice?"

I first posed this question first to myself. Now I pose it to you as readers, as I hold a personal tension between my life as a dyed-in-the-wool second-wave feminist from the 1960s and my work as a gender affirmative mental health theorist and practitioner in the twenty-first century. As a feminist, I am all too aware of the harm patriarchy has done to both women and men, of the sexism and misogyny that remains alive and well, of the dangers of a radical masculinity that promotes war and power-mongering over peace and empathy. In that trope, the tensions between masculine and feminine, and the sex binary of male and female, provide an accurate and invaluable GPS in guiding our efforts toward gender equality and shared distribution of power. Yet, as a gender specialist, I am learning each day, particularly from the children who are leading the charge, that gender in two boxes is becoming an anachronism, an artificial concept reified by our Judeo-Christian ancestors beginning in the Age of Enlightenment, now replaced by the model of gender multiplicity—or, if you will, gender infinity. This includes rainbow kids, gender smoothies, gender Priuses, among many others.[1] Through the lens of this dialectic between aging feminist and modern gender affirmative practitioner, I would like to share with you how my thinking has evolved about male femininities—pondering the girl in the boy, the boy in the girl, the girl who was once a boy, the boy who was once a girl, the child who says, "I'm neither."

An Introduction to the Small ts

First, let me introduce you to this population of young people who hopefully will give us some insight to the problematic at hand: What exactly is a male femininity in the context of the growing number of people who have lived in different genders or in the margins of the binary? What do these children of the twenty-first century see that is different from what those of us see who have lived in only one gender perceive—that is, we cisgender folks, or those of us in whose psyches the male-female, masculine-feminine binaries were imprinted the day we were born?

We hear much about the LGBT community, but the T has often been an afterthought, or an accepted but barely embraced cousin. We are now witnessing a turnabout, with the Ts—the transgender and gender-nonbinary folks—taking their place at the table: revamping theory, confronting transphobia, demanding their rights, and challenging the hegemony of the cisgender binary. Yet, until very recently, a subgroup of Ts, which I will call "small ts," has remained less visible and rarely acknowledged: young children who either object to the gender others expect them to be, based on their designated sex at birth, or who resist the cultural norms and prescriptions for gender performance. We're going to bring an even smaller set of those small ts into sharp focus in deconstructing the concept of male femininities: boys who defy the rules and regulations for binary male performative gender, and boys who everyone originally thought were girls until they made it known that they were actually boys. The first group are known as our gender-expansive boys, the second our transgender boys. A good number, but not all, of the former group are our "proto-gay" boys, exploring gender on the way to discovering their gay identities, and a number at some point may assert a nonbinary gender self. A good number in the latter group will move through childhood consolidating a masculine gender identity, with or without later medical interventions (e.g., puberty blockers, gender affirming hormones, surgeries)—a consolidation that, by necessity, will integrate an original "feminine" socialization experience with their present male identity and expression.[2]

As I understand the language construction of "male femininities" as a term, "male" stands as the adjective, referencing boys or men, and "femininities" represents the noun/subject—that is, characteristics our culture stereotypically attribute to girls and women. So, just to make the query more complicated, are we also talking about people who used to be males but have now entered the field of femininity (girlhood or womanhood)? These would be the people everyone thought were boys or men until they themselves discovered this to be wrong. I think we must talk about those folks as well. Therefore, we will need to expand our subject pool of small ts to include our transgender children who started out being perceived as boys, discovered themselves to be girls, let that be known to others, and, if fortunate, have been given the green light to live their lives as the affirmed girls they know themselves to be. These are the children and youth that bring their past masculine socialization into their present feminine existence.

We know that the content of the tropes of masculinity and femininity vary significantly from one culture to another and demonstrate distinctive shifts from one historical period to the next,[3] but we have yet to identify a culture in which gender categories do not exist at all.[4] What, therefore, can we learn from these children—the small ts—who, with increasing cultural permission, reorganize the existing Western gender tropes of femininities in males by either crossing over from one gender to the other or replacing femininity/masculinity with an any-and-all mosaic rather than an either-or gender binary?

## The Boy Once Believed to Be a Girl

Let me introduce you to one of these children: a real-life child with a camouflaged identity. When our story begins, Angelica was nine years old. As long as she could remember, she rejected "girls'" clothes and veered toward what she described as gender neutral garb. The last time she wore a dress she was four years old. By her own account, it was "an awful, miserable time." Her distress at being perceived as female had been intensifying over the last four years, leaving her anxious and downtrodden, enough that her parents brought her to see a therapist. Entering the therapist's office with timid steps, she began her first session by announcing, before even sitting down, "I know who I am, but I don't know how to do it." What unfolded is that she knew that she was a boy. Over the next year, with that point clarified both for the therapist and her parents, Angelica engaged in what is known as a social transition, changing her name to Angel, asking that people use "he/him/his" as pronouns, getting a haircut, and purchasing clothes in the boys' department. Angel insisted on announcing these changes to his fourth-grade class, and eventually—again at his own insistence—visited each of the other classes to introduce himself as Angel, explaining that he was a transgender boy once thought to be Angelica. As the school year progressed, he kept a watchful eye on the rules and regulations of boyhood, adopting some but rejecting others, but generally socializing himself into the world of boys. What never disappeared from his life as Angelica was his personality and physical features, which showed him to be a delicate, gentle, but sturdy soul, with a love of theater and acting, which was the center of his life—characteristics typically assigned as forms of femininity.

As exemplified by Angel, the transgender boy emerges from the "feminine" that was expected of him to a declaration of the masculine that is him. But that masculine will not necessarily have the same meaning as it would for a cisgender boy, because it will be an amalgam of what was and what is. Although many transmasculine children will say, "I've always been the gender I am now. It's just you who got it wrong," they nonetheless will have had an earlier socialization experience in which they were perceived to be female and had mirrored back to them the images and expectations for a girl. This can have either minimum or maximum effect, but rarely does it have no effect.

Often, upon first socially transitioning, a transgender boy will present himself as hypermasculine, repudiating any trailing signs of femininity as if they were the plague. Typically, this is to both fortify himself and make clear to others that he is a *real* boy, no matter what others (or he, before his gender self-discovery) had thought in the past, no matter what others may continue to think about real boys having to have been born with a penis and XY chromosomes (witness the bathroom battles in school districts, halls of justice, and legislative bodies throughout the United States in the second decade of the twenty-first century).[5] The color pink can stimulate in the transgender boy an apoplectic response. Baby dolls are given away, destroyed, or sent to the attic. However, observations by parents, teachers, and therapists indicate that, over time, this vigilant hypermasculinity softens as the child's gender identity is affirmed by his social environment. The dolls, if still in the house, may be recovered from the attic. The color pink may make a return on a T-shirt worn with nary a frown. What we are witnessing here is a developmental unfolding and psychological synthesis—a coalescence of the dual experiences this child has had, first being socialized into "girl" culture and then, later, anthropologically learning the ropes of boy culture, not just as a child who heretofore identified with boys, but who now *is* a boy.

We can ask when this child traversed from being a girl to being a boy—did nature, nurture, or culture trigger the transformation? The answer is that we really do not know, but those of us who have developed an affirmative model for understanding children's gender development draw on the theory of a gender web, with each child's gender being an interweaving of all three of those components to generate their own unique gender self.[6] Within that conceptualization, what we do know is that nurture and culture are the two strands of the web that teach a child what it means to be the gender that they are in the social context in which they live and perform that gender accordingly. For the transgender boy like Angel, growing up in the United States, he began life with an effort by others to socialize him toward femininity and then entered a new domain in which he is making every effort to adapt to the male culture with which he identifies. In that effort, he finds himself synthesizing the elements of his past female life with his present male life. Is that male femininity, feminine masculinity, or another entity altogether—a pangender position, neither masculine nor feminine, but a mixture of both?

To date, no transgender child has been identified as transgender at birth. Instead, they find themselves transitioning later, once their psyche is developed enough to inform them of their authentic gender. It is far more likely, then, that a transgender boy's sense of maleness is more nuanced and fluid than it is for the boy who was designated male at birth, who knows himself as male and abides by the normative structures in the culture. If we consider masculinity and femininity as social constructs, the transgender boy has had the experience of being raised within both feminine and masculine tropes. I am recalling the experience of a newly transitioned transgender eleven-year-old boy who transferred to a new school where no one knew his history as a perceived girl, and for which he had had to leave all his close female friends behind. I asked him how things were going in his new school. He said fine, except he really had to get used to the "boy" stuff. I asked what he meant. His reply: "Well, when I see one of my new friends, he just comes up and hits me on the arm. My girl friends always came up and asked how I was feeling. It's really weird."

In that vein, Nick Kreiger, a transgender man who did not transition until early adulthood, writes of his pretransition thoughts, when he was still Nina: "I just don't want to be some douchebag guy," like the one who would greet you by hitting you on the arm.[7] Later, post-transition, placing a photo of himself on the refrigerator from when he was Nina, Nick reflects: "As I stuck the magnet to my photo, I recognized the young woman in the picture, felt her life inside of me, and knew it would remain there, wherever I went."[8] By Nick's self-report, Nina comes with a history of feminine socialization experiences, either embraced, repudiated, or accommodated, ambivalently or unconsciously.

The concept of "male femininities" includes a call to evolutionary survival: the need for men to become more cooperative and collaborative in order for the species to survive.[9] In essence, then, the transgender boy or man will, by default, lead the charge. They neither have to educate nor retrain themselves; it comes with the territory of their life trajectory from female to male. Ironically, in biological terms, it is often perceived that, over the millenia, a reduction in testosterone has been the key to male femininity.[10] For example, a man who has been castrated will often be perceived as a man who leans toward the feminine; the sex offender whose testosterone is suppressed will be expected to be less aggressive. In contrast, the transgender male, if choosing hormone interventions, receives an infusion of testosterone, with a simultaneous suppression of estrogen. He may more easily arrive at a male femininity than his cisgender counterparts, even in the presence of increased testosterone. This plausibility suggests that it isn't hormones, but prior gender socialization (the "Nina" within them), along with other biological factors, that may be the linchpin in the development of a male who also holds the female.

If you mix red and blue, you have purple. If you mix girl and boy, by taking a child who was originally socialized as a girl and allowing them to be their authentic gender as a boy, you may no longer have male femininity or feminine masculinity, but a whole other state of being.

Let us also consider the transgender boy from another angle: the masculine in the girl before she transitioned to her boyhood. Here I call on the writings of a mother about her transgender son. In *My Daughter He*, Candace Waldron recalls that, early on, "Kendra not only dressed differently than her peers, her play was also different. She never wanted to play house or dress dolls."[11] Okay: so, the gender-nonconforming little girl. Yet Waldron also goes on to lament, "I loved her femininity. . . . My daughter would never in a million years so trample her girl side to become all boy. And if she did, I might be angry forever with the boy in her for overpowering the beloved girl. I felt protective of this tender, special girl and angry with the impulsive, inscrutable boy."[12] Here we bear witness to a mother coming to terms with the reality that she has a transgender son: a plea for the feminine of old to enter the masculine of new—in essence, a call for her child to embody male femininity if ever she was to transition to male, as indeed she did. Yet, paradoxically, this mother also fully recognizes that the masculine has always been there for Kendra (later, Kai) as well. The transgender boy not only brings the feminine socialization of the past into his affirmed gender self; he also packs in the masculine traits and expressions that coexisted with that earlier female socialization experience. Now we come to Candace's wish for Kai's future: "I was sending out into the world a boy who was raised as a girl to become a man—hopefully a conscious, responsible, loving, and sensitive man."[13] Kai writes back to his mother about the kind of man he sees himself becoming: "I like my feminine qualities. I'm even proud I was a cute baby. It doesn't bother me that you will still have old pictures of me around. I sometimes wish I didn't have to commit to one gender or another. I'd be all right living in between if I could."[14]

Both mother and son experience a duel between gender dualities. A boy with a history of feminine socialization also carries a history of masculinity within a female child, as a transgender man carries a history of his feminine self. Therefore, Kai, as an emblem of male femininities (if we so choose to hold on to this concept), leaves us with questions: Why *does* Kai have to commit to one gender or another? Why do these qualities have to be allocated to one gender or another? Why can we not transform them simply into traits, qualities, and preferences, rather than continually gendering them?

## The Girl Who Was Believed to Be a Boy

In attempting to draw all the vectors of male femininity, I came to the realization that if we are going to address male femininities, we also have to include the boys who become girls: our transgender girls. Before a transgender girl knows and lets it be known to others that she is a girl, not a boy, she often lives and is perceived as a feminine boy. Given the sexism of our culture, feminine gender presentations among little boys are not taken lightly, resulting often in an even stronger dose of male socialization. At its extreme, such boys are taken to mental health professionals who perform reparative therapy to eradicate the feminine and fortify the masculine.[15] Their girl toys are taken away from them; they are forced to play with boys and engage in "boys'" activities; and the male adults in their lives are asked to come in closer to model and shape more masculine behaviors. Typically, these children resist and frequently continue toward either a gay or transgender identity—if they make it there alive, given the high rates of suicidality among LGBTQ+ youth.[16] Those who go on to become transgender girls will, like transgender boys, maintain a history of the other gender socialization that they bring into their newly articulated female selves. Ultimately, they, too, will mix the hues of male and female from their past with her present socialization to create an entirely new shade of gender.

Yet this particular story takes an untoward turn, much more so than for transgender boys. The perceived repudiation of the masculine to embrace the feminine is not always taken kindly by a hegemonic, male-dominated world. Rather than being celebrated as an entrance into a kinder, gentler world, the child's turn to the feminine can be experienced as a profound threat by those around them. As a result, this form of male femininity, when it surfaces among youth on their way to becoming transgender girls, can actually be dangerous.

The tragic story of fifteen-year-old Larry King, who died before he could clearly articulate a female gender identity, is a case in point. Although cast as a gay boy, there were plenty of indications that he was a transgender girl.[17] He began to urinate sitting down; he wore female clothes; he asked to be called "Latisha"; and, shortly before his death, he began telling people at his foster group home that he was a girl. But to his school, the family, and social world, and to the media, he was known as a boy who exaggerated the feminine—in his manner of dress, in his walk, in his seductiveness toward boys, for which he was shot and killed by a fellow classmate, Brandon McInerney. His crime: male femininity. It is a precarious—if not lethal—proposition for anyone, not just youth, to bring the feminine into the patriarchal inner ring of the masculine. This is the plight of the boy on the way to becoming a girl.

In McInerney's trial for the murder of Larry King, who had just begun going by the name Latisha, there was much support for Brandon as a victim of Larry King's unwelcome advances—actions that were documented as actually having happened. We often hear this called the "gay panic defense." Ken Corbett had the opportunity to interview Larry/Latisha special resource teacher, who lamented that, in paying so much attention to Larry's "feminine" behaviors, the school failed to recognize the bigger problem: the murderous violence of a young man driven by radical and—one might say—insecure masculinity. As Corbett explains: "Brandon's normal-boy masculinity shielded him from sight. Boys will be boys. And one of the ways that they get to be boys is that they get to be invisible. Lost in the glare of Larry's 'problem' femininity was Brandon's presumed and invisible masculinity."[18] Unfortunately, that invisible masculinity rears its head when challenged with the entrance of femininity into its ranks, leaving in its wake a word of caution about the potential risks of male femininity in a transphobic world. In Corbett's words, "The regulatory regime moves with particular vigilance and diagnostic overdrive in the face of feminine masculinity.[19] Once again, this time to eliminate the risk, we are pointed toward dismantling the gender binary altogether and replacing it with an amalgam of "people" traits that heretofore have received gender-divided and gender-divisive labels of male/female, masculine/feminine.

Candace Waldron wanted her transgender son to be an empathic and caring rather than a rambunctious and impulsive boy. Yet when the vector goes in the opposite direction—a boy transitioning to a girl—that same badge of femininity is hardly seen as the bastion of a solid future society, but as a threat to an unsteady present social order, in which male dominates and man is king. Ironically, that is the very reason that transgender women are not welcomed by certain radical feminists, who assert that they had been raised with male privilege.[20] In these feminists' eyes, transgender women not only fail to grasp the meaning of female oppression, but continue to oppress from the inner depths of their socialized male privilege. This perspective is concerning on several counts: in trying to foster, nurture, and disclose their female selves, transgender women have hardly basked in the glories, but rather buckled under the weight, of the male dictates imposed on them before their transition. Secondly, we now have a cohort of very young transgender girls who have hardly had an opportunity to live in the glory of male privilege. Albeit with their history of male socialization a short one, they, like their older counterparts, are typically dissociated from, rather than associated with, the trope of dominating masculinity, and like Larry/Letisha King, may fear for or even lose their life as a result of that brand of masculinity in others. Lastly, it is one thing for patriarchal adherents to throw their swords; it is even more disconcerting when the attacks come from feminists who one would hope would be allies.

Listen to the words of a mother describing her transgender daughter: "Daniel always preferred playing with girls rather than boys. In the toy box at Grandma Clela's house the old doll was his favorite. Daniel liked to sew, cook, and clean house."[21] After Daniel's transition to Danielle, "she was bubbly, exuberant, and optimistic about her new life, as the person who had been hidden inside began to emerge. She began letting go of the male role she had tried to maintain. She still had demons of the boy sitting on her shoulder always whispering that the male was still present, but they were becoming quieter."[22] It saddens me to think that this ebullient young person would be shunned, harassed, or even attacked by others. It also made me think about the boy on Danielle's shoulder: Why should he have to go away? Why couldn't he simply live with the girl who is emerging, in a happy amalgam of boy and girl, past and present? If we embrace the notion of male femininities, wouldn't that peaceful coexistence epitomize those joined worlds? If we embark on dismantling the binary concept, would this still not be the essence of a new gender: not a binary, but a mosaic?

## Boys Who Remain Boys and Incorporate the Feminine

These I believe would qualify as the population to which the term "male femininities" might best be applied. They are boys now and always have been. They are not striving to be gentler human beings by borrowing the characteristics culturally ascribed to women, or searching for the feminine in themselves. They are just being themselves: gender upstarts who do not abide by the cultural dictates of "This is for girls, and this is for boys." Through word and action they assert, "Who said pink is a girl color? It's a people color. And, you know what, it used to be a boy color. Pink is a color, not a gender."

In the 1970s feminists seized the opportunity to challenge sexism and the cultural dictates of what we now refer to as "gender expressions," or the "doing" of gender (i.e., the activities we engage in; the clothes we choose to wear; the manner in which we walk, talk, and feel). With new icons of little boys playing with dolls, as memorialized in Charlotte Zolotow's groundbreaking and stereotype-busting 1972 children's book, *William's Doll*, coupled with new mantras of "Boys Can Cry," and Girls Don't Just Become Mommies," we have seen a phenomenal shake-up ensued in previously conservative and sexist gender-binary mores.[23] Apart from the clarion call of the feminists, there independently existed a group of boys pejoratively tagged as the "sissy boys" who pushed far beyond the boundaries of boys crying or carrying a doll. Regretfully, they did not fare so well—were either bullied or sent to programs like the clinic run by Dr. Richard Greene at UCLA to be fixed. The gender-expansive boys of today are the next generation of those gender upstarts and outcasts, but this time they are finding a place at the table, although there is no denying that bullying and rejection of "feminine" boys persists to the present.

Second-wave feminists demanded freedom from constricting and oppressive gender for all boys, so that they could discard reflexive "macho" shields and more freely emote, relate, and feel. As they did then, gender-expansive boys claim that freedom as their own, but that freedom goes far beyond a performative act encouraged by their elders. It is a deep and declarative sense of self; it is just who they are. In the interplay between nature, nurture, and culture that shapes every individual's sense and expression of their unique gender self, for these boys nature appears to play a strong role.[24] With that said, they would also feel compelled, either overtly or covertly, to march to the beat of their own tropes, which don't repudiate the feminine or the masculine but embrace both. Some of these boys will identify as heterosexual and cisgender, with expansive gender expressions. Many will grow up to join the community of gay or queer men, with sexual orientation toward men. Others may grow to identify as genderqueer or gender nonbinary, or perhaps as identities we cannot even yet conceive, as the gender revolution pushes forward into the future.

In their contemporary iteration, these are the boys with growing confidence to push back:

> Third grade gender-expansive boy wears his pink butterfly shirt to school.
> Fifth grade boy: "You can't wear that pink shirt. Only girls wear pink shirts."
> Third grade boy: "Well, I'm a boy, and I'm wearing this pink shirt, so I guess boys can."
> Another third grade gender-expansive boy comes to school wearing his purple unicorn shirt.
> Fourth grade boy taunts him: "Why are you wearing that purple unicorn shirt?"
> Third grade boy shoots back: "Why AREN'T you wearing a purple unicorn shirt?"

The gender affirmative model puts these third grade boys' responses under the umbrella of gender resilience, which is defined as the confidence to articulate one's gender with authenticity and aplomb, with tools for confronting the questioning, condemnation, or rejection from others who do not accept who they are. Yet, even more to the point, here is evidence of a group of boys who create a gender mosaic of self that dispenses with the gender-divided categories of masculine and feminine to affirm the gender that is them.

Over a decade ago I wrote about this phenomenon in a piece called "Raising Girlyboys."[25] Although I would no longer use that term, I think I was then trying to capture what I'm attempting to articulate here about the problematic of male femininities: "A girlyboy extends beyond the boy who incorporates a bit of the feminine within him. He plays at the edge of reality, refusing to accept the socially defined borders of male/female. Ludovic, the seven-year-old main character in the movie *Ma Vie en Rose*, defines it most succinctly: '... you have to understand, I'm a girlboy.'"[26] In essence, a girlboy or girlyboy—known today as a "gender-expansive boy," or "pink boy" by some—is a boy who challenges the cultural binary concepts of gender. He crosses over, in his play, in his dress, in his fantasies. What we have here is any/all rather than either/or.

## Transcending Male Femininities

In his book *Nina Here Nor There*, Nick Krieger describes his own gender configuration: "Some people see it as a binary, a spectrum, a continuum, or a rainbow. But when I envision my own gender it is with my eye to the lens of a kaleidoscope that I spin and spin and spin."[27] In 2018, Ara Halstead, a high school student in Olympia, Washington, wrote in the *New York Times*: "Toward the end of my junior year, I realized that I was gender-fluid—that my gender floats between identities. Some days I feel more feminine, some more masculine, and some days I'm somewhere in the middle."[28] Lori Duran, in *Raising My Rainbow*, shared a touching letter from her gay brother about her gender-expansive little boy, C.J.:

> As C.J. continued to not phase out of his fantastically pink phase, I began to realize that C.J. and I are different. You and Matt [C.J.'s dad] are going to raise him to be proud of who he is, to relish his creative use of purple, pink, and all the other non-grey colors. He feels safe to twirl, flit, flip, skip, and bounce. C. J. has what I didn't have. C.J. has a home that loves him for who he is, not who they want him to be.[29]

I include these three accounts in the conclusion of this discussion to alert us to the phenomenal change in the air that might transform the entire discourse on male femininities into a perhaps utopian future of postbinary gender infinity, in which gender neither disappears nor remains locked in boxes, but spins, twirls, flip-flops, and floats.

Gender will always be a relational phenomenon. As Lori Duran's brother Michael highlights for us, it is not just who a gender-expansive boy is, but how his parents mirror back to him a positive image—as neither expressing his male femininity nor being a feminine boy, but as being free to be C.J. To conclude with the wisdom of a gender-expansive nine-year-old of my acquaintance: "Why does it have to be that boys are rough, and girls are sensitive? Don't people realize it's just personalities? It doesn't matter if you're a boy or a girl or neither. You're just your personality." When we can arrive at adopting that wisdom in raising our children and expand those "personality options" to all children, "male femininities" may indeed become an anachronism. Perhaps the new cohort of parents who are bringing their children into the world as "theybies" rather than girl babies or boy babies are breaking ground in that endeavor. The future will tell us.[30]

NOTES

1. Diane Ehrensaft, *Gender Born, Gender Made* (New York: Experiment, 2011); Diane Ehrensaft, *The Gender Creative Child* (New York: Experiment, 2016).
2. Jack L. Turban and Diane Ehrensaft, "Research Review: Gender Identity in Youth: Treatment Paradigms and Controversies," *Journal of Child Psychology and Psychiatry* 59, no. 12 (2017): http://dx.doi.org/10.1111/jcpp.12833.
3. Will Roscoe, *Changing Ones: Third and Fourth Genders in Native North America* (New York: St. Martin's, 1993); Judith Butler, *Undoing Gender* (New York: Routledge, 2004); Jenny Nordberg, *The Underground Girls of Kabul* (New York: Broadway, 2015).
4. Deborah Rudacille, *The Riddle of Gender* (New York: Random House, 2006).
5. Jacob Tobia, "Why All Bathrooms Should Be Gender-Neutral," *Time Magazine*, March 23, 2017, http://time.com.
6. Colt Keo-Meier and Diane Ehrensaft, eds., *The Gender Affirmative Model: An Interdisciplinary Approach to Supporting Transgender and Gender Expansive Children.* (Washington, DC: APA, 2018); Ehrensaft, *Gender Born, Gender Made*; Diane Ehrensaft, "From Gender Identity Disorder to Gender Identity Creativity: True Gender Self Child Therapy," *Journal of Homosexuality* 59, no. 3 (2012): 337–56; Ehrensaft, *Gender Creative Child*; Marco Hidalgo, Diane Ehrensaft, Amy C. Tishelman, Leslie F. Clark, Robert Garofalo, Stephen M. Rosenthal, Norman P. Spack, and Johanna Olson, "The Gender Affirmative Model: What We Know and What We Aim to Learn," *Human Development* 56 (2013): 285–90.
7. Nick Krieger, *Nina Here Nor There* (Boston: Beacon, 2011), 76.
8. Krieger, *Nina Here Nor There*, 96.
9. R. L. Cieri et al., "Craniofacial Feminization, Social Tolerance, and the Origins of Behavioral Modernity," *Current Anthropology* 55, no. 4 (2014): 419.
10. Cieri et al., "Craniofacial Feminization," 419.
11. Candace Waldron, *My Daughter He* (Rockport, MA: Stone Circle, 2014).
12. Waldron, *My Daughter He*, 122.
13. Waldron, 181.

14 Waldron, 229.
15 Richard Green, *The "Sissy Boy Syndrome" and the Development of Homosexuality* (New Haven, CT: Yale University Press, 1987).
16 Ann P. Hass, Phillip L. Rogers, and Jody L. Herman. "Suicide Attempts among Transgender and Gender Non-Conforming Adults: Findings of the National Transgender Discrimination Survey," Williams Institute, UCLA School of Law, January 2014.
17 Ken Corbett, *A Murder over a Girl: Justice, Gender, Junior High* (New York: Henry Holt, 2016).
18 Corbett, *Murder over a Girl*, 149.
19 Ken Corbett, *Boyhoods: Rethinking Masculinities* (New Haven, CT: Yale University Press, 2009), 97.
20 Michelle Goldberg, "What Is a Woman? The Dispute between Radical Feminism and Transgenderism," *New Yorker*, August 14, 2014, https://www.newyorker.com.
21 Just Evelyn, *Mom, I Need to Be a Girl* (Imperial Beach, CA: Walter Trook, 1998).
22 Evelyn, *Mom*, 25.
23 Charlotte Zolotow, *William's Doll* (New York: Harper & Row, 1972).
24 Milton Diamond, "Sex and Gender Are Different: Sexual Identity and Gender Identity Are Different," *Clinical Child Psychology & Psychiatry* 7, no. 3 (2002): 320–34.
25 Diane Ehrensaft, "Raising Girlyboys: A Parent's Perspective," *Studies in Gender and Sexuality* 8, no. 3 (2007): 269–302.
26 Ehrensaft, "Raising Girlyboys," 271.
27 Krieger, *Nina Here Nor There*, 198.
28 Ava Halstead, "My Gender-Fluid Senior Prom," *New York Times*, May 13, 2018, www.nytimes.com.
29 Duran, Lori. *Raising My Rainbow* (New York: Broadway, 2013), 36.
30 Alex Morris, "It's a Theybe," *New York Magazine*, April 2018, https://www.thecut.com.

# 6

## Trapped in the Glass Closet

*Feminine Straight Men and the Politics of Coming Out*

TRAVIS BEAVER

A few days after posting my study recruitment flyers—"Are you ever mistaken for being gay? Would you like to share your experience?"—around Austin, Texas, I received an email that began, "Several friends have sent me photos of your flyer, sooooo [sic] I'm thinking we should chat :)." I met the sender two weeks later at a coffee shop for what turned out to be a fascinating conversation. Sean, a twenty-seven-year-old white man, arrived slightly late, damp with sweat.[1] He apologized for both and explained that he had traveled by bike. Sean is about six foot one with a medium build. He had a five o'clock shadow, even though it was ten in the morning, and his dark brown hair was neatly coiffed, with long, slicked-back bangs that elongated his face, revealing a slightly receding hairline. Several times over the course of the interview, he nonchalantly ran his fingers through his bangs. He was dressed in a pink and mauve striped tank top, tight cut-off black jean shorts that ended a couple of inches above the knee, and flip-flops. Although dressed casually, appropriate for the Texas summer heat, I noticed in professional photos online that Sean's sartorial style and expensive salon haircut came closest, out of all the men in my study, to approximating the stereotypical image of the metrosexual. In contrast to the initial nervousness I detected from other interviewees, Sean came across as confident and gregarious from the moment he sat down.

When I asked how Sean found out about my research project, he laughed, his large hazel eyes twinkling, as he explained that two friends texted him photos of my flyer within the same hour. Even though they worried that this might offend him, he recounted:

It really [laughs] kind of cracked me up. One of them was like, "I'm sorry, does this offend you?" [laughs] I was like, "No, not at all!" Because I'm very open about this, about this in my life, so it was just really funny. I was, like, you know, ten years ago I would have been concerned about something like that, but now it's just a funny thing that happens.

In fact, Sean *is* "very open" about being mistaken for gay, or what he refers to as the "not gay thing," and his career is centered on this phenomenon. Sean described himself to me as a "social justice comedian": he makes a living performing a comedy show, primarily at universities, in which he talks about the way stereotypes—or what he calls "snap judgments"—lead to oppression. His act largely focuses on gender and sexuality, and his jokes draw from his personal experiences of being read as gay. When asked why he decided to participate in my study, he said, "I've joked for a long time about this thing happening, the 'not gay thing,' I call it, because it's not really, it's not universal in any way. Everybody experiences it in weird, different ways, and I've always joked about creating a little 'not gay' community [laughs], like a 'not gay' support group [laughs]." In addition to his comedy show, Sean has written a book that attempts to explain social constructionist theories about gender and sexuality to a popular audience.

When I asked Sean to give examples of times he had been mistaken as gay, he replied, "Oh my gosh! Yeah, I've got a Word document that I started about a year and a half ago, so this isn't even comprehensive, but I just started writing down the times when people misread me as gay. It's up to like 260 unique things." When I laughed and raised my eyebrows at what sounded like a strange obsession, Sean justified the list as being "material" for his comedy routine and writings on gender and sexuality. In response to my inquiry about items on this list, he said:

> I've got them broken down into categories like lifestyle choices, like, if I know the lyrics to *Wicked*, or whatever. And then, like, ways that I act, ways that I dress, and, um, then there's this one and I just call it "wild-cards." So, for example, I was doing a comedy show a couple months ago and after the show this, like, fourteen- or fifteen-year-old girl was like, "I'll tell you how I knew you were gay!" Because I tell some stories on stage about people misreading me as gay—and I was like, "Well, first of

all you missed the point [laughs], but let's hear it [laughs]." And she goes, "You've got a gay forehead." And I was like, "What does *that* mean?" And she was like, "Well, not your forehead, but, like, if you were to peel your skin back and look at the skull, and then take a bunch of gay people and look at their skulls, I bet you'd have the same foreheads." I'm like, "Oh, my god! You just invented phrenology. That's terrifying." [Laughs] Let's lock you up preemptively.

After being briefly sidetracked by this story, he continued giving examples on the list:

So, like, the way that I dress, my hair, my eyebrows [laughs], like, these are all different people. Someone said my lips—like, that I have "gay lips." And I don't know what that means. Fingernails—pretty much every aspect of my physical self [laughs]. Other than my legs—I have very straight legs, someone told me once, which is weird. So that's funny. And then people will tell me why they knew I was straight, which is, like, the next level of this, which is even weirder. And then, like, my interests—like, I talk about musical theater and dancing and stuff like that. My mannerisms, my voice, the words that I use, uh, people say that I "talk good" [said in mocking voice, laughs] So, I smell good.

While Sean is unique in his recording and cataloging of these instances, his experience of being "misread as gay" for the reasons listed above is shared by several men whom I interviewed for this study. Regarding this list, Sean asserted, "I read them and I, like, think they're hilarious." Yet, he quickly added, "they're remnants of a sad culture and, like, a kind of oppressive culture that we live in."

Sean contends that he is not bothered, and is mostly amused, when people "misread" him as gay, although this was not always the case. As a college undergraduate, he was especially alarmed by "mistaken for gay" incidents and worried that these might be accurate perceptions of his sexuality. He said that he often found himself coming out as straight or "not gay." After visiting the gender and sexuality resource center on his college campus, Sean said he realized that being perceived as gay had "nothing to do with [his] sexuality and pretty much everything to do with [his] gender." Sean describes himself as a "feminine person." He hopes that speaking publicly about his experiences will help expand the boundaries of what it means to be a straight man by demonstrating that men can be heterosexual *and* feminine.

Masculinities scholars have found evidence that heterosexual masculinities are transforming to incorporate practices that have been stereotyped as "gay" or "feminine."[2] The meaning of these changes, particularly in regard to issues of power and inequality, have been the subject of ongoing debates within the field. Scholars who utilize the framework of "inclusive masculinity theory" argue that the expansion of socially acceptable behaviors for heterosexual men stems from the declining significance of homophobia in the construction of masculinity. Proponents of this theory optimistically claim that these changes in heteromasculinities are indicative of greater sexual and gender equality, including a world in which masculinities are no longer organized hierarchically.[3] The concept of "hybrid masculinities" provides a more convincing interpretation of these transformations. Scholars utilizing this concept argue that, instead of heralding gender and sexual equality, the selective incorporation of practices coded as "gay" and/or "feminine" into the gender performances of class-privileged, white straight men actually works to reproduce and obscure various forms of inequality.[4] These gender performances, for example, allow men to appear politically progressive and to distance themselves from aspects of masculinity that are becoming increasingly stigmatized, like being overtly homophobic. Yet this discursive distancing is largely symbolic as these men still benefit from heteromasculine privilege and often do little to change the larger gender order.

A key insight of social constructionist perspectives on gender is that configurations of gender practices vary across space and time. In other words, there are no static forms of masculinity or femininity.[5] The concept of hybrid masculinities is useful because it highlights how straight-identified men can incorporate and recode practices that have historically been coded as "gay" or "feminine" into their performances of masculinity, and that they often do so in ways that perpetuate inequality. Yet the concept of "hybrid masculinities" doesn't exhaust the possibilities of the way men's engagement in practices coded as "feminine" are interpreted in social interactions. Men who incorporate these practices into their gender performances do not always see themselves—nor are they always seen by others—as being masculine. Moreover, there is a risk of conflating "masculinity" with "whatever men do" when men's engagement in "feminine" practices is conceptualized as indicating new configurations of masculinity, as opposed to being conceptualized as male femininity. As some gender scholars have pointed out, defining masculinity as "whatever men do" reifies differences between men and women while leading researchers to overlook female masculinity, or women's embodiment of masculinity and engagement in practices coded as "masculine."[6] It has also meant that male femininity has been largely ignored and has remained undertheorized.[7] When male femininity is discussed in gender studies literature, it tends to be in relation to effeminate gay men.[8]

In this chapter, I shine a light on an unstudied group of men, hiding in plain sight: effeminate straight men with significant experiences of being misread as gay. I collected data through life history interviews with twenty straight-identified men. The men in the study ranged from twenty-three years old to fifty years old, with an average age of thirty-one. Three of the men identified their race/ethnicity as "Hispanic," and the rest identified as white. In terms of class, the majority of respondents grew up in lower-middle- to middle-class families, even though many of them are currently engaged in service industry jobs. Three respondents explicitly talked about growing up working-class. All but three respondents had at least a bachelor's degree, and even the three without degrees had attended college. All but one of the interviews were conducted in person; one interview was conducted by phone. In the interviews, I asked questions about the participant's sexual and gender identity and about "mistaken for gay" incidents.

In the following section, I explain why the men in my study describe themselves as feminine. For the purposes of this chapter, I define "male femininity" as men's engagement in practices and/or embodiment of characteristics that are culturally ascribed to women and are therefore coded as "feminine." Then, I show how the men in my study negotiate the continuing conflation of gender presentation and sexuality. Because many of these men describe themselves—and claim to be viewed by others—as "feminine," they are often assumed to be in the closet when they make claims to a straight identity. I argue that the concept of the glass closet works to erase the possibility that men can be effeminate and still desire women.

## More Feminine than Masculine: Attributes of Male Femininity

Male femininity continues to be construed as an indisputable sign of same-sex desire in American culture. Indicative of this conflation of gender and sexuality, the majority of men in my study believe they are read as gay due to their engagement in practices coded as feminine. Several of the men in my study self-identify as "feminine" or "effeminate" men on account of their practices, interests, comportment, or emotional traits. For example, Sean, whom I introduced at the start of this chapter, said he considers himself a "feminine person." When asked why, he replied:

> For a lot of reasons—okay, my voice, the way that I speak, the way that I approach people in a very deferent way. Um, so, other ways . . . the way that I dress, I would say I dress femininely, the way that I take care of my hair, or any other grooming stuff, I would say would be more feminine. And the way, I mean, my hand gestures, just a lot of things that are, that I've realized are very subconscious that I do are just read as more feminine than masculine. I don't have swagger, you know?

In fact, Sean's manner of speaking could be categorized as stereotypically feminine on account of his "uptalk": a rising intonation at the end of a declarative statement. In popular discourse, uptalk is primarily associated with young women and is believed to connote a lack of confidence. Regarding his style, Sean self-identifies as metrosexual. When asked about his clothing choices, he talked about wearing slim-fitting pants, V-neck shirts, and colorful clothing: "I like colors. Like, I think colors are just for fun."

Jared, a thirty-year-old white man who grew up in a small town outside of Austin, Texas, identifies with goth subculture; his sartorial style could be described as Edwardian dandy. He is tall and rail-thin with a narrow face and large, protruding brown eyes. He showed up to our interview at a local coffee shop with his black hair slicked back and wearing a slim-fitting black button-down shirt, black slacks, and black oxfords. His affected comportment was delicate and proper: he sat with his legs crossed, elbows pulled in, one hand resting on top of the other on the table. Although he did not have makeup on, I have seen Jared at dance clubs around town with a powdered face and wearing black eyeliner. Similar to Sean, Jared unabashedly described himself as "effeminate." I asked Jared if his gender presentation had changed over time, or if he had always considered himself to be effeminate. He replied:

> Well, it wasn't until about eighth grade that I started embracing more of that effeminate aesthetic. I started wearing makeup in eighth grade. Before then I was a lot more casual. I do believe that that came around the time when I started getting more into music and identifying myself with the message of certain genres, particularly the goth subculture and New Romantic. So, at that age, I started to embrace that more, and through that I think that my style started to change. And I became more effeminate because I felt like I identified with that.

Jared's explanation of his femininity is different than Sean's. Sean attributes the qualities about him that are read as "more feminine than masculine" to his subconscious, whereas Jared connects his effeminacy to a conscious identification with goth subculture. At another point in the interview, I asked Jared, "What does it mean when you say you're effeminate? What is it that makes you effeminate?" He answered:

> My demeanor. Just pretty much my air. I do wear makeup from time to time. I really appreciate the New Romantic movement of the eighties. And I appreciate the Edwardian aesthetic of the early turn of the century and also that of the Victorian period. So, you know, all of these things I would consider to be effeminate because they're more romantic in nature. And also I think that most people would perceive me as effeminate because of these things, so therefore I would have to classify myself as being effeminate through that as well.

In the first quote, Jared contrasts his effeminacy with an earlier period in his life when he was more "casual," which is how he describes most men. When asked to explain what he meant by that, he said, "Casual in that [most men] aren't naturally wanting to go an extra mile to accentuate certain aspects of themselves style-wise. They would rather just look more laid back. It's more a question of comfort rather than style for most men. And myself in relation to that I see myself as more stylized, more accentuated." In making this comparison, Jared draws on a popular discourse about gender that juxtaposes the "naturalness" of masculinity to the "artificiality" of femininity.

Both Sean and Jared discuss a range of self-attributes that they designate as feminine, particularly in comparison to men who have "swagger" or a "casual" appearance. This comparison, and the description of their femininity, points to the somatic, behavioral, and aesthetic dimensions of gender. Sean and Jared would likely describe Clint, a fifty-year-old white man whom I interviewed, as having both "swagger" and a "casual" appearance.

Clint arrived to our interview wearing a turquoise T-shirt with a pink peace sign on it, baggy cargo shorts in a plaid pastel print, and flip-flops. Although the color scheme of his outfit could be coded as feminine, the fit of his clothing, along with Clint's body type and comportment—short and stocky with muscular arms, broad shoulders, and a wide stance—could be described as masculine. Clint's shaved head and piercing eyes gave him an intensity that was only slightly offset by his stylish designer glasses. I noticed that his arms and legs were hairless (he later told me that he saw the flyer for my study at the salon where he gets waxed), and that this accentuated his muscular frame. When I asked Clint to talk about his gender, he said, "I would say that I'm masculine—physically masculine, I guess, is the key thing." He told me he was never harassed or bullied because of his gender presentation, unlike many of the men in my study. Yet, despite his masculine appearance, Clint told me:

> Yes, physically I'm a man. Emotionally, you know, [I'm] probably closer to a woman just from the standpoint of empathy and emotional connectedness and sensitivity, and these are kind of stereotypical things, but whatever. So very, kind of like a mixed bag. I mean, some typical male things like I'm super active, super physical, kind of just driven. But then a lot of aspects of it, even in the way I approach work, it's like, you know, very, a very empathetic way to do the kind of work that I do, which is hard because my job is to go into companies that are financially distressed and figure out how to fix them. So, a lot of times it's like firing a lot of people or shutting down plants or, you know, just a lot of stuff that is kind of, like, you know, dick moves of the corporate world.

Even though Clint defines his physical appearance and some of his behavioral traits—being "active," "physical," and "driven"—as masculine, he also claims to possess emotional traits that are stereotypically associated with women and femininity. While his description of himself as masculine was uncharacteristic of most of my other interviews, his portrayal of himself as sensitive and empathetic was similar to the way other men in my study talked about their emotional traits.

In addition to possessing "feminine" emotions, some of the men in my study also talked about having and pursuing interests that are coded as "feminine." Jared and Sean alluded to this when they characterized their investment in a stylized aesthetic as something that makes them feminine. Along with his interest in fashion and grooming products, Sean also mentioned his love for musical theater and dancing as interests that are considered to be feminine. Like Sean, William, a thirty-one-year-old Latino man who described himself as "more feminine than a typical man," also talked about having feminine interests. He told me, for example, about his disinterest in sports and his enjoyment of musicals and other elements of popular culture, like musical group the Spice Girls, which are not considered "manly."

In sum, the men in my study described a range of practices, traits, and interests to illustrate their "femininity" or "effeminacy."[9] For Sean and Jared, along with other men I interviewed, having a stylized aesthetic and engaging in particular grooming practices to achieve it are labeled as "feminine." The conscious cultivation of an aesthetic is contrasted with the "casualness" or lack of concern and effort that "typical"—read masculine—men put into their appearance. This is also what the label "metrosexual" is intended to describe: straight men's engagement in aesthetic and consumption practices typically associated with women and urban gay men.[10] Yet, as my interviews show, metrosexuality does not exhaust the dimensions of male femininity. In addition to aesthetics, several men told me that their emotional traits, comportment, and interests also characterized them as "feminine." Some men in my study, like Sean, who called himself a "feminine person . . . for a lot of reasons," identified with all of these attributes. Others, like Clint, who characterized himself as "physically masculine" and a "mixed bag" in terms of gender, only identified with some aspects of being a feminine man.

## Negotiating the Conflation of Gender Expression and Sexuality

For the most part, the men in my study claimed a special moral esteem for themselves on account of their "feminine" qualities. Far from being ashamed of their effeminacy, it was not uncommon to hear men in my study invert the masculine/feminine status hierarchy. For example, Jared, the Edwardian dandy, proclaimed, "I'm effeminate. I recognize that. I embrace that. I wish more men were in order to counteract the principles that I feel like keep men down and keep them from showing their emotions." In Jared's interpretation, masculinity is constrictive and harmful to men's well-being, particularly because he believes masculine norms require an unhealthy repression of emotions.

Although men like Jared profess to embrace femininity, they also recognize the ways that gender nonconformity complicates their claims to a heterosexual identity. While I was in the early stages of designing this study, Jared, an old acquaintance from the Austin music scene, posted the following status on Facebook: "For the last time, world, I'm not gay!" I immediately asked if I could interview him for my project. During our interview, I asked whether anything in particular had sparked his exasperated declaration on Facebook, which led to the following exchange:

JARED: Well, I have another friend who is also effeminate and we were activity partners—we like to go out and dance, we like going to the same places. We were both always very well-dressed, very formal—ties, dress shoes, slacks. And I think there is a misperception that if a man always looks too good or is always dressing up that they must be gay. And so, when we would go out together, even though we were both straight, we were often misperceived as being gay and with one another, because we were always out with one another.

TRAVIS: And how did you know in those situations? Was it people asking or . . .

JARED: It was a way in which I read through social cues, through others and the way they looked at me, and the way I wouldn't get as much reception from women when I was hanging out with him. It was also the way in which they came up to us and they just assumed that we were gay. Like, "Oh, you guys are so cute together." Or, you know, "Are you guys gay?" They would just ask us and we would both get frustrated in just constantly being misinterpreted. But yet at the same time we understood how we would [be misinterpreted], considering the way we knew we were.

Although Jared described other instances when he experienced physical violence and verbal harassment for being read as gay, in this story he encountered women who intended to compliment him and his friend by telling them they looked "cute" together. He is frustrated because he thinks he receives less romantic interest from women when out with this friend on account of their being "misperceived" as a gay couple. He rejects the "misperception" that effeminacy always signifies same-sex desire, yet he also recognizes that his gender presentation, particularly when coupled with his friend's effeminacy, leads to being "misinterpreted" as gay.

When asked to explain why they thought people read them as gay, several respondents pointed to their "feminine" traits and practices. Parker, a forty-seven-year-old white man, sent the following email in response to my flyer, which asked, "Are you ever mistaken for gay?:"

> I spent a year of college in east Arkansas (not my choice). Somebody wrote "FAG" on my door.
>   I don't care about football, or most any team sport. I like to cook and tend to dress well, don't mind dressing up for fancy dinners out.
>   but I'm attracted to women, not men. My wife was amused when a guy recently asked me "are you gay?", not realizing I was with my wife and mother of our three kids.
>   oh yeah, that happens to me . . . it doesn't bother me. I just quit caring so much what other people think. if somebody doesn't like me, I figure they have something wrong with them. I'm not trying to fit in.
>   yes, I have like 60 pairs of shoes. . . . but that doesn't make me gay, just well heeled. [punctuation in the original]

I quote Parker's email because it highlights several themes that emerged in my research. First, the men in my study talked about a range of "mistaken for gay" experiences, from the violent and threatening to the fairly benign and amusing. Of course, similar kinds of incidents were interpreted differently by respondents: some men shrugged off being called "fags" while others felt threatened by it; and, while Parker's wife was amused, other women were unsettled or annoyed by questions pertaining to their partner's sexual identity.

Second, most—but not all—of the men in my study connected being read as gay to being perceived as effeminate. Similar to Jared, Parker recognizes that his engagement in activities coded as "feminine" (i.e., enjoyment of cooking, dressing well, obsessing about shoes, his eschewing of "masculine" activities like team sports) are read as signs of same-sex desire; hence his listing of these activities are immediately followed by the statement "But I'm attracted to women, not men." However, he rejects the idea that these activities are inherently or essentially "gay:" "Yes, I have, like, sixty pairs of shoes. . . . but that doesn't make me gay, just well heeled." Instead of identifying their interests, traits, and practices as "gay," some of the men in my study, like Parker and Jared, opt to identify as "feminine" straight men, even as they recognize that this identity category is not typically validated in American culture.

Third, Parker and other men in my study attempt to signal and authenticate their heterosexuality through references to female partners or desires for women. In his email, for instance, Parker makes sure to draw attention to his "wife" and to the fact that he has three children. He not only signals his heterosexuality through this statement but also locates himself within a normative nuclear family structure. In Jared's case, he explains part of his frustration with being mistaken as gay as relating to the decreased romantic and sexual attention he receives from women who "misperceive" his sexuality. While this may be an honest expression of his feelings and perceptions, this account also functions as a performance of heterosexuality.

Negotiating the conflation of effeminacy and same-sex desire is a tricky task for the straight-identified men in my study. Their sexual identity work involves walking a fine line that requires conveying their heterosexuality to others while not coming off as defensive about it. Here is how Sean describes the conundrum of communicating his heterosexuality to people:

> I didn't want to tell people I was straight because the mentality that I was taught when I was a kid, and it is still reinforced all the time, is that if you are defensive about your sexuality then you are gay. Right? Which

is screwed up. It's just, I mean, there's research which shows that more homophobic people *might be gay*. Um, but to defend your sexuality, or just to describe your sexuality. But in any case even just saying you have a sexuality means you are gay, right?

In this quote, Sean points to the widely held belief that defensiveness about one's heterosexuality reveals repressed same-sex desires. Proclamations of straightness—either explicitly stated or implicitly communicated by, for example, talking excessively about sexual interest in women—are often interpreted as overcompensation for insecurities about one's sexual identity. For this reason, declarations like Jared's ("For the last time, world, I am not gay!") run the risk of being seen as protesting too much. Likewise, being homophobic is also considered to be a sign of closetedness. This belief is legitimated through scientific studies reported on in the popular press in articles with titles like this one in the *New York Times*: "Homophobic? Maybe You're Gay."[11]

Sean also points to the normative status of straightness when he says, "Just saying you have a sexuality means you are gay." As with other dominant identity categories, the dominance of heterosexuality means that it usually goes unmarked. One aspect of a heteronormative culture is that most people are simply assumed to be straight. Yet this assumption of straightness does not always extend to straight-identified men like Sean who see themselves, and claim to be perceived by others, as feminine. Sean refers to having your straight identity read correctly by others as a "bro privilege": "I wrote this article that was [called] 'Thirty Bro Privileges,' or, like, masculine dude privileges, and it was mostly a snarky thing but it was, like, privileges I don't have as being a feminine dude, even though I still have male privilege and straight privilege, I don't really have, like, 'bro privilege.'" Sean went on to list a few of the items in his article: "A bro privilege would be not having to come out as straight, not having to convince someone you were dating that you were dating, not having to defend the way that you dress, not having to defend the products that you buy for your face—things like that." As someone who speaks and writes about privilege, Sean is careful to distinguish between the "frustrations" of being mistaken for gay or having to account for aesthetic practices and the "genuine roadblocks" faced by gay and lesbian people. He also acknowledges that he has straight privilege and male privilege, but contends that these privileges are mediated by his feminine gender presentation. As a "feminine dude," Sean has to "come out as straight" while not appearing defensive about this heterosexuality.

Like Jared and Parker, Sean's identity as a feminine straight man relies on disarticulating gender from sexuality: his gender identification, being a "feminine guy," does not determine his sexual orientation. Sean hopes that he can serve as a role model for other feminine straight men by being public—through his comedy shows, books, and web presence—about his experiences with gender and sexuality. He said he receives emails from men who have anxieties about being read as gay and who "take comfort in knowing that like I am a straight guy who is comfortable talking about these things. And is a straight guy who is misread as gay and isn't terrified of that." As previously discussed, Sean knows that focusing his comedy and writing on being "mistaken as gay" can be interpreted as a sign of insecurity about his sexuality, or even as homophobia: "In a lot of ways it can be taken as, 'Well, why are you so defensive?' or 'What's wrong with being gay?' Like, *nothing* is wrong with being gay, I'm just not that, you know?"

## Trapped in the Glass Closet: Attributions of Internalized Homophobia

The concept of homophobia was intended to explain not only fear and hatred that is directed at gay people but, equally important, that is also internalized by gay people. As a concept developed during the gay rights movement of the 1970s, it offered a psychological explanation of why some gay people were in the closet and why some resisted calls by activists to come out and publicly embrace their "true" sexual identity. Activists argued that growing up in a society that pathologized homosexuality resulted in fear and self-loathing of same-sex desires. As Sean points out above, the idea of internalized homophobia remains highly salient in popular discourses about sexual identity. Straight-identified men who are believed to be gay, or who are caught engaging in same-sex behavior, like former US senator Larry Craig, are often accused of being "closet cases" by gays and straights alike. For those on the liberal side of the US political spectrum, being homophobic is often interpreted as projecting one's own fears of being labeled as gay.[12] Given this popular discourse, it makes sense that many of the men in my study told me they were "comfortable" admitting that they found some men attractive, were "secure" about their sexual identity, and were not homophobic. While ostensibly true, these disavowals of homophobia, demonstrated by the admission of finding some men attractive, can be interpreted as facets of their heterosexual identity work.

While only a few of the men I interviewed acknowledged or admitted to having experienced anxieties about their sexual orientation, several others recounted times when they had been accused of being closeted. For example, Jared told me that even a woman he was dating asked if he was gay. When I asked what she said in response to his assertion that he was straight, he told me: "She said, 'You've got be at least bi. Tell me! You've got to at least be bi. I can't understand you being the way that you are and not being at least bi.' It's like, 'I think it's a matter of time before you come out of the closet.'" Jared also talked about his annoyance with "assertive" gay men who hit on him at clubs. When I asked how he responded to them, he replied:

> If they're touching me I push them away. If they ask me for my number I tell them—well, if I can tell they're gay, I tell them flat out right away, "I'm not gay, just so you know." A lot of the time they think, "Oh, whatever, you just haven't come out of the closet yet." And they take it personal, like being rejected. [Many of these men] don't believe me because they think that, "Well, maybe you just haven't owned up to it yet. You just haven't come out of the closet and it's just a matter of time so let me be that guy to push you in that direction." You know, "I'll show you what you really want" kind of thing.

As Jared tells it, he is assumed to be a "closeted" gay man who has not yet "owned up" to being gay. Essentially, Jared describes the experience of being put in the glass closet by gay men who are frustrated by his rejection of their advances. In his telling, there is also an excitement for gay men who want to pull him out of the closet by showing him "what he really wants" to do sexually.

While some masculinities scholars argue that boys and men can now engage in practices coded as "gay" or "feminine" without this threatening their heterosexual identity, this is clearly not the case for all men.[13] As I demonstrate in this chapter, straight men who are perceived as effeminate still contend with the "gender inversion model of homosexuality," which holds that gay people usually possess characteristics associated with the "opposite" sex. Gender-nonconforming individuals who claim to be straight, or who do not openly proclaim to be gay, are often characterized as being in the glass closet, which means that their "true" sexuality is considered to be readily apparent. In other words, being in the glass closet means that one's sexual identity is an open secret.[14]

## Conclusion

In the post-Stonewall era, coming out of the closet has been viewed as a necessary act both for individual psychological well-being and for the collective achievement of gay rights.[15] Individuals who remain "closeted" are often viewed as self-loathing gays who suffer from internalized homophobia.[16] Although scholars have studied how the politics and imperatives of visibility impact members of LGBTQ communities differently based on race, gender identity, geography, and occupation, little research has focused on how these politics impact people who self-identify as heterosexual.[17] This research begins to address that gap.

The straight-identified men in my study have undoubtedly benefited from the increasing visibility and acceptance of gay people. In fact, some of them report being valorized in certain contexts for engaging in practices that have been coded as "feminine" and "gay." Many of the men in my study experienced pleasure in being mistaken as gay; they reported being flattered when gay men flirted with them, and several expressed genuine enjoyment of the attention they received in these encounters. Moreover, "mistaken for gay" incidents validate my respondents' feelings that they are more enlightened than the conventionally masculine man, who is framed as retrograde due to his objectification of women, inability to express a range of emotion, and lack of style.[18]

However, I also found a great deal of ambivalence about the experience of being a straight-identified man who is read as gay in social interactions. While my respondents certainly benefit from heterosexual privilege, most of them also recounted painful experiences of being targets of both explicit, overt homophobia and more subtle microaggressions on account of being perceived as effeminate and, therefore, gay. In many of these stories, a straight identity, and sexual desire for women, did not protect these men from homophobia. My respondents' experiences show that one need not be gay or identify as gay to be the target of homophobia. In interaction, it is enough to be perceived as gay, and these attributions of a gay identity are most frequently based on gender nonconformity.[19] Ultimately, the misreadings of sexual identity experienced by the men in my study demonstrate the persistent conflation of gender presentation with sexual identity—a conflation that underwrites systems of violence against all forms of male femininity.

While stereotypes about effeminate gays and mannish lesbians still exist, gay and lesbian individuals and communities have challenged the conflation of gender and sexuality.[20] The politics surrounding these struggles over gender presentation in LGBTQ communities are complex and contentious. On the one hand, gender normative gays and lesbians are sometimes seen as assimilationists who benefit from "passing" as straight. On the other hand, lesbian and gay-identified people who do not conform to gender norms are often accused of undermining the struggle for gay rights.[21] According to this argument, "flamboyant" gays reaffirm stereotypes and harm efforts to normalize same-sex desire. These debates notwithstanding, within gay and lesbian communities there has long been a recognition that a range of gendered presentation and behavior exists among those who identify as gay.

Aside from social categories like "metrosexual," which allowed that some straight men were beginning to engage in "feminized" practices largely associated with urban gay men, and "tomboy," which attempts to safely contain masculine behavior by girls within early childhood, there has been far less recognition of the diversity of gender presentation among straight-identified people. This oversight is exacerbated by discourses about the "closet" that can erase the possibility of being straight and gender-nonconforming. Despite progressive intentions, popular discourse about "closet cases" or "latent homosexuals" can work to reproduce heteronormativity. The belief that effeminacy is a definitive sign of same-sex desire relies on a notion of gender essentialism that strengthens the normative link between heterosexuality and conformity to gender norms. Heteronormativity is as much about upholding and reproducing binary gender norms as it is about policing sexuality. The experiences of feminine straight men who are mistaken for being gay highlight the persistence of gender policing even in the context—and sometimes purportedly in the service—of increased LGBTQ visibility.

NOTES

1. All the names in this chapter are pseudonyms.
2. Kristen Barber, "The Well-Coiffed Man: Class, Race, and Heterosexual Masculinity in the Hair Salon," *Gender & Society* 22, no. 4 (2008): 455–76; Eric Anderson, *Inclusive Masculinity: The Changing Nature of Masculinities* (New York: Routledge, 2009); Mark McCormack, *The Declining Significance of Homophobia: How Teenage Boys Are Redefining Masculinity and Heterosexuality* (London: Oxford University Press, 2012); Tristan Bridges, "A Very 'Gay' Straight? Hybrid Masculinities, Sexual Aesthetics, and the Changing Relationship between Masculinity and Homophobia," *Gender & Society* 28, no. 1 (2014): 58–82; Tristan Bridges and C. J. Pascoe, "Hybrid Masculinities: New Directions in the Sociology of Men and Masculinities," *Sociology Compass* 8, no. 3 (2014): 246–58; James Joseph Dean, *Straights: Heterosexuality in Post-Closeted Culture* (New York: New York University Press, 2014).
3. "Inclusive masculinity theory" was developed by Eric Anderson (see *Inclusive Masculinity*). This framework has been subject to numerous convincing critiques on theoretical, methodological, and empirical grounds. See Bridges, "Very 'Gay' Straight?"; Bridges and Pascoe, "Hybrid Masculinities"; Sam de Boise, "I'm Not Homophobic, 'I've Got Gay Friends': Evaluating the Validity of Inclusive Masculinity," *Men and Masculinities* 18, no. 3 (2015): 318–39; Rachel O'Neill, "Whither Critical Masculinity Studies? Notes on Inclusive Masculinity Theory, Postfeminism, and Sexual Politics," *Men & Masculinities* 18, no. 1 (2015): 100–120; Mike Parent, Amber Batura, and Kiyra Crooks, "Homohysteria: A Commentary and Critique," *Sex Roles* 71, no. 3 (2014): 121–25; Sarah Diefendorf and Tristan Bridges, "On the Enduring Relationship between Masculinity and Homophobia," *Sexualities* 23, no. 7 (2020): 1264–84; and Sarah Diefendorf and Tristan Bridges, "On the Enduring Relationship between Masculinity and Homophobia: Reply to McCormack," *Sexualities* 23, no. 7 (2020): 1299–309.
4. Demetrakis Demetriou, "Connell's Concept of Hegemonic Masculinity: A Critique," *Theory and Society* 30, no. 3 (2001): 337–61; Bridges, "Very 'Gay' Straight?"; Bridges and Pascoe, "Hybrid Masculinities."
5. Raewyn Connell, *Masculinities: Knowledge, Power, and Social Change* (Berkeley: University of California Press, 1995).
6. Jack Halberstam, *Female Masculinity* (Durham, NC: Duke University Press, 1998); Mimi Schippers, "Recovering the Feminine Other: Masculinity, Femininity, and Gender Hegemony," *Theory and Society* 36, no. 1 (2007): 85–102; C. J. Pascoe, *Dude, You're a Fag: Masculinity and Sexuality in High School* (Berkeley: University of California Press, 2007).
7. Schippers, "Recovering the Feminine Other."

8  Peter Hennen, *Faeries, Bears, and Leathermen: Men in Community Queering the Masculine* (Chicago: University of Chicago Press, 2008); David Halperin, *How to Be Gay* (Cambridge, MA: Belknap Press of Harvard University Press, 2012).
9  Some men used the term "feminine" to describe themselves, others used the term "effeminate," and some used both terms interchangeably.
10  David Coad, *The Metrosexual: Gender, Sexuality, and Sport* (Albany: State University of New York Press, 2008).
11  Richard M. Ryan and William S. Ryan, "Homophobic? Maybe You're Gay," *New York Times*, April 27, 2012, www.nytimes.com.
12  Michael Kimmel, "Masculinity as Homophobia: Fear, Shame, and Silence in the Construction of Gender Identity," in *The Masculinities Reader*, ed. S. M. Whitehead and F. J. Barrett (Cambridge: Polity, 2001), 266–87.
13  Anderson, *Inclusive Masculinity*; McCormack, *Declining Significance of Homophobia*.
14  Eve Kosofsky Sedgwick, *Epistemology of the Closet*, 2nd ed. (Berkeley: University of California Press, 2008).
15  Steven Seidman, *Beyond the Closet: The Transformation of Gay and Lesbian Life* (New York: Routledge, 2003).
16  Heather Love, *Feeling Backward: Loss and the Politics of Queer History* (Cambridge, MA: Harvard University Press, 2007).
17  Jeffrey Q. McCune, *Sexual Discretion: Black Masculinity and the Politics of Passing* (Chicago: University of Chicago Press, 2014); David Valentine, *Imagining Transgender: An Ethnography of a Category* (Durham, NC: Duke University Press, 2007); Mary L. Gray, *Out in the Country: Youth, Media, and Queer Visibility in Rural America* (New York: New York University Press, 2009); Catherine Connell, *School's Out: Gay and Lesbian Teachers in the Classroom* (Berkeley: University of California Press, 2014).
18  Bridges, "Very 'Gay' Straight?"
19  Pascoe, *Dude, You're a Fag*.
20  Connell, *Masculinities*; Hennen, *Faeries, Bears, and Leathermen*.
21  Jay Clarkson, "The Limitations of the Discourse of Norms: Gay Visibility and Degrees of Transgression," *Journal of Communication Inquiry* 32, no. 4 (2008): 368–82.

7

## Two-Spirit, Not Trans

*Joshua Whitehead's Erotic Sovereignty*

LISA TATONETTI

On March 6, 2018, the nation's oldest organization dedicated to promoting and recognizing queer literary arts announced their finalists for the Thirtieth Annual Lambda Literary Awards, one of whom was a brilliant young Indigenous writer and theorist, Joshua Whitehead (Oji-Cree). Whitehead was nominated for his debut book, *Full-Metal Indigiqueer*, an innovative collection of poetry narrated by a hybridized cyber trickster. On March 14, Whitehead respectfully withdrew his book from contention. His nuanced letter to Lambda organizers, published by TIA House, speaks directly to the difficulties of fitting queer Indigenous people into preexisting Western gender categories.

The diversity of Indigenous gender categories has historically been referenced in the twentieth and twenty-first centuries by non-Native activists as a way of validating the long-standing existence of identities now deemed queer, but that would not have been queer in Indigenous cultural contexts. This practice of cultural appropriation has been traced by Scott Morgensen in his landmark book *Spaces between Us*, which shows how non-Native queer communities in the 1960s and 1970s deployed the term "berdache"—a word missionaries and settler anthropologists used for nonbinary Indigenous peoples—to authorize settler claims to gay rights.[1] That term, which was subsequently rejected by Indigenous activists due to its troubling etymology and deployment, became a way for non-Native people to craft a queer history that was used in equal rights discourses. Such arguments, as Morgensen demonstrates, activate a settler sleight-of-hand in which queer Indigeneity is invoked to support white queer rights claims and then conveniently disappeared as non-Indigenous folks continue to inhabit tribal lands and often also commodify Native identity markers.

Whitehead's letter, "Why I'm Withdrawing from My Lambda Literary Award Nomination," circulates in the wake of the complicated relationships between the less-than-parallel histories of settler and Indigenous queerness. In terms of this collection, Whitehead's explanation of why his poetry can't be categorized as "trans" offers a particularly relevant entrance into a discussion of how and why queer Indigeneity doesn't fit neatly within a book about male femininities.

In his "Lammy" nomination rejection, Whitehead describes himself as "a 2SQ (Two-Spirit, queer Indigenous) person" who inhabits a nehiyaw (Cree) space of 2SQ-ness.[2] That tribally connected Two-Spiritedness informs both his understanding of self and his subsequent rejection of settler categories of queerness. Whitehead's discussion of the disconnect between his Lammy nomination in the category of "trans poetry" and queer Indigeneity as he lives it is worth quoting at length. He explains:

> I recognize the difficulty of categorizing Two-Spirit (2SQ) within Western conceptualizations of sex, sexuality, and gender. I cling to Two-Spirit because it became an honour song that sung me back into myself as an Indigenous person, a nehiyaw (Cree), an Oji-Cree; I have placed it into my maskihkîwiwat, my medicine bag, because it has healed and nourished me whenever I needed it. To be Two-Spirit/Indigiqueer, for me, is a celebration of the fluidity of gender, sex, sexuality, and identities, one that is firmly grounded within nehiyawewin (the Cree language) and nehiyaw world-views. I think of myself like I think of my home, manitowapow, the strait that isn't straight, fluid as the water, as vicious as the rapids on my reservation, as vivacious as a pickerel scale. I come from a nation that has survived because of sex and sexuality, as post-contact nations that deploy sex ceremonially. My gender, sexuality, and my identities supersede Western categorizations of LGBTQ+ because Two-Spirit is a home-calling, it is a home-coming. I note that it may be easy from an outside vantage point to read Two-Spirit as a conflation of feminine and masculine spirits and to easily, although wrongfully, categorize it as trans; I also note the appropriation of Two-Spirit genealogies by settler queerness to mark it as a reminder that Western conceptions of "queerness" have always lived due

in part to the stealing of third, fourth, fifth, and fluid genders from many, although not all, Indigenous worldviews.³

I would be remiss if I didn't first point to Whitehead's gorgeous prose; he is both a talented creative writer and a brilliant theorist, as are so many of his contemporaries—such as Billy-Ray Belcourt (Driftpile Cree Nation), Erica Violet Lee (Cree), and Lindsay Nixon (Cree-Métis-Saulteaux)—as well as the influential queer Indigenous writers who came before him, perhaps most notably, in terms of their theoretical work, Paula Gunn Allen (Laguna Pueblo), Beth Brant (Bay of Quinte Mohawk), Connie Fife (Cree), and Janice Gould (Koyangk'auwi). Whitehead differentiates between Western and Cree understandings of genders and sexualities in a way that marks how Cree Two-Spirit identities supersede dominant categories. Thus, while acknowledging the recognition as an honor, Whitehead also makes visible how it *simultaneously* functions as an erasure of the specificity of Two-Spirit presents, histories, and identities. His Lammy withdrawal emphasizes, then, how dominant conceptions of LGBTQ identity can gesture toward Two-Spirit categories even while subsuming Two-Spirit under settler understandings of gender.

Though some might see such contemporary differences as simply a matter of semantics in which the expansive nature of trans should be able to stand in for, or directly parallel, the concept and practice of Two-Spirit identities, Whitehead describes his Two-Spiritness as an embodied knowledge that functions radically differently. To consider the facets of this difference, I first offer a bit of history for readers new to queer Indigenous writing, theories, and lives and then turn to Whitehead's fiction to consider how experiences of male femininity and Two-Spiritness can both coalesce and radically diverge in the contexts he imagines.

## Two-Spirit Histories

The term "Two-Spirit" did not come into common usage until the late 1980s and early 1990s. After being used informally, it was presented at the third annual intertribal Native American / First Nations gay and lesbian conference in 1990 as a replacement for "berdache." First seen in Jesuit documents from the late 1600s, the word "berdache" emerged in English from Arabic, Spanish, and French translations of loaded expressions like "kept boy" or "male prostitute," which have negative connotations in their respective cultural contexts.[4] In light of such troubling histories, Queer Indigenous people came together at this historic conference to reject not only the problematic anthropological term but also the loaded settler ideologies to which it is so closely allied.

To offer further context, non-Native invaders, including the Spanish, French, and English, physically and psychologically attacked gender-expansive—non-cis, non-heteronormative—Indigenous people at, and after, contact. In one of the most cited examples of this genocidal oppression, Vasco Núñez de Balboa and his crew seized and murdered some forty Two-Spirit people, whom he identified as men dressed as women, by throwing them to his war dogs to be torn apart on their 1513 expedition to Panama. Balboa was by no means alone in such practices. These continued attacks on nonbinary peoples' bodies were accompanied by years of psychological violence perpetrated by priests, missionaries, church and government boarding and residential schools, and Judeo-Christian heterodoxy. Here, then, lies the painful irony of later settler populations invoking queer Indigenous people and traditions to authorize their identifications and rights.

However, even more than rejecting pejorative connotations and settler ideologies, Two-Spirit is intended to evoke the particular histories *and* particular presents of Native North America. Since time immemorial on Turtle Island, most Indigenous nations had names and social and/or ceremonial places for nonbinary peoples. To offer one example, the Diné (Navajo) have four gender positions—female (*Áád*), male (*Ka'*), *Náadleehí*, and *Dilbaa'*—and gender shifts play a part in their creation narratives.[5] While the contemporary term "Two-Spirit" was never intended to be translated into Indigenous languages, it emerges from the Ojibwe phrase *Niizh Manidoowag*.[6] *Niizh Manidoowag, Náadleehí, Dilbaa', winkte* (Lakota), *Badé* (Crow), and many more such names/gender positions are linguistic traces of Two-Spirit histories and roles within Indigenous nations. In some cases, such roles are extant (as Brian Gilley, of Chickasaw/Cherokee descent, notes in *Becoming Two Spirit*) in some cases not, and in some cases they are being resurrected by present-day Indigenous people.[7] Just as genders and sexualities are fluid and, for many, changeable over a lifetime, so, too, are Indigenous traditions active and vibrant constructs, as the present-day usage of Two-Spirit demonstrates.

In contrast to hegemonic categories of gender and sexuality, non-cis gender roles among Indigenous nations have been more often identified with occupation than sexual object choice. There are not, then, one-to-one correlations between categories like lesbian, gay, bi, transgender, transsexual, and the term Two-Spirit, even though, as Two-Spirit Chickasaw scholar Jenny L. Davis explains, "people who identify as Two Spirit are frequently asked by researchers, media, and others outside their community to position their identity as either female or male."[8] While the hypothesis, evidenced from oral tradition and extant archival evidence in existing photographs and written accounts, is that Two-Spirit people sometimes had partners who seem to be what Western eyes would perceive as "same sex," these third and fourth gender positions operate outside such binaries. This is exactly the distinction to which Whitehead refers when he states, "I note that it may be easy from an outside vantage point to read Two-Spirit as a conflation of feminine and masculine spirits and to easily, although wrongfully, categorize it as trans."[9]

To build off of Whitehead, the "two" in "Two-Spirit" often misleads non-Two-Spirit folks into reifying an existing binary in which "male" and "female" or "masculine" and "feminine" are two preexisting roles that somehow meld together in this Indigenous understanding of gender. However, such reliance on hegemonic dualisms entirely misses the point that Two-Spirit peoples inhabit/inhabited *different, tribally specific* gender positions operating within and through Indigenous knowledge systems. Evidence suggests, for example, that, unlike men who identify as gay and seek same-sex partners as objects of desire, historically Two-Spirit people would not have been in romantic or sexual relationships with one another. Two-Spirit people would partner with *other* genders or at times not partner at all. As a result, while Two-Spirits subvert current dominant norms around gender and sexuality, thereby fitting the category of "queer," as it is now understood, within their home cultures they would not necessarily been perceived as subverting norms or having same-sex/same-gender relationships.

## Femme Narratives and Heteropatriarchal Resistance

Whitehead's creative work addresses both the ways in which these understandings of Two-Spirit circulate in contemporary Cree culture and also the ways in which such folks, in the form of his fictional and poetic avatars/characters, run up against very real barriers of homophobia, transphobia, misogyny, and settler hegemony that cause a Two-Spirit person to be perceived as performing male femininity rather than a tribally recognized third or fourth gender. While Two-Spirit roles and identities have, at times, been simplified and romanticized, the worlds that Whitehead creates extend no such trite or easy answers; thus his readers encounter twenty-first-century Two-Spirit realities, which are named and highly valued, *and* they simultaneously see the infiltration and ramifications of Judeo-Christian prohibitions against queerness.

In *Jonny Appleseed* (2018), Whitehead's first novel, the titular character has moved to Winnipeg from the Peguis First Nation Reserve, an Indigenous nation with a population of Ojibway and Cree descent located in what is currently the province of Manitoba, Canada. The novel opens with the narrator's explanation: "I figured out that I was gay when I was eight. I liked to stay up late after everyone went to bed and watch *Queer as Folk* on my kokum's [grandma's] tv."[10] The narrative subsequently moves between flashbacks to the narrator's coming of age on the reserve and several days during which he raises money to return to the reserve for his stepfather's funeral.

Despite the fact that he is a Two-Spirit person, Jonny, the compelling central character who narrates the book, in many ways fits into the paradigm of a gay man who inhabits a non-cis space of male femininity. Reminiscing about his early years as a "brown gay boy on the rez," Jonny notes that, although he wasn't out, "the others at school knew I was different. They called me fag, homo, queer—all the fun stuff."[11] Jonny's self-identifications and gender role-playing situate him as femme throughout the text. In fact, Whitehead himself describes Jonny as "a hyper-femme, contemplative, seductive existentialist."[12] To offer just a few examples, as Jonny prepares to move from Peguis to Winnipeg he feels "like Elle from *Stranger Things* holding weights much too heavy for little girly-boys."[13] Likewise, after his move he calls himself "an urban NDN, Two-Spirit femmeboy" and trades on this identification in his sex work, where non-Natives' romanticized visions of Indigeneity become Jonny's capital.[14] A self-identified "bad girl," Jonny regularly meditates on both the boundaries and possibilities of gender. Remembering an incident of being refused entry to a sweat lodge because he wore a skirt, Johnny notes, "When I think of masculinity, I think of femininity."[15] When taken together, these descriptions suggest Johnny views his male femininity as part inexorable force and part finely honed craft.

To consider exactly how Jonny *crafts* rather than simply inhabits a non-cis gender role requires a turn to how and where he inhabits femininity. A key marker in these gender performances can be found in his experiences around makeup and the rituals connected with it. One of Jonny's early encounters with cosmetics is with his best friend and lover Tias's babysitter, who would give them "makeovers" in which she painted their faces and nails. This was, he explains, "a tradition we wholeheartedly signed up for."[16] Disturbingly, the boys' joy in this play is met with violence when Tias's adoptive father discovers the nail polish and viciously cuts Tias's nails to a bloody mess as punishment. This is not, then, a narrative of easy acceptance where, because Jonny is Indigenous, his coming of age as a Two-Spirit person is inherently easy. Instead, what *Jonny Appleseed* presents is a world in which the titular character faces a sharp divide between the hostility of male responses to queerness and the acceptance of his close female relatives, particularly his mother and kokum to whom his Two-Spirit identity is acknowledged with warmth and support.

When Jonny is a prepubescent boy in a bath with his mother, for example, he describes her approval for his non-cis gender play, saying: "I built myself a pair of breasts just like my mother's using the soap from my head. 'Momma, you think I'm pretty?' I'd ask and she'd reply, 'M'boy, ain't no one ever looked better.'"[17] His mother consistently reacts to Jonny's femme gender performances with complete equanimity. As opposed to the aforementioned trauma Tias and Jonny experience when Tias's father confronts them upon seeing their nail polish—an item that is clearly marked in his eyes as an accoutrement of femininity and, by association, of the boys' potential queerness—Jonny remembers loving reactions to his displays of non-cis attire and behaviors, which, as in this example, he often calls to his mother's attention as he seeks and finds approval for his femininity.

Embodied familial ties undergird Jonny's interactions with his kokum, who, like his mother, accepts his femininity with little fanfare. His earliest experience with makeup is, in fact, with his kokum. He describes this memory, which is captured in a laughing photo of the two, with deep emotion: "She would apply her powders and lotions to my face with such grace and softness that I would fall asleep, smelling of talc and lilac. She would push back my hair with her hand and tickle my widow's peak with her fingers, applying concealer to the scar there. I like thinking that she is impressed on my forehead even now—that the stories in her body are written on mine."[18] Read comparatively, this scene shows the radical difference between Jonny's experiences with Tias's father and, later, his own stepfather, two men who police gender and threaten Jonny and Tias if they fail to perform cisgendered masculinity. Here, with his kokum, we see Jonny *invited* into a ritual marked as feminine. Moreover, he is not just grudgingly allowed to inhabit practices marked female; rather, he is welcomed into the fold of femininity with love and, to use his words, "grace."

Importantly, Jonny particularly highlights the somatic exchange he shares with his kokum as an affective engagement he holds in his body as well as his memory. This somatic memory becomes part of an archive of Indigenous knowledge that Jonny carries with him. Speaking of such embodied practices, Tanana Athabasan scholar Dian Million discusses affective exchange in Indigenous writing. In her award-winning article, "Felt Theory," Million considers the impact of Native women's personal narratives that transform "an old social control, *shame*, into a social change agent."[19] She further points to "the importance of felt experiences as community knowledges that interactively inform our positions as Native [writers and] scholars."[20] I would argue that Jonny's exchange with his grandmother demonstrates Indigenous women's affective power: Jonny's kokum fosters his incipient femininity by literally stroking her approval into his body. To return to Jonny's claim that "the stories in her body are written on mine," we see his kokum offer an embodied tale of gender expansiveness through her caress.[21] That story, which not only allows for but also *cultivates* gender-expansive possibilities, is shared through a felt experience that subsequently nurtures and sustains him after he leaves the reserve for Winnipeg.

Jonny's mother, like his kokum, invites Jonny into the rituals that surround the construction of certain forms of femininity. When Jonny watches her getting ready to go out at night, his mother offers him makeup tips coupled with advice on men. As she puts on makeup that "border[s] more on drag than natural," she tells Jonny, "This is eyeshadow, but you can also use it to color your lips if you're out of lipstick, remember that.... You want to snag yourself a man? Then you best slather this shit around your eyes.... Smoke your eyes and they'll be begging to smudge you. That's a fact."[22] Her invitation to him suggests her realization that gender is, after all, just drag, as Butler noted nearly thirty years ago and Indigenous people have known for millennia. Like his kokum, Jonny's mother invites him into a femininity that, while bounded by particular rules and rites, is an expansive space in which there is room and grace enough for all. Through repeated stories like these about his mother and kokum, Jonny makes clear that in these women's eyes he is welcome to follow his own desires about his gender and sexuality.

His mother and grandmother's acceptance of Johnny's femininity and their related—if unspoken—recognition that gender is a construct that he can rightfully inhabit is decidedly absent in the attitudes of some of the men he depicts in his memories of the reserve (as the previous example with Tias's father suggests). If femininity is something Jonny can be taught, heteronormative masculinity is something that is expected by the authority figures in his life regardless of the existence of Two-Spirit roles in Ojibway and Cree cultures. Jonny comments: "The men in my life liked to pressure me to butch myself up and ridicule me for my feminine ways."[23] As with his memories of his mother and grandmother, Jonny again highlights his complete understanding that gender acts and expectations are performance, as seen in the phrase "butch myself up." Furthermore, the "practical skills" the men pressure Johnny to perform include "how to use tools, start a fire, hunt, and skin animals"—all futile exercises for Jonny, who has "no aptitude" for such training.[24] However, his aptitude (or lack thereof) is clearly not the point of the pressure to adhere to normative masculinity, which demands at least the appearance of cisgender conformity.

Significantly, Jonny's commentary on this memory challenges romanticized concepts of Two-Spirit identity; instead of the easy acceptance we see in his maternal line, Whitehead here depicts the lack of understanding that can exist for gay, queer, or Two-Spirit roles and peoples in some Indigenous contexts. As a result, while the masculine practices he references relate to Native subsistence practices, they are also firmly situated in a dominant gender binary by the men who demand them. *Jonny Appleseed* suggests, then, that straying from cisgender practices can have very real consequences for a person assigned male at birth, no matter how that person might perceive their gender. In fact, Jonny says that "'Man up' was the mantra of [his] childhood and teenage years."[25] To offer just one example, when Jonny comes home from a fourth grade dance and excitedly tells his family he waltzed with a boy, his mother and kokum laugh and "pat him on the arm."[26] In stark contrast, his stepfather, Roger, takes his belt and beats Johnny until he bleeds, yelling all the while: "'Boys don't'—*smack*—'dance with'—*smack*—'boys'—*smack*."[27] The divide between male and female responses in this scene, which could not be more evident, illustrates the heteropatriarchal imperative that, when in the company of men who identify as straight and cis, Jonny should act "butch" no matter what or who he feels himself to be.

Roger's words and violence signify his investment in contemporary gender expectations that align with a paradigm of colonial masculinity. Such tensions have recently been the subject of Indigenous masculinity studies, a rising field in which scholars like Kim Anderson (Cree/Métis), Brendan Hokowhitu (Ngāti Pūkenga), Robert Alexander Innes (Plains Cree, Cowessess First Nation), Sam McKegney (settler), and Ty P. Kāwika Tengan (Kanaka Maoli) undertake critical analyses as well as on-the-ground community, private, and governmentally supported programs that promote constructive and healthy masculinities for Indigenous men. In the introduction to *Indigenous Men and Masculinities*, the first critical collection on the subject, Innes and Anderson note that "the performance of Indigenous masculinities has been profoundly impacted by colonization and the imposition of a white supremacist heteronormative patriarchy."[28] Likewise, in *Masculindians*, his powerful collection of interviews with Indigenous writers, activists, and cultural leaders, Sam McKegney comments that "affirmations of biological maleness and celebrations of masculine power always risk trading in biological essentialisms and being conscripted into chauvinism and misogyny, especially when masculinity becomes conflated with strength and dominance," as it is in settler configurations of gender.[29] This conflation has undoubtedly occurred among the male authority figures in Tias's and Jonny's lives, who—in marked contrast to Jonny's mother and kokum—place a settler paradigm of masculinity above the physical and psychological well-being of their children and families.

## Two-Spirit Futures

The counter to these harmful iterations of masculinity comes in the aforementioned female approval and also in the text's turn to a Two-Spirit ideology. In Whitehead's novel, powerful dreams of Two-Spirit people promote healing and integrate genders and sexualities that now might be perceived as queer into the Oji-Cree context of the novel. Much as Whitehead himself rejects the term "trans," so, too, does Jonny, who explains to a self-proclaimed "tranny chaser" client that he is "Two-Spirit, not transgender."[30] Though "femme" might delineate a particular gender performance, Two-Spirit marks the person Jonny is and the future *Jonny Appleseed* envisions. It's useful here, then, to return to Whitehead's description of his own Two-Spiritness to consider what this means in the world of his novel: "I cling to Two-Spirit because it became an honour song that sung me back into myself as an Indigenous person, a nehiyaw (Cree), an Oji-Cree; I have placed it into my maskihkîwiwat, my medicine bag, because it has healed and nourished me whenever I needed it. To be Two-Spirit/Indigiqueer, for me, is a celebration of the fluidity of gender, sex, sexuality, and identities, one that is firmly grounded within nehiyawewin (the Cree language) and nehiyaw world-views."[31]

Whitehead's character experiences this same homecoming when he is welcomed into the space of Two-Spiritness by his female relatives. What to dominant culture would be the gender-nonconforming behavior of male femininity is simply who he is and how they relate to him from their Nehiyaw worldviews. When Jonny is eight and beading a thunderbird as a gift for a crush, his mother comments "Don't be thinking I don't know who this is for—you like that Walker boy. I'm fine with that, son, Creator, he made you for a reason—you girl and boy and that's fine with me, but what's not fine is you selling yourself short."[32] In this scene,

Jonny's Two-Spirit identity is, as we've seen previously, a nonissue for his mother; what counts instead is his self-worth—she is appalled that Jonny could give something of himself away to someone who "don't give two hoots about" him.[33] His kokum has the same nonchalant reaction to his gender identity when, crying, he comes out to her (he thinks) in a phone call after he's moved to Winnipeg. Entirely unsurprised, she comments, "Jonny, m'boy, your kokum old but she ain't dull. You's napêwiskwewisehot, m'boy, Two-Spirit. You still my beautiful baby grandkid no matter what you want to look like or who you want to like."[34] She gets off the phone to make frybread, telling Jonny "kisâkihitin," that she loves him (or, more accurately, "You are loved by me").[35] Just as when she stroked her love into his body while she put makeup on him, here, too, the affirmation of Jonny as simultaneously Two-Spirit and loved comes to him as medicine, a healing he remembers, holds, and treasures in a world that too often offers him pain rather than approbation.

While these examples could, to an outside reader, seem to simply parallel the experiences of any non-cis gay boy coming out to his family, Whitehead is as careful to distinguish these roles and beliefs in his fiction as he is in his life. While Jonny performs a female-identified gender or male femininity, he *is* Two-Spirit, and the novel emphasizes the fact that such an identification is tied to particular cultural affiliations, which is perhaps best seen in the dreamscapes we encounter throughout the text. In one example, Jonny dreams of and makes a jingle "dress that had the colours of the medicine wheel: black, yellow, and red."[36] His acknowledgment that he would not have been able to wear such regalia on the rez today due to the infiltration of the sort of colonial heteropatriarchy already discussed doesn't temper the productive effects of sewing his dream into reality. Like his memories of his kokum, Jonny's realized dream in which he wears regalia usually reserved for women assigned female at birth has the power to heal. Jonny recognizes and values this power as seen in his comment after making the dress: "I am my own best medicine."[37]

Million theorizes that such "intense dreaming" is an Indigenous practice of transformation.[38] Among culturally connected Indigenous people, dreaming, she explains, "is the effort to make sense of relations in the worlds we live, dreaming and empathizing intensely our relations with past and present and the future without the boundaries of linear time. Dreaming is a communicative sacred activity."[39] There are two dreams, in particular, in *Jonny Appleseed* that bring this truth home for Jonny and the reader. The first is Jonny's dream of a regenerating and fecund world in which "treaty land has awakened."[40] This world, which he traverses naked, is animated by the erotic: the "buds drip" and the "berries are thick with juice."[41] As he hears a round dance song, Jonny voices his love for the land in Cree and is mounted by Maskwa, a bear, who recognizes him as an Oji-Cree feminine man. As a result, Jonny comes on—or, more appropriately, into—the land, saying, "All of this treaty land is filled with me."[42] At the scene's conclusion, Maskwa recognizes and names Jonny's Two-Spirit identity and also reiterates his love, much like his Kokum did, not only seeing Jonny for who he is but also telling Jonny he is loved, always: "Kâkike, he huffs, kisákihitin kâkike."[43] This world, with its integral tie to the land, is entirely informed by an Indigenous cosmology. The sacred dreamspace Jonny describes joins him with a specifically Cree spiritual world in which the generative power of Two-Spirit desire calls forth erotic sovereignty: spirituality, land, and Two-Spirit desire are unified.[44]

If "dreaming is a communicative sacred activity," then we can recognize the final dream in the text, which Jonny's mother shares with him when he returns to the reserve, as a powerful message from the creator. In it, Jonny and his mother are pushed away from a riverbank where "big-ass Native men in regalia" line the banks, spearfishing unsuccessfully for salmon.[45] His mother explains that when Jonny finally penetrates this male-dominated dream space he is mocked as a "girlboy" until he spears the first fish.[46] In the aftermath of his success, Jonny gains respect, and it is he, in the end, who teaches the men to fish and feed the people. The dream ends with Jonny's kokum smiling and telling his mother, "That boy of yours, Karen, he is his own best thing."[47] This particular dream is perhaps the weightiest in the text, since it is predicted by his kokum, who tells Jonny's mother to watch and share with him an important dream that she'll have about him. Like Jonny's dream of his jingle dress and his dream of Maskwa and the animate treaty land, Jonny's Two-Spirit identity again becomes medicine. In his first dream of the dress, that medicine nourishes him; in the second, his Two-Spiritness feeds both him and the land itself. In this final dream, Jonny sustains the people who make up his nation by not just feeding them, but teaching subsistence practices that will sustain them. This is the epitome of erotic sovereignty in which Two-Spirit people take on generative, culturally specific roles that augment Indigenous nationhood.

Million argues that "to 'decolonize' means to understand as fully as possible the forms colonialism takes in our own times."[48] Whitehead's novel underscores this point—his readers are not offered an easy celebration of Two-Spiritness that romanticizes Indigeneity. Jonny has no choice but to face the insistent mandates of settler-identified masculinity; in the process, he experiences the physical and psychological pain caused by a cis heteropatriarchy that tries to erase his very existence. By concretely depicting the dangers of these encounters, Whitehead demands a rejection of settler imaginaries, and, particularly, of settler masculinity, a form of colonialism that still has violent power today. But while he acknowledges such ongoing colonial infiltrations into Indigenous worldviews, they define neither Whitehead, as we see in his Lammy rejection, nor his protagonist, as we see in his novel. The dreamscapes of *Jonny Appleseed* allow Whitehead to imagine better, to imagine differently, to see Jonny, in all his femme glory, as medicine. Thus, even as Jonny claims a queer femme identity—or what some might call male femininity—he narrates his life in a way that defines and privileges an Oji-Cree Two-Spirit ideology. As a Two-Spirit person, Jonny is "his own best thing," and, moreover, his mother's dream argues, the best thing for the nation. Whitehead's embodied dreamscapes ultimately claim the productive possibilities of erotic sovereignty in which Two-Spirit people tenderly and fully inhabiting their genders, desires, and nations is the very best medicine of all.

## NOTES

1. Scott Lauria Morgensen, *Spaces between Us: Queer Settler Colonialism and Indigenous Decolonization* (Minneapolis: University of Minnesota Press, 2018).
2. Joshua Whitehead, "Why I'm Withdrawing from My Lambda Literary Award Nomination," The Insurgent Architects' House for Creative Writing, March 14, 2018, https://www.tiahouse.ca.
3. Whitehead, "Why I'm Withdrawing."
4. For more on the term's etymology, see Kylan Mattias de Vries, "Berdache (Two-Spirit)," *Encyclopedia of Gender and Society*, vols. 1–2, ed. Jodi O'Brien (Thousand Oaks: CA: Sage, 2009), 62–65. In *Spaces between Us*, Morgensen notes that "this Orientalist term arose first to condemn Middle Eastern and Muslim men as racial

enemies of Christian civilization, by linking them to the creation of berdache (in translation) as "kept boys" or "male slaves" whose sex was said to have been altered by immoral male desire" (36).

5  There are Two-Spirit/Queer Diné folks who claim and live within these categories today; hence my use of present tense—queer Indigenous people are not artifacts of the past. However, it would be disingenuous not to also acknowledge that there are Diné people who reject the current or historical existence of such identity categories or define them more narrowly. See also Jennifer Nez Denetdale's "Securing Navajo National Boundaries: War, Patriotism, Tradition, and the Diné Marriage Act of 2005," *Wicazo Sa Review* 24, no. 2 (2009): 131–48; and *The Status of Navajo Women and Gender Violence*, a 2016 report from the Navajo Nation Human Right Commission. The latter document, of which Denetdale is a coauthor, is the result of four years of extensive discussions, public forums, and a two-day workshop with Navajo traditional practitioners. The hearings, which, notably, were held by the Navajo Nation about and for Diné people, affirm Diné gender perspectives citing the existence of three sexes and four genders.

6  See trans Anishinaabe scholar Kai Pyle for an excellent discussion of Anishinaabemowin terms for Two-Spirit people. Pyle, "Naming and Claiming: Recovering Ojibwe and Plains Cree Two-Spirit Language," *TSQ* 5, no. 4 (2018): 574–88.

7  See Brian Gilley, *Becoming Two-Spirit: Gay Identity and Social Acceptance in Indian Country* (Lincoln: University of Nebraska Press, 2006).

8  Jenny L. Davis, "Refusing (Mis)Recognition: Navigating Multiple Marginalization in the US Two Spirit Movement," *Review of International American Studies* 12, no. 1 (2019): 66.

9  Whitehead, "Why I'm Withdrawing."

10  Joshua Whitehead, *Jonny Appleseed* (Vancouver: Arsenal Pulp, 2018), 7.

11  Whitehead, *Jonny Appleseed*, 8, 9.

12  Whitehead, "Chat with Joshua Whitehead," 49th Shelf, July 2, 2018, https://49thshelf.com.

13  Whitehead, *Jonny Appleseed*, 22.

14  Whitehead, 45. For those unfamiliar, "NDN" is slang/text-speak for Indian among many Indigenous folks.

15  Whitehead, 89, 79.

16  Whitehead, 73.

17  Whitehead, 67.

18  Whitehead, 105.

19  Dian Million, "Felt Theory: An Indigenous Feminist Approach to Affect and History," *Wicazo Sa Review* 24, no. 2 (2009), 54.

20  Million, "Felt Theory," 54.

21  Whitehead, *Jonny Appleseed*, 105.

22  Whitehead, 124.

23  Whitehead, 172.

24  Whitehead, 172.

25  Whitehead, 79.
26  Whitehead, 173.
27  Whitehead, 173.
28  Robert Alexander Innes and Kim Anderson, "Introduction: Who Is Walking with Our Brothers?," in *Indigenous Men and Masculinities* (Winnipeg: University of Manitoba Press, 2015), 4.
29  Sam McKegney, "Into the Full Grace of the Blood in Men: An Introduction," in *Masculindians: Conversations about Indigenous Manhood* (East Lansing: Michigan State University Press, 2014), 8.
30  Whitehead, *Jonny Appleseed*, 99.
31  Whitehead, "Why I'm Withdrawing."
32  Whitehead, *Jonny Appleseed*, 63.
33  Whitehead, 63.
34  Whitehead, 48.
35  Arden Ogg, "You Always Come First with Me and 'Order of Persons in Cree," Cree Literacy Network, February 12, 2016, http://creeliteracy.org.
36  Whitehead, *Jonny Appleseed*, 80.
37  Whitehead, 80.
38  Dian Million, "Intense Dreaming: Theories, Narratives, and Our Search for Home," *American Indian Quarterly* 15, no. 3 (2011): 313–33.
39  Million, "Intense Dreaming," 315.
40  Whitehead, *Jonny Appleseed*, 69.
41  Whitehead, 69.
42  Whitehead, 40.
43  Whitehead, 40.
44  The concept of erotic sovereignty is built from the work of Audre Lorde and Beth Brant, among others. The term "sovereign erotic" originates with Qwo-Li Driskill, who explains, "When I speak of a Sovereign Erotic, I'm speaking of an erotic whole ness healed and/or healing from the historical trauma that First Nations people continue to survive, rooted within the histories, traditions, and resistance struggles of our nations." Driskill, "Stolen from Our Bodies: First Nations Two-Spirits/Queers and the Journey to a Sovereign Erotic," *Studies in American Indian Literatures* 16, no. 2 (2004): 51. For more on this history, see Lisa Tatonetti, *The Queerness of Native American Literature* (Minneapolis: University of Minnesota Press, 2014).
45  Whitehead, *Jonny Appleseed*, 205.
46  Whitehead, 206.
47  Whitehead, 207.
48  Million, "Felt Theory," 55.

PART 3

# Embodying Male Femininities

The authors in this section of the book explore what it means to alter, modify, and cultivate bodies in ways that produce or project male femininities. While the body has long been the purview of medicine and science, scholars in the humanities and social sciences have recently begun to think about how the body, self, and society interact. It is only though our bodies that we experience the social world, so it makes sense that the body is an inescapable part of gender, sex, and sexuality.

All of the readings in this section reveal the dialectical relationship between bodies and culture, or the ways that our bodies are shaped by and shape culture. They also elucidate the ways in which bodies are gendered subjects and objects; bodies are purposeful and reflexive, as well as disciplined by social and cultural norms. Moreover, the readings in this section demonstrate how the neat distinctions between male/female, man/woman, and even nature/culture are upended through the processes, practices, and performances of embodying male femininities.

Perhaps more so than any other section of this volume, the readings in "Embodying Male Femininities" encompass a unique assortment of disciplinary styles, research methods, and mediums. While KC Councilor uses a comic to explore his relationship to masculinity through the process of gender transition, Stephanie Bonvissuto offers us a personal interview with renowned trans activist Julia Serano. We also include three empirical chapters that explore what happens when men grow breasts, become pregnant, and use cosmetic enhancements, and what these changes in embodiment might mean for making sense of male femininities.

In the previous section, on "Configuring Male Femininities," we explained that gender is a social construction. But you might also be asking yourself, if gender is socially constructed, what does that mean for the material differences we find between our bodies? The idea that masculinity and femininity are socially constructed does not mean that breasts, penises, and uteruses are not real, or that human reproduction does not require eggs and sperm. What it does mean, however, is that these biological realities are not the end-all for how we experience social life. As some of the readings in this section demonstrate, men can grow breasts (as Bishop explains), and in this brave new world of ours, men can become pregnant (as Ingraham-Waters relays). As you shall see, breasts and pregnancy belong to biological processes, but they are also imbued with gendered meanings—meanings that are often used to legitimate gender inequality. For example, explanations that men cannot breastfeed or become pregnant have served to justify the feminization of care work and the gendered division of labor.[1]

We use what we believe to be natural embodied differences to justify all sorts of things about the gender binary. Take testosterone, for example: a hormone fundamental to the way we culturally conceptualize masculinity. We have been told that men have higher levels of testosterone than women, *and* that testosterone causes men to be aggressive. We take biological explanations and use them to validate our social behavior. Well, quite a bit of evidence demonstrates that masculine behavior actually produces testosterone, and that testosterone is a physiological response to aggression, activity, and social status, rather than their cause.[2] Testosterone increases, for instance, when men win in sports, and deceases when they lose.[3] It also decreases when men are intimately involved with caring for children.[4] Thus, the physiology of our bodies is gendered by social processes, and our seemingly natural bodies are actually the sustained product of gendered practices and ideologies.

In addition to illustrating the social meanings of gendered embodiment, the readings in this section highlight how bodies can be both subject and object. Bodies are active, purposeful, and regulated by social norms; it is impossible to separate bodies and our understanding of bodies from cultural meanings and social context. How we assign meaning to bodies emerges through culture and through lived experiences. The body is a subject that individuals experience, create, and negotiate. We construct, preserve, and challenge socially structured gender relations through our appearances and behavior. Seeing bodies as subjects illuminates the extent to which people do not merely *have* bodies, but also *do* bodies. Bodies are always being performed in ways that meaningfully construct and demonstrate our selves and social identities. The bodies body is a vessel for communicating how subjects see themselves, how they want to be perceived by others, and where they locate themselves in society.

Both Councilor and Serano explore the ways individuals can use the process of gender transition to express a gender identity through the body, and reveal the ways that imagined appraisals—or the way we perceive others view us—reflect onto the self and body in an interpretive process. In the comic, KC Councilor shows how enhancing male sex characteristics in the body can transform social interactions. With the cultural genitalia of shorter hair, men's clothing, and a wider jawline, Councilor becomes a body read as male and is thus permitted to take up more space, get drinks more quickly, and is afforded more physical autonomy than when he was read as a queer female.[5] Moreover, Councilor illustrates that as some trans men become more socially recognized as male, they can become more comfortable expressing femininity and engaging in stereotypically feminine behaviors. As scholars have shown,[6] this is because there is increased reliance on highly gendered behavior when sex is ambiguous, but when sex category is more obvious, there can be more gender flexibility, like wearing pink or crying at a wedding.[7] Later in this section, Bishop documents a reversal of this process. Unlike trans men who shift their gender presentation and modify their bodies to align their appearance with their identities, Bishop's interviews with men who unexpectedly grow breasts shows what happens when bodily change itself is a catalyst for expanding modes of gender expression.

Where psychosocial processes, social interactions, and cultural interpretations are important for experiences of embodiment, so, too, are processes of objectification. Larger structural forces and social discourses also influence our decisions about how we shape and present our bodies. Some of the readings in this section explicitly highlight the consequences of objectification. Ingraham-Waters documents the way different stakeholders police and surveil the bodies of imagined and actual pregnant men; Berkowitz examines the increasing objectification of aging men's bodies through the anti-aging industry, Big Pharma, and the beauty industry. Perhaps because of the forces of objectification, in different ways both of these chapters reveal the limits of subversion for male femininities.

Finally, the readings in this section turn the spotlight on the illusory binaries of masculine/feminine, male/female, man/woman, and natural/

cultural through the embodiment of male femininities. Sex, sexuality, and gender are not discrete identity categories, but are malleable and flexible. As they expose the instabilities of these categories, the empirical studies and personal narratives in "Embodying Male Femininities" illuminate the extent to which bodies and identities have endless possible combinations. Many of the authors featured here demonstrate that folks can move through the world identifying as a feminine man, a crossdresser, genderqueer, a trans woman, a masculine woman, and a trans man at different points in their lives. And each of these identities provides a unique experience of femininity and masculinity, for how they do body is differentially read and interpreted by oneself and by interlocuters.

These readings belie any existence of a natural body unmarked by collective norms, cultural discourses, and technological interventions. The idea of a natural body is illusory, and, even more, what we imagine as natural is temporal and transient. We live in a reality of gender affirming surgeries, assisted reproductive technologies, and cosmetic enhancements, all of which expose the encroachment of technology onto human bodies and the fictitious distinction between nature and culture. Male pregnancy, trans bodies, Botoxed, and even bra-donning men are all contemporary conjectures in which bodies and technology become conjoined. In 1985, Donna Haraway notoriously used the phrase "cyborg bodies" to refer to the breakdown of the nature/culture dichotomy and the false distinction between the organic and the technological.[8] The bodies you will read about here are indeed cyborgs—techno bodies that expose the postmodern destabilization of the human/nonhuman binary and the divide between nature and culture. However, as you read, we urge you to keep in mind the extent to which technology is always embedded in power relations and the ways in which these bodies are constituted within gender, race, class, and a host of other inequalities.

This scholarship demonstrates the complex ways that folks who embody male femininities negotiate new and unanticipated interpersonal and cultural scripts. Dislocating femininity from the female body allows us to question the association between embodiment and gender, complicating the relationship between technologies, sexed bodies, and gendered identities. We hope that the readings in this section encourage readers to imagine a world more accepting of gender diversity, with expanded opportunities for men to modify their bodies in ways that highlight the liberating potential of femininities.

NOTES

1 R. W. Connell, *Teachers' Work* (New York: Routledge, 1985); R. W. Connell, *Gender and Power: Society, the Person, and Sexual Politics* (Stanford, CA: Stanford University Press, 1987).
2 Robert M. Sapolsky, *The Trouble with Testosterone and Other Essays on the Biology of the Human Predicament* (New York: Simon & Schuster, 1997); Alan Mazur and Alan Booth, "Testosterone and Dominance in Men," *Behavioral and Brain Sciences* 21, no. 3 (1998) 353–97; Alan Booth, Douglas A. Granger, Alan Mazur, and Katie T. Kivlighan, "Testosterone and Social Behavior." *Social Forces* 85, no. 1 (2006): 167–91.
3 A. Booth, G. Shelley, A. Mazur, G. Tharp, and R. Kittok, "Testosterone, and Winning and Losing in Human Competition," *Hormones and Behavior* 23, no. 4 (December 1989): 556–71; Booth et al., "Testosterone and Social Behavior."
4 Lee T. Gettler, Thomas W. McDade, Alan B. Feranil, and Cristopher W. Kuzawa, "Longitudinal Evidence That Fatherhood Decreases Testosterone in Human Males," *Proceedings of the National Academy of Sciences* 108, no. 39 (2011): 16194–99.
5 Suzanne J. Kessler and Wendy McKenna, *Gender: An Ethnomethodological Approach* (Hoboken NJ: Wiley, 1978).
6 Raine Dozier, "Beards, Breasts, and Bodies: Doing Sex in a Gendered World," *Gender and Society* 19, no. 3 (2005): 297–316.
7 KC Councilor, L. Barry, K. C. Kay, and L. A. Kozik, *Between You and Me: Transitional Comics* (Berkeley, CA: Drawbridge, 2019).
8 Donna Haraway, "A Manifesto for Cyborgs: Science, Technology, and Socialist Feminism in the 1980s," *Australian Feminist Studies* 2, no. 4, (1985): 1–42.

# 8

## Dear Masculinity

KC COUNCILOR

9

## An Interview with Julia Serano

STEPHANIE BONVISSUTO

It is difficult to imagine having any meaningful dialogue about the complex experiences of being transgender in the United States today without mentioning Julia Serano's name and work. Her sociopolitical trilogy—*Whipping Girl: A Transsexual Woman on the Scapegoating of Femininity*, *Excluded: Making Feminist and Queer Movements More Inclusive*, and *Outspoken: A Decade of Transgender Activism and Trans Feminism*—has been a part of academic and activist discussion for over a decade. Indeed, the "Trans-Woman's Manifesto" holds revered space on many feminist and gender studies course syllabi. She has also published numerous articles in publications such as *Time*, the *Guardian*, *MS. Magazine*, *Out*, and the Daily Beast. She analyzes current issues of gender and politics through an unapologetic feminist lens that holds many social movements accountable for their philosophies, politics, and subsequent actions.

Not everyone finishes her chapters, books, or articles feeling pleased—but Serano has not shown up to please people. Perhaps because her record includes work not only as an academic/activist/advocate author, but also as an accomplished musician, spoken-word artist, and slam poet, she has come to appreciate what it means to be authentic in front of different audiences, even at the risk of their disapproval. (Although, given the favorable reviews her work has garnished, it seems she has more accolades than rebukes.) This legitimacy seems to embolden her words and theories against the criticism that sweeps through many of the conversations regarding gender identities today.

I was initially introduced to Julia Serano's work through women-only consciousness-raising groups—or, rather, in *response* to the microaggressive hostility I found within them—when I first came out as a queer woman/lesbian of transsexual experience. I often fought both to understand the vitriol I encountered in these supposedly safe spaces and to articulate my unique standpoints, to explain and defend myself. Over the course of countless discussions, the name "Julia Serano" and the book *Whipping Girl* kept circulating between us queer women. Since then Julia Serano's writings have become, for me, a go-to standard for the necessary articulations of the political intricacies that underscore the relations not only between cisgender and transgender communities, but between gender nonconforming people themselves.

That articulation continues here.

* * *

*How did you come to your authentic gender identity? What did that journey mean for you, especially during the time you began taking proactive steps?*

For me, it involved many smaller stages over a long period of time. As a young child, I assumed I was a boy because that's what everyone told me I was, even though something always felt wrong about it. Around the time I was eleven, I consciously realized that I wanted to be a girl, or should be a girl—words sort of fail here. This was the late 1970s, so I didn't have labels like "transgender" to explain myself. I guess you could say that I identified as "a boy who wanted to be a girl" back then. Since I couldn't really change the "boy" part, anatomically speaking, I explored my gender through feminine dress and imagining stories where I could be a girl. Later, as a young adult, I became aware of the identity "male crossdresser" and embraced that for a number of years. It seemed relatively safe—or at least less drastic—for me to imagine myself as a male who was expressing their feminine side on occasion, rather than contemplate the possibility that I might actually be "transsexual." But, over time, it became more and more clear to me that what I enjoyed most out of crossdressing wasn't expressing femininity, but having others see me as female.

I guess I came full circle, and realized that the primary driving force was the same one that I recognized as an eleven-year-old: that I should be a girl rather than a boy. The journey itself was a mixture of frightening and empowering. Each new stage started out scary, because what I was doing (exploring my gender, expressing femininity) was obviously taboo, and I was confused about what it all meant and where it might lead, and afraid of being found out. But, by the end of each stage, I would come to embrace who I was.

*As an out transsexual, trans-rights activist and advocate who not only embraces a visible femininity but espouses a political femininity, what did masculinity mean to you before starting transition, and what has it come to mean to you now? What did femininity mean to you before and what has it come to mean now?*

In my writings, I have countered some of the more condescending attitudes that some cisgender feminists have expressed toward femininity—viewing it as oppressive and artificial, and presuming that women who embrace femininity must be doing it in order to fit in or appease others. I'm afraid to say that that's pretty much how I viewed masculinity when I was younger. I presumed that masculinity must be some kind of act or performance, because it didn't resonate at all with me personally. I thought: "Why would anyone want or choose to be masculine?" It made absolutely no sense to me.

In subsequent years, especially upon getting to know trans men, butch women, and others on the trans masculine spectrum, I came to understand that some people just are masculine—it comes naturally to them, often despite their socialization to the contrary. Nowadays, I view masculinity, femininity, and other gender expressions as ways of being that resonate with some people, but not everyone. As long as it's not compulsory, and not "toxic" (i.e., reliant on dominating other people), I no longer have any qualms with masculinity.

*I was wondering if you could deconstruct a little more what you mean by "ways of being." We as a binary-gendered culture tend to process gender (and sexuality) as either social constructs (implying choice/nurturing) or as innate features (implying being "born that way"). Do "ways of being" encompass both, or even more than both?*

Even more than both. In my book *Excluded*, I have a chapter called "Homogenizing versus Holistic Views of Gender and Sexuality," where I go into this in great depth. But, to quickly summarize, I make the case that strict-nature and strict-nurture arguments are not only overly simplistic and ignore the full breadth of evidence, but they also fail to explain the great diversity in gender and sexualities that we see in the world. I instead forward a more holistic view, one in which countless biological factors (including both shared biology and individual biological variation) and countless social and environmental factors (including shared culture and unique individual experiences) come together in an extraordinarily complex manner to produce certain trends but also a wide range of exceptions to those trends. I forwarded that model not only because I believe it is true, but also in the hopes that we can finally move beyond dwelling on why people turn out the way they do, and instead focus more on challenging the hierarchies, expectations, and meanings that we project onto gender and sexual difference.

*Where had you or might you have had encountered male femininity along your gender journey? If so, how may have your understanding of it changed? If so, did it influence your identity at the time?*

Most of my early experiences with male femininity came from crossdresser culture, which was somewhat unique in that it usually involved having an entirely separate female or "en femme" persona or identity. As an eventual trans woman, it's obvious why I gravitated toward that community! I was aware of other expressions of male femininity, such as drag or men who were feminine in other ways. I appreciated their existence, but I wasn't really influenced by them, as my goal wasn't to be a feminine man—what I wanted was to be seen as a woman.

*How do you approach male-femininity currently? Are you indifferent to its presence?*

These days, I don't really think about male femininity much per se. I have friends who are feminine men, or crossdressers, or drag performers, or AMAB (assigned male at birth) genderqueer femmes, and so on, and I appreciate their gender diversity. And I can relate to many of the obstacles and presumptions they face, having faced similar difficulties myself in the past. But, these days, I find myself thinking about femininity in a more general sense, rather than thinking specifically about male femininity.

There is a tendency for femininity to be viewed as artificial and inferior to masculinity in our culture, no matter who is expressing it. These assumptions become amplified when the feminine person is viewed as or presumed to be male. In *Whipping Girl*, I described this as the intersection of oppositional sexism and traditional sexism, or "trans-misogyny." Anti-feminine sentiment—or femmephobia, or whatever you want to call it—also intersects with other forms of marginalization. These days, I'm more interested in considering this broad intersectional approach to femininity, rather than focusing specifically on "male femininity" (as I did in some of my earlier writings).

*How might you respond to the expectation that male-femininity would be a chapter in the story of any male-to-female transsexual?*

I grew up during a time when virtually all trans people were forced to live as a member of their birth-assigned gender throughout childhood and often into adulthood. Many of our narratives involve periods of experimenting with "male femininity" or "female masculinity," but this was often by necessity, as that was the only option or outlet available to us to explore or express our genders at the time.

But, nowadays, with the growing acceptance of gender-affirming approaches to trans children, this is no longer the case. Increasing numbers of younger trans women have never had a "male femininity" stage, because they were able to socially live as girls and women without ever having lived much (if any) of their lives identifying or being perceived as male. To be clear, I don't expect "male femininity" to disappear entirely, as there is a lot of diversity with regard to gender expression, identity, and embodiment. But I do believe that male femininity stages will be significantly less common among trans women moving forward.

*Your occupations—as activist, advocate, author, musician, even as spoken-word artist—often locate you under the figurative if not literal spotlight. It is, one imagines, a unique social relation in that you must foster a special relationship with an audience who in turn may or may not generally share, let alone understand the nuances of, your gender journey. What might you feel you need to project to them regarding your gender identity?*

I used to think about this a lot shortly after my transition. Nowadays, I honestly don't really give it much thought. Because I can't really control what people think. People tend to read me as a (cisgender) woman these days. If they become aware that I'm trans—which is likely when I'm performing, since it's a regular subject of my writings, songs, etcetera—I know some people will still see me and accept me as a woman, while others may view me as a feminine or defective "man," and still others will lump me into some "not-quite-man-not-quite-woman" third category along with other trans and gender nonconforming people. All of this is outside of my control. Regardless of how I dress or act, audiences will come to their own conclusions regarding my gender, based upon their own beliefs and prejudices. My job is to be authentically me and share my thoughts and art with the world, even if some people don't get it or refuse to respect my identity.

*Halberstam's formulation of female masculinity potentially serves as a disruption of patriarchal discourses through which gender-based power exerts itself, especially at the level of the body. Should we expect the same of male femininity? Where might we find the starting points or limits of such destabilizations? In 2018, with a plethora of gender identities available in certain popular segments of Western culture, what can male femininity come to mean?*

Within feminism, and gender and queer studies, there have been many claims about how certain identities and expressions supposedly destabilize binary/patriarchal notions of gender, and concerns about whether these identities and expressions may eventually be co-opted or assimilated by the mainstream, thereby losing their revolutionary power. I have never been a fan of such framings, because if some genders are seen as inherently "radical," then others must be inherently "conservative." Around the time that I was writing *Whipping Girl* in the mid-aughts, it was common for transsexuals, and especially feminine trans women, to be accused of "reinforcing gender" or being "conservatively gendered." Even though, in our day-to-day lives, absolutely no one in the cisnormative mainstream views us as gender conforming or reinforcing the gender binary.

Most people in our culture adhere to a strict binary understanding of maleness/masculinity and femaleness/femininity. In that context, anyone who fails to neatly conform to those ideals—including those who express male femininity—will seemingly disturb or disrupt that system to some degree, whether that is their intention or not. However, if we hope to someday dismantle existing binary/patriarchal gender structures, then somewhere along the line, male femininities, female masculinities, and other gender-nonconforming expressions and identities will cease to be unexpected or noteworthy.

I think our goal should be a world that embraces gender and sexual diversity, and that is free of sexism and gender hierarchies (along with other forms of marginalization). In such a world, we should expect that ways of being that seem disruptive and radical to us today will simply become accepted and passé.

*How do you imagine male femininity mattering differently for cisgender men than for trans women?*

In many cases, quite significantly. Obviously, there are some trans women who never identify as male in their lives, so they might not even relate to the concept. For those of us who did identify as male at some point in the past, we may reinterpret any previous experiences with male femininity as merely a phase or stage we passed through on the way to realizing our trans womanhood. Or in retrospect, we may not consider ourselves to have ever been truly "male" in the first place.

I also think that expectations regarding femininity are very different between the two groups. Cisgender men are expected to be masculine, or at the very least "not feminine." So any expressions of femininity they exhibit will defy those expectations, and may garner consternation or derision as a result. For trans women, those expectations are reversed. Once we transition and begin publicly identifying as women, the expectation is that we should be feminine. And if we are seen as insufficiently feminine, people may not take our identities seriously. Butch, tomboyish, and androgynously presenting trans women are often interrogated for their gender expression, garnering reactions like, "Why should I take you seriously as a woman if you're going to dress like that?"

While cisgender men who embrace "male femininity" and trans women may have very different personal experiences and understandings with regards to femininity, we do share something in common. We are all navigating our way through a world where femininity is routinely dismissed and delegitimized, and where transmisogyny ensures that trans and gender nonconforming expressions of femininity are especially ridiculed and punished.

*Where does/can male femininity enter current conversations about nonbinary/genderqueer and other non-normative identity constructions?*

Transgender activists of the 1990s forwarded the idea of "transgender" as a big umbrella that includes all people who defy societal gender norms to in some manner. The purpose for this wasn't to insist that we are all the same—we obviously differ quite a bit in our identities and our experiences. Rather, the reason was twofold. First, we should all band together because we are oppressed by the same system: the gender binary. Second, these trans activists recognized that the individual subgroups we may inhabit are not entirely discrete. For instance, in the course of my life, I have identified as a male who was exploring femininity, a crossdresser, a genderqueer, and a trans woman.

For these reasons, I believe that there are plenty of constructive conversations that can be had between AMAB feminine people, whether they identify as cisgender men, nonbinary, or even trans women. For such conversations to take place, it is important for all of us to recognize our potential similarities (e.g., our experiences overcoming male/masculine socialization, the forms of discrimination we may face) while also recognizing our many differences. I have moved through the world as a man, a genderqueer, and a woman at different points in my life, and each was a very different experience. And the femininity I expressed in each of those contexts was read and interpreted differently by others. So we should refrain from making too many assumptions about what we may have in common. But, at the same time, we do have a mutual interest in working across these differences in order to challenge sexism, gender norms, and anti-feminine sentiment.

*Do you think the binary presuppositions that underscore male femininities would limit non-normative gender constructions? In other words, emerging from a long-standing binary-gendered Western society, does male femininity cast a particular gravity that male-to-female transsexuals or AMAB-female-spectrum people may find difficult to break free from?*

Yes, this most certainly happens, as seen in the long-standing tensions that have existed between trans women, crossdressers, and drag queens. While we may differ from one another with regard to our identities, expressions, and embodiments, outsiders who hold a strict binary mindset tend to lump all of us together as "feminine men" (especially if they refuse to acknowledge trans women's and nonbinary gender identities).

I remember when I first came out to people about my decision to transition, and I had a number of people ask me why I couldn't just wear feminine clothing without going on hormones. It is a very common misconception that those of us who transition do so in order to express femininity rather than a deep-seated understanding that we are (or should be) female. This is precisely why some trans women prefer to distance themselves from other AMAB gender-nonconforming folks or forward the notion that they are "true transsexuals" while these other groups are merely "sexual deviants."

I think the way forward is through education and making the cisnormative majority understand that there are many facets of gender (e.g., identity, expression, embodiment), and lots of variation that exists within them.

*What might you suggest the cisnormative majority could do to assist in creating that particular future?*

As an activist, I appreciate the idea of holding the dominant/majority group accountable and compelling them to work to end the form of marginalization in question. But in this particular case, I think it's a bit more complicated than that, as many of us who are gender diverse fail to recognize this multiplicity ourselves.

In our culture, we are all socialized to view gender and sexuality in a strict binary fashion: men are masculine, women are feminine, and as "opposite sexes" they are naturally attracted to one another. Those of us who are gender or sexual minorities (in whatever way) often initially embrace simplistic theories that explain our existence and experiences, but not those of others. For instance, a trans woman who claims to have a "female brain trapped inside a male body"—that may make sense for her, but it doesn't explain why there are feminine men and crossdressers. Similarly, these later groups may claim to be "letting their feminine side out"—which may be how they see their situation, but it doesn't explain why trans women exist. The problem with these sorts of explanations is that they portray the gender or sexual minority in question as a valid "exception to the rule," while keeping the rule (i.e., the gender binary/heteronormativity/cisnormativity) largely intact.

Such "single exception" theories are extremely prevalent, and they perpetuate hierarchies within our own ranks. You can see this in the many gay and lesbian folks who are antagonistic toward bisexuals, or the many cisgender feminists who are antagonistic toward trans people, or the constant tensions between various transgender and trans-adjacent subgroups, and so on. And it's not unusual for such individuals to share these attitudes and beliefs with the straight cisgender majority, who will then further spread this misinformation.

This is why I've written extensively about making feminist and queer/LGBTQIA+ movements more inclusive, a big part of which involves accepting this heterogeneity, and to stop policing autonomous and consensual expressions of gender and sexuality. If we can all get on the same page on this, it will be far easier for us to press the straight cisgender majority to advocate on behalf of this multiplicity, too. But so long as we continue to forward "single exception" theories, and buy into gender and sexual hierarchies ourselves, this will remain an uphill battle.

## 10

# Unexpected Breasts, Unexpected Pleasures

*Exploring Cisgender Men's Breast Development and Bra Wearing*

KATELYNN BISHOP

Male breasts, or breasts that develop on the bodies of cisgender men (disparagingly called "man boobs") [1] are often mocked and represented as unattractive, funny, or embarrassing.[2] This bodily development is associated with fatness and aging—commonly objects of fear and disgust in Western culture.[3] And because breasts are popularly regarded as feminine, they are seen as "out of place" on male bodies.[4] But, far from an anomaly, male breast development actually affects a significant proportion of cisgender men, particularly (but not exclusively) during puberty and older age.[5] These men's perspectives have rarely been considered in the academic literature on gender, masculinities, and embodiment, though their experiences raise important questions. How do they feel about their breasts, and how do they manage them? How does their development of breasts impact their sense of masculinity? Do they ever regard their breasts positively?

This chapter addresses these questions through analysis of qualitative interviews conducted with fourteen breasted men. Using a feminist approach to embodiment that understands the meanings of bodies as emerging both through culture and through lived, embodied experience, I demonstrate how these men confront and refigure the meanings of male breasts.[6] The men I interviewed—who were recruited through a broader study on bra-wearing practices—did not seek to remove their breasts through exercise or surgery, which are marketed to breasted men as options to "masculinize" their bodies. Instead, they opted to wear bras to manage sensations associated with breast development such as tenderness and sensitivity. While these men were initially dismayed by their breast development and hesitant to begin wearing bras, some of them came to find unexpected pleasures through wearing them and through appreciating (and even intentionally enhancing) their breasts. My analysis details these men's reactions to their breast development and decisions to wear bras, emphasizing the unexpected pleasures that emerged, which serve as a counterpoint to negative and stigmatizing representations of male breasts, and as a resource for reimagining bodies and gender.

## Uncovering the Meanings of Male Breasts

From a medical standpoint, breasts are comprised primarily of mammary glands (also called glandular tissue or breast tissue) and fat. Mammary glands—which have the capacity to produce breast milk—are present in both males and females, and it is relatively common for male and female infants to have swollen breast tissue. Similar to females, it is common for males to experience swelling of the breast tissue during puberty. Male breast development at puberty is typically temporary—the swelling tends to subside after three years, at most.[7] However, many men develop swollen breast tissue in middle age, which is often a more lasting development. The medical term used to describe male breast development is "gynecomastia," which refers to the enlargement of glandular tissue in males.[8] According to the Mayo Clinic, as many as one in four men develop gynecomastia between the ages of fifty and sixty-nine.[9] Additionally, some men (including men with and without gynecomastia) develop fatty deposits in the chest area. This development is medically termed "pseudogynecomastia," although it may visually appear similar to gynecomastia.[10] While the medical terminology used to define these bodily features implies pathology or abnormality, the fact that they are quite common might prompt us to think of them less as "disorders" and more as common bodily developments.[11]

This discussion thus far has acknowledged only two types of bodies—male and female. Yet the existence of *intersex* people complicates these categories.[12] Intersex is a broad category that encompasses several types of bodily variations that diverge from the socially defined categories of male and female, including variations in the makeup of genitals, internal sex organs, and chromosomes, as well as in the way the body produces and processes hormones.[13] Gynecomastia is not typically thought of as an intersex condition in and of itself, though men with the variation called

"Klinefelter syndrome," which is defined by the presence of one of more "extra" X chromosomes (i.e., XXY, XXXY, rather than the more typical male chromosomal makeup of XY) may develop gynecomastia and other female-associated secondary sex characteristics.[14] Many men who develop gynecomastia are otherwise "sex-typical"—in other words, they do not have any other bodily features that would be defined as "intersex."

While medical perspectives define breasts and bodies through their biological functions and cellular makeup, sociologists and feminist scholars emphasize the layers of cultural meanings that shape our reactions to bodies.[15] One of the few scholars to discuss male breasts, Robyn Longhurst, theorizes social reactions to male breasts and reports on interviews with four breasted men.[16] Drawing on feminist philosophers, Longhurst argues that these features make us uncomfortable because they upset the neat distinctions between male/female and man/woman.[17] Longhurst explains that we expect male bodies to be firm and solid, whereas female bodies—which are associated with menstruation, lactation, and pregnancy—are expected to be soft and fluid.[18] Longhurst's four interviewees report on the self-consciousness they feel about their breasts, demonstrating how men respond to the social stigma associated with male breasts. However, Longhurst says that she refrained from asking these men questions about what embodied sensations they experienced, whether they regarded their breasts as erotic, and whether they considered wearing bras, as she perceived these topics to be too sensitive to broach directly.

This chapter addresses Longhurst's call for other scholars to further explore the experiences of breasted men and expands on her analysis by considering their positive perceptions of their breasts. Before presenting my analysis, I contextualize these themes within the scholarship on masculinities—a field that emphasizes the social construction of the multiple forms of masculinity, and the shifting meanings of masculinities across time and space.[19]

## Men, Body Image, and Beauty Practices

Feminist scholars and activists often critique the "objectification" of women's bodies through their display in media images.[20] At least since the 1980s, men's bodies have increasingly been objectified,[21] resulting in men paying more attention to, and becoming dissatisfied with, their appearance.[22] As men have become increasingly concerned with their appearance, they have also adopted bodily practices typically defined as "feminine," such as undergoing cosmetic surgery,[23] removing body hair,[24] and visiting beauty salons.[25] Although participation in these practices might be interpreted as a sign of femininity, one key finding across these studies is that men tend to define their participation in these practices in ways that bolster their masculinity, rather than detract from it. For instance, Elizabeth Haiken finds that men justify their use of cosmetic surgery as a way to increase their ability to earn money—a traditionally masculine goal.[26] Matthew Immergut observes that cultural representations of men's removal of body hair portray this practice as a way to enact control over nature.[27] Kristen Barber notes that men's beauty salons are masculine spaces where the masculinities and social status of upper-class, white, straight men are bolstered through the feminine labor of women salon workers.[28]

Aging leads some men to become more self-conscious about their bodily appearance and bodily function, because younger men's bodies are typically valorized as the masculine "ideal," and aging is culturally perceived as "de-gendering" both men's and women's bodies.[29] In a meta-analysis of ninety-eight studies on men and aging conducted between 2000 and 2015, Edward H. Thompson and Kaitlyn Barnes Langendoerfer argue that older men, recognizing their physical limitations, maintain their masculinity through expressions of intelligence, rather than through their bodies.[30] Other studies examine men's negotiation of bodily changes related to sexual function; the pharmaceutical Viagra, for example, has become culturally synonymous with men's efforts to maintain their masculinity as they age.[31] Meika Loe reports that men say that their use of Viagra restores their sense of masculinity;[32] however, a relatively high percentage of men who try the drug are dissatisfied with its effects and ultimately discontinue their use of it, which points to the limits of technology.[33] Despite scholarly attention to a variety of aspects of men's embodied experience of aging, their reactions to their development of breasts have rarely received attention.[34]

## How I Came to Study Breasted Men

This project emerged unexpectedly from a broader study of bra-wearing practices. When I put out a recruitment call seeking interviewees to speak about their experiences, I expected to hear primarily from cisgender women. However, I had phrased the call somewhat open-endedly, as I was interested in speaking to anyone who had ever worn bras, including genderqueer folks and trans men and women. I had not considered the possibility that my respondents would include cisgender men, but after being contacted by and interviewing one cisgender man, I attempted to recruit more. My email inbox quickly filled up—clearly this was a topic that many men were dealing with, and, while several of them confessed to me that they had not spoken to anyone about these experiences before, they were eager to break their silence.

I ultimately conducted interviews with fourteen masculine-identified people who wear bras to manage their breast development. This group is composed of eleven cisgender men and three male-identified individuals with Klinefelter syndrome. Despite biological differences between these groups, the subjects all identified themselves—and have been perceived by others—as masculine for much of their lives, and their initial breast development was involuntary and generally unexpected. These interviewees' ages ranged from thirty-three to seventy-five, with their ages distributed relatively evenly across this range. Among them are truck drivers, an engineer, a nurse, bankers, and managers. Most identify their gender simply as male or masculine, although one identifies as gender-fluid. They primarily describe themselves as middle-class or upper-middle-class; one identifies as white and Native American, and all others identify as white; one describes his sexuality as fluid, and all others identify as heterosexual. Though these men reported developing breasts at various points during the course, of their lives, from puberty to older age, this analysis focuses specifically on what they shared about their experiences during adulthood.

Conducting interviews with cisgender and intersex men required methodological flexibility, as many of them were not accustomed to discussing this aspect of their lives openly and were uncomfortable with face-to-face or real-time forms of communication. Three of these interviews took place over the phone, one via video chat, and one with a text-based chat service. Seven of the interview participants preferred to participate solely by email; in these cases, I asked them to share a bit of initial information about their breast development and the purposes for which they used bras. I then followed up with a tailored set of questions. After they sent their responses, I typically asked two or three rounds of follow-up questions. Four additional interviewees addressed an initial round of questions via email and subsequently participated in follow-up conversations over video chat.

As a relatively young white woman, I differed from these interviewees in gender and, for many, in age. Rather than impeding conversations, I suspect that my gender generally made men more willing to open up to me about these sensitive experiences. They often asked me for reassurance about whether their bodies or bodily practices were "weird" or "abnormal," and even, in one case, advice about how to broach the topic of wearing bras with his wife. I was empathetic to the fact that, as research participants, they desired affirmation that I, as a researcher, would perceive—and ultimately represent—them in ways that were affirming, rather than stigmatizing. I frequently assured them that other men I had interviewed had shared similar experiences, and I offered my own beliefs that gender is much more complex than often assumed, and that promoting awareness of this fact is valuable.

## From Feeling to Looking: Men's Initial Awareness of Their Breasts and Decisions to Wear Bras

The process through which men became aware of their breasts followed a typical pattern: they initially experienced bodily sensations of pain, sensitivity, or tenderness in their chests, which prompted them to visually evaluate themselves. By looking at their chests, they became aware that they had experienced significant breast development. For instance, Charles explained that he had first noticed tenderness in his nipple after accidentally jamming it into a box at the age of sixty-three (one year before I interviewed him).[35] When the tenderness persisted, he consulted a doctor, who diagnosed him with gynecomastia. Though he said he was aware that he had always had "puffy" nipples and a more pronounced chest, neither he nor his wife had noticed that it had increased significantly in size until his experience of pain prompted them to look more carefully. Another white man, Keith, sixty-four years old and a registered nurse, remembered feeling a sensation of heaviness in his chest after a day of heavy yard work. He thought he might be experiencing a cardiac event and took his vital signs; later, in the shower, he examined his chest and realized that it had grown—what he later describes as one and a half cup sizes in the span of three months.

After becoming aware of their breast development, men worried that others would notice their breasts and sought a solution that would simultaneously conceal their breasts and minimize their discomfort. While some of the men I interviewed considered other options, they typically rejected these options as too cumbersome or invasive. Mark, fifty-four, recounted: "After some research on the web I decided to give a sports bra a try. All the other options looked a lot less comfortable—the compression garments and ace bandages especially looked hideous and time-consuming to apply." Surgery was not a reasonable solution for thirty-five-year-old Jason, who explained: "Surgery was not an option, for several reasons. I just had surgery only a year or so ago before my gynecomastia and that did not go so well. The expense of such surgery, which my insurance would not cover. Also, finally my doctors did not know what was causing it and could therefore not guarantee they would not grow back." Although the men hesitated about wearing them due to their association with femininity, bras provided a satisfying and practical solution to these problems. As Jason reported: "A bra helps with my daily life. It relieves the pain. I don't feel so self-conscious about gynecomastia when they are not bouncing or causing me grief. I guess a bra helps put my breasts in the background." After deciding to try bras, men typically researched options online or, for those who were married, sought assistance from their wives, who were generally accepting of their decisions.

Although bras provided comfort, the men at first experienced anxiety about being "found out" as bra wearers. But, over time, most men came to find that others simply did not pay much attention to their chests, or, if their bras were noticed, they rarely evoked any significant reaction. Martin, fifty-seven, specifically linked the virtual invisibility of his chest to the male privilege of not having it subject to constant scrutiny: "Most of the time, it's very easy to hide wearing a bra. Nobody looks for it on a man. However, I would not want to be female, and have my breasts scanned visually by everyone, not just men. I can't imagine what adolescent women go through." Several men said that they were fairly certain that others had become aware of their bra wearing—for example, they described both coworkers and family members noticing bra straps when patting them on the back or hugging them—but that these incidents occasioned, at worst, brief funny looks. On the flip side, one man reported a positive reaction to his bra wearing. Ed, in his forties, said that a woman approached him and commented that she wished more larger-breasted men would wear bras because they look "untidy" without them.

## Unexpected Pleasures: Experimenting with Gender and Self-Expression

Despite their initial hesitation about wearing bras, many men experienced positive shifts in their relationship to bra wearing over time. For some, wearing a bra became a means to achieving acceptance of their breasts or a more positive body image overall. And, in several cases, men branched out from wearing the most plain and simple bras possible to seeking out and enjoying colorful ones with embellishments, such as lace. These men varied in how they connected these shifting attitudes and behaviors to their masculinities, from viewing their bra wearing practices as making them "more of a man" to thinking of wearing bras as a way of "indulging" their "feminine side."

Keith was unique among the men I interviewed in describing his bra wearing—including his willingness to wear more "feminine styles"—as bolstering his masculinity. For Keith, mastering the complex task of selecting a properly fitting bra was indicative of masculinity. "In my opinion," he offered, "if a guy needs a bra, and he goes and gets, uh, fitted properly, and makes himself look nice, he's more of a man, because it's quite a challenge . . ." Keith narrated at length his efforts to master the highly technical task of fitting; through describing these efforts as an intensive form of labor and making reference to his background in technology and engineering, he arguably codes bra shopping as a masculine pursuit: "[My background is in tech and engineering] and I said if I had to, you know, build a bra for my body type, what would be needed, uh, and I did a lot of reading about all the different types of bras, and, gosh, it's almost overwhelming. . . . I looked on YouTube, and I did Internet searches, and I went to every bra fitting site I could find, I learned all about the shape of my breasts, I must have put in well over forty hours in learning about this [so I wouldn't go out and spend] money on something to find that it doesn't work for me."

Keith selected bras based on a logically derived and purely functional set of criteria, and in so doing was able to justify decisions to wear more "feminine" styles: "A couple of the bras that fit me really well, are, uh, very, how should I say, feminine, very sexy looking, full coverage, uh, they're very nice looking, um, so I said, 'Well, am I going to take something that doesn't fit just right, or am I gonna take this other one that's more sexy looking and that fits right and is comfortable? I'll take the sexy one.'" Although Keith did not discuss deriving pleasure from wearing feminine bras in particular, he did gain satisfaction through carefully shopping for them. He says that through this process he came to appreciate his body and gained satisfaction through taking better care of it.

Whereas Keith treated the aesthetic characteristics of his bras as simply incidental to his selection of them, other men consciously opted to become more adventurous. Some viewed their decision to wear bras that might be defined by some as "feminine" not as feminine behavior, but as an individual form of self-expression. Jason, for instance, said that once he overcame his fear that wearing colorful or embellished bras would threaten his masculinity, he was able to view this practice simply as an expression of his unique personality:

JASON: At first, I was about trying to preserve my "man hold" when it was never endangered. I thought I should stick to only plain and neutral color bras.
KATELYNN: And what caused you to change your thinking about that?
JASON: I'm not a plain person, never have been. Every piece of clothing reflects that of me, except for bras at first. I also have never been one to go along with the flow. I'm unique and proud of it. However, when it came to bras, I think I was trying to prove I was still a man, I don't know. I just kind of woke up and realized a bra with color or lace would not degrade me. I started to accept my new piece of clothing, and my personality started to show through once I started accepting a bra did not make me and it certainly would not break me. From

there I started experimenting with other styles, too. . . . I even have a bra that makes me feel special/sexy.[36]

Through refiguring the wearing of colorful, embellished bras as a form of self-expression that does not threaten his masculinity, Jason arguably expands narrow social conceptions of masculinity.

In contrast to Jason, as other men branched out from plain bras to more embellished styles, they saw themselves as incorporating elements of femininity into their self-expression. Kevin, in his thirties, who first developed breasts as a teenager, said he initially viewed bras as a "necessary evil" in dealing with the physical discomfort caused by gynecomastia. For years, he alternated between accumulating bras and purging his collection, due to his inability to accept his need to wear bras. A couple of years before the interview, he says that he was able to reach a place of self-acceptance about wearing bras, which enabled him to experiment with new styles:

> So I just kind of gave up on not wearing a bra, and then at that point it was kind of like a self-acceptance exercise, so it's, okay, this doesn't reflect on my manhood, this doesn't reflect on who I am, this is just about my own comfort and support, and it's not a big deal. . . . And then it was kind of this experience of like, "Wow, look at all these different varieties of bras, I'm gonna," you know, "since now bras are, like, for me, and I'm not gonna fight it anymore," it was kind of a, an evolution of, "I wanna try that one," or "That one looks interesting," or, "Oooh," you know, "that one's actually kind of cute, I'm gonna go look at it," and I just, I don't know, I just started giving myself permission to, you know, start to join them, instead of fighting them, or recognizing them as a necessary evil or whatever.

He said he has now embraced self-expression through bras and picks the most colorful ones possible, prefers sports bras with cutout details, and enjoys lace. Although Kevin uses language that parallels Jason's in describing his realization that wearing a bra did not threaten his "manhood," he does go on to describe some of his bra-wearing behavior as feminine. At the same time, he performs identity work by marking a boundary between his behavior and crossdressing. He speaks somewhat disparagingly about crossdressers and distinguishes his behavior from theirs by reference to the fact that he is not attempting to appear *as* a woman, despite incorporating elements of femininity into his self-expression.

In contrast to Kevin's efforts to distinguish his behavior from crossdressing, for Taylor, thirty-seven and with Klinefelter syndrome, bra wearing was a path toward embracing occasional cross-gender presentation. He described how he shifted from trying to maintain his masculinity while wearing bras through selecting the plainest options available, to accepting that, in his view, bra wearing and masculinity are simply incompatible: "I was, like, so concerned about trying to, you know, "Oh, even if I have to wear a bra, I'll still try to keep it masculine." . . . [But then I realized] that makes absolutely no sense, that's not even remotely possible." He went on to describe the first time he wore a bra that was anything other than plain: "I was getting fitted, and [the salesperson] brought the styles over, and this one bra, I saw it and I thought it was really nice, it was like, um, I wanna say like a periwinkle color, and it had some lace embellishments, and I just thought it was really beautifully made, and it fit perfectly, even she said so, she was like, "It really fits you nicely," I was like, "It really does, but it has like, you know . . ." She was like, "If you like it, what's wrong with wearing it?" I was like, you know, she had a point."

When I asked him what he did after purchasing the bra, he continued: "I think, uh, I went home, you know, I guess I probably got changed and took a shower, and put it on, and I kind of like looked in the mirror and I admired it, and I was like, you know what, this actually really is nice, I'm gonna treat myself to it, I don't remember if I went directly afterwards, but I'm sure I went out, you know." Taylor reports that not only has bra wearing helped him to accept that his breasts are a part of himself, but that he now enjoys presenting more completely as "female" at times, wearing women's clothing and makeup.

Whereas the pleasures Jason, Kevin, and Taylor discussed deriving from bra wearing were linked primarily to self-expression, Charles, sixty-three, volunteered that he derived sexual pleasure from wearing bras. Similar to the other men, Charles explained that he started out wearing plain bras; in his case, he preferred them in his skin tone because they were easier to conceal, and his wife was more comfortable with him wearing bras that were less feminine. But boredom led him to experiment with other styles, he said: "As time went by though, I got bored with the plainness of the nude bras and began branching out to other colors and even a little bit of frill. My favorite bras right now are a leopard print one and a pink embroidered frame one." Charles had alluded earlier in the interview to deriving sexual pleasure from wearing bras; when I asked him if he could elaborate on this, he responded: "I don't really understand why it can also be a turn-on. It isn't always, but sometimes it is. Maybe it's a fantasy to crossdress or to be a 'sissy'. Most of my life I have felt that I have had to repress my 'feminine side' in order to be manly. I have always loved to touch soft, silky things, but guys' clothes aren't supposed to be soft or silky. Now that I have gotten older, I feel less inhibited, so I'm able to indulge these feelings a little. Sometimes it just really feels good to 'indulge' the feminine."

The sexual pleasure Charles derives from wearing bras seems to stem simultaneously from the tactile aspects of bras—that is, their softness and silkiness against his skin—and his feeling that he is engaging in "forbidden" behavior. While Charles's experience is significant in pointing to the potentially erotic dimension of this form of gendered expression, it is important to note here that because I did not ask directly about experiences of sexual pleasure connected to wearing bras, I am unable to speculate about whether other men had similar experiences.

### Further Pleasures: Men's Modification of Their Breasts

While the men described above found unexpected pleasures in embracing new sartorial options and came to accept their breasts in the process, a couple of men offered that they ventured beyond experimentation with fashion products and opted to more permanently enhance their breasts. These men's decisions cut against widely held assumptions about gender, identity, and embodiment, in that they intentionally modify their bodies with the goal of developing a feature commonly defined as "feminine," while continuing to identify as men. Although it is important to emphasize that these men were a small minority among the men I interviewed, their experiences are compelling and worthy of exploration.

For Nathan, the desire to enhance his breasts emerged directly from his experiences wearing bras. Though he had been self-conscious about his chest for much of his life, wearing bras had led him to feel pride in it, and this feeling extended to a desire to develop his breast tissue further. While Nathan did not share details about the methods he used to induce breast development, he offered his recollections on the thought process leading to the decision and the conversation he had with his wife: "I think that for me personally, it's like someone who feels like they were born in the wrong body or someone who is gay/bi, it's just how they were born and for me it feels normal and 'right.' Before trying to increase the volume of my breast tissue, my wife and I talked about it deeply and why I wanted to do it. I didn't know how to explain it to her other than to say that it just felt like it's the way I'm supposed to be." Nathan drew on popular discourses that portray sexuality and gender identity as "essential" elements of the self, although, interestingly, his feeling that this is the way he is "supposed to be" stands in contradiction to the shame he felt over his chest development earlier in his life. It seems that his experience wearing bras, along with the support and affirmation provided by his wife, enabled him to experience his breasts as an authentic and positive aspect of his body and self.

For Mark, a fifty-four-year-old man who says his wife describes him as "too hetero," the desire to enhance his breasts was less directly related to his experiences wearing bras, and more due to his experiences with the process of breast development itself. He describes his involuntary development of breasts as an "opportunity" to more intentionally explore something he had long wondered about: "I've always been curious as to what it's like for women to go around with, uh, breasts, you know, I am, [what they call] a breast man, they're attractive to me, so I've wondered for a very long time what it would be like, and now that I have this, uh, opportunity, well, you know, I'm getting on in years, and maybe I'm not making as much testosterone, so I'm more predisposed, to uh, to having them, to begin with." Mark said that breast implants and estrogen had always been out of the question for him, but, because of the changes occurring in his body, herbal supplements (which he felt might not have had an effect on him before the reduction in his testosterone production) became a viable way to experiment with increasing his breast size. His initial development of breasts might be conceptualized as providing a form of "embodied permission" to explore breast development further. As he explained, "I'll aid my body's changes but not provoke them excessively." Mark said that he realized that the supplements were taking effect when he noticed his wife (whom he did not inform about his use of the supplements) glancing at his chest—though the change garnered some attention, he had not received any explicit commentary or criticism about his breasts. Nevertheless, he clarified that there was a limit to how far he felt he could safely go: "I'm six foot tall, you know, broad-shouldered, and, well, an A cup is okay, you know, I can get away with that, um, uh, socially when I'm out and about, I don't think anybody would, I don't know what other people would think of, seeing it, um, but I think people could ignore it if they so choose, but anything bigger than that, it's like um, hmm, I really haven't seen guys wandering around here with like, C cups [laughing] . . . I'm in the Bible Belt . . . I don't wanna get uh, get me, or anybody around me in trouble because of it." Although Mark's ability to experiment with breast development was not unlimited, the relative lack of scrutiny of his body by others gave him the opportunity to embark upon a bodily experience that he found enjoyable.

Reimagining Bodies, Genders, and Pleasures

The pleasures these men came to find through embracing their unanticipated breast development and bra wearing were unexpected not only by them, but by me as a researcher. In many ways, their reactions to developing breasts contradict what might be expected, given previous findings about men's body image and bodily practices. With the exception of Keith, they did not attempt to define their bra wearing in ways that bolster their masculinity, as other researchers have observed men do in relation to grooming practices and cosmetic surgery. And, in contrast to men's use of Viagra to overcome bodily changes associated with aging, these men eschew more invasive technologies and adopt an everyday consumer product to manage breast development. In so doing, they pioneer new definitions of masculinities and novel configurations of bodies, behaviors, and identities. Their use of the product to manage their breast development, rather than opting for medical solutions, also refigures male breast development as a routine bodily development, rather than a medical disorder.

These men's experiences open up new ways of thinking about bodies, genders, pleasures, and desires. Through expanding their gender expression in response to an unexpected bodily change, their experiences diverge from scholars' general observations about the interrelationships between bodily change, identity, and desire. For instance, research on transgender identity focuses on the intentional body modifications trans people make to align their outward appearance with their felt gender identity.[37] In previous work, I have discussed how trans men's body modifications—which are intentional, yet never fully controllable or predictable—refigure sexuality and desire in unexpected ways.[38] These breasted men's experiences represent a reversal of this process; that is, rather than shifting their gender presentation and modifying their bodies to align their appearance with their identities, for these men bodily change itself is a catalyst for expanding modes of gender expression and for the desire for further body modification. Further, whereas we might expect social actors to react to involuntary bodily changes, such as gaining weight or aging, by attempting to resist these changes and restore their bodies to their previous state, these men instead react by relinquishing control and taking pleasure in these changes. Future research might examine the impact of other involuntary bodily changes on gender expression and desires.

From a feminist perspective that sees the loosening of the constraints around gender expression as a form of social progress, the unexpected pleasures experienced by these breasted men are encouraging. They seem to gesture toward a world where there is wider latitude to challenge gender expectations, and where creative forms of gender expression and bodily pleasures emerge serendipitously. However, it is necessary to account for how these men's positions of relative privilege allowed them the opportunities for these pleasures. Unlike cisgender girls and women, their appearance and sexual expression was not scrutinized and policed.[39] And, unlike trans and queer people, they did not face harassment or violence for violating gender expectations.[40] Instead, they repeatedly found (to their surprise and relief) that others simply did not carefully scrutinize their bodies. The fact that the men noticed the changed appearance of their chests only after embodied sensations prompted them to look demonstrates the primacy of sensation to their embodied experience—in contrast to girls and women, who commonly perceive themselves as visual objects as a result of their objectification by others.[41] This relative freedom from scrutiny and objectification, which can likely be attributed to the intersections of these men's age, race, gender, and sexuality, afforded them space to refashion their bodies in unexpectedly pleasurable ways. As feminists endeavor to create a world more accepting of gender diversity, we may aim to expand opportunities not only for all to express their gender and modify their bodies in desired ways, but to widen opportunities for unexpected pleasures.

NOTES

1  The term "cisgender" is used to describe someone whose gender identity aligns with the sex/gender assigned to them at birth.
2  Robyn Longhurst, "'Man-Breasts': Spaces of Sexual Difference, Fluidity, and Abjection," in *Spaces of Masculinities*, ed. B. van Hoven and K. Hörschelmann (New York: Routledge, 2005), 165–78.
3  Kathleen F. Slevin, "'If I Had Lots of Money . . . I'd Have a Body Makeover': Managing the Aging Body," *Social Forces* 88, no. 3 (2010): 1003–20; Marilyn Wann, "Foreword, Fat Studies: An Invitation to Revolution," in *The Fat Studies Reader*, ed. E. Rothblum and S. Solovay (New York: New York University Press, 2009), xi–xxv.
4  Longhurst, "Man-Breasts."
5  Ronald S. Swerdloff, and Chiu Ming Ng, "Gynecomastia: Etiology, Diagnosis, and Treatment," *Endotext*, October 22, 2017, https://www.ncbi.nlm.nih.gov.
6  Iris Marion Young, "Breasted Experience: The Look and the Feeling," in *The Body in Medical Thought and Practice*, ed. D. Leder (Dordrecht: Kluwer, 1992), 215–30.
7  Swerdloff and Ng, "Gynecomastia."
8  Glenn D. Braunstein, "Gynecomastia," *New England Journal of Medicine* 328 (1993): 490–95.
9  Mayo Clinic, "Enlarged Breasts in Men (Gynecomastia)," https://www.mayoclinic.org.
10  Braunstein, "Gynecomastia."
11  Medical researchers point out that the causes of gynecomastia can range from benign to serious (Swerdloff and Ng, "Gynecomastia"). I am not advocating that anyone avoid seeking medical evaluation, to ensure that bodily changes are not indicative of an underlying health problem. Nevertheless, I aim to suggest that reconceptualizing male breast development in ways that avoid pathologizing and negative connotations may have positive social effects.
12  Georgiann Davis, *Contesting Intersex: The Dubious Diagnosis* (New York: New York University Press, 2015).
13  Anne Fausto-Sterling, "The Five Sexes: Why Male and Female Are Not Enough," *Sciences,* March–April 1993, 20–24. Although medical professionals typically use the term "disorders of sex development" (see Davis, *Contesting Intersex*), I use "intersex" to convey my perspective that these bodily states are benign biological variations, rather than "problems" to be solved.

14  Mayo Clinic, "Klinefelter Syndrome," https://www.mayoclinic.org.
15  Susan Bordo, *Unbearable Weight: Feminism, Western Culture, and the Body* (Berkeley: University of California Press, 1993); Chris Shilling, *The Body and Social Theory* (Newbury Park, CA: Sage, 1993).
16  Longhurst "Man-Breasts."
17  Luce Irigaray, *This Sex Which Is Not One* (Ithaca, NY: Cornell University Press, 1985); Julia Kristeva, "Approaching Abjection," *Oxford Literary Review* 5, nos. 1–2 (1982): 125–49.
18  Margrit Shildrick, *Leaky Bodies and Boundaries: Feminism, Postmodernism and (Bio)ethics* (New York: Routledge, 1997).
19  R. W. Connell, *Masculinities* (Berkeley, CA: University of California Press, [1995] 2005).
20  Bordo, *Unbearable Weight*; Naomi Wolf, *The Beauty Myth: How Images of Beauty Are Used against Women* (New York: Morrow, 1991).
21  Susan Bordo, *The Male Body: A New Look at Men in Public and in Private* (New York: Farrar, Straus & Giroux, 1999); Rosalind Gill, Karen Henwood, and Carol McLean, "Body Projects and the Regulation of Normative Masculinity," *Body & Society* 11, no. 1 (2005) : 37–62.
22  Sarah Grogan and Helen Richards, "Body Image: Focus Groups with Boys and Men," *Men and Masculinities* 4, no. 3 (2002): 219–32.
23  Elizabeth Haiken, "Virtual Virility, or, Does Medicine Make the Man?," *Men and Masculinities* 2, no. 4 (2000): 388–409.
24  Elena Frank, "Groomers and Consumers: The Meaning of Male Body Depilation to a Modern Masculinity Body Project," *Men and Masculinities* 17, no. 3 (2014): 278–98; Matthew Immergut, "Manscaping: The Tangle of Nature, Culture, and Male Body Hair," in *The Body Reader: Essential Social and Cultural Readings*, ed. L. J. Moore and M. Kosut (New York: New York University Press, 2002), 287–304.
25  Kristen Barber, *Styling Masculinity: Gender, Class, and Inequality in the Men's Grooming Industry* (New Brunswick, NJ: Rutgers University Press, 2016.)
26  Haiken, "Virtual Virility."
27  Immergut, "Manscaping."
28  Barber, *Styling Masculinity*.
29  Catherine B. Silver, "Gendered Identities in Old Age: Toward (De)Gendering?," *Journal of Aging Studies* 17 (2003): 379–97.
30  Edward H. Thompson and Kaitlyn Barnes Langendoerfer, "Older Men's Blueprint for 'Being a Man,'" *Men and Masculinities* 19, no. 2 (2015): 119–47.
31  Meika Loe, 2004. *The Rise of Viagra: How the Little Blue Pill Changed Sex in America* (New York: New York University Press, 2004).
32  Meika Loe, "The Viagra Blues: Embracing or Resisting the Viagra Body," in *Medicalized Masculinities*, ed. D. Rosenfeld and C. Faircloth (Philadelphia, PA: Temple University Press, 2006), 21–44.
33  Loe, "Viagra Blues."
34  Longhurst, "Man-Breasts."

35  All names are pseudonyms, and all quoted interviewees identified as white.
36  I have preserved the use of punctuation and other symbols when quoting from text-based interviews (i.e., interviews conducted via email or messaging services).
37  Susan Stryker and Stephen Whittle, eds., *The Transgender Studies Reader* (New York: Routledge, 2006).
38  Katelynn Bishop, "Body Modification and Trans Men: The Lived Realities of Gender Transition and Partner Intimacy," *Body & Society* 22, no. 1 (2016): 62–91.
39  Peggy Orenstein, *Girls and Sex: Navigating the Complicated Landscape* (New York: Harper, 2016).
40  Kristen Schilt and Laurel Westbrook, "Doing Gender, Doing Heteronormativity: 'Gender Normals,' Transgender People, and the Social Maintenance of Heterosexuality," *Gender & Society* 23, no. 4 (2009): 440–64.
41  Sandra Lee Bartky, "Foucault, Femininity, and the Modernization of Patriarchal Power," in *Writing on the Body: Female Embodiment and Feminist Theory*, ed. K. Conboy, N. Medina, and S. Stanbury (New York: Columbia University Press, 1997), 129–54; Barbara L. Fredrickson and Tomi-Ann Roberts, "Objectification Theory: Toward Understanding Women's Lived Experiences and Mental Health Risks," *Psychology of Women Quarterly* 21, no. 2 (1997): 173–206.

# 11

## Brotox and the Retreat from Male Femininity

DANA BERKOWITZ

Botox is not just manly now, it's going to change the world.[1]

In a recent article in *Forbes*, aptly titled "'Brotox': It's Time for Men to Come Out of the Closet," journalist Peter Lane Taylor begins, "Every guy needs to admit this one honest truth: Feeling that you're getting old sucks, no matter what your age. We all look in the mirror every morning and judge ourselves by how we look."[2] Lane's commentary is indicative of a new trend, whereby more men than ever are concerning themselves with their appearance. The US male grooming market is valued at a whopping $38 billion.[3] More and more men are using anti-aging products, removing their body hair, visiting beauty salons, undergoing cosmetic surgery, and using Botox.

Yet, even against the backdrop of men's unprecedented foray into this terrain, words like "hygiene" and "grooming" continue to pervade descriptions of men's bodily self-care. Reserving the language of beauty only for commodities designated for women allows men to repudiate any association with femininity, homosexuality, and vanity and to preserve the gender binary. Consistent with this, most men's skincare brands have made every effort to differentiate themselves from the female beauty industry. Men's products are either distinguished by the stipulation "For Men," as in Kiehl's for Men or Aveda for Men, or they are given unequivocally manly names, such as Everyman Jack and Gameface Moisturizer. With Botox, a cosmetic procedure once aggressively marketed only to women, this distinction is even more magnified. For men Botox Cosmetic has been branded with its own nomenclature, Brotox, a name that connotes masculinity so clearly that nobody would be confused that this is a product only for someone with a penis.

Botox Cosmetic—the brand name of the drug botulinum toxin—is *the* anti-aging wonder drug of the moment: marketed as a quick, easy, and safe way to temporarily improve the look of wrinkles on the upper part of the face.[4] With over seven million Botox procedures in the United States in 2019 alone, Botox is currently the most popular cosmetic procedure on the market.[5] Even through the overwhelming majority of its consumers are women, a small but growing number of men are beginning to go under the needle. Today, close to half a million men have used Botox, comprising slightly less than 6 percent of total Botox procedures.[6]

These statistics mirror general trends in cosmetic surgery and further expose how larger social forces such as media, medicine, the pharmaceutical lobby, and the beauty industry are increasingly regulating men's bodies. Where once men were immune to the pressures of bodily objectification and self-surveillance, this no longer rings true. Big Pharma and the beauty industry are beginning to realize that they are ignoring an untapped consumer base and are finding innovative ways to market to men. Advertisements targeting men are on the rise, as are aesthetic centers catering specifically to them. This trend is a global one: Manology in Australia, the Club House in Manhattan, and Maffi Clinic in Arizona are just a few of business ventures being launched around the globe specializing in aesthetic treatments *just for men.*

The rise of Botox use among men ushers in a new set of questions about male femininities, or men's participation in embodied practices symbolically coded as feminine. As Botox becomes increasingly included in the body modification practices of more and more men, how are they taught to make sense of this gendered boundary crossing? What do media and marketing messages about Botox communicate to men about how to interpret their identities, bodies, and selves?

In this chapter I explore the ways that aesthetic centers, dermatologists, and cosmetic surgeons market Botox Cosmetic to men. What can these advertisements reveal about the ways men's bodies are regulated and disciplined by dominant discourses about masculinity and gender more broadly? I address these questions through an analysis of twenty-two advertisements for Botox targeting men. My findings expose how these marketing messages for Botox reconfigure the practice from one of feminine vanity and frivolity to a normal, rational, masculine strategy for self-care.

## Men, Masculinities, and Body Work

To say that bodies are gendered means that the bodies we see and interact with on an everyday basis are not natural, but the sustained product of gendered practices and ideologies. Our bodies are at once gendered subjects and objects—active, purposeful, and reflexive, as well as regulated by social and cultural norms. For men, this means that the body is a site both for the enactment of masculinity, and for its profound governance.

There is a deep-seated and reciprocal relationship between the appearance and utility of men's bodies and masculine identity. As R. W. Connell affirms, "True masculinity is almost always thought to proceed from men's bodies" and today, middle-class men are increasingly defined by their physiques, style, and appearance.[7] Health, fitness, and attractiveness are new benchmarks for measuring masculinity. With the recent increase in media and marketing attention to men's bodies, a growing number of scholars have interrogated men's responses to this trend, specifically the way men today wrestle with and negotiate these messages alongside established constructions of masculinity.[8]

Some scholars see men's entrée into this traditionally feminized landscape as indicative of some degree of the blurring of traditional gender boundaries. Most others, however, tend to agree that this trend highlights that dominant practices of masculinity adapt to changing social conditions by appropriating from femininities and other less powerful masculinities, and that they do so in ways that repudiate femininity and marginalized masculinities rather than welcome them.

For example, the emergence of the metrosexual man popularized in the 1990s reveals the ways that hegemonic masculinity can selectively poach from femininities and gay masculinities without polluting or threatening its dominance. A cosmopolitan man who is polished, fashionable, and brand-obsessed, the metrosexual engages in a repertoire of embodied aesthetic labor previously regarded as feminine or gay. He frequents high-end barbershops, wears form-fitting expensive suits, spends hours at the gym, and cares for his skin. On the surface, it might seem that the metrosexual is the embodiment of a new male femininity. However, scholars have pointed out that when marketing messages instruct metrosexual men on proper aesthetics and style, they empty these from any association with the feminine, selling them on the idea that these consumer choices preserve their privileged gendered location rather than endanger it.[9] In other words, embedded in the instruction manual for the metrosexual is the assumption that femininity be renounced at all costs. Further, scholars have critiqued the metrosexual archetype as "depoliticized consumerism masquerading as freedom,"[10] exposing the metrosexuality's deep roots in performances of whiteness, class privilege, and heterosexuality.[11]

Similarly, men's narratives about their participation in feminized body work reveal that they tend to define it in ways that reinforce their masculinity. Researchers have found that men who seek cosmetic enhancements construct themselves as active consumers, reconfiguring feminized aesthetic labor as a masculine and rational body management strategy.[12] Elizabeth Haiken finds that, beginning as early as post–World War I, when male soldiers sought reconstructive surgery following facial disfigurement, they rationalized their choice to undergo surgery as motivated by pursuits of economic security, as a means to secure a good job and to be able to provide for their family—all traditionally masculine ideals.[13] Likewise, in his study of aesthetic surgery, Sander Gilman documents how penile implants were configured as an achievement of masculinity.[14]

Masculinity scholars have also speculated how men's boundary crossings into feminized beauty work might be understood against a cultural and historical backdrop of shifting gender relations where men feel a collective loss of established hegemony. In a prolific history of American manhood, Michael Kimmel documents a perpetual condition that he refers to as a "crisis" in masculinity where social and political changes have caused men to feel a loss of power and control over a world in which gender relations are no longer fixed and stable.[15] He argues that one of the ways men have always negotiated this "crisis" has been to seek comfort in controlling the one thing they can—their bodies. Lending empirical muscle to Kimmel's framework, Atkinson's conversations with men who underwent cosmetic surgery in Canada demonstrated that cosmetic surgery was a response to shifting power balances between men and women due to the current "crisis" in masculinity.[16] In her ethnography of Viagra, Loe found that the men she spoke with talked about Viagra as restoring their sense of manhood.[17] In my own research on magazine articles about men and Botox, I discovered that the threat of women invading masculine social territories was used to fuel men's anxiety about their masculine identities, selves, and bodies. Many of the Botox providers with whom I spoke framed Botox as a means to help men cope with increasing competition in the workplace from women and younger applicants.[18] In this paper, I build upon my earlier work to further interrogate the messages projected by Botox advertisements targeting men.

## Studying Visual Advertisements

I conducted a visual discourse analysis of promotional materials for Botox targeting men. Most of these advertisements are from cosmetic surgery and aesthetic centers in America, but a small handful are from the UK and Australia. This promotional material not only transmits knowledge about Botox but also reveals a great deal about Western cultural norms about gender, our investments in masculinity, and the repudiation of male femininities, while in addition telling us a great deal about aging bodies, class privilege, whiteness, and heterosexuality.

Guided by principles of purposeful sampling in constructivist grounded theory research, a research assistant and I conducted a Google Image search for Botox advertisements for men during the spring of 2018.[19] My assistant first conducted a search in February 2018 using the search terms "men Botox ads," "advertisements for Botox for men," and "Brotox." After sifting through the first one hundred of these images—omitting those without words, those that were not advertisements, those that did not picture a man, and those that were either gender neutral or catered to women—I came up with a total of fourteen advertisements. Next, I conducted the same search in both March and April 2018 using the same search terms. After omitting redundancies and making sure that each image met the criteria detailed above, I collected a sample of twenty-two total advertisements.

Next, I critically analyzed each advertisement using techniques outlined by Adele Clarke's visual discourse analysis.[20] Beginning with my guiding research question of how Botox, an explicitly feminized cosmetic procedure, is marketed to men, I systemically coded each advertisement, asking the following questions: How does the ad reflect assumptions about gender, masculinity, and femininity? How does it reflect assumptions about social class, race, ethnicity, age, and sexuality? What meanings are embedded in its words and imagery? For whom was the advertisement produced and directed? How do these meanings reflect social, cultural, economic, and historical contexts? What is not being said or pictured in these advertisements? And what can these invisibilities and silences reveal?

Following the completion of open coding, I moved to a more formal process of focused coding whereby I categorized images and fleshed out their meanings in relationship to one another. An iterative process, I moved back and forth between coding the images, reading the scholarly literature on masculinities and body work, and scrutinizing the mainstream media for information about men and Botox.

## Selling Brotox: Visual Advertisements

In what follows, I detail the typology of four categories of advertisements that emerged in my analysis: 1) generic ads marketing Botox for men; 2) ads marketing Botox to men using hypermasculine tropes and images; 3) ads marketing Botox as a tool for career security and advancement; and 4) ads marketing the male Botox user as a family man. While I discuss each of these separately in my analysis, I want to note that these themes were not discrete categories; rather, they often overlapped.

### *Brotox: Botox for Real Men*

I coded the majority (n=11) of advertisements under the category "generic ads marketing Botox to men." In many ways, the images in these ads could be used to market any personal care product to men, such as cologne, deodorant, or aftershave. In fact, only two out of the eleven ads even picture a needle; most simply feature the face of a conventionally handsome man staring confidently into the camera. Representing the idealized Botox user, the men in these ads are white and approximately thirty-five to sixty-five years old, and they look like white-collar professionals in the worlds of business, law, or fashion.

In three of the ads, men are pictured without a shirt, prominently highlighting their broad shoulders and sculpted frames. In the eight

Figure 11.1. Advertisement from Dr. J. Roberto Ramirez Gavidia's plastic surgery and rejuvenation spa in Nashville, Tennessee.

other ads, men are clothed either in swanky business suits or casual (yet pressed) T-shirts. One ad for a plastic surgery clinic in Woodbury, New York, features a shirtless man somewhere between the ages of thirty-five and forty with shadowy scruff; full, chin-length dark hair; and sensually puckered lips. Below the model's chin appears the phrase, "Be Manly, Not Wrinkly" and underneath in large black block letters the word "BROTOX." A similar ad for a plastic surgery and rejuvenation clinic in Nashville, Tennessee, shows an equally chiseled man with luxurious dark hair and a perfectly trimmed beard nonchalantly looking over his shoulder. As with the previous ad, the phrase "Brotox: Botox for Real Men" is the only other thing in the image. Pictured in the majority of these ads are white men who seemingly care about their appearances and can afford to do so, the type who sculpt their bodies at boutique fitness centers, always wear expensive clothing, and use pricey "just for men" skincare products. Intentionally aligned with metrosexual images of male femininity, the men in these ads are symbolic of a necessary accommodation to changing contemporary social norms about men and masculinity.

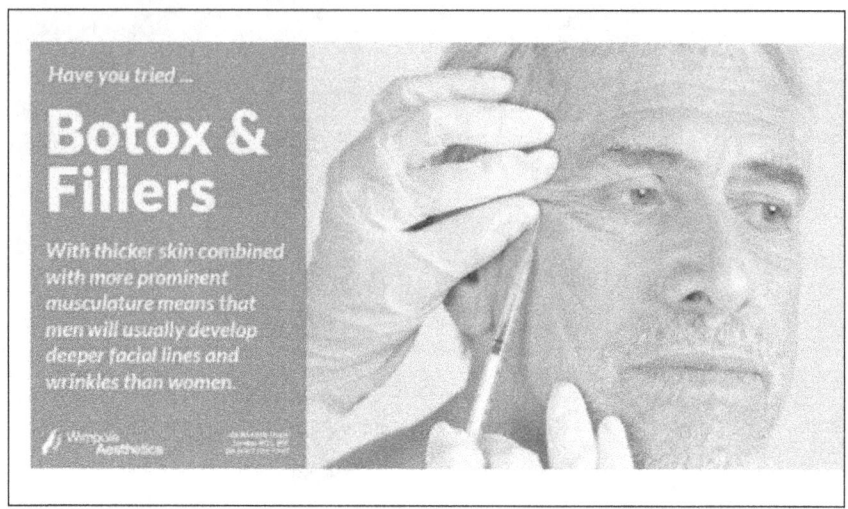

Figure 11.2. Advertisement from Wimpole Aesthetics in London.

Even though many of these men are strikingly handsome, a handful of the models look like regular guys. For example, one ad for an aesthetic center in London pictures an older man with prominent wrinkles being injected with Botox in the outer corner of his eye, an area colloquially known as "crow's feet." To the right of the image, the ad reads, "Have you tried Botox and Fillers? With thicker skin combined with more prominent musculature means that more men will develop deeper facial lines and wrinkles than women." Statements like this that construct men and women's facial skin as opposites reify cultural ideologies about the gender binary—specifically that masculinity be constructed in opposition to femininity. Likewise, the tactic of emphasizing that men have thicker skin and the potential for more prominent wrinkles was intentionally used as a justification that men used Botox for different reasons than women. Consider the fact that the man is visibly aged; now try to imagine a similar ad with a woman. Nowhere in my ten years researching Botox's aggressive marketing to women did I come across an ad featuring a woman with visible lines and creases and lines on her face. The image in this ad illustrates how media images of aging men are far more diverse than those of aging women, providing men a sense of refuge in their bodies that women do not possess. Moreover, the ad deliberately uses the man's wrinkled face to transmit the message that men can use Botox and still preserve a corporeal façade of masculinity untainted by the feminization of beauty ideals.

Finally, embedded within this group, was the theme that Botox was about fitting in, not standing out. Elsewhere I have documented that the objective of Botox is to create a face that passes as natural. In order to avoid the stigma of going overboard, the female Botoxed visage needs to publicly pass as one that has not undergone any obvious technological intervention.[21] This theme, I found, was also prevalent in advertisements for Botox for men. One ad featuring an attractive everyman says, "Look like you got 8 hours of sleep: Botox should make you look well rested, not well done." Another, for a medical spa in Washington reads, "Everyone will notice but nobody will know." The intention of Botox is not to draw the collective gaze to technologically altered flesh; rather, Botox is meant to make men look more relaxed, less stressed out, and younger, all while passing as natural. For men, the pressure to look natu-

Figure 11.3. Advertisement from Ambrosia Medspa in Kirkland, Washington.

ral is even more compounded by the cultural necessities of preserving the masculine character of their faces and avoiding the stigma of excessive vanity. In her historical analysis of cosmetic surgery, Elizabeth Haiken demonstrates how countering any impression of vanity was an essential component of the industry's successful marketing to men.[22] Considered a deviation into the feminine, the stigma of vanity long prevented men from becoming consumers of cosmetic surgery or any other product intended to enhance physical appearance. Ensuring that "everybody will notice but nobody will know" allows men to maintain the appearance of masculine hegemony, protecting them from the powerless aspects associated with a feminine culture of beauty.

*Botox, Bourbon, Burgers, and Beer*

Five ads were coded under the category "marketing Botox to men using hypermasculine tropes and images." In this group of ads, beer, bourbon, burgers, and sports are used as symbolic cues to convince men that trying Botox would not threaten their heteromasculinity. Employed to decontaminate Botox from its association with the feminine, these ads created a recognizable gendered narrative embedded with masculine archetypes like athletics and alcohol. For example, one ad for a dermatology clinic in Knoxville, Tennessee, pictures a chef's hat with barbeque tools on a picnic table. In bold black letters reads: "Botox, Bourbon, and Burgers." The caption underneath states, "Join us for delicious burgers paired with bourbon sampling and learn why Botox is the #1 anti-aging treatment for men." Emblematic of heteromasculinity, the idea of grilling up some burgers while enjoying a bourbon tasting aligns men, however imperfectly, with straight masculine culture. Another ad from the same clinic promoted a Botox and bourbon event where interested male consumers could learn about how Botox can "soften their lines, not their edge" while sipping some Bourbon and eating some light snacks. In this ad, the imagery of a refined man wearing a business suit and holding a rocks glass helped to distinguish Botox not only as a practice for women but also as a requisite for the maintenance of bourgeois masculinity. These promotional materials situate Botox as part of a classed and gendered body project where middle-class men come to identify with and embody these cultural norms.

It is also worth noting that the fine print of these ads indicates that, even though this dermatology clinic seems to be targeting men, with their hypermasculine images of beer, bourbon, and burgers, these promotions are actually directed at their already existing women clientele. This clever marketing strategy rewards their women clients with complimentary Botox and chemical peels if they bring the man in their lives into the clinic to learn about Botox's Botox. Thus, in this case, the women serve as consumer liaisons, luring men into a space otherwise coded as feminine.

As most men are uncomfortable with Botox, motivating them with free burgers, beer, and bourbon creates a consumer experience that is both masculine and heterosexual. The next two advertisements—from Pure Life Medical Spa in Largo, Florida—blend beer, Botox, sports, and rock and roll to create such an unapologetically heteromasculine experience. The first ad offers free beer, one facial area of free Botox, and the opportunity to meet a former music publicist and former football player. The second ad, promoting a "Men's Night Event," brings together the strange bedfellows of Botox, beer, and a book signing from a Major League baseball announcer. As heterosexual masculine institutions, sports and rock and roll have historically provided men the space to express violence, aggression, unrestrained dominance, and heterosexual prowess. Moreover, both institutions are entangled with the consumption of beer and liquor. These ads communicate heteromasculinity by selling men on a high of sports, rock music, booze, and hegemonic masculinity. Moreover, unlike the advertisements that use women as consumer liaisons, these bypass women altogether. In so doing, they project the impression that these events are not simply *masculine spaces*, but *men-only spaces*. They reveal that fashioning a homosocial space that excludes women is crucial to selling any product to men designed to enhance their physical appearance and that could possibly be coded as feminine.

I also want to point out the not-so-subtle ways that these ads appeal to a mostly white, class-privileged, sophisticated consumer through the pseudocelebrities they feature. They advertise a a meet-and-greet with a music publicist (not a rock and roll front man) and a sports announcer (not a sports player). The only player interested consumers can actually meet is a former punter—not exactly known as the most aggressive po-

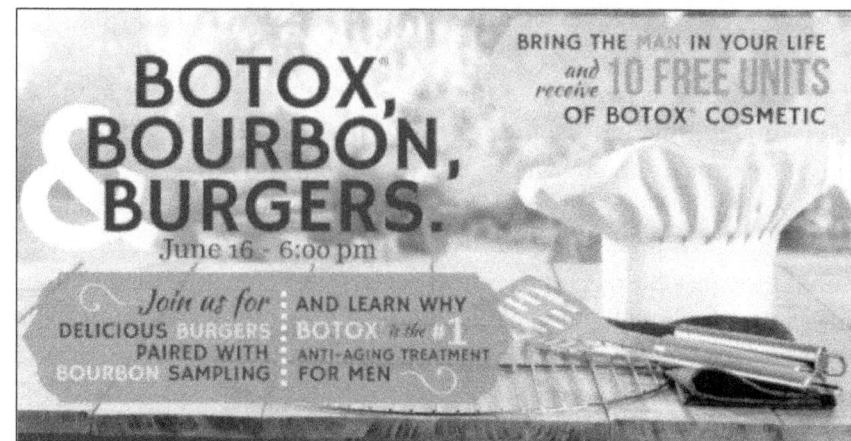

Figure 11.4a–b. Advertisements from Southeastern Dermatology in Knoxville, Tennessee.

Figure 11.5a–b. Advertisements from PureLife MedSpa in Largo, Florida.

Figure 11.6. Advertisements from BergerHenry ENT Facial Rejuvenation Center in Philadelphia, Pennsylvania.

sition in a football team. Hence, while these men represent masculine archetypes, they are symbolic of a softer, tamer masculinity than that of the linebacker or rock star. In a similar vein, the final ad in this category features Deion Sanders, iconic Black athlete and sports broadcaster, and the first male celebrity spokesperson for the project, pictured sandwiched between two white men above the caption "Botox Cosmetic isn't just for women." A former football and baseball player, Sanders is currently a sports announcer, and his status as an icon in all three of these domains, added to the fact that he is Black, are being used to attract a wide variety of men across race and class lines. Nonetheless, it is Sanders's status as a sports commentator more than as an athlete that allows him to embody a safe and subdued Black masculinity that can be used to appeal to Botox's mostly white and professional target audience. Allergan's decision to feature Sanders in their ads reflects the sort of masculinity that they are trying to sell—a predominantly white, middle-class aesthetic—to men who are concerned with preserving their social advantages.

*Looking Good Is My Key to Success*

Three ads fell under the category "marketing Botox as a tool for career security and advancement." In these ads, Botox for men was constructed as a sensible and necessary upgrade to maintain their competitive edge in the workplace. Capitalizing on men's insecurities about continuing to be desired professionally once their age begins to show, these ads take advantage of the mounting pressure men can feel to look young and vital in order to maintain their careers.

For example, one advertisement for a cosmetic and plastic surgery office in San Diego features an attractive Black man (one of only two Black men in my entire sample, the other being Deion Sanders) with the caption "Looking Good Is Key to My Success." Similarly, a series of ads from an aesthetic clinic in the UK that I originally found on an article in LinkedIn featured the torso of a man, wearing an expensive watch and a suit, hovering over documents. Next to him was the caption "Botox for Men. Would you get it for your career?" One ad says, "Men in high stress or competitive jobs such as sales are more likely to get Botox or Cosmetic treatments," while another one reads, "We are more likely to buy off someone we find attractive." These ads bring to light the ways that Big Pharma and the beauty and anti-aging industries use the masculine domain of the workplace to convince men to pay closer attention to their physical image. This marketing has worked. Fear of becoming a victim of corporate layoffs and anxiety about diminished economic and social prestige has led increasing numbers of professional men to use anti-aging interventions, especially Botox. In fact, data suggests that Botox injections increase in times of economic downturn.[23]

Cast as an appearance intervention that can yield economic benefits for men, these ads project the idea that having a wrinkled brow in the workplace is a risk. By framing Botox Cosmetic as a sensible body management strategy for men and locating that strategy within the realm of career enhancement, these ads make room for an alliance between Botox and masculinity. Such marketing tactics shift men's aesthetic labor from the feminine realm of beauty and vanity to the more acceptable masculine territory of career investment.

It is also useful to examine this group of advertisements against the backdrop of the "crisis" of masculinity, in which men experience uncertainty regarding shifting gendered norms and expectations. Some men feel a visceral loss of power as their ownership over institutions once held as bastions for establishing their dominance are gradually chipped away. In this particular case, it is women's real or imagined boundary crossings into the professional workplace that are used to fuel a panic

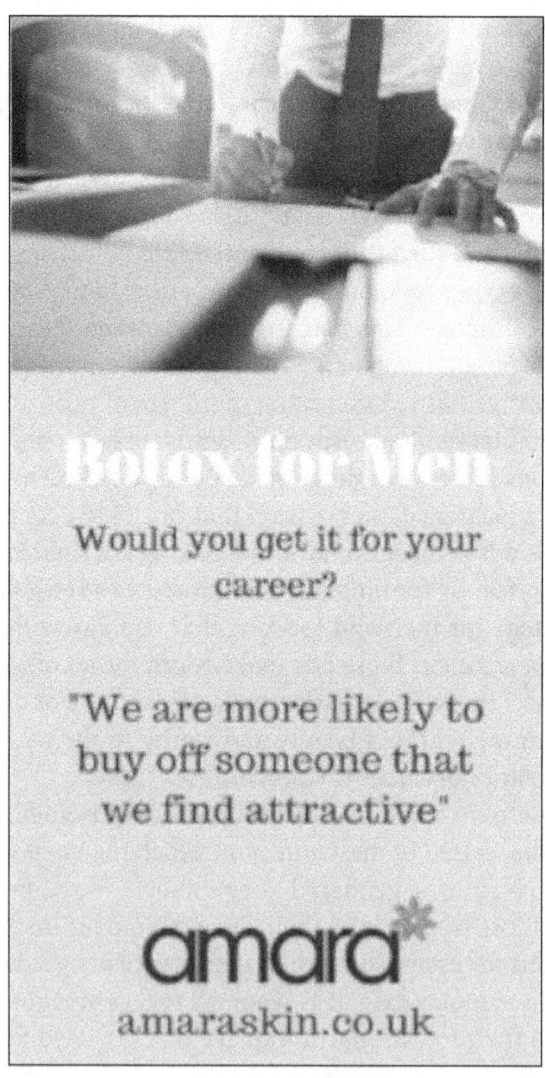

Figure 11.7a–b. Advertisements from Amaraskin, UK.

over men's aging faces and bodies, convincing them to go ahead and give Botox a try.

It is equally compelling to consider the ways these advertisements expose the ways Botox is transforming our cultural imaginary about masculine features and aging men. According to a recent article in *Forbes*, men's brow creases, once seen as distinguished, "don't represent industry experience the way they used to, so being able to come across seasoned as well as youthful is often the ticket to nailing your next big promotion against the Millennial who's leveraging age against you."[24] Although employment-based ageism disadvantages women more than men, it seems that we are seeing some changes where, for men, the privileging of a young-looking face is beginning to replace the importance of seniority in the workplace.[25]

## *My Wife Is the One Who Suggested I Look into Botox Cosmetic*

Finally, three of the ads were coded under the category "marketing the male Botox user as a family man and father." Interwoven throughout these advertisements is the assumption that this ideal family man was heterosexual, white, and class privileged. Two of the ads offered promotional deals for Father's Day specials. Using this holiday as a publicity campaign allowed aesthetic centers to appeal to the average man, given fatherhood's deep links to today's hegemonic archetype of the American male. Men currently rank marriage and children among their most valued goals, and the current modern ideal of fatherhood expects men to be active and nurturing parents.[26] As many women are well aware, this long-term investment of both economic and emotional commitments to children has the potential to deeply etch itself in one's brows.

Both of the Father's Day ads advertise promotions where men can buy twenty units of Botox and get the other twenty units for free. One, for an aesthetic and wellness practice in Plano, Texas, features a handsome middle-aged white man with prominent brow wrinkles, crow's feet, and jowls. Overlaying his photograph is the caption "196 Hangovers, 4 Heartbreaks, 135 Sunburns, 3 Teenagers. Hide the Evidence." Just as cosmetic surgery has been marketed to women as a means to "hide the evidence" of pregnancy and childbirth, this advertisement employs a similar tactic, albeit one directed at fathers whose faces bear the imprint

Figure 11.8a–b. Advertisements from Rosemary Bates Wellness Spa, Plano, Texas; and Turkle & Associates Medical Skin Care and Laser Center, Carmel, Indiana.

of raising teenage daughters (note that his wrinkles could not possibly be from raising teenage sons).

In addition to concealing the facial creases that result from fatherhood, this ad also promises to erase the traces of leisure masculinity on men's faces—notably sunburns and hangovers. The man pictured in this ad does not look as if his sunburn came from working in a construction yard, nor was his hangover a consequence of downing too many Budweisers at the local dive bar. Rather, he looks like a man who spent too many hours at the golf course and then finished off his day with a few too many martinis before coming home to his family. This ad cleverly fuses configurations of hedonistic masculine consumerism with the trope of the family man, in so doing providing men the space to embody a bourgeois masculinity that is at once dutiful, reliant, and self-indulgent.

Another ad, for a medical skin care and laser center in Indianapolis, features a middle-aged white man with less pronounced wrinkles than the man in the previous ad, but with slightly grayer hair. The caption above him reads, "My wife is the one who suggested I look into Botox Cosmetic. I'm glad I did. BROTOX: Botox for Men." Although we don't know for sure, there is some anecdotal evidence suggesting that one of the reasons men try Botox for the first time is per the suggestion of their women partners, once again revealing the ways that women can serve as consumer liaisons. More than this, however, I want to consider what this ad and the others in this group project about the significance of maintaining a heterosexual front for men who are curious about Botox. Penetrating these ads is the message that guys who use Botox are regular family men, married to women, and, most important, heterosexual. Because heterosexuality is a vital ingredient in the construction and maintenance of hegemonic masculinity, projecting a heterosexual front in the marketing of Botox to men is a crucial component of its merchandising. Using the catchphrase "My wife is the one who suggested I look into Botox Cosmetic" steers men safely into the realm of heterosexuality, assuring them that their sexuality will not be called into question if they veer into this precarious feminine terrain.

## Brotox and the Repudiation of Male Femininity

Although social scripts about masculinity are shifting to the extent that it is expected for heterosexual, class-privileged white men to take care of their appearances, there is a limit to how much work they should put into their bodily self-care, and Botox Cosmetic injections definitely cross the limit. Even though Botox is not yet—and likely will never be—part of the socially acceptable grooming repertoire for heterosexual men, male Botox consumers are on the rise, as are Botox advertisements targeting men. Examining these promotional materials reveals the ways men's bodies are regulated by dominant discourses about masculinity, femininity, and heterosexuality. Men who embody aspects of feminine beauty culture are stigmatized as failed, feminized, or gay. As such, these practices of male femininity and the bodies that inhabit them must be reconfigured as heteromasculine—a strategic process that requires reifying cultural ideologies about the sex/gender binary. Thus, rather than rupturing societal norms of masculinity, these ads redefine them as an adaptation to changing gender relations and consumerist pressures. As found by other researchers who have studied men's grooming practices and cosmetic surgery, instead of risking even the slightest brush with male femininity, these advertisements redefine Botox injections in ways that bolster men's fragile masculinity. Whether framing Botox as a normal component of masculine self-care and as a rational tool for career advancement, marketing it to the average family man, or using hypermasculine tropes and images, each of these ads shares in common their repudiation of femininity, homosexuality, and vanity.

In addition to telling us a great deal about the insecurity around masculinity and the perpetuation of male hegemony, these ads illuminate how other institutionalized inequalities are preserved and disseminated. First, by featuring images of older men proudly flaunting their wrinkles and grey hair, these ads reproduced gendered ageism. The very fact that I have yet to see an ad for Botox that shows a woman with even the slightest crease on her face or a single strand of gray hair reveals a great deal about the privileges of male embodiment. Moreover, the contemporary ideologies of masculinity presented in these advertisements construct men's aesthetics as a way to appropriate class status, creating a class-privileged masculine Botox consumer and reflecting a white bourgeois ideal. Thus, both the process and outcome of marketing Botox to men is as much about whiteness and class privilege as it is about heteromasculinity.

Returning to the guiding question of this volume, what does this all mean for the embodiment of male femininity? Unfortunately—though not surprisingly—the proliferation of ads marketing Botox to men neither pioneer new definitions of masculinities nor present an opportunity to destabilize and denaturalize binary gender systems. Perhaps this is because, even more so than other body work such as high-end hairstyling and even cosmetic surgery, Botox conjures up images of feminine frivolity and vanity. Moreover, as I have documented elsewhere, Botox is a technology that is used to create and maintain the illusion of an ideal feminine face unable to express negative emotions.[27] Because of this, in order to sell men on the possibility of becoming a Botox user, dermatologists, cosmetic surgeons, and other providers need to find innovative means to butch Botox up, so to speak, in ways that minimize any chance that it will be perceived as feminine. Big Pharma and the beauty and anti-aging industries strategically repackage youth and beauty to men in ways that both appropriate from and repudiate femininities. In the end, these marketing tactics reveal how a feminized technology can be reframed along established masculine lines of hegemony in order to reproduce existing power dynamics.

NOTES

1 Jim Atkinson, "The Next Great Drug," *Esquire*, July 2003, 50–52.
2 Peter Lane Taylor. "Brotox: It's Time for Men to Come Out of the Closet," *Forbes*, May 31, 2016, https://www.forbes.com.
3 "Global Men's Grooming Products Industry," Report Linker, July 2020, https://www.reportlinker.com/.
4 Botox Cosmetic is one of the three FDA-approved brand names of botulinum toxin injections, the others being Dysport and Xeomin.
5 American Society for Aesthetic Plastic Surgery, 2019, http://www.surgery.org.
6 "Statistics, 2019."
7 R. W. Connell, *Masculinities* (Berkeley: University of California Press, 2000).
8 Michael Atkinson, "Exploring Male Femininity in the 'Crisis': Men and Cosmetic Surgery," *Body and Society* 14, no. 1 (2008): 67–87.
9 Kristen Barber, *Styling Masculinity: Gender, Class, and Inequality in the Men's Grooming Industry* (Rutgers, NJ: Rutgers University Press, 2016).

10 Michael Kimmel, *Manhood in America: A Cultural History* (New York: Oxford University Press, 2011).
11 Barber, *Styling Masculinity*.
12 Atkinson, "Exploring Male Femininity"; Suzanne Fraser, *Cosmetic Surgery, Gender, and Culture* (New York: Palgrave Macmillan, 2003).
13 Elizabeth Haiken, *Venus Envy: A History of Cosmetic Surgery* (Baltimore, MD: Johns Hopkins University Press, 1997).
14 Sander L Gilman, *Making the Body Beautiful: A Cultural History of Aesthetic Surgery* (Princeton, NJ: Princeton University Press, 2000).
15 Kimmel, *Manhood in America*.
16 Atkinson, "Exploring Male Femininity."
17 Meika Loe, *The Rise of Viagra: How the Little Blue Pill Changed Sex in America* (New York: New York University Press, 2004).
18 Dana Berkowitz, *Botox Nation: Changing the Face of America* (New York: New York University Press, 2017).
19 Kathy Charmaz, *Constructing Ground Theory: A Practical Guide through Qualitative Research* (London: Sage, 2014).
20 Adele Clarke, *Situational Analysis: Grounded Theory after the Postmodern Turn* (Thousand Oaks, CA: Sage, 2005).
21 Berkowitz, *Botox Nation*.
22 Haiken, *Venus Envy*.
23 American Society for Aesthetic Plastic Surgery, "Statistics, 2017," http://www.surgery.org.
24 Taylor, "Brotox."
25 Colin Duncan and Wendy Loretto, "Never the Right Age? Gender and Age-Based Discrimination in Employment," *Gender, Work and Organization* 11, no. 1 (2004): 95–115.
26 Scott Coltrane, "Fathering: Paradoxes, Contradictions, and Dilemmas," in *Handbook of Contemporary Families: Considering the Past, Contemplating the Future*, ed. Marilyn Coleman and Lawrence Ganong (Thousand Oaks: Sage, 2004), 224–43.
27 Berkowitz, *Botox Nation*.

12

Pregnant Men and Their Reconfigurations of Pregnancy

MARY INGRAM-WATERS

During the long months of 2020 and the pandemic-imposed quarantine, Danny Wakefield, a thirty-four-year-old transmasculine and nonbinary person who uses masculine pronouns, publicly documented and celebrated his male pregnancy. Reaching tens of thousands of followers on Instagram, on Facebook, and through his website, Wakefield shared the news of his pregnancy, his struggles with severe morning sickness, his changing body, his excitement and anxieties, his interactions with health care providers, and the birth of his child on November 28, 2020.[1] In a post to his Instagram account dated May 2, 2020, Wakefield wrote, "My hope is that I can raise awareness through showing up as my beautiful, masculine, male identified pregnant-self and help y'all learn how to be more inclusive."[2] This sentiment, that men can be pregnant and should be celebrated in their maleness and their pregnancy, is consistent across his posts, his use of images, his writings, his interviews with different media sources, and his December 28, 2020, op-ed in *Newsweek*.[3] Wakefield's deliberately curated presentation of male pregnancy, in which he draws on his masculine gender identity while simultaneously embracing and challenging the culturally feminine behaviors, expectations, and processes of pregnancy, can be read as an example of male femininity.

In this chapter, I will consider male pregnancy as male femininity. Put another way, we will look at male pregnancy as it sits at the intersection of what we think about masculinity and femininity. We will discuss the real male pregnancies of trans men and trans masculine persons like Danny Wakefield, and the imagined male pregnancies in films, television, art, and fan fiction communities. Male pregnancy offers a lens to see the push and pull of male femininities. While Danny's male pregnancy embraces male femininity with a two-pronged goal of celebrating the potential of male-identified bodies and expanding how we understand who can be pregnant, other conceptualizations of male pregnancies are tied to male femininities in ways that engender very different cultural responses. In films and television shows, male pregnancy is extremely rare, and, in all of the examples discussed here, presented as a male femininity. That means that these films and shows depict cisgender men as pregnant in ways that juxtapose characters' unquestionable normative masculinity with stereotypically feminine behaviors associated with pregnancy. These sources always show male pregnancy as an outlandish, shocking farce that reinforces normative cisgender and heterosexual masculinity. For media fan communities, male pregnancy—or "mpreg"—is a fan-fiction and fan-art trope that embraces cisgender men who become pregnant usually as a result of sexual relations with other cisgender men. Fans love or hate mpreg for the same reason: the seriousness with which male pregnancy is presented as a male femininity. Here, male pregnancy as male femininity means that cisgender men can participate in the stereotypically feminine behaviors of pregnancy and, in doing so, expand what it means to be masculine.[4] In Lee Mingwei and Virgil Wong's art installation *POP! The First Human Male Pregnancy*, male pregnancy is also a male femininity, meaning that a cisgender male engages with stereotypically feminine behaviors associated with pregnancy. While they aim for seriousness instead of comedy, they still draw on shock value in the same way as films, shows, and fan communities do.[5] Taken together, all of the male pregnancies considered in this chapter can be read as male femininities and as such, often come across as shocking in how they bring together masculinity and femininity. But, as we will explore throughout, the goals for those presenting male pregnancies differ greatly.

Let us start with a general question: What is pregnancy? Biologically, pregnancy is the process by which a person gestates a fetus to birth. Within a few months of being pregnant, most bodies change such that they are visibly, physically pregnant. Pregnancy is also a rich cultural process imbued with shared values and meanings, often celebrated with distinctive rituals and customs such as having a baby shower, wearing maternity clothing, and seeking specialized health care. While many providers increasingly refer to pregnant patients in gender-neutral terms, for almost everyone else in the world, pregnancy is so strongly associated with females as to be taken for granted and assumed to be a natural condition.

Pregnant cisgender females are subject to commonly held stereotypes—for example, expectations that they will be moody or crave odd combinations of foods. Strangers and acquaintances alike often feel like they can freely comment on or even touch pregnant cisgender females' bodies. Pregnant cisgender females are highly visible members of society, and, as such, they experience very specific societal expectations with respect to their pregnancies. Pregnancy is also codified into laws and policies such as maternity leave, custody designations, and reproductive rights. Thus we can see that cisgender female pregnancy is normative in its configuration of gender, science, and bodies.

Now we can ask: What is male pregnancy? Male pregnancy is the biological process by which a trans man or a transmasculine person gestates a fetus to birth; it is also the imagined biological process by which a cisgender man gestates a fetus to birth. Elsewhere, I have argued that pregnancy is so closely tied to femininity that a male version of it must engage with pregnancy's normatively gendered cultural and biological markers in order to be intelligible as pregnancy.[6] In one of the texts that I will examine closely in this chapter, installation artist Lee Mingwei is filmed wearing a belly pillow that makes his cisgender male body look pregnant. He walks slowly and with a bit of a waddle, his hands often braced against the small of his back. He so invokes the look and behaviors of pregnancy that some people he encounters, and some viewers of the film, respond to him as though he is pregnant. He could arguably have a large midsection for any number of reasons and yet, coupled with his behavior, his otherwise male body can be read as pregnant. Because we can hold up male pregnancy to female pregnancy, we can experience it as though it is real and see it as a male femininity, even if we go on to have a range of different reactions.

In the next section, I will discuss how film, television, art, and fan communities imagine male pregnancy as a shocking distortion of gender, science, and bodies. I will also show how male pregnancy manifests as a male femininity and how, as such, male pregnancy can be used to reaffirm or even expand normative masculinity at the expense of femininity.

## Imagined Male Pregnancy

In one of the most popular English-language filmic depictions of male pregnancy, the 1944 film *Junior*, Arnold Schwarzenegger plays Dr. Alex Hesse, a cisgender male scientist who experiments on himself and becomes pregnant. Schwarzenegger's character's pregnancy is rendered as a farce.[7] For humor, the film draws on common pregnancy tropes such as strange food cravings, swollen ankles, fainting, emotional volatility, and increased sexual urges. Schwarzenegger's body quickly takes on an exaggerated form of pregnancy, as seen in the film's publicity poster (see fig. 12.1). These physical changes are also played for laughs, as he struggles to find appropriate well-fitting clothing, gets winded easily, and often has to urinate. The poster is easily a reflection of normative pregnancy: note Schwarzenegger's comically surprised expression as he splays his hand on his huge lower abdomen. His romantic interest and cisgender female coparent, played by Emma Thompson, radiates supportiveness and happiness, as an expectant father might, while his doctor and fellow cisgender male scientist, played by Danny DeVito, looks confident and happy as he listens through a stethoscope to Schwarzenegger's belly. His pregnancy is recognizable though impossible, except through fictional scientific means, because it mirrors the cultural expectations for normative pregnancy while reconfiguring the particular mix of gender, science, and bodies. In this outlandish case, a highly masculine body with a penis can be pregnant because of experimental science.

Readers may recall that Arnold Schwarzenegger, who also served as governor of California from 2003 to 2011, has enjoyed a long and successful acting career, playing iconic hypermasculine roles in movies such as *Predator*,[8] *Commando*,[9] *Total Recall*,[10] and *True Lies*,[11] though he is most well known for playing the Terminator in that long-running blockbuster film series of the same name.[12] Prior to acting, he was a professional, highly decorated bodybuilder. Part of what makes *Junior*'s portrayal of male pregnancy so funny is that it juxtaposes a definitively feminine process with an icon of extreme masculinity. Although viewers are clearly invited to laugh at Schwarzenegger as he experiences pregnancy, his masculinity is always safe, and by the end of the film, he is "man enough" to go through childbirth, albeit through C-section.

Figure 12.1. Promotional poster for *Junior*. https://en.wikipedia.org.

Two earlier films, *A Slightly Pregnant Man*[13] and *Rabbit Test*,[14] in addition to a much-discussed episode of *Star Trek: Enterprise*, "Unexpected,"[15] offer a similar reconfiguration of pregnancy: masculine cisgender men who suddenly and comically experience pregnancy and its accompanying femininities, triumphing in the end with their masculinity intact. In the 1973 film *A Slightly Pregnant Man*, Italian actor Marcello Mastroianni plays a working-class everyman who finds himself pregnant due to changes in his hormonal makeup from an increased consumption of chicken. Mastroianni, like Schwarzenegger, is famous for playing iconic masculine characters, and perhaps even more notorious for his numerous off-screen trysts with his fellow actresses. Like Schwarzenegger, despite the humorous depiction of his pregnancy, his masculinity is safe. In *Rabbit Test*, comedian Billy Krystal, in his film debut from 1978, becomes pregnant after a one-night stand. Upon its release, this film was resoundingly panned by critics and viewers alike. Since then, it has accrued cult film status for its funny depictions of a feminine pregnancy experience against a masculine body. Though Krystal is not comparable to Schwarzenegger as an action hero or Mastroianni as a ladies' man, his role in the film is solidly masculine. As in the other two films, Krystal's character, despite his pregnancy, successfully engages in a romantic heteronormative relationship with a cisgender woman. In the *Star Trek: Enterprise* episode, "Unexpected", which first aired in 2001, Commander Trip Tucker, played by actor Connor Trinneer, is accidently impregnated through prolonged, though nonsexual, contact with a female alien. Unlike in the three films, Tucker is not truly pregnant, but, rather, a host for a developing fetus, but he does experience pregnancy in recognizable and humorous ways, such as feeling nauseous, tired, overly emotional, and bloated. Though he doesn't sexually consummate a heteronormative romantic relationship during the episode, his character and T'Pol, a cisgender female Vulcan officer, already have an established, long-simmering sexual tension that continues to play out here. Tucker is an attractive, masculine cisgender man, who, like the others discussed above, can carry a pregnancy without endangering his masculinity.

The three films and the *Star Trek: Enterprise* episode imagine male pregnancy as a male femininity that cisgender, heterosexual men can embody with absolutely no threat to their masculinity. In each case, male pregnancy is a stunning, unforeseen event, brought about by weird, out-of-control science. The men, all of whom are cisgender and heterosexual, remain so while they undergo a recognizable feminine cultural and biological process. Male pregnancy is a joke because it juxtaposes well-known pregnancy tropes with unquestionably masculine bodies. It is funny to see the same person who can play the aloof and heartless Terminator also cry uncontrollably while watching sappy television.

In media fandoms, male pregnancy—also known as "mpreg" or "male preg"—is a much-maligned fan-fiction trope that usually conforms to a vision of cisgender masculinity[16] and normative family relations.[17] Here, mpreg is similar to comedic film and TV portrayals in that it almost uniformly demands a clear, unyielding presentation of masculinity. Further, mpreg is possible due to unexpected science or magical interventions. And, while mpreg does mimic normative pregnancy tropes, it does so as high drama rather than comedy. One other notable distinction for the mpreg trope is that mpreg is a form of "slash"—that is, it occurs as a consequence of romantic, sexual contact between two cisgender masculine men. Here, normative pregnancy's reconfiguration is that masculine men can become pregnant as a result of sexual contact, coupled with unnatural science or magic.

While male pregnancy is nearly always portrayed similarly to normative female pregnancy, there is one very important point of departure: childbirth. Childbirth either happens surgically or is hand-waved away. In *Junior*, Schwarzenegger's character gives birth through a C-section. In *Rabbit Test*, the camera angles away as the baby is born. Mpreg nearly universally requires C-sections, as fans demand that masculine bodies remain masculine.[18] When speaking about the prevalence of surgical births, one prominent fan-fiction author, Akahannah, stated, "I find the idea of a pregnant male growing a vagina and then delivering a baby to be more traumatizing than a c-section."[19] For real, rather than imagined, pregnancy, C-section births only occur about one-fourth of the time. For mpreg fans, avoiding the birth canal is essential for maintaining the credibility of an imagined pregnant male's masculinity.

Fans of mpreg embrace male pregnancy as male femininity. Fans write, review, comment on, recommend, and amplify what they collectively recognize as good mpreg, which takes male pregnancy seriously in how it incorporates the features of an authentic pregnancy, with stereotypically feminine behaviors, expectations, and, to some extent, biological processes.[20] For mpreg fans, masculine cisgender men can be nurturing, emotional, and invested in their pregnant bodies. They can bond with their partners over their pregnancies. They can worry about their babies. Their masculinity is intact despite embracing normative feminine behaviors and biological processes. However, mpreg is a maligned trope, in that, for many fans, the seriousness with which mpreg brings together masculinity and femininity is itself a phenomenon worthy of scorn.[21]

Thus far, we have considered imagined male pregnancy as male femininity. We have seen how films, television, and fanfic authors reconfigure cisgender male bodies, science, and gender expectations associated with pregnancy in ways that always garner shock value. We have also seen that male pregnancy as male femininity can actually serve to reinforce normative masculinity when it is presented as a joke, as it is in films and shows. But we have also seen how male pregnancy as male femininity can expand normative masculinity when it is taken seriously, as it is in mpreg fan fiction. However, we also note that mpreg is a punching bag for larger fandom communities precisely because it does take male pregnancy so seriously. In all of these cases, it is the presence of the feminine, from stereotypical pregnancy tropes to actual vaginas, that renders the cultural shock. In the next section, I take a closer look at an art installation that imagines male pregnancy as a cutting-edge scientific breakthrough.

## Male Pregnancy: A Case Study

Renowned installation artists Lee Mingwei and Virgil Wong's online installation *POP! The First Human Male Pregnancy*, and its accompanying short film, *When Men are Pregnant*, provide us with a case study of imagined cisgender male pregnancy.[22] We can look closely at the installation and the film for their portrayal of male pregnancy, and, unlike the texts discussed above, we can analyze their reception through online comments left by viewers. Both texts offer a liminal space for audiences to vicariously experience Lee's pregnancy.[23] The website presents Lee's pregnancy as a highly stylized and realistic—if risky—biomedical intervention. It prominently features graphs of medical information, clips of ultrasounds, and radiographic images of Lee's pregnant male body. Video clips include Lee speaking with his doctor, played by Wong, about how male pregnancy stands to reshape the boundaries of gender. Here, male pregnancy reconfigures normative pregnancy by emphasizing the possibilities of science and technology to purposefully, rather than accidentally, displace pregnancy from female bodies.

For more than fifteen years, Mingwei and Wong's *POP! The First Human Male Pregnancy* ran as publicly available, interactive, Internet-based performance art. Now, the website is available only as an internet

# PREGNANT MEN AND THEIR RECONFIGURATIONS OF PREGNANCY | 173

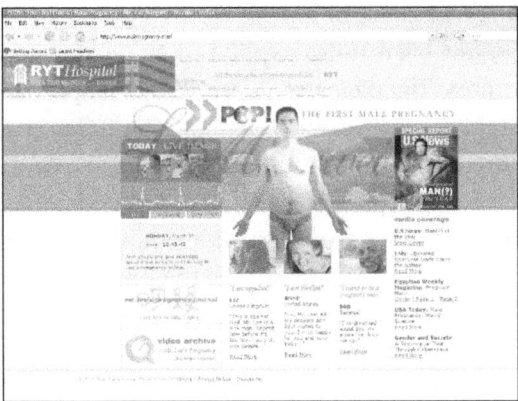

Figure 12.2. Home page, *POP! The First Male Pregnancy*. Source: www.malepregnancy.com, last accessed December 2014.

archives.[24] To reflect the end of the *POP!* installation, Lee's professional website now links the entry, *The Male Pregnancy Project* to a short film associated with the *POP!* installation, *When Men Are Pregnant*, directed by Sofie Lepault and Capucine Lafait that has been hosted on YouTube since 2006.[25]

Lee and Wong's installation opens with a highly technoscientific home page (see fig. 12.2) that shows Lee in the forefront, wearing only blue underwear, with an enlarged abdomen, indicating an advanced stage of pregnancy. He immediately presents as a cisgender, Asian male, relatively young, in his thirties. His underwear is somewhat fitted and, while plain, a traditionally masculine style with a Y-front design to accommodate a penis. Thus, Lee and Wong immediately juxtapose Lee's pregnant abdomen with his genitals, challenging viewers to think about the limits and potential of male bodies. The picture of Lee's pregnant body is surrounded by various smaller images that are recognizable as medical in nature: charts of fetal growth and Lee's weight and blood pressure, even a video clip of an ultrasound. Lee's file, so to speak, is framed by banners that indicate that a medical establishment, RYT Hospital Dwayne Medical Center, is actively monitoring Lee's pregnancy.

One click away the home page leads to a page dedicated to "The Science of Male Pregnancy."[26] A striking image of an X-ray of Lee's naked, pregnant body takes up about half the screen (see fig. 3). Similar to the previous image, but even more explicit, is the juxtaposition of a fetus directly over a penis. The page's text describes male pregnancy as similar to an ectopic pregnancy, meaning that it is a high-risk and highly medicalized procedure that is still grounded in realistic medical science. Ectopic pregnancies are pregnancies that occur outside of a uterus and are usually considered so dangerous that they are terminated immediately upon detection.[27] Lee and Wong outline the process of male pregnancy as beginning with Lee taking hormones to "prepare his body" to host a fetus and placenta. Then, an embryo, created though in vitro fertilization, is implanted in his now-hospitable abdomen. From there, his pregnancy progresses "naturally" and thus can be supervised in the typical medical fashion for high-risk pregnancies. He expects to have his baby delivered by Cesarean section. In this image, Lee and Wong are able to take the already normalized and medicalized technologies of pregnancy and extend them to a cisgender male body in a manner that is realistic and convincing. Indeed, when scientists and practitioners who specialize in reproductive technologies speculate about the possibility of cisgender male pregnancy, they often describe it as similar to an intentional ectopic pregnancy.[28]

The film *When Men Are Pregnant* follows Lee, sporting a large pregnant belly, as he walks through downtown New York City, the site of the fictional RYT Hospital. He encounters strangers, some of whom comment on his pregnancy. One cisgender woman exclaims, "It's about time!" and then goes on to talk about how her sister, who gave birth to six children, was exhausted from what she described as the gendered burden of pregnancy. Lee's cab driver, a cisgender man, is friendly and jokes with him, but also says that all the religions he knows of would view Lee's pregnancy as "unnatural." Lee meets with his doctor, played by Wong, who in later scene will say to the camera, "He is a man that is very comfortable in that role. It's not that he's becoming a woman. He's a man." At another point in Lee's walk, he stops and appears to converse with an interviewer, telling him that male pregnancy makes people uncomfortable because "it challenges the very foundation of what is it to be men and what is it to be a woman [sic]." The seven-minute film is primarily motivated by two goals: conveying a realistic pregnancy that is recognized by the greater public who encounters Lee as he

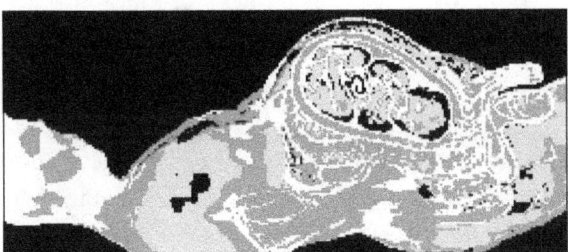

Figure 12.3. Radiographic image of Lee. Source: www.malepregnancy.com, last accessed December 2014.

walks through the city, and persuading that public that cisgender men who become pregnant are absolutely still men. Though Lee does not use the word "cisgender," he implies its applicability to himself with his and Wong's emphasis on his male identity and the film's inclusion of the penis-centric radiographic image (fig. 3). Whether they welcome or shun it, strangers recognize Lee's pregnant body as it reflects normative female pregnancy.

*When Men Are Pregnant*, which is hosted on YouTube, has been moved at least once, which has resulted in an inaccurate count of total page views and user comments. Since 2006, it has had 726,912 views and has received 821 comments.[29] In my analysis of the most recent 125 comments, I found that, more than any other type of claim made, commenters stated that the film was a hoax. Thirty-four comments said that the film (and presumably, male pregnancy more specifically) was a hoax. These comments generally resembled the following two examples: user Adam Misaki's "Fake" and Thao Ngo's "this is fake LOL". Thirty-one commenters posed questions or offered speculative explanations about the mechanics of male pregnancy—for instance, user FriedFrudda's entry "How is male pregnancy possible?" and Dawon Field's "How many weeks is he at in his pregnancy?" Other commenters offered scientific explanations:

> NAMI KITTY: This is real, let me explain this first. Yes this can happen, this requires a surgery to have some type of synthetic womb and then they can do invertro [*sic*] from there. Genetics can be used from the man but doesn't have to be, commonly it is a donor. Men are origi-

nally females in the womb, therefor they actually do have the ability to lactate as well. In 10 to 20 years this may be a common surgery for this to occur. Hopefully this helps anyone whom is confused.

SADIE A FOSHEY: wow some of yall actually believe this is real? wowwwwwww take a friggin second to think about the logistics of it- how would the egg get there? howwould it grow? where would it grow? what does the doctor mean by"abdominal cavity"? use some common sense, guys."

Three other users offer complimentary comments, including Amanda Khanyezi's "its [sic] wonderful that a man is having a baby," and Mega Master's "I think it's wonderful a man is having a baby. It's a little strange at first, but it reminds a lot of the Sims 4." By way of explanation, eight commenters assert that Lee is gay or trans. Three commenters comment on Lee's race in a negative and racist manner, with Anastasia Abeyta writing, "Oh my . . . he's Asian." Another three comments are outright negative, with Troy Mason writing that Lee's pregnancy is "an abomination to human kind and against all that noble and good with our race!!!" Two comments indicate that women are now useless. Forty-one comments have nothing to do with the concept of male pregnancy, with twenty of those seeming to relate to having been forced to watch the film for a school project.

These 125 comments do not represent the views of all of the people who have watched the film, nor all of the comments left in response to it. Rather, they are a convenience sample of only the most recent responses left by commenters who self-selected to leave a response. They cannot necessarily be read at face value, as some commenters may have been motivated to write for a range of reasons that have nothing to do with their actual thoughts about male pregnancy. However, we can still look at the spread of themes that emerge from this recent snapshot. For those who dismissed the film as a hoax, we can see that they are engaging with normative female pregnancy for the purpose of rejecting a male version; in other words, they know what pregnancy is, and Lee's pregnancy is not it. For those who had questions about details of the pregnancy ("how many weeks is he at his pregnancy?"), they are trying to make sense of male pregnancy through their understanding of normative female pregnancy and the menstrual cycle. For those who left compliments ("it's wonderful"), they, too, are recognizing male pregnancy as intelligible in light of normative female pregnancy, because congratulations and positive reactions to a pregnancy are socially appropriate responses.

For those who made scientifically themed comments, we can see more nuance in the way they draw on science in relation to bodies in discussing whether male pregnancy is real or not. For the person who says it is real, relatively recognizable reproductive technologies—in the form of a "synthetic womb," "invertro" (presumably a misspelling of in vitro), and "genetics" from the "donor"—are invoked to tie male pregnancy, again, to normative female pregnancy. For Sadie A Foshey, questions about the "logistics" of how and where the egg would go and grow signal that the film's use of recognizable reproductive technologies is not convincing in making male pregnancy feasible. Yet, even in its rejection of the video as authentic, the comment uses the language of normative female pregnancy to assess the possibility of male pregnancy.

The eight comments about Lee's presumed sexuality and gender status also reveal another front for the interpretative work of male pregnancy as male femininity. For the commenters who suggest that Lee is gay, male pregnancy is intelligible with respect to normative female pregnancy through the implication that Lee is not a real man because he is not heterosexual. For the commenters who assume that Lee is a trans man, Lee's male pregnancy is explainable due to his presumably female reproductive organs; therefore, his pregnancy is not really a male pregnancy because he is not, for those commenters, legitimately male. Though the film emphasizes Lee's cisgender status and remains absolutely silent about his sexuality, these two sets of comments show that male pregnancy can be effectively explained away in terms of gender and sexuality.

Comments on Lee's race are overwhelmingly inflammatory, and, as such, are shortened in this analysis. However, even abridged, comments like "Oh my . . . he's Asian" are grounded in the racist trope that Asian cisgender men are effeminate.[30] This presumption translates into an apparent lack of masculinity, which here seems to undergird a logical connection between Lee's Asian identity and his ability to be a pregnant man. For the comments that offer an overall criticism, male pregnancy is pitted against what is natural for "human kind" and "all that is noble and good." For those commenters, the very idea of cisgender male pregnancy threatens to disrupt the natural order of humanity.

Similar to the earlier discussed examples of imagined male pregnancy, Lee and Wong's installation situates male pregnancy as male femininity. They rely primarily on experimental yet recognizable medical science to explain it, and they make Lee's status as a cisgender male explicit by emphasizing his normative gender identity and his masculine body as a point of departure. Those who comment on the film *When Men Are Pregnant* also engage with normative female pregnancy to either deny the possibility of male pregnancy or to understand it as real. Pregnancy is intelligible for Lee and Wong and for the commenters of the film, though they certainly lack consensus about whether or not Lee's male pregnancy is—or can be—real.

For Lee and Wong, POP! *The First Human Male Pregnancy* and *When Men Are Pregnant* reconfigure the boundaries of masculinity and femininity by mapping normative female pregnancy onto a cisgender male body through the use of exceptional medical technologies. Viewers who leave comments on the film largely reject the concept of male pregnancy, denying the possibilities of even extensive technological interventions, and take aim at Lee's gender, sexuality, and race as a means of further rejecting his representation of male pregnancy.

## Trans Men's Male Pregnancy

Thus far, we have focused on imagined male pregnancy as it exists in films, shows, fan works, and art. Trans men's male pregnancy is real. Thomas Beatie—the most famous case—and other trans men and trans masculine individuals (including Danny Wakefield, introduced at the beginning of this chapter), who refer to their pregnancies as "male pregnancies," offer a series of breaks in the concept of normative female pregnancy.[31] By insisting on their identity as men, while using their reproductive organs to gestate a fetus, they challenge the boundaries between gender and reproductive physiology. Precisely because they assert their masculinity as distinct from, though accommodating to, their pregnant bodies, Beatie and Wakefield, among other pregnant trans men, faced a tremendous public backlash over their legitimacy as men and experienced mixed reactions on numerous fronts as to whether or not their bodies were actually capable of pregnancy.

Trans men and transmasculine persons who become pregnant do not have homogenous experiences of pregnancy.[32] In one study of trans men's understandings of their pregnancies, researchers noted that trans men sometimes thought of themselves as surrogates for their babies because they couldn't fully reconcile their pregnancies with normative female pregnancies.[33] In another study, some trans men reported emotional distress and gender dysphoria due to seeing their bodies change in ways that either they read or feared others would read as feminine.[34] Yet, in both studies, some trans men were happy, or at least at peace with their bodies, during pregnancy. In a third study that included participants who felt that they balanced their gender identity with their pregnancy, Damien W. Riggs writes "that it is indeed possible for pregnancy to be detached from its normative relationship to particular embodied identities (i.e., female), and to instead reconceptualise pregnancy as a role that can be fulfilled by any embodied identity (albeit one that occupies a body capable of bearing a child)."[35] Taken in concert, this body of work suggests that pregnant trans men and trans masculine persons negotiate new scripts, often at a personal level, that incorporate their gender, body, and pregnancy. They may look at their own bodies and see them as useful technologies for carrying a pregnancy. They may hide their pregnancies from others to avoid a confrontation about perceived contradictions between their gender and their pregnancy. They may suffer emotional distress due to dissonance between their gender and pregnancy's physiological demands. They may be able to see pregnancy as a process that need not be gendered at all—in other words, that their gender does not stand in contradiction with their pregnancy.

Returning to Danny Wakefield, we can see him wrestling with many of factors noted in the existing research on trans men's pregnancy. For example, at times he seems to understand his pregnancy as kind of surrogacy. In some of his social media posts, Wakefield refers to himself as a "seahorse," drawing on the fact that male seahorses carry fertilized eggs in a pouch until they are ready to hatch.[36] In a *Newsweek* op-ed, he writes: "I had been on testosterone for nine years, and now I have been off testosterone for a year in order to carry Wilder, and it's like parts of my body from my past are visiting. It's just been a really comforting feeling of welcoming a friend back, knowing that it's not going to be forever. So even if moments do feel dysphoric or uncomfortable, that's OK."[37] In this single quote, Wakefield expresses a multitude of different thoughts about his male pregnancy: that his body is different from the one he has purposefully chosen, but that the difference is OK because it is also a choice; that the feminine parts of his body are necessary in order to carry his child; that the feminine parts of his body that have reemerged will be short-lived; and that feelings of gender dysphoria and general discomfort are natural and manageable. In his posts, interviews, and writings, he overwhelmingly projects happiness, excitement, and highly relatable anxiety about the birth process and his desire to be a good parent.

In documenting his pregnancy, Wakefield is clear about two of his goals: to be visible for other trans individuals, and to educate the general public to be inclusive regarding "pregnant folks." He is also committed to transparency, describing an intensive monitoring of his social media channels by a team of five individuals who censor negative comments, sometimes at the rate of "hundreds . . . a day."[38] Echoing the findings of other studies on the backlash to trans men's pregnancies, Wakefield describes receiving hateful and violent comments; intrusive questions about his anatomy, sexuality, and relationships from strangers; and references to his former gender identity, all with an underlying effort to delegitimize his gender and his ability to call his pregnancy "male."

In this section, we have discussed the real male pregnancy of trans men and trans masculine persons. In doing so, we have acknowledged that they don't have uniform experiences. In reviewing existing research and looking more closely at Danny Wakefield's documented male pregnancy, we have seen how the intersection of masculinity and femininity can be fraught and even dangerous for pregnant trans men.

## Male Pregnancy and Reconfigurations of Gender, Science, and Bodies

In both real and imagined male pregnancy, pregnant men embody femininity through their reconfiguring of normative female pregnancy through new and unexpected connections between gender, science, and bodies. Looking at different cases helps us understand where male pregnancy intersects with normative female pregnancy to produce male femininities for different stakeholders. For trans men, male pregnancy and normative female pregnancy align physiologically, at the level of female reproductive organs, and culturally, at the expectations they and others have for their bodies. Because the use of female reproductive organs to carry pregnancies effectively engenders those organs as socially feminine, trans men experience a range of reactions, all of which reconfigure pregnancy's gendered norms: they think of their bodies as a gender-neutral technology that can function as a surrogate; they hide their bodies and maintain the distinction between their maleness and their female reproductive organs; they suffer cognitive dissonance between their own expectations for their gender and those of pregnancy; they embrace their bodies as both male and capable of being pregnant. Pregnant cisgender men in film are presented as humorous because their gender identities are secure, even as their bodies perform the highly feminine work of pregnancy. Pregnant cisgender men in mpreg are also secure in their masculinity, though their experiences with pregnancy are very dramatic. For Lee and Wong, male pregnancy and normative female pregnancy can also align physiologically with the use of novel medical science, though, like all of the other examples of imagined pregnant men, Lee's delivery is a planned C-section. Lee and Wong draw on science to purposefully transform a cisgender male body so that it can undergo a pregnancy. Similar to the other representations, they present pregnancy as male femininity—a deliberate embracing of feminine behaviors and biological processes—by emphasizing Lee's pregnancy in relation to his maleness, eschewing any cognitive dissonance between Lee's gender identity and expectations for pregnancy, and (very similar to some trans men) embracing his body as both male and also capable of pregnancy. If we look at the commenters on *When Men Are Pregnant*, as a reflection of another set of stakeholders, we continue to see how normative female pregnancy operates as a touchstone, mostly through dissensus around male pregnancy. These commenters are, for the most part, unwilling to see alignment between normative female pregnancy and male pregnancy, with many dismissing Lee's pregnancy outright as a hoax or a fake. Since Lee and Wong are established artists, calling Lee's performance a "hoax"—a strong word that implies a deliberate attempt at trickery—seems especially harsh. Lee himself has sometimes attributed his motivation for this work as being in awe of his sister's pregnancy experience.[39] For the few commenters who seem to positively engage with the film and with male pregnancy, they do so by using sense-making strategies that indicate ties between normative female pregnancy and male pregnancy.

In this chapter, we have analyzed real and imagined male pregnancy and have seen repeatedly how it exists in conversation with normative female pregnancy. We have noted the new and different configurations of gender, science, and bodies, which produce different stakeholders' versions of male pregnancy. Regardless of how trans men feel about their gender or their bodies, they have to operate vis-à-vis highly gendered scripts for pregnancy. Similarly, imagined male pregnancy must incorporate many of the scripts of normative female pregnancy in order to be intelligible as pregnancy. Though both real and imagined male pregnancy demonstrate the flexibility of those normative scripts, they also show the high stakes for bringing masculinity and femininity together.

NOTES

1 Danny Wakefield, Facebook, https://www.facebook.com.
2 Dannythetransdad, May 2, 2020, Instagram, https://www.instagram.com.
3 Danny Wakefield, "I'm Trans Masculine and Just Gave Birth to My First Child," *Newsweek*. December 28, 2020, https://www.newsweek.com.
4 Mary Ingram-Waters, "Writing the Pregnant Man," *Transformative Works and Cultures* 20 (2015): n.p.
5 Mary Ingram-Waters, "Gender, Sexuality, and Technology in Male Pregnancy: An Analysis of Lee Mingwei and Virgil Wong's Installation, POP! The First Human Male Pregnancy," *Sexualities* 19, no. 1–2 (2016): 138–55.
6 Ingram-Waters, "Writing the Pregnant Man," 20.
7 *Junior*, directed by Ivan Reitman (Los Angeles, CA: Universal Pictures, 1994).
8 *Predator*, directed by John McTiernan (Los Angeles, CA: Twentieth Century Fox, 1987).
9 *Commando*, directed by Mark L. Lester (Los Angeles, CA: Twentieth Century Fox, 1985).
10 *Total Recall*, directed by Paul Verhoeven (Van Nuys, CA: Carolco Home Video, 1990).
11 *True Lies*, directed by James Cameron ( Los Angeles, CA: Twentieth Century Fox, 1994).
12 *The Terminator*, directed by James Cameron (Los Angeles, CA: Hemdale, 1984).
13 *A Slightly Pregnant Man*, directed by Jacques Demy (France: Koch Lorber Films, 1973).

14 *Rabbit Test*, directed by Joan Rivers (Los Angeles, CA: AVCO Embassy Pictures, 1978).
15 *Star Trek: Enterprise*, season 1, episode 5, "Unexpected," directed by Michael Vejar, aired October 17, 2001, on UPN.
16 Mary Ingram-Waters, "When Normal and Deviant Identities Collide: Confessions of an Aca/Fan,"*Transformative Works and Cultures* 5 (2010): n.p.; Ingram-Waters, "Writing the Pregnant Man," 20.
17 Berit Åström,"'Let's Get those Winchesters Pregnant': Male Pregnancy in Supernatural Fan Fiction," *Transformative Works and Cultures* 4 (2010): n.p.; Louisa E. Stein, "'This Dratted Thing': Fannish Storytelling through New Media," in *Fan Fiction and Fan Communities in the Age of the Internet*, ed. Karen Hellekson and Kristna Busse (Jefferson, NC: McFarland, 2006), 245–60.
18 Ingram-Waters, "Writing the Pregnant Man."
19 Ingram-Waters.
20 Ingram-Waters.
21 Ingram-Waters.
22 Lee Mingwei is Taiwanese and thus orders his surname first.
23 Irina Aristarkhova, "Man as Hospitable Space: The Male Pregnancy Project," *Performance Research* 14, no. 4 (2009): 25–30; Mary Ingram-Waters, "Gender, Sexuality, and Technology in Male Pregnancy: An Analysis of Lee Mingwei and Virgil Wong's Installation, POP! *The First Human Male Pregnancy*," *Sexualities* 19, nos. 1–2 (2016): 138–55.
24 See https://malepregnancy.com; and Lee Mingwei, http://www.leemingwei.com.
25 "The World's First Male Pregnancy," YouTube video, 7:29, September 21, 2006, https://www.youtube.com.
26 "Male Pregnancy," https://web.archive.org.
27 "Ectopic Pregnancy," American Pregnancy Association, 2017, http://americanpregnancy.org.
28 Ingrid Peritz, "Miracle Birth Signals Male Moms?," *Globe and Mail*, August 15, 2003, https://www.theglobeandmail.com.
29 Sophie Lepault and Capucine Lafait, "When Men Are Pregnant," YouTube video, 7:29, August 20, 2006, https://www.youtube.com.
30 Yen Ling Shek, "Asian American Masculinity: A Review of the Literature," *Journal of Men's Studies* 14, no. 3 (2006): 379–91.
31 Taylor Cruz, "Thomas Beatie and Reactions from the Trans Community" (unpublished manuscript, Arizona State University, 2011); Judith Halberstam, "The Pregnant Man," *Velvet Light Trap* 65 (2010): 77–79; Mary Ingram-Waters, "Gender, Sexuality, and Technology in Male Pregnancy: An Analysis of Lee Mingwei and Virgil Wong's Installation, POP! *The First Human Male Pregnancy*," *Sexualities* 19, nos. 1–2 (2016): 138–55; Eve Shapiro, *Gender Circuits: Bodies and Identities in a Technological Age*, 2nd ed. (New York: Routledge, 2015); Jasper Verlinden, "Transgender Bodies and Male Pregnancy: The Ethics of Radical Self-Refashioning," in

*Machine: Bodies, Genders, Technologies* (Heidelberg: Universitätsverlag Winter, 2012), 107–36.

32  Simone A. Ellis, Danuta M. Wojnar, and Maria Pettinato, "Conception, Pregnancy, and Birth Experiences of Male and Gender Variant Gestational Parents: It's How We Could Have a Family," *Journal of Midwifery & Women's Health* 60, no. 1 (2015): 62–69.

33  Ellis et al., "Conception, Pregnancy."

34  Alexis Hoffkling, Juno Obedin-Maliver, and Jae Sevelius, "From Erasure to Opportunity: A Qualitative Study of the Experiences of Transgender Men around Pregnancy and Recommendations for Providers," *BMC Pregnancy and Childbirth* 17, no. 2 (2017): 332.

35  Damien W. Riggs, "Transgender Men's Self-Representations of Bearing Children Post-Transition," in *Chasing Rainbows: Exploring Gender Fluid Parenting Practices*, ed. Fiona Joy Green and May Friedman (Ontario: Demeter, 2013), 9–10.

36  Dannythetransdad, Instagram, August 26, 2020, https://www.instagram.com.

37  Wakefield, "I'm Trans Masculine."

38  Wakefield.

39  Irina Aristarkhova, "Man as Hospitable Space: The Male Pregnancy Project," *Performance Research* 14, no. 4 (2009): 25–30.

PART 4

# Performing Male Femininities

The authors in this section explore the ways that male femininities are performed on varying stages, both metaphorical and literal. These readings each highlight the ways that men manage their feminine performances as a means of navigating their personal relationships, challenging structural inequalities, and upending their own assumptions about their gender identities. Each author shows us how men can enact male femininities to meet different social and interpersonal needs and expose how feminine performances for men can be colored by, one the one hand, risk and surveillance, and by pride, gratification, and pleasure, on the other.

Gender performativity—the idea that gender is something that we "do," rather than something that we "are"—is one of the most enduring concepts in contemporary gender studies. As Candice West and Don H. Zimmerman observed more than thirty years ago, gender is "the activity of managing situated conduct in light of normative conceptions of attitudes and activities appropriate for one's sex category . . . [and] . . . not simply an aspect of what one is, but, more fundamentally, it is something that one does, and does recurrently, in interaction with others."[1] By performing gender, we give meaning to gender and gender identities.[2] In other words, we are not "born" with gender; through the act of "doing" gender, we achieve gender.

Rather than occurring "naturally," gender performances are learned and performed during interaction with others. These performances act to reinforce gender further until our gender performance and our gender identity become so intermingled as to appear to be one and the same. As a result, we come to believe that gender is natural and inevitable. Yet we only behave in gender appropriate ways because we learn gender appropriate behaviors and behave in gender appropriate ways in public to perform our gender roles because that is what comes "naturally." But, when it comes to gender performances, what is considered "appropriate" is entirely socially constructed.

When we perform our genders in ways that are expected, they tend to be invisible. Because so many of us follow gender norms, we rarely notice that we are all constantly performing gender in one way or another. Only when our performances disrupt expectations do the existence of those expectations become evident. When individuals perform appropriately, they are rewarded; when they do not, they are punished. For men, performing masculinity comes with little risk: boys are rewarded for being "tuff" and admonished when they are not. Men are praised when they meet societal expectations of a "good" man, such as providing for their families, being athletic, and achieving prominence in certain occupations. Yet, if they behave in effeminate ways, enter occupations that society has deemed to be feminine, and display emotions, they are scorned. Given that so many rewards accrue to men who perform masculinities, and so much scorn if they perform femininities, why and how would they come to perform femininities at all?

### The Complex Performances of Male Femininities

Conceptualizing the performativity of male femininity is not as cut and dry as it might seem. For example, while many of the readings in this section discuss drag as a means by which men perform male femininities, there are many other ways that male femininities can be performed, some of which are less deliberate. Several of the readings in this section highlight the various reasons and motivations for performing drag while revealing the importance of geography and social context for the way folks make sense of their own and other's gender performances. The readings in this section expose how social context makes gender performances different, even when they seem similar.[3]

We begin with a personal voice essay from Ray LeBlanc. In recalling his first drag experience, LeBlanc reflects on how drag allowed him to embody both the "feminine and masculine, familiar and strange" and to craft his body beyond the socially constructed meaning of "maleness." For LeBlanc, drag provided him the opportunity to reconcile his inner turmoil associated with masculinity and gave him new insights about the ways that gender, sex, and sexuality are complicated by the newfound confidence that accompanies drag performance intermingled with experiences of sexism and transmisogyny.

In the first empirical study in this section, Amy Stone demonstrates how, within certain contexts, drag can give drag performers a chance to connect with family members and the larger community in unexpected ways. Within the context of Mardi Gras, Stone finds that drag can provide performers with a sense of accomplishment, helping to establish them as "outstanding, artistic, popular and valued members of the community," and with a route to cultural citizenship that demonstrates that they, and other members of the LGBTQ community, can contribute to civic life in important ways. From this piece we can see that social context offers both limitations to and opportunities for the occurrence of male femininities. Within some contexts, the performance of femininities may be shunned, but, within others, such as Mardi Gras, it is rewarded.

Further demonstrating the importance of social context, Han's piece on gay Asian drag queens demonstrates the opportunities that drag can offer to challenge both racism and the centrality of masculinity within gay communities. Among gay Asian drag queens, Han finds that drag—and thus gender—is more than "just an act," but additionally a way of exploring conflicting gender identities. For gay Asian drag queens, drag makes it possible to confront dominant narratives within gay communities regarding what is considered "desirable" both in terms of gender and race.

In their article on gay Latinx men, Smith and colleagues show how male femininities are performed in the most intimate of encounters, revealing that, within certain sexual contexts, such as the gender presentation of their sexual partners, gay Latinx men "make choices that often align with undesirable expectations to conform to traditional gender norms or perform freely as feminine." In so doing, they demonstrate the outdatedness of the gender binary as a means of examining modern day gender performances, which are often contextual rather than individual. In other words, depending on context, men may engage in masculinities, femininities, or male femininities.

Finally, Elroi Windsor's essay recounts the author's personal experiences as a member of the radical cheerleading group the Cheerbois. Windsor urges us to think about what it means to consider a performance feminine, masculine one, or some combination of both, and what factors we should bear in mind when we think about gender performance as being "gendered" in the first place.

Taken together, the readings in this section highlight the ways that masculinity, femininity, and male femininity are performances. They also challenge the very notion of what it means to "perform" gender in the first place and the components of the performance that allows it be read as either masculine or feminine. Moreover, they reveal that gender performances are relational, situated, and contextual, providing us an opportunity to explore how this matters for the way we and others make sense of gender performances.

NOTES
1. Candice West and Don H. Zimmermann, "Doing Gender," *Gender and Society*, 1 (1987): 127, 140.
2. Judith Butler, *Gender Trouble: Feminism and the Subversion of Identity* (New York: Routledge, 1990).
3. Tim Carrigan, Bob Connell, and John Lee, "Toward a New Sociology of Masculinity," *Theory and Society* 14, no. 5 (1985): 551–604.

## 13

## Welcome to the Stage

*Power, Practice, and the Performance of Drag Queening*

RAY LEBLANC

Walking into Joe's Bar, I felt as if I was entering a historic landmark.[1] What seems like fifty years worth of accumulating dust can easily give that impression. But the tiny square bar also held visible reminders of the joy and trauma its patrons have experienced over the decades, alluding to its historic past. Joe's, like most spaces in queer nightlife, was one of the original refuges for LGBTQI people living in rural Louisiana. The metal entry door was kept locked—a reminder of police raids and homophobic attacks. Although a locked door may not make the place the most accessible for potential patrons, an off-duty drag queen usually watched the security monitor and would push the door open for customers, greeting them with a full-bodied hug. Inside, the dim lights and low ceiling were a stark contrast to the lively conversations, booming music, and towering drag queens that filled the bar. Walking around Joe's without losing a crown or a wig was a testament to the poise and athleticism of the most accomplished performers.

Nevertheless, the crowd was forgiving to first-time drag queens, so I was pleased when the bar's show director offered me a spot. For over a year, I had been visiting local gay bars and talking to drag queens about their experiences for my master's thesis. At that point, I had not yet read about any other scholars who were both studying drag and doing drag.[2] Fueled by a desire to stand out, and of course, my own curiosity, I frequently told the queens that my ultimate goal was to perform. Sharon Coxx, the show director, held me to this promise. And now I was terrified for my onstage debut.

When I arrived at Joe's in full drag, Sharon led me to the farthest corner of the bar behind a pool table to the "backstage" area. Passing through a white sheet hung across a string, we walked into chaos. Clothing and beauty products covered every surface. Three performers leaned toward mirrors propped atop old dressers, fighting for any sliver of lighting. Sharon sat in "the office"—a closet with a computer—and asked if I had decided on a drag name. "Hegemony Flowers," I told her, with some reservation. "What?" she asked, bewildered. "Okay—Gem Flowers, and hopefully they don't think it's Jim like a man."

The men got dressed, moving frantically between each other, asking for help with difficult clasps and dodging random pool sticks. I stood there, silent in embarrassment and fear, and watched in awe. Adding another layer of dark black liner to her eyes, Molly Hart asked if I had had a drink yet to loosen up, and I nodded. She remarked that the bar might start paying queens a $30 stipend. Everyone groaned about the small crowd, slow night, and few tips, but I was thankful that not many people would witness whatever tragedy I was about to perform. Finding a vacant mirror, I anxiously critiqued my reflection, not completely happy with what I saw, despite the eight hours of preparation it had taken me to transform myself. Most first-timers have a "drag mother" to paint their faces, and a few performers offered to the first few times I came to the bar in drag. But I wanted to do my own makeup and styling. To borrow the words of my fellow queens, I was "busted" and "dusted": a face "like a brick," and "a body like a hog." I was a butch queen, obviously out of place. What had I gotten myself into?

It was my turn to perform. The emcee, Miss Lady, was an older Cajun queen with a deep, raspy voice that rattled the walls. She gave me a grand introduction: "It's her first time performing—Gem is a beautiful stone, show her some love!" With no escape, I nervously looked up at the paint-chipped ceiling and then walked to the stage.

Piano riffs cued me in as I nervously tousled my long, curly brunette wig, turned my back to the audience, and closed my eyes. I had chosen Carrie Underwood's nostalgic track "Before He Cheats" for its short, yet dramatic, narrative. When the lyrics began, and I turned to face the blinding spotlights, my legs trembled. I wobbled back and forth on the warped wood, unable to find a solid foundation on which to stand. The audience was barely visible—uninterested patrons engaged in conversation, older men swirling their drinks. The wig's cheap lace prickled my forehead. False eyelashes weighted down my lids, and the corners of my eyes itched and watered. Several waistbands of pantyhose dug into my pelvis, reaching for my ribs through the hip and butt pads.

When I glanced at the mirrored wall, I saw my reflection once again, but this time there was an unrecognizable body: at once both feminine and masculine, familiar and strange, crafted through contradicting processes of gendered meanings and practices. As a drag queen, I wanted to purposefully craft my body and stretch my flesh beyond rigid biological and social understandings of maleness. I emerged a queer assemblage of femininities and masculinities, traversing the boundary between performing woman and being man through my own personal negotiations of gender play. Looking at myself, I saw the embodiment of femininity, a body I was always taught to repudiate. For me, drag queening was a way to reconcile this turmoil and explore my gender creativity.

I descended the stage to seek out tippers. Through clouds of smoke, I could see shy smiles and blushing cheeks. I emphatically caressed barstools, stumbling only slightly. Then, I approached a man playing with the straw in his drink and successfully utilized a drag queen's most powerful tool—direct eye contact. He gave me one dollar, and I repeated the procedure on three others. Although four dollars failed to compensate any costs I had incurred to transform into a drag queen (well, maybe half a set of fake lashes), accepting the bills from their fingertips was at once intimate, empowering, and validating. I returned to the stage and stroked my padded hips to draw attention away from my eyebrows breaking through their gluey prison, when a man in the audience yelled out: "I'll give you a dollar if you let me kiss you!"

"At least ten dollars for that," Miss Lady mouthed to me from the edge of the stage. The man drunkenly ran up onstage, held my face, and shoved his tongue into my mouth. With all of my will, I pushed back, clenched my jaw, and closed my mouth tight. With the corner of my eye I looked at Lady and knew she understood the visceral and naked vulnerability that permeated my body. She mouthed a soft apology. She had dealt with men like this, who felt entitled to our bodies, a million times before.

As a drag queen, I was initiated into an economy of consumption, rewards, and exploitation. I knew that professional queens were important community figures and political representations of LGBTQI visibility. But, for many, their celebrity status was complicated by minimal monetary gain, social marginalization, and even violence. Although during my performance I felt empowered, my experience was penetrated by both sexism and transmisogyny. Expressing femininity through my male-assigned body, I was caught between contradictory and complementary ideas about gender, sex, and sexuality. Going out in drag attracted forms of harassment I had never experienced before, ranging from strangers commanding me to smile to propositioning me for sex. If I was out of drag, this same man probably would not have even spoken to me, let alone demanded a kiss. I would most likely laugh in his face if he did. But here, now, onstage before an audience, limping in six-inch heels, with a corseted waist and the illusion of breasts, I remained silent to his advances.

The man was aggravated that I didn't open my mouth. "Come on, I paid for a real kiss!" he fussed, but Lady led him back to his seat, using her seasoned emceeing abilities. I hid behind a cigarette machine to review my tips, and Lady came by to encourage me to perform again soon. "I'm sorry about that," she quipped, "but it's part of the business. It pays for the water bill, you know? For the water bill."

NOTES

1 All names of people and businesses are pseudonyms.
2 See Leila Rupp and Verta Taylor, *Drag Queens at the 801 Cabaret* (Chicago: University of Chicago Press, 2003). Most researchers study drag from the audience, but Steven Schacht is put into drag for a first-timer's pageant: see "Turnabout: Gay Drag Queens and the Masculine Embodiment of the Feminine," in *Revealing Male Bodies*, ed. Nancy Tuana, William Cowling, Maurice Hamington, Greg Johnson, and Terrance MacMullan (Bloomington: Indiana University Press, 2002), 155–70.

# 14

# "In My Dad's Gun Room, There's an 8×10 Picture of Me in Drag"

*Drag and Respect in the Deep South*

AMY L. STONE

Joshua and I sat on his couch while he described the first costuming he did as a member of his Mardi Gras krewe, an organization devoted to putting on a ball every year during the winter Carnival season in Mobile, Alabama. In recalling his first year performing during Carnival, he described the ten-foot-tall debutante-shaped float that he'd constructed and how it felt being perched on top of it in full drag. Costuming like Joshua's are part of what makes this ball a popular event for thousands of Carnival attendees every year, garnering the krewe respect and prestige among Mobile residents. Joshua's father, an elderly man from rural Louisiana, came to the ball the first time Joshua performed drag during Mardi Gras. As Joshua reminisced about his father's attendance, the two of us smiled at the incongruity of him watching his son being wheeled around the convention center dressed as a debutante. A few months later, Joshua went home to discover in his father's gun room an 8x10 picture of him, which his father described as "a great conversation piece." For Joshua, drag became an unexpected source of connection with his father, a man who, before he attended the ball, knew little about gay culture. Although male femininity is often something that divides men from one another, Josh's story revealed that drag is one way that gay men can gain respect in their urban communities as well as in their own families.[1]

Drag, as a form of male femininity, is complex. Drag queens are simultaneously consumed as a spectacle by heterosexuals, treated as fundraising celebrities within the LGBTQ community, and marginalized socially and romantically by other gay men.[2] Scholars have shown that drag's function is deeply dependent on context; the geographical and physical location, the identity of the former, and the composition of the audience all shape the meaning of the performance. In this chapter, I analyze drag performances in the Deep South, by both white and Black gay men, during two Mardi Gras masque balls in Baton Rouge, Louisiana, and Mobile, Alabama. I argue that, because drag fits into the lauded aesthetics of the masque balls, performing drag provides krewe members recognition and respect from the larger community. In this context, drag helps members of the Southern LGBTQ community make a place for themselves in the city as a form of cultural citizenship. This respect, however, is conditional; family members appreciate drag only if it is performed within the context of Mardi Gras as an "amateur" performance, and the performers maintain symbolic boundaries between drag and transgender identification. My findings suggest that certain forms of male femininity have the potential to accrue respect, but that this respect comes only when male femininity is transitional or fleeting and for a specific purpose or "good cause."

## Background: Mardi Gras

Although most people associate Mardi Gras with a weekend of debauchery in New Orleans's French Quarter, Mardi Gras is celebrated all over the South, from Houston, Texas, to Pensacola, Florida, during several weeks in the winter Carnival season. The season includes private, formal adult events as well as family-friendly street parades. The focus of this chapter is on the adults-only masque balls run by private organizations called "krewes," or mystic societies, which are often organized around race, gender, class, and sex categories.[3] Masque balls are costumed affairs attended by guests who are invited through the krewe members' social networks. Most krewes crown their own royalty—"kings" or "queens," or emblems of the group—at the ball, recognizing longtime members. These balls include refreshments, decorations, music, and a theme-based tableau of acting, dancing, or visual displays. Dress codes for most balls require floor-length gowns for women and tuxedos for men. While, on their invitations, many straight krewes explicitly forbid cross-dressing, LGBTQ krewes allow guests to select which formal wear they think suits them best.

LGBTQ krewes are common throughout the Gulf South, with gay men having their own in New Orleans, Baton Rouge, and Lafayette. There are also "all-inclusive" krewes in the eastern Gulf South that were formed by members of the LGBTQ community but that welcome all potential members regardless of race, gender, or sexuality. In both Baton Rouge and Mobile, the oldest gay and lesbian organizations are Mardi Gras krewes started in the early 1980s (the Krewe of Apollo and Order of Osiris, respectively).[4] Mobile is often described as the birthplace of the American Mardi Gras tradition, with celebrations dating back to the 1700s. The city hosts over twenty-five parades and sixty-five formal balls organized by over seventy krewes or secret societies—an impressive number for a city of less than two hundred thousand people.[5] The krewe tradition for gay men dates from the 1950s, and Mobile currently boasts four krewes that serve the LGBTQ community. The largest of these, the all-inclusive Order of Osiris, is composed primarily of white gay men and lesbians and hosts a yearly masque ball attended by almost two thousand people. The city of Baton Rouge did not develop its own krewes and carnival traditions until after World War II.[6] Moreover, Krewes for the LGBTQ community did not form until the 1980s. Baton Rouge has two LGBTQ krewes: the Krewe of Apollo, and the Krewe of Divas. The Krewe of Divas is exclusively for drag queens and serves as more of a troupe than a typical krewe. The Krewe of Apollo for gay men hosts a ball that is attended by over one thousand guests during Carnival season.

## Drag in Context

In Leila Rupp and Verta Taylor's ethnographic study, *Drag Queens at the 801 Cabaret*, the participants defined drag queens as "gay men who dress as [women] but don't want to be women or have women's bodies."[7] The drag I observed in both of the Carnival krewes that I observed was similar: a performance by gay men dressed as women, although the drag performed in the gay bars in each city include trans women or drag queens with breast augmentation.

Drag is often studied as a socially meaningful experience for performers,[8] and as a "performance of protest" for the audience that destabilizes and challenges gender.[9] The experience and impact of drag, for both audiences and performers, is deeply contextual.[10] Esther Newton argues that "drag as performance and camp as a sensibility are cultural schema used by individuals and by collectivities to signify, constitute, and advance particular agendas in specific situations."[11]

Carnival drag operates within the context of the region and festival. Cross-dressing pageantry such as "women-less weddings" and "powder puff football" have long served as temporary rituals of reversal in Southern churches and schools.[12] Drag is "a way of life" in many Southern LGBTQ communities, integral to bar and community life,[13] and it may also serve as a support system for transgender people.[14] Drag is not uncommon during festival events like Mardi Gras,[15] as cross-dressing fits into carnival culture norms of inversion and performance.[16]

However, festival events are not free and open, and, even within the typically transgressive Carnival season, drag has been contested and regulated. In 1962, New Orleans police raided the ball of the first known gay krewe, the Krewe of Yuga, due to the strict regulation of cross-dressing and gay visibility during the festival.[17] During Carnival in Rio de Janeiro, gay visibility through drag, which has become more visible over time, and was been regulated by the state and festival organizers. While gay visibility in Carnival in Rio did not guarantee acceptance during the rest of the year, it did gradually help advance gay rights.[18]

Festival spaces create opportunities for amateur cross-dressing and drag, motivating men who do not routinely engage in either to do so. Despite the significant academic attention given to drag in the last few decades, scholars still know little about the experiences of amateur drag performers, as most research focuses on drag performed in gay venues by professional or semiprofessional drag queens.[19] In a study of drag during a protest march, Tristan Bridges argues that, "while professional drag performers may intend to disrupt essentialist notions of gender and identity, more casual performances of drag often do not have the same effect, nor are they intended in the same ways."[20] My work contributes to this scholarship by examining amateur drag performers during Carnival events that are attended by diverse audiences.

## Drag, Citizenship, and Respect

Drag is one of the most identifiable aspects of gay culture,[21] and shows like *Ru Paul's Drag Race* have made it part of the "gaystreaming" of gay culture for a mainstream audience.[22] However, research has documented that often members of the LGBTQ community downplay forms of gender nonconformity such as drag in order to establish respectable social identities[23]—a practice that Kenji Yoshino describes as "covering" minority cultural differences.[24] In my study, I found that LGBTQ people who do drag were not expected to "cover" their differences, but they did often need to account for this way of "doing gender" to friends and family members.[25]

Social recognition and appreciation of queer cultural differences is part of cultural citizenship: the right to be recognized as an equal subject, worthy of respect and granted the "right to be different," particularly culturally different.[26] Cultural valuation recognizes minority group differences and considers them "valid possibilit[ies] for the conduct of life."[27] Michèle Lamont describes the "recognition gap" as the lack of respect for or valuation of the social worth of marginalized groups and individuals.[28] In my study, I examine the ways that doing drag during Mardi Gras becomes a source of respect for and valuation of queer cultural difference. This respect and recognition is not without pressure to cover or account for gender nonconformity; however, I show that, within some contexts, drag serves as the means by which gayness becomes more accepted by heterosexuals, and that drag can be a source of cultural citizenship for members of the LGBTQ community. In a limited way, gay men who do drag during Mardi Gras events gain validation from the heterosexual participants in these events, including their own family members.

## Methods

This research is part of a multiyear, four-city study of LGBTQ incorporation into festival life in the South and the Southwest. I began studying Mardi Gras in Baton Rouge and Mobile in the summer of 2013 and left the field in the winter of 2016. I attended the ball for the Order of Osiris and Krewe of Apollo during two Carnival seasons; additionally,

I attended other Mardi Gras events, including the other LGBTQ krewe balls, parades, and non-LGBTQ balls and events. I had access to both major krewes, and I attended a range of private events during each ball weekend, including royalty receptions, members' brunches, ball setups and dress rehearsals, and dinners with family members. Outside of Carnival season, I attended krewe events such as pool parties and fundraisers.

In addition, I made summer trips to Mobile and Baton Rouge to conduct interviews and conduct archival research. I interviewed twenty-nine members of LGBTQ krewes (eighteen in Mobile, eleven in Baton Rouge). The interviewees were almost exclusively Southerners born and raised in the Deep South. The interviewees were predominately white, middle-aged, middle-class gay men and lesbians: eight women and twenty-one men. All interviews in Baton Rouge were with gay men; twenty-five interviewees identified as white, while the remaining four identified as Black. Most interviewees worked in occupations such as gym teachers, bus drivers, and nurses. Interviewees ranged in age from twenty-nine to eighty-three years old with an average age of fifty. During my four years of ethnographic research, I spoke with dozens of other LGBTQ krewe members and participants in Mardi Gras, as well as their family members, friends, and ball guests.

## The Most Fabulous Carnival Event in Town

Drag played a role in the cultural distinctiveness and popularity of both Carnival krewes in their respective cities. Yet drag manifested differently in each krewe. Due to the focus on the queen of the ball, it was more central for the Krewe of Apollo, whereas, for the Order of Osiris, drag fit into a tradition of grandiose costumes. The visibility of drag during the events meant that performers had to account for their use of drag to family and friends, particularly to parents who attended.

When I first met members of both LGBTQ krewes, they bragged that their ball was the most popular one in town, and that their tickets sell out first. Both krewes had reputations for throwing a well-decorated ball with an extravagant tableau attended by social and political elites such as the mayor and school superintendent. In Mobile, municipal newspapers described Osiris as "Mobile's most fabulous mystic society."[29] Accounts of the ball emphasized the table decor, the drag and costume tableau, and the fun atmosphere, favorably compared to other Carnival balls. The Osiris ball was described as "definitely the one tableau you never want to miss";[30] "the only call out in town you actually want to watch, as the decorations are fabulous"; and "carried out to perfection."[31] Reviews of the Krewe of Apollo emphasized their ball's grandeur, along with the fundraising for their HIV/crisis fund. One particularly ebullient review called an invitation to the Apollo ball "one of the most coveted of Carnival season.... No one can argue that Apollo's New Orleans-style tableau isn't one of the most elaborate in town; people are talking about the costumes for weeks afterward."[32] One Apollo member told me, "We've had people trying to get into our ball because it's *so much more* than the regular balls."

In Mobile, where throwing an extravagant ball is a valued part of Mardi Gras, these compliments are meaningful. During their interview, a lesbian couple from Osiris explained to me the complexities of Mobile and its obsession with partying; to do Mardi Gras *well* means to get respect. For both krewes, this reputation was built on the aesthetics of the ball, of which drag was an important component.

## Apollo: All about the Queen

Drag was central to the tableau, in which krewe members paraded down a runway dressed in extravagant costumes and elaborate backpieces that sometimes extended four or five feet above their heads. During the dress rehearsal for one ball, I spoke with the boyfriend of Stan, a slender, twenty-something white man who was costuming for the first time. The boyfriend explained that Stan had to do drag because the ball captain was concerned that there was "not enough drag" in the show. This routine performance was reported regularly in local newspapers, where krewe members' drag names were included in the ball. For example, in a review of an Apollo ball with a disco theme, the local newspaper described the scene: "Ball Captain Lester Mut made his entrance as Jennifer Marlowe, the Disco Queen, a Caucasian cross between Diana Ross and Donna Summers . . . Joe Boniol, Ball Lieutenant Jim Omohundro and Rick Hamilton emerged from a pink bus in costumes reproduced from the musical *Priscilla, Queen of the Desert* and boogied to such disco hits as 'I Love The Nightlife,' 'I Will Survive,' and 'Shake Your Groove Thing.'"[33] Pervaded by an appreciation of gay—specifically, drag—culture, the article affirmed drag's positive contributions to the Krewe of Apollo ball.

Krewe members emphasized the drag performed by the queen, an Apollo member who reigns over the krewe for the year. In this men's krewe, "royalty" was a king/queen pairing, with the queen always a man in drag. The new royalty was dramatically revealed at the end of the masque ball as the grand finale. Many krewe members said that the ball is "all about the queen," because the queen's grand finale and distinguished gay masque balls from straight balls, which have a cisgender woman as queen. According to one man in his thirties, it was "similar to a wedding [where it's all about the bride]. There's probably the aspect of seeing a man look like a woman. And you probably can't tell it's a man." The queen's drag differentiated the krewe from other festival events in the city. Like a wedding, participants' attention is focused on the production and performance of femininity—in this case, male femininity. The performance draws from the heteronormativity of rituals like weddings while simultaneously challenging them. For example, when ball attendees "can't tell [the queen] is a man" yet everyone knows it, it queers the heteronormativity of the king/queen pairing at the ball. The production of this male femininity becomes the marked difference between the gay men's ball and other balls in Baton Rouge.

Male femininity as an elaborate production was a central part of the Apollo ball. Although there was an abundant amount of drag in the tableau, the queen's drag was often the most elegant and closest embodiment of female impersonation. According to one Apollo member, "The queen's costumes are always better, there's always more rhinestones, there's always more attendants, better-looking tables, and everything else, and always lots more help than the king has. The king just has to put on a pair of pants, the queen has to do her hair, has to do her face, she has put on her pantyhose and everything else." In this description, the production of the queen reproduced tropes about femininity requiring elaborate additions to the body, including makeup and pantyhose, in order to be perceived as authentic. The process of using makeup, padding, and clothing to produce male femininity for drag queens is already an involved process, but the work to create a queen extended this production even further.³⁴ And the emphasis on the queen privileged the most dramatic productions of male femininity.

The queen's value centered on her beauty more than her ability, talent, or creativity. This stands in direct contrast to findings on professional drag queens, whose talent and creativity are equally important as their beauty, if not more so.³⁵ An older krewe member noted that queens are often selected not based on their drag experience but their physical appearance. Charles, a former queen, light up when describing how much he enjoys being "pretty" in the role: "You're not really putting on a show, you're just looking pretty and elegant, and looking royal. You're not walking, you're not dancing, you're not moving, you're just being pretty." Another queen noted that the performance is much less like drag and more like being "regal," because "you have to look your best." Being queen of the ball was different from a typical drag queen performance, which required lip-synching, singing, or dancing; the emphasis on the queen's beauty contributes to the excessive valuation of appearance for femininity more generally.

## Osiris: Never Too Big, Never Too Much

The ethos of Osiris focused on grandeur and fabulousness, regardless of the type of costume or decoration in the tableau. One of the founding members of Osiris had a motto—"Nver too big, never too much"—and the krewe gave an annual award to the member who lived up to it. In newspaper accounts, some of this fabulousness was attributed to gay aesthetics; as one reviewer commented, "The gays do it up right."³⁶ The group was described as "Mobile's most fabulous mystic society, and the one most qualified to tell you which tie goes with which dress shirt."³⁷ Another article opined, "Well-manicured hands down, The Order of Osiris has the most entertaining ball of them all. And this year, the organization made up of gay and lesbian members, once again, did not disappoint."³⁸ These references to "well-manicured hands" and fashion advice build on cultural understandings of gay culture as "fabulous," attuned to aesthetics, consumerism, and fashion, reducing LGBTQ culture to its most visible and frequently consumed aspect: the culture of gay men—often assumed to be fashionable gay white men. Yet the participation of lesbians in the group was not completely obscured:

newspaper reviews mentioned the number of women in tuxedos at the event or noted references to lesbian culture in the tableau, such as *Xena: Warrior Princess*.

As the Order of Osiris is a mixed-gender group, both men and women members performed drag and cross-dressed. However, Osiris was not invested in drag being a regular part of their tableau. One older gay man described the difference between Osiris and Apollo as "We costume, they're a glorified drag show." There were two royalty figures every year at the ball, and the royalty could be a king or a queen; some years saw two queens or two kings, and butch lesbian members have promenaded as the latter and gay men have debuted as the former. The three emblems of the krewe, or minor royalty figures, were also gendered feminine or masculine. The figure of Isis, for example, was always feminine, and, the first year I attended, Joshua did drag in the role. During the tableau portion of the ball, krewe members donned such elaborate costumes as a robot, a gingerbread boy, and an alien. For members of the group who enjoyed cross-dressing, costuming provided unlimited opportunities for gender bending. Two male members consistently costumed in drag, while others did so sporadically. At one ball, two men with hairy legs and large stomachs were costumed as Tinkerbell fairies, in skimpy neon-colored tutus and sports bras, dancing and throwing beads at attendees. An older gay man who typically did more masculine costuming performed as Dr. Frank N. Furter from *The Rocky Horror Picture Show*. At the Osiris ball, drag was just one possible option for grandiose and creative costuming.

## Drag and the Ball Audience

The social relations of Mardi Gras are rich. Most ball attendees are friends, acquaintances, or coworkers of krewe members; as a consequence, krewe members who perform drag for these events do so in front of their parents and other family members. Two-thirds of the krewe members I spoke with have had parents attend the ball, and almost everyone had other relatives who came. For those whose parents do not attend the ball, it was typically because they had passed away or were sick or disinclined to travel outside of their rural communities.

Two krewe members intentionally did not invite their parents. One gay man told me he wanted to enjoy the ball and not "babysit" his family.

The attendance of parents was deeply meaningful for krewe members; it signified their support and acceptance of their gay and lesbian adult children. When reflecting on the experience of having their parents attend, krewe members expressed strong feelings of anxiety, joy, and gratitude, often with teary eyes. They also described their parents' transformation from skeptics to avid supporters; once family members attended a ball, they enjoyed it and often developed deep investments in their children's involvement in the krewe.

Unlike drag shows, family participation in Carnival balls is ritualized in Mardi Gras throughout the Gulf South, particularly the attendance of family when one of their own is crowned royalty—a ceremony that entails processions and "callouts" for family members to come onstage with their royal relatives. When Ernest was crowned the Queen of Apollo, his rural Louisiana family, who were familiar with the expectations surrounding the event, attended the ball, wearing their own crowns and pins from their own krewes. In his preentrance video, over one thousand attendees cheered when Ernest described how meaningful it was to him that his father was there.

Family involvement in Mardi Gras krewes, which was often reconciliatory, produced a subtle level of recognition of the accomplishments of LGBTQ people. Some scholarship suggests that carnivalesque displays like talk shows and drag shows can positively change audience members' perceptions of LGBTQ individuals.[39] The attendance of family members, especially parents, became symbolic of progress. My informal interview with Aubrey, a slender young Black man and the youngest member of Apollo, was one of the most memorable in our discussions about parents and drag. Aubrey's mother, who came to the ball for the first time, had seen him in drag before, was invested in him "looking good," and helped him dress from time to time. And yet he came up to her at the end of the ball, tears streaming down his face, to tell her how delighted he was that she was there.

Many older krewe members affirmed that the increasing attendance of parents—particularly fathers of gay sons—signaled progress in gay rights and acceptance in the South. Not surprisingly, gay men expected their fathers to have the most issues, coming to a ball where men kiss each other and wear drag. Leonard, an older gay man from Baton Rouge, remembered a meaningful moment ten years earlier, when a queen's father decided to come at the last minute. Leonard recalled the intense anxiety everyone had about "the daddy" being there the year his son was queen. Both parents attended the post-ball brunch, where the father stood up and announced, in an emotional speech to the krewe, that he was proud of the "brotherhood" and love among the gay men there—using the same trope of brotherhood, unity, and chosen family that the Apollo men use for themselves, while simultaneously supporting the femininity of his son. Leonard recalled that "the daddy cried, and we all cried." Weeping, itself often a marker of femininity, became an emotionally cathartic bonding experience between the krewe members and "the daddy." In this account, the support of "the daddy," one krewe member's parent, became socially significant for the entire group, signaling not only the parent's acceptance of the group but also the feminine performance of the queen.

## I Don't Say I'm a Drag Queen, I Do Drag for the Ball

These acts of recognition were not without complications. When krewe members accounted for drag performances at Carnival balls to their parents and other family members, they often reinforced symbolic boundaries between amateur or charity drag and professional drag or transgender identification. Family members were most supportive of drag as something that gay men occasionally *do* rather than as a reflection of feminine identification or desire, suggesting that male femininity is most acceptable as a transitory performance.

Both krewes reinforced these boundaries when resisting depictions of the events as a drag show. Several Apollo men specified to me that the tableau was not a drag show, and that their group was different in this respect from the Krewe of Divas: whereas the Krewe of Divas was just a drag queen troupe, Apollo followed a long tradition of gay Carnival. Through the construction and maintenance of these symbolic borderlines, male femininity as a permanent or stable state was judged as inferior or less desirable.

This boundary between amateur and professional drag/transgender identity was reinforced when krewe members educated parents about drag. They described concerns about their parents' exposure to drag at the balls, as most of them had not been in queer spaces before. Although other aspects of the event could also have been viewed disreputable (e.g., same-sex touching, scantily clad individuals), members were mostly concerned about their parents' reaction to drag in particular. Charles, a slender white middle-aged Apollo krewe member with an affinity for storytelling, did not invite his parents because he did drag at the ball as the queen. Charles's father was an evangelical minister who reacted contentiously to his coming out. Throughout the interview, Charles and his partner focused on the ways that he reconciled the relationship, stressing that his father frequently comes over to the house now, goes on vacation with the couple, and prefers to spend holidays with them. While his parents met krewe members, Charles never invited his parents to the ball. His drag operated as an open secret; his parents were at his house while he applied rhinestones on costumes, and his closets included dresses and wigs. However, he maintained, "I've been very selective about what I've shared with them about the krewe. I don't wanna go overboard with them. We're in a good place now, and I don't wanna do too much." When he talked about his current relationship with his parents, Charles was overwhelmingly positive, emphasizing that he never imagined it could be so good. He did not want to emotionally overwhelm them and disrupt their comfort with his sexuality by adding concerns about male femininity as well.

Other krewe members accounted for their drag by emphasizing the reason or motivation for their performances to maintain the boundary between amateur drag and professional drag or transgender identity. Ernest remembered that he "did a lot of prep work [with a family member] beforehand to say, you know, it's just like Halloween. It's a costume, it's dress-up, it's makeup. No matter if you're becoming a vampire or a ghost or a woman or a man, I don't wanna be this person, I'm just performing as this character." Other men explained to their family members that it was a costume, or "for charity." Many men in the krewes only performed drag at krewe events like the ball. All but two members I formally interviewed suggested that they only do drag within the context of the krewe—or, according to one member "for Apollo." One former queen commented that "I don't say I'm a drag queen, I do drag for the ball," but also noted that he won a number of local contests doing drag. One masculine younger gay man in line to be king said, "I do it for charity, and I make a comedy out of it and I do the best I can just to raise money." However, some krewe members had deep investments in their drag performances; one older member waxed eloquently about his dream performances and looked forward to doing them at the ball every year. By emphasizing that they do drag "for Apollo" and "for charity," krewe members constructed their drag performance as a flirtation with male femininity, unmotivated by their own gender identity. Drag became something they *did* for reasons like charity and group solidarity rather than expressed something they *are*. This emphasis on their motivations made drag a more palatable form of male femininity for parents (and perhaps also themselves). While parents could embrace transitory gender transgressiveness when it was for a good cause or to honor their sons' commitment to the organization, a stronger commitment to gender nonconformity was deeply challenging for them. Stressing motivations and differentiating between amateur and professional drag allowed gay men to secure respect for their performance without compromising that respect due to the disreputability of "wanting to be a woman."

## Rethinking Drag and Respect

Drag can be a source of respect for gay men in the Deep South. Lesbian and gay participants experience Mardi Gras balls as an accomplishment that establishes their contributions as valued members of the community. Within the context of a masque ball with a reputation for being the most spectacular Carnival event in town, drag becomes a route to cultural citizenship, demonstrating the ways in which the LGBTQ community can contribute to a civic festival. This research raises important questions about what it means to be a member of the community and how cultural differences can unexpectedly be embraced during urban festivals. It also challenges dominant understandings of male femininity, of which drag is a part, as an inherently disreputable or disconnecting experience for gay men. In this study, drag connects gay men in the Gulf South with their families as well as the broader community.

This recognition and respect is not without its complications or limitations, as gay participants navigate pressure to distance their drag from transgender identities and professional drag. In their accounts to parents and family members, gay men emphasize the ways that their performances fit within the amateur drag of many festivals. This boundary work dampens the potential of drag to protest gender essentialism.[40]

Overall, my findings highlight the ways that amateur drag as a form of male femininity can be a source of validation for participants in the South, but this male femininity is perceived as most reputable when it is a fleeting performance rather than an enduring gender identity. This transient male femininity fits into an extensive history of young, presumably heterosexual men and civic officials cross-dressing as part of public rituals like "powder puff football" and fraternity hazing.[41] Male femininity that is enacted temporarily with a clear, defined purpose may erase potential stigma or ambivalence about the practice. The impact and meaning of drag as a form of male femininity thus depends on the context in which it is performed.

NOTES

1 C. J. Pascoe, *Dude, You're a Fag: Masculinity and Sexuality in High School* (Berkeley: University of California Press, 2011).
2 Dana Berkowitz and Linda Liska Belgrave, "'She Works Hard for the Money': Drag Queens and the Management of Their Contradictory Status of Celebrity and Marginality," *Journal of Contemporary Ethnography* 39, no. 2 (2010): 159–86; Niall Brennan and David Gudelunas, *RuPaul's Drag Race and the Shifting Visibility of Drag Culture* (London: Palgrave Macmillan, 2017); Eve Ng, "A 'Post-Gay' Era? Media Gaystreaming, Homonormativity, and the Politics of LGBT Integration," *Communication, Culture & Critique* 6, no. 2 (2013): 258–83; Leila J. Rupp and Verta A. Taylor, *Drag Queens at the 801 Cabaret* (Chicago: University of Chicago Press, 2003).
3 Samuel Kinser, *Carnival, American Style: Mardi Gras at New Orleans and Mobile* (Chicago: University of Chicago Press, 1990).
4 Brian J. Costello, *Carnival in Louisiana: Celebrating Mardi Gras from the French Quarter to the Red River* (Baton Rouge: Louisiana State University Press, 2017); L. Craig Roberts, *Mardi Gras in Mobile*. Charleston, NC: History Press, 2015).
5 Roberts, *Mardi Gras in Mobile*.
6 Costello, *Carnival in Louisiana*.
7 Rupp and Taylor, *Drag Queens*, 31.
8 Ashley A. Baker and Kimberly Kelly, "Live Like a King, Y'all: Gender Negotiation and the Performance of Masculinity among Southern Drag Kings," *Sexualities* 19,

nos. 1–2 (2016): 46–63; Eve Shapiro, "Drag Kinging and the Transformation of Gender Identities," *Gender & Society* 21, no. 2 (2007): 250–71.
9   Rupp and Taylor, *Drag Queens*.
10  Tristan S. Bridges, "Men Just Weren't Made to Do This: Performances of Drag at 'Walk a Mile in Her Shoes' Marches," *Gender & Society* 24, no. 1 (2010): 5–30; Peter Hennen, *Faeries, Bears, and Leathermen: Men in Community Queering the Masculine* (Chicago: University of Chicago Press, 2008); Esther Newton, *Mother Camp: Female Impersonators in America* (Chicago: University of Chicago Press, 1979); Shapiro. "Drag Kinging."
11  Esther Newton, "'Dick (less) Tracy' and the Homecoming Queen: Lesbian Power and Representation in Gay Male Cherry Grove," in *Inventing Lesbian Cultures in America*, ed. Ellen Lewin (Boston: Beacon, 1996), 161–93.
12  Brock Thompson, *The Un-Natural State: Arkansas and the Queer South* (Fayetteville: University of Arkansas Press, 2010); John Howard, *Men Like That: A Southern Queer History* (Chicago: University of Chicago Press, 1999), 51–52; Douglas E. Foley, *Learning Capitalist Culture: Deep in the Heart of Tejas* (Philadelphia: University of Pennsylvania Press, 1990).
13  Baker and Kelly, "Live Like a King, Y'all."
14  Baker A. Rogers, "Drag as a Resource: Trans* and Nonbinary Individuals in the Southeastern United States," *Gender & Society* 32, no. 6 (2018): 889–910.
15  Howard Philips Smith, *Unveiling the Muse: The Lost History of Gay Carnival in New Orleans* (Jackson: University Press of Mississippi, 2017); Amy L. Stone, "Crowning King Anchovy: Cold War Gay Visibility in San Antonio's Urban Festival," *Journal of the History of Sexuality* 25, no. 2 (2016): 297–322; Amy L. Stone, *Cornyation: San Antonio's Outrageous Fiesta Tradition* (San Antonio: Trinity University Press, 2017).
16  Kinser, *Carnival, American Style*.
17  Smith, *Unveiling the Muse*.
18  James N. Green, *Beyond Carnival: Male Homosexuality in Twentieth-Century Brazil* (Chicago: University of Chicago Press, 2001).
19  Hennen, *Faeries, Bears, and Leathermen*; on nonprofessional drag, see Esther Newton, *Cherry Grove, Fire Island: Sixty Years in America's First Gay and Lesbian Town* (Durham, NC: Duke University Press, 2014).
20  Bridges. "Men Just Weren't Made," 18.
21  Newton, *Mother Camp*; Esther Newton, *Margaret Mead Made Me Gay: Personal Essays, Public Ideas* (Durham, NC: Duke University Press, 2000).
22  Ng, "'Post-Gay' Era?"
23  Yuvraj Joshi, "Respectable Queerness," *Columbia Human Rights Law Review* 43, no. 2 (2012): 415–67; Shane Phelan, *Sexual Strangers: Gays, Lesbians and Dilemmas of Citizenship* (Philadelphia: Temple University Press, 2001).
24  Kenji Yoshino, *Covering: The Hidden Assault on Our Civil Rights* (New York: Random House, 2007).

25 Candace West and Don H. Zimmerman, "Doing Gender." *Gender & Society* 1, no. 2 (1987): 125–51.
26 Renato Rosaldo, "Cultural Citizenship and Educational Democracy," *Cultural Anthropology* 9, no. 3 (1994): 402–11.
27 Phelan, *Sexual Strangers*, 16.
28 Michèle Lamont, "Addressing the Recognition Gap: Destigmatization and the Reduction of Inequality," in the presidential address at the 112th Annual Meeting of the American Sociological Association, Montréal, Québec, August 13, 2017.
29 Masked Observer, "Masked One Gets Fabulous," *Press-Register* (Mobile, AL), February 14, 2011, http://infoweb.newsbank.com/.
30 N. Helton, "Azalea Gay Old Time at the Order of Osiris Ball," *Press-Register*, January 19, 2010, http://infoweb.newsbank.com.
31 "Well, the Good Times Have Already Started Rolling in the Port City, and I've Been Catching," *Lagniappe* (Mobile, AL), June 1, 2009, http://infoweb.newsbank.com.
32 Pam Bordelon, "Apollo Turns 30," *Advocate* (Baton Rouge, LA), January 20, 2011, http://infoweb.newsbank.com.
33 "Local Krewe of Apollo Spins 'The Disco Ball,'" *Advocate*, January 15, 2012, http://infoweb.newsbank.com.
34 Rupp and Taylor, *Drag Queens*.
35 Rupp and Taylor.
36 "Well, the Insanity Has Begun," *Lagniappe*, June 1, 2009, http://infoweb.newsbank.com.
37 Masked Observer, "Masked One."
38 Boozie Beer Nues, "Osiris and the Land of Oz, 'Prostidude' and Pitt Stains," *Lagniappe*, January 26, 2010, http://infoweb.newsbank.com.
39 Joshua Gamson, *Freaks Talk Back: Tabloid Talk Shows and Sexual Nonconformity* (Chicago: University of Chicago Press, 1998); Rupp and Taylor, *Drag Queens*.
40 Bridges. "Men Just Weren't Made."
41 Thompson, *Un-Natural State*; Howard, *Men Like That*; Foley, *Learning Capitalist Culture*.

## 15

# The Fierce World of Gay Asian Drag

C. WINTER HAN

By now, it should be apparent to anyone studying "gay men" that a significant amount of academic ink has already been spilled on examining masculinity among members of this group, however that membership is defined. Thus far, academic studies have explored everything from gay websites,[1] gay athletes,[2] among rural gay men,[3] masculinity and HIV,[4] masculinity as it relates to sexual behaviors and desires[5], masculine portrayals of gay men on television,[6] and even masculinity in ex-gay movements.[7] In fact, so much ink has been spilled on writing about masculinity among gay men that it seems scholars who study gay men are even more infatuated with "masculinity" than gay men themselves.

The tendency of many queer theorists to center masculinity when examining the experiences of gay men is not surprising, given that masculinity has come to represent a central cultural value among gay men. As famed gay writer Edmund White noted several decades ago:

> This masculinization of gay life is now nearly universal. Flamboyance has been traded in for a sober, restrained manner. Voices are lowered, jewelry is shed, cologne is banished and, in the décor of houses, velvet and chandeliers have been exchanged for functional carpets and industrial lights. The campy queen who screams in falsetto, dishes (playfully insults) her friends, swishes by in drag is an anachronism; in her place is an updated Paul Bunyan. Personal advertisements for lovers or sex partners in gay publications call for men who are "macho," "butch," "masculine" or what have a "straight appearance." The advertisements insist that "no femmes need apply." So extreme is this masculinization that it has been termed "macho Fascism" by its critics.[8]

As can be expected, the rise in the cult of masculinity has been coupled with a growing increase in anti-feminine attitudes among many gay men.[9] Masculinity is not only normalized; it is also eroticized. For example, scholars have found that gay men prefer men with stereotypically masculine traits such as muscular bodies and wealth as potential sexual partners.[10]

However, the type of masculine—and gender-normative—homosexuality exalted by large segments of the gay community is often not available to nonwhite men precisely because gay masculinity depends on whiteness to mark gay men as "normal." Gay men of color, in contrast to gay white men, have largely been deemed gender nonnormative, whether they be "too" masculine or not masculine enough.

Gay Asian men, specifically, have been constructed as failing to meet the new masculine norm expected of, and valued by, the gay community. If gay white men are the normal men, marked by gender normative behaviors, than Asian men are the opposite to which they can be compared. Contemporary examples of gay Asian men being used to gender normalize gay white men in both gay media and mainstream media are legion from television shows, movies, advertisements, and even comic books.[11]

Not surprisingly, racist comments against gay Asian men are often submerged in gendered stereotypes. For example, on his blog, Bathhouse Diaries, a gay white man responding to an online posting by a gay Asian man about racism in the gay community wrote: "While white men have masculine underwear parties where guys take off their shirts and expose rippling stomach muscles, Asian gay men have 'Miss Asia' beauty pageants with Asian men dressing in drag. . . . With Asians, almost all of them do drag or walk like a faggot, are skinny, limp wrist. . . . If Asian gay men want to be accepted, try acting like a man."[12] The racialized gender narratives found in both gay and popular media about Asian men are not surprising, given the rather long history of racializing gender and sexuality. As Nayan Shah notes, "The racial caricatures that circulated in the nineteenth and twentieth century media of effeminate [Asian] men . . . reinforced the perception of the 'Oriental' race as gender atypical and sexually nonnormative, bereft of sexual agency."[13]

In order to examine the experiences of men who do not meet the standards of hegemonic masculinity, several scholars have attempted to apply the concept of "alternative" masculinity to Asian men.[14] While informative, an overarching application of the alternative masculinity framework may have the unintended consequence of reessentializing gender by arguing that any and all gendered practices performed by men that are nonhegemonic can be read as an alternative form of masculinity. While it may be certainly true that such practices are, indeed, alternative forms of masculinity, it is also possible that they may be a form of "male femininity" as well—that is, much in the way that masculinity is possible without men, femininity may be possible without women.[15]

In this essay, I argue that rather than fighting against the stereotypes of femininity by performing an alternative form of masculinity, gay Asian drag queens engage in a particular type of disidentification, embracing a unique gay male femininity in order to acquire situational power within the gay community and challenge dominant gay narratives about race, gender, and desirability. Rather than a direct appropriation of femininity, I use David Halperin's argument that "gay male femininity" is not necessarily an embrace of the femininity associated with women, but a unique form of femininity specific to gay men.[16] Thus, I examine the way that gay Asian drag queens construct a "gay femininity" independent of what it means to be a "real" woman. Rather than mimic or satire gender, the femininity performed by gay Asian drag queens should be understood outside of the notion of femininity performed by women. Through drag, gay Asian drag queens construct a form of femininity that challenges the masculinity promoted by the larger gay community, thereby challenging heteronormative constructions of gayness itself.

## Gay Male Femininity

According to Todd VanDerWerff, the 1999 film *Flawless*, written and directed by Joel Schumacher and starring Philip Seymour Hoffman as Rusty, a transgender drag performer, was a "potentially disastrous film." Given the now rather lengthy list of straight actors "playing gay" with varying degrees of calamity, VanDerWerff's assessment wasn't far off the mark. Yet the film—despite receiving what could only be considered, at best, a lukewarm critical reception—managed to bring to light a number of important issues within the gay community often ignored by more critically acclaimed "gay movies."[17]

In one particularly memorable scene, Rusty and a small coterie of drag queens meet with members of the Log Cabin Republicans, a gay conservative group, in order to discuss the upcoming Pride Parade. As can be expected, members suggest that they put forth a "united front" by marching together on foot—a thinly veiled attempt at suggesting that nobody march in high heels or dance provocatively on a float. After asking them if they aren't ashamed that they raised a "shitload" of money for Bob Dole's campaign, only to have them send it back, Rusty comments, "You are right. We are different. But not in the way that you mean. We're different, because you are all ashamed of us, and we are not ashamed of you. All right? Because as long as you get down on those Banana Republican knees and suck dick, honey, you're all my sisters, and I love you, I do. God bless you, and fuck off."

While the scene certainly touches upon the growing divide between self-described "straight-acting gays" and the allegedly more flamboyant drag queens, its greater significance is that it demonstrates the failure of gay masculinity to win full acceptance from those who can never see them as fully a man. Just as important, the scene also exemplifies how gay men use gay male femininity as a source of resistance that challenges what it means to be a member of a marginalized group. Unlike the Log Cabin Republicans, the drag queens understand that assimilation—as well as an active attempt to counter stereotypes by appropriating the dominant group's norms, values, and behaviors—will never lead o full acceptance. Instead, they actively resist assimilation not only by defying conventional gender norms but also by embracing those who are not embraced by others. So, while getting down on Banana Republican knees may lead to rejection by those whom the Log Cabin Republicans so desperately want to be accepted by, it is that very "deviant" act that is embraced by Rusty and the other queens.

But what exactly is "gay femininity"? In the simplest sense, it is "not the qualities and characteristics of women but the non-standard formation of gender and sexuality that is distinctive to gay male culture."[18] It isn't simply the absence of masculinity, the presence of femininity, or a combination of the masculine and the feminine. Rather, it is a collection of distinct cultural practices that can be considered "its own phenomenon, or range of phenomena . . . [that is] . . . something quite distinct from the various kinds of femininity exhibited or performed by (some) women."[19] More important, it disaggregates both sex and sexual orientation from gender and gender performances, helping us to deessentialize gender. As David Halperin states: "As a proxy identity, 'femininity' is a clear expression of gay male gender dissidence, a rejection of standard, canonical, established forms of heterosexual masculinity. But that doesn't mean that gay 'femininity' necessarily signifies an actual identification with women. However much it may refer to women, which it obviously does, it is not always or essentially about women. It is its own form of gender atypicality, and it has to do specifically with gay men themselves."[20] To demonstrate his point, Halperin provides a number of different examples of gay male femininity that may "refer" to women, but are not necessarily or essentially "about" women. For example, while worshipping a pop culture (or operatic) diva may not be incredibly masculine, but it also isn't necessarily feminine, as the term applies to women. As the author notes, women do not "collect Cher or Madonna videos for fear of being thought unwomanly."[21] Similarly, while straight women may arguably enjoy Broadway musicals more than straight men do, they don't have the same "intensely solitary, wildly ecstatic, excessively sentimental childhood experience of the musical" as many gay men.[22] Among these many different examples of gay male femininity, perhaps the quintessential example can be found in the art of drag queening.

## The Precarious Position of Drag Queens

Contemporary theorizing about drag queens generally follow two different threads. On the one hand, some theorists argue that drag queens reinforce the gender dichotomy as well as dominant assumptions about gender, while other scholars argue that drag queens destabilize gender categories by demonstrating that gender is performative. Adding more complexity to the problem is the acknowledgment that even if drag queens disrupt essentialized notions of gender, they nonetheless help to maintain the gender order by privileging the emphasized femininity featured in drag performances.

One of the reasons it is difficult to theorize drag may be due to the fact that there are multiple forms of drag, as well as disagreement regarding what constitutes it, and who can perform it. For example, Esther Newton divides drag into two overarching categories: the glamour queens, who attempt to present a highly elaborate illusion of female performance, and the comedy queens, who often use crass and vulgar comedic routines while performing a style of drag associated with "camp."[23] Steven Schacht identifies four renditions of drag: highbrow female impersonators, female illusionists, professional glamour queens, and professional camp queens.[24] In contemporary parlance, there may be upward of a dozen or more of these different categories.[25] Yet there is also a common understanding that the two primary types of drag identified by Newton continue to provide the overarching typology for drag, at least in the larger cultural imagination.[26]

A secondary problem, of course, is that drag is a performance rather than performative. While all performative acts are performed, not all performances are performative. Unlike gender identity, which is constructed and reinforced by continuous performances that become performative, "drag identities" are not necessarily constructed through repeated performances. Unlike being a woman, "being" a drag queen is an activity that requires a conscious act of transformation from being a man to being a drag queen through the deliberate presentation of an alter ego. Men who perform drag know full well that they are "boys in dresses," performing an illusion of a women, and that they are men, almost delighting in declaring their manhood to the audience.[27] More important, the audience, too, is fully aware that the performers are men. Yet the subversive nature of drag rests on the assumption of gender performativity more than gender performances per se.

Thus, drag is not necessarily a transcendence of gender, or a parody of it. While drag kings often experience gender transcendence through drag, drag queens may not.[28] In fact, drag queens recognize their performances as just that—performances. Thus, unlike drag kings, drag queens may view themselves not as having transcended gender boundaries, but as having put on a convincing impression of a woman, while all along identifying as a man.[29] Thus, drag performances are conscious presentations of an illusion of which both drag queens and the are fully aware. Drag queens are judged positively as presenting an image of realness not based on their ability to fool others that they are biologically female, but on their ability to present realness based on a "collective gay male fantasy of a real woman, a larger-than-life and more graceful than a swan woman who demands attention. Ironically, the ultimate goal of a drag queen is not to blend in but to stand out."[30]

But arguing that drag is entirely an "act"—that is, merely a performance—would also be missing the point. For many drag performers, drag is not simply an "act," but a way of exploring their own conflicting gender identities. Consider what Brigitte Bidet, hostess of the drag show Tossed Salad at Atlanta's My Sister's Room, had to say on a June 2018 episode of the NPR talk show *1A*. When asked how she got her start in drag, Bidet answered: "I had just finished going to school for dance so I was, you know, a nice little starving artist and I would go out to the clubs and watch the drag shows but when I was like on the dance floor dancing I felt super feminine like with the way I wanted to move and I was like, how can I make that not feel so uncomfortable for me and then I watched all these queens and I, you know, arrogantly thought I would do a better job than them, but that motivated me to get into it."[31] Clearly, for Bidet, drag is not only a performance, but a way of exploring an addressing a "feminine attribute" that she found uncomfortable as a man.

Drag can also transcend the boundaries of erotic desires. As Verta Taylor and Leila J. Rupp have observed, it is not uncommon for heterosexual men and women to be sexually aroused and excited by drag queens.[32] While it is likely that the feminine presentation of drag queens arouse straight men, as the gender presentation of drag queens may lead straight men to perceive them as a "gender other," it is also quite possible that straight women are aroused by "gay male femininity," as the femininity performed by drag queens may be perceived by straight women as the "other."

Rather than think of drag as either transcending or reinforcing gender boundaries or hierarchies, it may be possible to perceive it as a practice by which an alternative form of femininity can be practiced regardless of the performer's sex or gender identity . While controversial, the increasing visibility of "faux queens"—biologically female, woman-identified drag queen performers—demonstrates that the femininity associated with drag queens is not necessarily linked to women, given that faux queens must also adopt an alter ego to perform this particular version of femininity.[33] In other words, the performance of femininity typically associated with drag queens does not come "naturally" to women. For example, in the 2004 comedy movie *Connie and Carla* staring Nia Vardalos and Toni Collette as two female performers who are forced to go underground, disguised as drag queens, after witnessing a murder, the two women create personas anchored in male femininity to convince the audience, as well as their new friends and acquaintances, that they are men in dresses instead of biological women. In one pivotal scene, Connie must take off her drag in order to convince Jeff (played by David Duchovny) that she is a "real" woman. It is in the ability of drag queens to present an alternative form of femininity not bound by sex or gender identity where drag is most subversive.

## Gay Asian Drag in Context

Gay Asian men, as well as other men of color, experience high levels of racism within the gay community.[34] Much of this discrimination is evidenced by the difficulty that many of them report in finding potential sexual partners, specifically because of their race. As one gay Asian man told me regarding his first experiences in the gay community:

> It was hard at first. Like the first time I went to a gay bar, and try to date and, you know. Guys didn't look at me like that and I had a really hard time. And it took me a while to realize that a lot of it had to do with me being Asian. I hadn't realized, I guess, how much my being Asian would hinder my, I guess, ability to date men. I just assumed that I would come out, meet a man, and be happy ever after. Um, or happily ever after, whatever. But it didn't happen.

The rejection of gay Asian men as potential sexual partners isn't only raced but also deeply gendered. A part of what makes gay Asian men seem less desirable to gay white men is their perceived femininity within a sexual context that values masculinity. One Asian drag queen had this to say: "Being Asian, you know, you're perceived as somewhat less masculine. Like, they immediately assume that you're a bottom, that you're feminine, that you're going to be submissive. And that's a turnoff for lots of guys. So you definitely have these stereotypes about Asian guys that work against you when you're trying to meet guys."

To manage the dual stigmas of race and gender within the gay community, gay Asian men engage in a number of different management strategies, some which include directly challenging the stereotypes that Asian men are more feminine or exclusively take the sexually submissive role.[35] These strategies have mixed results, however.[36] As David Halperin notes, "You can't overcome social denigration merely by inverting its terms, by attempting to substitute positive images for negative ones. . . . There is no safety in so-called positive representations, especially when you don't have the social power to make them stick."[37] Specifically, negative stereotypes exist because they serve a purpose for the dominant group. In terms of gay Asian men, their feminization serves the purpose of presenting gay white men as masculine by comparison, giving them a basis for their claim of "straight-acting." Because of the vested interest in gay white men maintaining gay Asian men as the feminine other, attempts to directly confront these stereotypes will always be met with resistance.

Whereas some gay Asian men attempt to confront stereotypes, for many others the rejection they feel in the gay community because of their race and perceived gender presentation, as well as the realization that directly challenging these stereotypes would be met with limited success, is a catalyst for doing drag. Because their rejection by other gay men is based on their perceived (lack of) attractiveness and sexual desirability, due to the perception of gay Asian men being more feminine than other men, drag provides them an opportunity to address both of these problems through an act of disidentification that embraces, rather than rejects, the feminine stereotype. As José Esteban Muñoz writes, "The process of disidentification scrambles and reconstructs the encoded messages of a cultural text in a fashion that both exposes the encoded message's universalizing and exclusionary machinations and recircuits its working to account for, include, and empower minority identities and identifications."[38] In discussing how she embraces the Asian male stereotype, one Asian drag queen stated, "Well, being Asian, how can I be anything else [but a glamour queen]? I mean, whatever I do, I'm going to be seen as exotic and femme. So yeah, I use that, I use that because it's what they expect." As this quote demonstrates, gay Asian men recognize that their stereotyping; more important, they are also aware that challenging stereotypes was not necessarily going to reverse them. Thus, rather than engage in a losing battle, many used these stereotypes to their advantage.

At the same time, doing drag also provide gay Asian drag queens with an opportunity to feel attractive and desirable within a context that defines them as neither. According to one gay Asian drag queen:

> As a boy, I never really felt attractive. I mean, I didn't think I was ugly or anything like that, but not really attractive, you know? I always felt sort of like, I didn't stand out or that people didn't notice me. And it didn't help that when I first came out, it seemed like nobody that I was interested in was interested in me. So that really hurts your self-esteem. Doing drag, I feel like I can be that beautiful, sexy, outgoing person. And it gives me the confidence to just go up to a guy that I wouldn't do out of drag.

While discussing racial stereotypes, one drag queen stated, "In general, you know, Asian women are just seen as sexier and more exotic than white women. So I use that, I use that a little bit." For many gay Asian drag queens, doing drag allows them to address their own insecurities about their appearance and perceived lack of desirability. Yet their newfound confidence also depends on larger societal narratives about both Asian men and women. First, Asian men are limited to the type of drag they can perform due to stereotypes about Asian men; however, they also know that they can be successful as glamour queens because of the stereotypes about Asian women.

Rather than attempt to increase their self-esteem by adopting what the larger gay community deems desirable, gay Asian drag queens take what is considered unattractive—being feminine—to its extreme. They not only embrace the stereotype; they enhance it. And, in so doing, they offer a direct challenge to the very definition of what counts as attractive and desirable.

In addition, many gay Asian drag queens actively challenge what it means to be both raced and gendered. Specifically, most gay Asian drag queens don't simply appropriate femininity and produce an exact replica of it. In fact, they engage in behaviors that would be considered incredibly unladylike, therefore unfeminine, if engaged by women, but that would also be considered "feminine" if engaged by straight cis-gender men. Among this, of course, is the gay art of shade and read, as well as the generous use of camp, despite not presenting as comedy queens, specifically through which they mock white standards of attractiveness.

Equally important are the ways that gay Asian drag queens embrace racial stereotypes as a form of disidentification. In their reading of Asian drag queens on RuPaul's TV show *Drag Race*, Enrique Zhang examines the ways that Asian drag queens perform Orientalist stereotypes, often playing into the non-Asian judge's conception of what it means to be Asian, in order to win competitions, thereby transforming the stigma of race into a positive.[39] While several Asian contestants on *Drag Race* have used Orientalist motifs in their performances, fan favorite Kim Chi, who was the runner-up on season 8, perhaps best exemplified the use of such practices, specifically for the purpose of challenging the dominant gay narrative of attractiveness and desirability. Unlike the other Asian drag contestants, Kim Chi did not rely on stereotypical Orientalist motifs but rather transformed and blurred both racial and cultural lines to create a look that was at once traditional and modern, using a Korean aesthetic sensibility that challenges what can be considered feminine. For example, in a number of competitions, Kim Chi donned avant-garde versions of traditional Korean hanbok that challenged the more typical drag aesthetics in favor of a traditional Korean silhouette.[40] Rather than relying on Orientalist tropes, she took cultural cues from both traditional Korean culture and contemporary Asian pop culture and then fused them into a drag performance.

In the season finale, Kim Chi subverted the dominant narrative of desirability in the gay community by specifically taking three characteristics deemed unattractive—being fat, femme, and Asian—and used them as a source of power in her final performance. Rather than hide or minimize these characteristics, she highlighted them, challenging the audience to see these traits as strengths rather than deficiencies. More important, she did so by specifically using a gay male feminine sensibility that moves femininity away from the aestheticof tightly fitted, curved silhouettes to the gay male feminine aesthetics of avant-garde design.

Interestingly, gay Asian men often perform drag in environments that primarily cater to gay white men. Within these spaces, the types of bodies, as well as racialized stylistic aesthetics, that are considered attractive are blatantly obvious through the display of various visual objects that mark cis-gender white men as being the most desirable.[41] Gay Asian drag queens challenge the centering of cis-gender white men in two specific ways. First, as mentioned above, cis-gender white men are often used as the punch line of jokes that not only deemphasize their desirability but highlights their femininity. In addition, many gay Asian drag queens specifically utilize cis-gender male backup dancers in their acts. While this is true of many drag queens, the use of these backup dancers by gay Asian drag queens pivots the center of attention from cis-gender male bodies to a feminine presenting body, positioning that feminine body as the center of desire.

The use of femininity provides gay Asian drag queens not only with a way of addressing their own sense of attractiveness and desirability—allowing them to personally move from being what one gay Asian drag queen referred to as an "ugly duckling" to a "beautiful swan"—but also with an opportunity to amass situational power within the gay community. For example, many gay Asian drag queens specifically credit getting access to leadership positions within gay organizations or being provided a platform to address important issues to the notoriety they gained through winning drag pageants and gaining a following within the gay community.[42] In this way, gay Asian male femininity works on multiple levels.

## Conclusion

In the past few decades, the mirage of the gender normative, "straight-acting" gay has come to represent the "gay community." While an argument could be made that this heteronormalizing of gay men and women have led to widespread acceptance of nonheterosexuals, it has not come without a considerable cost. One of the major problems with gay men's incessant insistence on "normality" is an increasing embrace of masculinity among gay men. Unfortunately, this focus may force some gay men to return to the closet, albeit a gendered one, for the sake of social acceptance, in the process reproducing forms of toxic masculinity common among straight male behaviors. Equally problematic is the fact that the promotion of the image of gay white men as gender normative depends on constructing other men of color as gender deviant. Because masculinity exists in opposition to femininity, gay white male masculinity depends on another group being defined as feminine and, thus, opposite to gay white masculinity. Not surprisingly, gay Asian men are routinely stereotyped as being more feminine than gay white men, not only by gay media but also by mainstream media.

While there may be multiple ways of challenging stereotypes, direct confrontation is often unsuccessful, specifically because members of the dominant group depends on those stereotypes for their own cultural, social, and structural privileges. Yet alternative forms of resistance exists. Specifically among gay Asian men, many engage in a form of disidentification through drag that embraces gay male femininity. While it would be easy to assume that gay Asian men simply reinforce gender hierarchies through an embrace of an emphasized femininity, this would be missing the point.

As Halperin reminds us, the "femininity" practiced by gay men is not necessarily the same as the femininities exhibited by women, nor does it signify identifying as a woman. Rather, when practiced by gay men, femininity is a "means by which gay men can assert particular, nonstandard, antisocial way of being, feeling, and behaving." Specifically for gay Asian drag queens, femininity is a way to challenge the dominant narratives about race, sexuality, masculinity, and desirability within the gay community. It is, in fact, "the beginning of a process of reversal and resignification: it is a way of claiming ownership of [their] situation with the specific purpose of turning it around, or at least trying to turn it to [their] account."[43]

An alternative reading of drag might suggest that, rather than gay male femininity, gay Asian drag queens may be practicing an alternative masculinity. While I certainly do not dismiss this possibility, relying on the concept of alternative masculinity to explain drag queen behavior may have the unintended consequence of seeing all gendered performances by men as being some "alternative" form of masculinity rather than a form of femininity. Thus, it may also lead to perceiving all forms of gender resistance as masculine rather than feminine.

Examining gay male femininity offers us a glimpse into femininity without women. Doing so allows us to disaggregate gender from sex. As Hale and Ojeda argue, examining gay male femininity is not only "helpful in freeing femininity from its heteronormative attachment to female bodies" but, more important, it also allows for the exploration of the ways that it can be used as a tool of resistance to misogyny.[44] Examining the performance of gay male femininity among gay Asian drag queens offers a new way of theorizing both femininity and masculinity. First, it is possible to theorize gender and gender performance outside of alternative frameworks for masculinity, even when performed by men. Second, it is possible to theorize femininity performed by men outside of the framework of deficiency or deviancy and instead chronicle the ways that gay male femininity, and other forms of femininity, may be empowering for men, both gay and straight, as well as women.

Because gay Asian drag queens reappropriate and attempt to recode what it means to be feminine in a space that not only values masculinity but also glorifies it and demonizes femininity, their experiences give us clues as to how femininity can be deployed in masculine spaces and even how the very masculine signals that mark those spaces can be used to dismantle masculine domination. In this way, gay Asian drag queens may help us better understand the conditions on which femininity can be used to subvert masculine domination.

## NOTES

1 Jay Clarkson, "'Everyday Joe versus 'Pissy, Bitchy, Queens': Gay Masculinity on StraightActing.com," *Journal of Men's Studies* 14, no. 2 (2006): 191–207.
2 Eric Anderson, *In the Gay: Gay Athletes and the Cult of Masculinity* (Albany: State University of New York Press, 2005).
3 David Bell, "Fam Boys and Wild Men: Rurality, Masculinity, and Homosexuality," *Rural Sociology* 65, no. 4 (2000): 547–61.
4 Perry N. Halkitis, "An Exploration of Perceptions of Masculinity among Gay Men Living with HIV," *Journal of Men's Studies* 9, no. 3 (2001): 413–32.
5 Nicholas Lanzieri and Tom Hildebrandt, "Using Hegemonic Masculinity to Explain Gay Male Attraction to Muscular and Athletic Men," *Journal of Homosexuality* 58, no. 2 (2011): 275–93.
6 Guillermo Avila-Saavedra, "Nothing Queer about Queer Television: Televized Construction of Gay Masculinities," *Media, Culture & Society* 31, no. 1 (2009): 5–21.
7 Christine M. Robinson and Sue E. Spivey, "The Politics of Masculinity and Ex-Gay Movement," *Gender and Society* 21, no. 5 (2007): 650–75.
8 Edmund White, "The Political Vocabulary of Homosexuality," in *The State of the Language*, ed. Leonard Michael and Christopher Ricks (Berkeley: University of California Press, 1980), 235–46.
9 Clarkson, "'Everyday Joe"; Martin Levine, *Gay Macho: The Life and Death of the Homosexual Clone* (New York: New York University Press, 1998); Kittiwut Jod Taywaditep, "Marginalization among the Marginalized: Gay Men's Anti-Effeminacy Attitudes," *Journal of Homosexuality* 42, no. 1 (2002): 1–28.
10 Josepha Schwartz and Josh Grimm, "Body Talk: Body Image Commentary on Queerty.com," *Journal of Homosexuality* 63, no. 8 (2016): 1052–67.

11 C. Winter Han, *Geisha of a Different Kind: Race and Sexuality in Gaysian America* (New York: New York University Press, 2015).
12 Bathhouse Diaries, "Racism or Preference (At the Baths)," Bathhouse Blues, http://www.bathhouseblues.com.
13 Nayan Shah, "Race-ing Sex," *Frontiers: A Journal of Women's Studies* 35 no. 1 (2014): 26–36.
14 Jachinson W. Chan, "Bruce Lee's Fictional Models of Masculinity," *Men and Masculinities* 2, no. 4 (2000): 371–87; Peter Chua and Diane C. Fujino, "Negotiating New Asian American Masculinities: Attitudes and Gender Expectations," *Journal of Men's Studies* 7, no. 3 (1999): 391–413; Yen L. Shek, "Asian American Masculinity: A Review of the Literature," *Journal of Men's Studies* 14, no. 3 (2006): 379–91.
15 Jack Halberstam, *Female Masculinity* (Durham, NC: Duke University Press, 1998).
16 David M. Halperin, *How to Be Gay* (Cambridge, MA: Harvard University Press, 2012).
17 Todd VanDerWerff, "In *Flawless*, Philip Seymour Hoffman Gave Warmth to a Transgender Stereotype," AV/Film, February 4, 2014, https://films.avclub.com.
18 Halperin, *How to Be Gay*, 320.
19 David Halperin, "What Is Gay Male Femininity?," In *American Guy: Masculinity in American Law and Literature*, ed. Saul Levmore and Martha C. Nussbaum (New York: Oxford University Press), 202–12.
20 Halperin, *How to Be Gay*, 318.
21 Halperin, 314.
22 Halperin, 317.
23 Esther Newton, *Mother Camp: Female Impersonators in America* (Chicago: University of Chicago Press, 1979).
24 Steven P. Schacht, "Four Renditions of Doing Female Drag: Feminine Appearing Conceptual Variations of a Masculine Theme," *Gendered Sexualities* 6 (2002): 157–80.
25 Paige Turner, "The 11 Most Common Drag Queen Styles," Queerty, June 3, 2014, https://www.queerty.com.
26 Tom Bartolomei, "Comedy Queens and Pageant Queens," Huffington Post, February 2, 2013, https://www.huffingtonpost.com.
27 Verta Taylor and Leila J. Rupp, "Chicks with Dicks, Men in Dresses: What It Means to Be a Drag Queen," *Journal of Homosexuality* 46 nos. 3–4 (2004): 113–33.
28 Leila J. Rupp, Verta Taylor and Even Ilana Shapiro, "Drag Queens and Drag Kings: The Difference Gender Makes," *Sexualities* 13, no. 3 (2010): 275–94.
29 Steven P. Schacht, "Gay Female Impersonators and the Masculine Construction of Other," in *Gay Masculinities*, ed. Peter Nardi (Newbury Park, CA: Sage, 2000), 247–68.
30 Han, *Geisha of a Different Kind*, 147.
31 B. Bidet, "Ask a Drag Queen," NPR, June 23, 2018, https//npr.org.
32 Verta Taylor and Leila J. Rupp, "Learning from Drag Queens," *Context* 5, no. 3 (2006): 12–17.

33 Meredith Heller, "Female-Femmeing: A Gender-Bent Performance Practice," *QED: A Journal in GLBTQ Worldmaking* 2, no. 3 (2015): 1–23; Raven Snook, "These Female Drag Queens Don't Give a Tuck if You Think They're Appropriating Gay Culture," Logo, January 17, 2018, http://www.newnownext.com.
34 Tony Ayres, "China Doll: The Experience of Being a Gay Chinese Australian," *Journal of Homosexuality* 35, nos. 3–4 (1999): 87–97; Denton Callander, Christy E. Newman, and Martin Holt, "Is Sexual Racism Really Racism: Distinguishing Attitudes toward Sexual Racism and Generic Racism among Gay and Bisexual Men," *Archives of Sexual Behavior* 44, no. 7 (2015): 1991–2000; Patrick A. Wilson and Hirokazu Yoshikawa, "Experiences of and Responses to Social Discrimination among Asian and Pacific Islander Gay Men: Their Relationship to HIV Risk," *AIDS Education and Prevention* 16, no. 1 (2004): 68–83.
35 Chong-suk Han, Kristopher Proctor, and Kyung-Hee Choi, "I Know a Lot of Gay Asian Men Who Are Actually Tops: Managing and Negotiating Gay Racial Stigma," *Sexuality & Culture* 18, no. 2 (2014): 219–34.
36 Han, *Geisha of a Different Kind*.
37 Halperin, *How to Be Gay*, 381.
38 José Esteban Muñoz, *Disidentifications: Queers of Color and the Performance of Politics* (Minneapolis: University of Minnesota Press, 1999).
39 Enrique Zhang, "Memoirs of a GAY!Sha: Race and Gender Performance on RuPaul's *Drag Race*," *Studies in Costume and Performance* 1, no. 1 (2016): 59–75.
40 Sydney M. Paluch, "The Dramaturgy of Drag," *CLAMANTIS: The MALS Journal* 1, no. 4 (2018): n.p.
41 Adam I. Green, "The Social Organization of Desire: The Sexual Fields Approach," *Sociological Theory* 26, no. 1 (2008): 25–50.
42 Han, *Geisha of a Different Kind*.
43 Halperin, *How to Be Gay*, 318.
44 Sadie E. Hale and Tomas Ojeda, "Acceptable Femininity? Gay Male Misogyny and the Policing of Queer Femininities," *European Journal of Women's Studies* 25, no. 3 (2018): 310–24.

16

# "The Reason You Can Suck a Dick Is Because Some Fem Once Got Beaten Up, Right?"

*A Case Study of Gender, Race, and Sexuality for Latinx Queer Men*

JESÚS GREGORIO SMITH, NIKOLA C. OSTMAN, AND SAMANTHA L. TORRES

While much has been written regarding queer men and gender, scholarly analysis has often been focused on White men and masculinity;[1] men who are seen as more masculine than White men, such as Black men;[2] or men seen as less masculine than White men, such as Asian men.[3] Less explored are the experiences of Latinx men, particularly queer Latinx men, and discussed even less are the ways members of this group understand femininity, or the embodiment of male femininities. According to scholar Mimi Schippers, male femininities are the "characteristics and practices that are culturally ascribed to women, do the cultural work of situating the feminine in a complementary, hierarchical relationship with the masculine, and are embodied by men."[4] By focusing on Latinx queer men and their relationship to preconceived notions of masculinity and femininity, gender performances, and their insights on possible structures beyond the gender binary, we argue that their gender roles and performances are strongly influenced by context in specific ways.

## Gender and Heteronormativity

According to cultural theorist Judith Butler, gender is "the repeated stylization of the body, a set of repeated acts within a highly rigid regulatory frame that congeal over time to produce the appearance of substance, of a natural sort of being."[5] In this sense, gender can be perceived as a scripted and rehearsed presentation and performance developed within a given society that needs "actors" to carry out the performances that convince us that traditional gender presentations are natural and organic as opposed to socially constructed. Central to this understanding of gender is a heterosexual desire that "binds the masculine and feminine in a binary, hierarchical relationship."[6] Heterosexuality, then, ingrains the societal assumption that men must have a natural attraction to women, thus "fusing masculinity and femininity together as complementary opposites."[7] As such, gender is understood as the comparing and contrasting of masculinity and femininity through the lens of heterosexuality. Within this framework, dominance and submission are also central to understanding the two, realized in heterosexual sex as the person doing the penetrating, dominating the person being penetrated. Heteronormativity, or the presumption that heterosexuality is the default in society and that other aspects of personal identity align with heterosexuality, is assumed in these relationships so that the dominance of men over women seems natural.[8]

Both the heteronormative model of gender roles and the hierarchical dominance/submission model of power within gender relations have been replicated with relationships between queer men. One study finds that, due to the strong hold traditional heteronormative gender roles have on same-sex relationships, verse men—or men who are willing to either top or bottom during anal intercourse—are more likely to submit to partners who appear more masculine, a pattern that reinforces the notion of masculinity asserting dominance within a hierarchy of those who penetrate over those who are penetrated.[9] Yet, while "bottoming" is often associated with femininity, those men who were penetrated did not feel any more feminine, indicating that the association between femininity and subordination is a result of external heterosexist societal beliefs that are not necessarily held by the receiving individual. Nonetheless, attributions of femininity continue to emasculate men who bottom during sexual intercourse.

## Hegemonic Masculinities and Femininities

Gender scholar Raewyn Connell sees gender as a process that catalogs people's interrelated synergies.[10] She argues that, for masculinity in the Western context, there are four major relationships: dominant/

subordinate; authorized/marginalized; complicit; and, the most influential, hegemonic. As described by Katie. L. Acosta and Veronica B. Salcedo, hegemonic masculinity is "a nearly unattainable ideal embodied by a few elite white men ... predicated upon the subordination of all other masculinities and femininity."[11] Hegemonic masculinities are a set of practices that normalize the dominance of elite White men while maintaining the subjugation of women and other men who exhibit gendered performances that do not align with them.

Expanding on Raewyn W. Connell's theory, Mimi Schippers introduces the concept of hegemonic femininities,[12] which "consists of the characteristics defined as womanly that establish and legitimate a hierarchical and complementary relationship to hegemonic masculinity," which then normalize the dominance of elite White men and the subjugation of other men and women.[13] Men who possess or exhibit feminine characteristics, such as desiring other men or being physically weak, "disrupt the assumed naturalized, complimentary desire between men and women" and disturb the physical strength and authority assumed in men's social position, resulting in their stigmatization.[14] Although Connell contends that there are varied expressions of masculinities among different populations,[15] Schippers argues differently.[16] She believes "femininity is always and already inferior and undesirable when compared to masculinity"—meaning men who exhibit behaviors like homosexual desire and weakness should be understood not as queer masculinities but as male femininities.[17] Context matters for male femininities, but the hegemonic nature of masculinities and femininities nonetheless influences gender roles in same-sex relationships.

### Masculinity, Femininity, and Gender Fluidity in Queer Men's Relationships

Research using hegemonic masculinity as a conceptual framework has found that heteronormative conventions are present even in interactions between gay men. For example, gender and sexuality scholar Shinsuki Eguchi, who has studied straight-acting rhetoric on online forums, finds that gay men differ on the fluidity of their acted straightness: some feel that they are naturally straight-acting, while others only behave that way in public, embracing more feminine mannerisms in private settings.[18]

There are two major implications of this finding: first, men who only sometimes act straight appear to do so out of necessity—it is only in acting straight or masculine that they can fit into the broader, societally accepted narrative of hegemonic masculinity. Second, straightness and masculinity are the idealized standards by which even (feminine) gay men hold themselves. Hierarchies negotiated in terms of gender performativity exist in queer men's communities, with straight-acting masculinity at the top and femininity at the bottom.

Scholar Andrew Reilly also uses hegemonic masculinity in their work on sexual positioning—that is, "topping or bottoming" for gay men.[19] By co-opting heteronormative attitudes, gay men are subject to the assumption that gendered power structures between women and men are transferable to the relationships of men loving men. With the resulting ideological camps of those who embrace feminine stereotypes and those who deny them, femininity has been further subjected to stigmatization and violence.[20] Men with straight passing privilege, in contrast, are less confident in their sexuality, more likely to conform to harmful hegemonic masculine ideals, and least likely to experience sexual liberation due to external perceptions associated with sexual positioning, outward appearance, and opportunities to exhibit perceived feminine qualities.[21]

## Sex Positioning, Gender Performance, and Latinx Queer Men

Top and bottom positioning and its relationship to gender hegemony are unique in the context of Latinx men. The hegemonic masculine dynamic many Latinx men subscribe to may very well be a result of the *activo/pasivo* model. The basis of the model, as laid out in the discussion of Latinx men's sexual behaviors by sociologist Salvador Vidal-Ortiz and colleagues, is that men who take the activo role are macho, have agency in sexual negotiations, and generally penetrate their partners, who take the pasivo role.[22] The difference between activo/pasivo and top/bottom is that men must be one or the other, with little room for versatility. To be activo or pasivo is a concrete part of one's identity; thus sex comes down to being less about negotiation and more about character judgment. While this system prevails throughout much of Mexico, it does not in other queer Latin communities, like those in the Dominican Republic, where the ideal sexual positioning is to be versatile. In essence, the values ascribed to sex positioning are context specific and, in this case, country specific.

Further, the constraints of masculine performances only subside when contextual factors allow it, such as comfort level, type of engagement (hookup vs. long-term relationship), and security with one's own identity as a gay man.[23] These factors typically result in more opportunities for fluid gender and sexuality. Alex Carballo-Dieguez and colleagues found that participants who were more comfortable with their own sexual identity had more sexual role fluidity.[24] By rejecting the notion of femininity as subordination, men who engaged in fluid sexual positioning—often referred to as "verse"—were likely to engage in multiple sexual positions without jeopardizing their self-perceptions as defined by the implications of sexual positioning. This may also be said of those who freely embraced gender performances rather than conforming to gender scripts.

Mimi Schippers asks, "What characteristics or practices of men are defined as feminine, contaminating, or disruptive? What are the male femininities?"[25] We seek to answer this question through a case study of six Latinx queer men. We first examine the characteristics and practices that the men define as masculine, and then explore those that they define as feminine. Altogether, we believe this will allow us to better understand gender dynamics as they pertain to these Latinx queer men.

## Data and Methods

The data for this project were derived from a larger project on race and sexuality called The Intersections of Race and Sexuality. This larger project included interviews with approximately thirty-four Black, Latinx, Asian, Indigenous, White, and mixed-race men who were at least eighteen years old and identified as queer men. This chapter serves as a case study of six participants who identified as Latinx or mixed with Latino, including an Afro-Latino Venezuelan American, a mixed Puerto Rican and White American, and several Chicano/Mexican American men. While most of the men identified as gay, two of them identified as bisexual, with one of them currently in a relationship with a woman. All men had some level of college education, though one of them, the mixed Puerto Rican man, did not complete college. Additionally, some men were highly educated, having been in or completed posteducational training in master's or PhD programs. The socioeconomic status of the men ranged from working-class, with an income around $24K, to upper-middle-class, with income ranging between the $60K to $90K. All participants were asked to provide pseudonyms for themselves to protect their identities.

To investigate perspectives from differing gender performances and sex roles, the research team derived questions from researcher Michelle Marie Johns and company's study on topping (insertive partner during anal intercourse) and bottoming (receptive partner during anal intercourse).[26] The team used specific questions such as "What does the term bottom mean to you? What about the term top?" and "What characteristics in your partner may lead you to take a top or bottom role?" to clarify and probe nuanced cognitions and expectations of sex roles and gendered behavior.

The interviews were transcribed by the research team verbatim. Using Schippers's theoretical framework on gender as a guide, we coded the transcripts looking for characteristics and practices by the men that are defined as masculine and feminine and the consequences of embodying those ideals.[27] The transcripts were closely read and annotated with sections labeled to explain the findings.[28] Following this initial process, the team regrouped to compare notes. To tease out nuances, a constant discussion took place alongside the analytical process. Thus, the team was able to come to conclusive agreements on what was being said in the transcripts and how they should be coded. We sought to carefully define *how* and *why* the participants described their perspectives and experiences in the way that they did.

The research team consisted of one Afro-Latino gay male, one mixed-race Filipino and White straight male, and one bisexual Latina. These factors could have impacted how the participants responded to the study, especially as relates to expressing sexual behavior, racial preferences, and gendered expectations. The team was aware of the social constructions of their identities and the impact of their identities on their relationships with the participants as they conducted, transcribed, and analyzed the interviews.

## Findings

Our analysis revealed that, for these men, gender is complex and must be considered through various contexts to fully understand its impact on their lives. Two major themes arose from these findings: (1) societal expectations around gender roles and performances for queer men are full of contradictions, making ideal gender performances and expectations unattainable. As a result, there is a need to (2) negotiate gendered presentations and expectations during sex.

Most striking about the responses was how the men made sense of femininity in their own lives. While femininity is seen as submissive in a sexual context, it is also a liberating force from the confines of masculinity, and engaging in sexual acts perceived to be "feminine" provides them with the opportunity for more accurate presentations of the self in a social context. In many cases, femininity also serves as a liberating force from the restrictive codes of masculinity. Latinx men's willingness to take on nonconforming gendered roles that were stereotyped as feminine during sexual encounters, such as bottoming during anal intercourse or giving oral sex, affirms past research that suggests that it is not so much that queer men take on "feminine" roles that is problematic but instead the heteronormative disposition that femininity is inferior to masculinity.[29]

### The Contradictions within Gendered Performances

For Latinx queer men, gender roles and performances were contradictory. This was due in part to issues of gender and race that influenced their understandings of the ideal man in US society, which was often at odds with their identity as queer Latinx men. Take, for example, forty-nine-year-old Mexican American Gilberto, who describes this ideal: "Most people will say tall, blond, blue eyes. All-American. Uh-huh. Captain America type . . . when people describe American boys you see this White, blonde, more or less, named Bob, but they would see this very handsome White person . . . you know, all-American." For Gilberto, the ideal man in US society is perceived as White, blond, and blue-eyed, with even a generic white name: "Bob." Interestingly, Gilberto's perception of what society finds desirable is inherently different from his own identity as Mexican American, which was perceived as contradictory to the White ideal and as working against expectations of desirability in some Latinx men with regard to their own race and masculinity.

While Latinx masculinity may differ in many ways from White hegemonic masculinity, structured expectations of gender were similar. Alex, a thirty-four-year-old bisexual Mexican American man married to a White woman, stated: "I think my race definitely structures . . . how long it's taken me to have this type of conversation . . . so I'm not, obviously, very open about my sexuality, even though I've . . . been with guys since I was seventeen, I've dated a couple guys . . . a couple women . . . but my racial identity says that I should be heteronormative, and therefore only be dating women." As a Mexican American man, Alex felt that his racial identity meant that he was expected to be heterosexual and thus unable to openly embrace his bisexuality, even though he had had previous relationships with men. To Alex, masculinity was not simply about embodying a stereotypical White man, as he described, but rather a *straight* Latino man who *only* desires women. Thus, masculinity was defined by an exclusive heterosexual desire for women.

Also, certain behaviors are perceived differently given different racial and cultural markers. In some Mexican American and Central American communities, straight men can engage in same-sex behavior and still be considered heterosexual if they are in the activo rather than pasivo role.[30] As a bisexual man who often identifies as the bottom during sex with men and who has had a long-term relationship with a man despite being married to a woman, Alex straddles a complicated position. He views people who bottom as "more submissive behaviorally, and [he]considers [himself] more of a bottom." This contrasts with tops, whom he considers to be "more physically aggressive, more dominating." By identifying as the submissive partner during sex, subservient to a more aggressive and dominant male partner, Alex makes it clear that he violates the expectations of straight Mexican men in this way, reaffirming the hegemonic masculine dynamic associated with the activo/pasivo model.[31]

Alex's perspective as a bisexual man helps to illustrate the contradictions of gender performance in the lives of some Latinx men. He describes the societal pressure to conform to a White hegemonic model of masculinity and the way it contrasts with a Latinx model of masculinity centered around family. Being pressured to conform to both societal and familial ideals, he explained:

> What society expects the ideal man to be is tall, White, strong, employed, dependable, a little rugged, those types of things . . . are the ideal man stereotype . . . Familial obligation and familial expectations play a significant role in that, like, as a man, what should you be doing or looking like to fill your role, or as close as you can get to that ideal man, and so if you're not fulfilling that for your family there might be a sense of pressure or insecurity there as a man . . . I think there is a lot more subconsciousness in there that is actually occurring. Consciously I think every man makes a choice to be that ideal man. Like, I will get up and go to work every day and support my family and all that. Subconsciously, I think there is a lot of anxiety and stress there that isn't talked about . . . Does it stress me out? Yeah, fuck, yeah, it stresses me out . . . because I don't necessarily fit in that box, even though I know how stupid that box is . . . I just know there is something stupid about that categorization, and that I still let it get to me.

Alex's story reveals two important things about hegemonic gender roles and performances. For one, the ideal man in US society is often perceived as White, rugged, and strong as well as employed and dependable. As a Latinx man, family plays a very important role in Alex's perceptions of masculinity because Latinos generally tend to engage in collectivist behavior due to cultural traditions and norms, including putting family obligations over one's own individual needs.[32]

Still, Alex makes clear that while, on the surface, men are expected to embody a specific "dependable" masculine presentation, underneath men can suffer from chronic anxiety over not achieving this ideal. As a bisexual man who takes on the more submissive role during sex, Alex contradicts the expectation of Latino men who only desire women. While Alex recognizes that the "categorization" around maleness and sexuality is "stupid" and not so simple, he remains adversely impacted by stress over his own categorization of what constitutes a man and how his masculinity can define his worth. Alex's narrative underscores how race, class, and performance influence gender expectations and how the contradictions inherent in hegemonic masculinity render it unattainable for the majority of men.

### Negotiations between Gender Performances and Expectations

Other participants highlighted the contradictions of femininity. Diego, a twenty-three-year-old Venezuelan Afro-Latino male, explains that feminine men have always had to fight for their humanity:

> I am on different Facebook groups and they're very open about telling off this whole stereotype of the masculine man. Like the masculine gay man never did anything for the gay community, it was always the trans or the very femme people who have broken through [barriers], which makes sense because, like, if they are the most oppressed, the most, like, publicly shamed, then, of course, they have a reason to fight, right? Like, if you are accepted or you are in the closet and only being masculine because of society, or whatever, or but then in secret you're very femme, then I think that there's that barrier. But then people that are openly persecuted break through.

In contrast to Alex and Gilberto's descriptions of masculinity as being strong, dependable, and heroic like Captain America, Diego says it is femininity that can offer resistance to a homophobic world. For example, Diego describes how gay masculine men "never did anything for the gay community" and credits revolutions in the gay community to trans and "very femme people." According to Diego, men who engage in overt masculine performances, remain in the closet, or perform "very femme" in secrecy cannot break barriers that deny gay men basic human rights and security. It is those who are most persecuted and "publicly shamed" for being femme who fight and "break through." It is femininity, in this case, that is the heroic gender performance. Carlos, a thirty-two-year-old queer Mexican, echoed Diego's sentiments:

> I am always bothered because the reason we are able to be who we are is primarily because of fem folks. Like, that is who protected us in front of the institutionalized and physical violence directed at queer folks. It has almost always been the [fem] folks, who are the first buffer to violence. So, I am always kind of like, "Go fuck yourself [to anti-femininity]. The reason you can suck a dick is because some fem once got beaten up, right?" That is kind of the history of queer liberation.

According to Carlos, queer liberation was possible because of "fem folks" who were marginalized for their queer identity and victimized for their failure to adhere to societal gender expectations. This resonates with Andrew Reilly's work on tops and bottoms, which points out that the censuring of femininity does a disservice to the strides of great change that feminine and gender nonconforming gay men have accomplished because of their femininity, not despite it, such as the Stonewall riots of 1969.[33]

## Contextual Contradictions

The contradictions in gender expectations and performances are compounded by the way that gender performance is negotiated within sexual contexts. For many queer men, masculinity and femininity were not static but, rather, fluid performances, especially when it came to sex. Take Chris, a twenty-six-year-old self-identified half Puerto Rican and White fem man, whose sexual behavior changes depending on who he has sex with: "I am adjustable, I guess you could say. So, it is like, if I see you are more, trying to, like, be the more dominant one, I will be a little bit more submissive. You know, depending on who you are. If you are more, like, feminine, I will be more, like, dominant. I do not know. I kind of feed off how they are in a way." Chris's statement demonstrates how, even if a man identifies as masculine or feminine in social contexts, gender roles and subsequent sexual positions are negotiable. Chris's "adjustable" nature allows him to play off the energy he gets from partners during sex as he adapts his behavior to fit the scenario. Chris's case demonstrates what Carballo-Dieguez and company saw as the comfort in one's sexuality that allows for more fluidity.[34] Similarly for Alex, time and comfort also allowed for sex roles and gendered expectations to become more negotiable as well:

> I am pretty introverted, and as a function of my introverted nature, I find myself more in the submissive role, which usually means I am more often than not a bottom. Having said that, as relationships evolve with me, I think that tends to get to a more even state, and so . . . as that comfort grows and you explore each other, I think those ratios balance out . . . I can tell you that the best sexual relationships that I have had

with men are the ones where we'd flip, and I feel like we are both getting something unique out of that experience, and experiencing the full thing, being both the top and the bottom . . . together, and I think that has been the most fulfilling type of sex that I've had.

Alex's reference to his "introverted nature," which positions him as a submissive bottom, speaks to what Ortiz and colleagues described as the concreteness of the activo/pasivo sex position to Mexican men's personalities.[35] In this sense, as a Mexican American man, Alex's bottom sex position goes hand in hand with his passive personality. Yet, for Alex, the evolution of the relationship and the time partners took to learn about each other's desires allowed for gendered expectations to become more negotiable during sex, in contrast to the rigidness of the activo/pasivo paradigm. Instead, this "comfort and type of relationship" angle in shaping the negotiations of sex positioning aligns with Andrew Reilly's work.[36]

## Femininity as Submissive

Men came to understand femininity in contrast to masculinity, reinforcing Schippers's point that masculinity and femininity are compared and contrasted through a heterosexual lens.[37] Some of the men described femininity as sexually submissiveness in contrast to the domineering qualities of masculinity. Alex explained how he came to see femininity in this way:

> If there is this unequal power dynamic and one person is clearly more aggressive, dominant, then the likelihood of them being the top is likely going to be really high. If they're pretty evenly tempered dynamically then . . . that becomes trickier, I think [long pause, then laughs] . . . Sorry, I don't know if I should be very graphic or whatnot, but . . . the first person to be oral, and so, if you go down on a guy, then the action of going down on a guy is a case of submissiveness. I think so, and so if you are the first person to go down on your partner, then you're saying, "I'm here to serve you in one way or another," and usually I think that leads to being a bottom.

As previously reported, Carballo-Dieguez and company's study found that verse men are more likely to submit to partners that are perceived as more masculine.[38] But what of men who perceive each other as having a similar disposition, or who are "even tempered"? Alex's response provides us a path to understanding. As previously noted, Schippers argued that, for male femininities, "femininity is always . . . inferior . . . when compared to masculinity."[39] Alex suggests that the act of going down on his male partner first reflects the subordination of individuals who "serve" masculine men in "one way or another," thus signifying male femininity in the sexual behavior of one man when both men share the same disposition.

The association of femininity with submissiveness was also supported by another participant, thirty-four-year-old queer Mexican American Oscar, who shared his thoughts on the behavioral risks feminine men take, such as being less likely to engage in safe-sex practices. On the topic of pressures to provide versus receive pleasure, Oscar stated: "I think the pressure to sort of provide a desirable experience, which usually translates into like a bareback experience, the pressure to provide that for tops I think is definitely a thing, yeah . . . I think it kind of goes in both directions, I think. I think for, for men who are, I think, who think of themselves as more masculine, there would be the idea that, like, there is a permission to be able to fuck without a condom." Oscar's explicitness reflects the sexual power dynamics previously highlighted by Alex. As in heterosexual spaces, gender roles influence sex roles, which then determine who has the permission to receive a pleasurable experience and who is pressured to deliver said experience. In both men's accounts, femininity during sex signals submission to dominant and masculine men. These accounts are in congruence with the contrasting and complementary nature of gender hegemony.

### Femininity as a Liberating Force from Masculinity

Although femininity was constructed as submissive, it was largely seen among the participants as a liberating force from the confines of societal scripts associated with masculinity. In many ways, embracing femininity offered freedom from a narrow and restricted idea of what it means to be a man. It also provided an avenue to more erotic capital, or the "the quality and quantity of attributes that an individual possesses which elicit an erotic response in another."[40] Diego helped illuminate this point in several unique ways, such as with the grooming of his hair: "First of all, I grew up with mom, my dad, and two brothers. My dad is very masculine and, like, very machismo and all that stuff, so things like doing your hair . . . like, when I was little, I even grew out my hair and . . . no one ever told me to put oil in it or do any sort of hair maintenance." Diego describes how his father was very masculine or "machismo," a racialized term used to describe Hispanic and Latino men. This "machismo" was so restricting that, when he was growing out his hair, no one taught him how to maintain it. The emphasis on his father's masculinity in relation to Diego's grooming habits makes sense if one considers how hair grooming in certain cultures is seen as a gendered activity. In this scenario, women groom themselves and take care of their hair whereas the machismo Venezuelan man does not. Thus, Diego's father never taught him how to maintain his hair, in turn limiting his capacity to properly care for all aspects of his body. This failure to establish basic grooming habits demonstrates how certain forms of masculinity are confining and limiting even outside intimate settings. Later in the interview, Diego explained that, when it comes to meeting new potential partners, his embodied masculinity was limiting, often making him wish he was more feminine presenting. When asked how others might perceive his gender performance, Diego responded:

> I feel like people in general either do not assume that I am queer . . . and I'm fine with that, I don't really care. I almost wish I was casually more feminine, like, not really because of the whole societal thing but, like, sometimes I kind of just feel like if I was more like gay presenting, I would be hit on more [by other men] than if people assumed I was straight, and that is kind of how people assume I am. I do not know, I feel like . . . I am missing out because I am not stereotypically gay presenting.
> So, you feel that you are almost being looked over by certain people?
> Yeah.

Mignon Moore's work on gendered representation in Black lesbian communities speaks to the way that desire is central to understanding gender displays, as the women dressed according to butch/fem gender roles that eroticized sexual interactions.[41] The case of Diego echoes Moore's findings. For Diego, as a bisexual Latinx man, his masculinity defaults him to a straight passing identity. This point is significant not only because Diego describes how masculinity can be limiting for his erotic capital but also how femininity provides a different form of erotic currency in the sexual market.[42] This femininity can be found in the "stereotypical gay presentation," which, according to Diego, would aid him in not being overlooked by others. In this sense, masculinity limits Diego's erotic capital while femininity would expand it, freeing him from the confinement of presumed heterosexual masculinity.

The compounding forces of masculine presentation and heteronormative assumptions are not exclusive to Diego. In fact, Alex described something very similar: "Like the idea that I've got . . . a very hetero life that I live, and that, based on appearances, I have to be that consistently and if I deviate from that, one way or another, then there's going to be some sort of judgment or awkward social engagement, or friendships might be lost or something . . . I think that is where the subconscious [anxiety] kicks in and you are like . . . , "OK, that is what my fears are.'" Like Diego, Alex describes masculinity as a sort of presentation or "appearance" that is perceived by others as "very hetero." His telling emphasis on the subconscious pressure he felt speaks to the impossibility of hegemonic masculinity as articulated by Acosta and Salcedo.[43] In this sense, masculinity is once again constrictive, limiting authentic self-presentations due to the powerful influence of "subconscious" fears. Where Alex describes the restrictions of masculinity, Diego shows how femininity can be liberating from pressures of constant performative masculinity and provide the opportunity to become a more authentic self.

### Femininity as a Means for Self-Actualization

Femininity powerfully impacted the lives of the participants by allowing avenues of opportunity for more meaningful self-actualization. Where some participants described feeling trapped by masculinity and forced to conform to the masculine script developed by heterosexist society, others felt that the opportunity for liberation presented by femininity meant that they could be more of their whole selves without censure. For example, Gilberto described how, while some people might see him as masculine, when he is around other gay men he allows himself to be more effeminate:

> [I'm] masculine but I can queen out every once in a while, so, yeah.
> *So, what situations do you queen out in, then?*
> I will when you get a bunch of friends and you're going to Pride or you're going to a club and you get a few drinks and you act a little crazy...
> *How would others perceive your gender performance?*
> Both! It's weird, it's like the straight people always think I'm straighter, and gay people think I am gayer, I guess 'cause maybe I feel more comfortable around gay people and maybe that's when I queen out a little bit more or something like that.

When asked about his gender performance, Gilberto states he is more masculine but caveats this by saying that occasionally he can "queen out"—meaning he can be more effeminate in his behavior. When pressed about the contexts in which he may perform in a more feminine manner, Gilberto clarifies that he does so when with "a bunch of friends," going to queer "Pride" events, or after having a couple of drinks at "the club." In this sense, while Gilberto suggests he is mostly masculine, under specific contexts he can deviate from strict masculine scripts and behave more effeminately. Furthermore, although Gilberto says both straight folks and gay folks might perceive him as masculine and feminine, he suspects that the reason why gay people might see him as more feminine might be related to the fact that he feels "more comfortable around gay people." This comfort allows him to relax the masculine presentation demanded by general social contexts and permit his effeminate side to be unapologetically free. Femininity, in Gilberto's case, is about the liberty to comfortably be oneself around friends or in queer spaces in contrast to being under heterosexual surveillance, where men are expected to perform in an overtly masculine way.

For Chris, who identified as more feminine presenting, changing in different contexts was more of a copout to him:

> [I'm] probably more, feminine.
>
> *Why do you say that?*
>
> Um. I do not know. I am real prissy. (Laughs) Real, um, I do not know. I just am. I am masculine-looking. Feminine-acting. How I am, my characteristics, the way I present myself.
>
> *Do you change your gender performance based on the people that you are with?*
>
> Oh, hell, no. (Laughs)
>
> *Why is that?*
>
> Because I am true to myself. And I really do not care what other people think about me.

Chris' experience mirrors Carballo-Dieguez and company's observations that men who rejected the notion of femininity as subordinate to masculinity were more comfortable with their sexual identity.[44] Chris embraces his feminine self, which he characterizes as masculine-looking but "feminine-acting" and "real prissy." Where he was once willing to adjust his gender performance during sex, outside of sexual scenarios Chris rejects changing his gender performance based on who he is with. As he states, he does not really "care what other people think about" his femininity, as he cares more about being true to himself.

## Moving beyond the Gender Binary

For the queer men we interviewed, the gender binary was not an accurate indication of true gender performances in their lives. This is because, depending on the context, they often would perform along a gender spectrum. Gilberto explains the problems of associating queer men with a strict binary:

> Well, yeah, you always think that the bottoms are queenier than the tops. And you know, if somebody is all queenie and then they say, "Oh yeah, I'm only a top," and then that is where people laugh . . . you know, so they assume just 'cause somebody is more femme or something like that that they would be a bottom and that if he is all butch and this and that that he will only be only a top, and that is not always the case.

The ways that Gilberto disrupts the assumption that the more feminine man is always the receptive partner during anal sex or the first to perform oral sex on his partner is similar to Alex's sentiment detailed earlier in this chapter. Gilberto's perspective pushes beyond the sexual/gender binary as he mentions how someone could be "all queenie" (i.e., femme performing) and still state that they are "only a top" when it comes to sex, a role often associated with masculine men. While Gilberto mentions that this sort of response from a femme man, assumed to be a bottom, might solicit laughter from others, he highlights that by only using society's White, hegemonic masculinity lens, one misses the variety and complexity of gender performances in the lives of Latinx queer men. This requires a point of view that moves beyond the binary and includes the fluidity of gendered performances.

Oscar also supported Gilberto's point that the expectations of the gender binary do not accurately reflect the realities of Latinx queer men. As previously mentioned, masculinity is not only ideologically reproduced but also embodied in corporeal ideals of "tall," "rugged" White men. Still, Oscar points out that this embodiment is not always so simple to interpret, explaining that "people read tall men as more masculine, but [he has] also seen the ways in which sometimes a taller, leaner, physique can be read as more feminine." Oscar makes a conscious effort to point out that while some might assume taller bodies are always read as masculine, the reality is that some "taller, leaner, physiques" may also be read as feminine in other contexts. Again, these assumptions built upon hegemonic masculinity norms do not always accurately capture the reality of Latinx queer men. Further complicating the gender binary is also the fact that there is a specific femininity enacted with and in gay or queer bodies. Carlos, a 30-year-old Latinx man, helps illustrate this point. He states:

> I mean, they definitely see me, I don't want to say in masculine terms, but, I mean, if there is a spectrum, they are definitely like, "That is a dude, that's a guy," and, I don't know, it's one of those things where I'm like, "Oh, yeah, I'm most really read as a gay man." Like, just, they are like, "Oh, that's a dude, but he has a higher-pitched voice, he carries his body in a certain way, that's a gay man," so.

> *(All right, but you do not know whether that is associated more with a masculinity or femininity?)*
>> I, I mean, I think it's, I don't know, like, for me it's like, it's its own thing, perhaps it falls closer to the feminine side because they're reading what they perceive as my gayness than my effeminacy? I don't know.

Carlos's comments reveal the need to move beyond binary conceptualizations of gender performance for queer men and instead consider how gender might be thought of as a spectrum. For instance, one can be read as a straight man based on the appearance of one's body but have a "higher pitched voice" and "carry" one's body in ways that can be understood as gay. While his voice and carriage could be simply understood as a "feminine performance," the reality is more that the performance resides in the liminal space between "gayness" and "effeminacy." In essence, to capture the uniqueness of this performance, we need to distinguish between differences in performances that are feminine and in male bodies of *all* sexual orientations and those that are considered feminine just because they are performed in gay bodies.

## Discussion

In this chapter we argue that gender roles and performances continue to influence the lives of Latinx queer men in context-specific ways. The narratives of these men revealed the persistent influence of white hegemonic masculinity in both queer communities and US society at large.[45] Further, these men also exposed the contradictions in gender hegemony for Latinx queer men because of its predication on a dichotomy that assumes heterosexual desire and (hetero)gendered social scripts.

These Latinx men also illuminated how hegemonic masculinity in America is not only contradictory, but unrealistic, and that it is precisely this unattainability that results in these men constantly having to negotiate their gender expectations and presentations, especially in the context of sexual behavior and relationships. Our analysis demonstrates that gender for Latinx queer men is anything but static, especially when it comes to sex. In addition, these men's narratives challenge the existing dichotomies that structure how we define masculinity and femininity.

Whereas they described hegemonic masculinity as brave and heroic, the Latinx men recognized that in different contexts, femininity was also as much, even more brave and heroic and embodied in Latinidad. In the case of historical protests for gay civil rights, some of the men pointed to the premier role Black and Latinx femmes and transwomen played in securing those rights. These findings rupture the stereotypes associated with racialized male femininities and advance knowledge on the extent to which different types of masculinities and femininities are produced in protest to white Western hegemonic masculinity. In other words, where the US ideal of masculinity was embodied in whiteness, constructing Latinx masculinity as excessive or "machismo" in contrast, the men in our study demonstrate that, for them, gender is fluid, and that they can even embrace and aspire to femininity in direct contradiction to Western gender ideals.

Depending on the context, the men with whom we spoke either did not see binary gendered presentations as accurately applying to them, or they used both masculinity and femininity as tools in interactions. When gender was understood as a tool, masculinity served as a shield, while femininity functioned as a sword. Specifically, some of the men described masculinity as a defense against the stigma associated with White conceptions of gayness[46] and feminized performances.[47] Functioning as a shield that helped some men fit into larger heteronormative culture, masculinity allowed some of the men, like Gilberto, to come off as masculine around straight friends, whereas they might "queen" out or be a little more themselves around other queer men. Yet other men, like Diego, used their femininity as a weapon that empowered them to be their more authentic selves around anyone, regardless of the dangers. For Schippers, hegemonic femininity worked to uphold the gender hierarchy in favor of masculine men, while male femininities were seen as contaminating and disruptive to the gender hierarchy.[48] Our findings in many ways challenge Schippers's work in that they emphasize how these Latinx men saw femininity as *a means to being* a version of their more authentic selves. Performing male femininities were a route to authenticity, whereby femininity was less about maintaining subordination and more of a vehicle to opportunity, fulfillment, and self-actualization.

We urge scholars to theorize gender performativity beyond the gender binary. Essentially, breaking down barriers enacted by the binary will allow us to rethink stereotyped aesthetics and assumptions. For example, some queer men might embody the stereotypical tall and lean man that is assumed to be masculine, but are feminine in performance or presentation, just as some hypermasculine men may sexually identify as "bottoms" and feminine men as "tops." Thus, the gender binary does not accurately reflect queer men's sexual and social behaviors. Given the recent Gallup survey that finds an increase in bisexuality and trans identity, as opposed to just gay and straight, this finding seems particularly pertinent to growing gender and sexual diversity in the United States.[49] While our study was circumscribed in several ways, such as its small sample size, its lack of variation in Latinx men (as most were Mexican or Mexican American), and its limited engagement with trans and nonbinary men, its strengths lie in the way it includes men who embrace feminine gender performances, bisexual men, and Puerto Rican and Afro-Venezuelan perspectives.

The interviews, albeit with a small sample of men, also provide a glimpse into the space between what is understood as "gayness" and feminine gender performance, or the proximity by which gender performances align with assumptions about sexual orientation and sexual positioning associated with gendered bodies. Our findings reveal the complexities of male femininity that are not only captured in one type of body or one type of sexual orientation, but a different approximation altogether.

NOTES

1 Jane Ward, *Not Gay: Sex between Straight White Men* (New York: New York University Press, 2015).
2 Jesus Gregorio Smith, Maria Cristina Morales, and Chong-Suk Han, "The Influence of Sexual Racism on Erotic Capital: A Systemic Racism Perspective," in *Handbook of the Sociology of Racial and Ethnic Relations*, ed. Pinar Batur and Joe Feagin (New York: Springer, 2018), 389–99.
3 C. Winter Han, *Geisha of a Different Kind: Race and Sexuality in Gaysian America* (New York: New York University Press, 2015).
4 Mimi Schippers, "Recovering the Feminine Other: Masculinity, Femininity, and Gender Hegemony," *Theory and Society* 36, no. 1(2007): 85–102, 97.
5 Judith Butler, *Gender Trouble* (New York: New York: Routledge, 1990), 33.
6 Schippers, "Recovering the Feminine Other," 91.
7 Schippers, 91.

8   Michael Warner, "Introduction: Fear of a Queer Planet," *Social Text* 29, no. 1(1991): 3–17.
9   Alex Carballo-Dieguez, Curtis Dolezal, Luis Nieves, Francisco Diaz, and Carlos Decena, "Looking for a Tall, Dark, Macho Man . . . Sexual-Role Behaviour Variations in Latino Gay and Bisexual Men," *Cultural, Health & Sexuality* 6, no. 2 (2004): 159–71.
10  R. W. Connell, *Masculinities*, 2nd ed. (Berkeley: University of California Press, 2005).
11  Katie. L. Acosta and Veronica B. Salcedo, "Gender (Non) Conformity in the Family," in *Handbook of the Sociology of Gender*, ed. Barbara J. Risman, Carissa M. Froyum, and William J. Scarborough (New York: Springer, 2018), 366.
12  Connell, *Masculinities*.
13  Schippers, "Recovering the Feminine Other," 94.
14  Schippers, 96.
15  Connell, *Masculinities*.
16  Schippers, "Recovering the Feminine Other."
17  Schippers, 96.
18  Shinsuke Eguchi, "Negotiating Hegemonic Masculinity: The Rhetorical Strategy of 'Straight-Acting' among Gay Men," *Journal of Intercultural Communication Research* 38, no. 3 (2009): 193–209.
19  Andrew Reilly, "Top or Bottom: A Position Paper," *Psychology & Sexuality* 7 no. 3 (2016): 167–76.
20  Reilly, "Top or Bottom."
21  Theo G. M. Sandfort, Rita M. Melendez, and Rafael M. Diaz, "Gender Nonconformity, Homophobia, and Mental Distress in Latino Gay and Bisexual Men," *Journal of Sex Research* 44 no. 2 (2007): 181–89.
22  Salvador Vidal-Ortiz, Carlos Decena, Hector Carrillo, and Tomás Almaguer, "Revisiting Activos and Pasivos: Toward New Cartographies of Latino/Latin American Male Same-Sex Desire," In *Latina/o Sexualities: Probing Powers, Passions, Practices, and Policies*, ed. Marysol Asencio (New Brunswick, NJ: Rutgers University Press, 2010), 253–73.
23  Reilly, "Top or Bottom."
24  Carballo-Dieguez et al., "Looking for a Tall, Dark, Macho Man."
25  Schippers, "Recovering the Feminine Other," 100.
26  Michelle Marie Johns, Emily Pingel, Anna Eisenberg, Matthew Leslie Santana, and José Bauermeister, "Butch Tops and Femme Bottoms? Sexual Positioning, Sexual Decision Making, and Gender Roles among Young Gay Men," *American Journal of Men's Health* 6 no. 6 (2012): 505–18.
27  Schippers, "Recovering the Feminine Other."
28  Hsiu-Fang Hsieh and Sarah E. Shannon, "Three Approaches to Qualitative Content Analysis," *Qualitative Health Research* 15, no. 9 (2005): 1277–88.
29  Brandon Miller, "Textually Presenting Masculinity and the Body on Mobile Dating Apps for Men Who Have Sex With Men," *Journal of Men's Studies* 26, no. 3 (2018): 305–26; James P. Ravenhill and Richard O. de Visser, "'It Takes a Man to

Put Me on the Bottom': Gay Men's Experiences of Masculinity and Anal Intercourse," *Journal of Sex Research* 55, no.8 (2018): 1033–47.
30  Vidal-Ortiz et al., "Revisiting Activos and Pasivos."
31  Vidal-Ortiz et al.
32  Anthony C. Ocampo, "Making Masculinity: Negotiations of Gender Presentation among Latino Gay Men," *Latino Studies* 10, no. 1(2012): 448–72.
33  Reilly, "Top or Bottom."
34  Carballo-Dieguez et al., "Looking for a Tall, Dark, Macho Man."
35  Vidal-Ortiz et al., "Revisiting Activos and Pasivos."
36  Reilly, "Top or Bottom."
37  Schippers, "Recovering the Feminine Other."
38  Carballo-Dieguez et al., "Looking for a Tall, Dark, Macho Man."
39  Schippers, "Recovering the Feminine Other."
40  Adam Isaiah Green, "Erotic Habitus: Toward a Sociology of Desire," *Theory and Society* 37, no. 6 (2008): 597–626.
41  Mignon R. Moore, "Lipstick or Timberlands? Meanings of Gender Presentation in Black Lesbian Communities," *Signs* 32, no. 1 (2006): 113–39.
42  Smith et al., "Influence of Sexual Racism."
43  Acosta and Salcedo, "Gender (Non) Conformity in the Family."
44  Carballo-Dieguez et al., "Looking for a Tall, Dark, Macho Man."
45  Eguchi, "Negotiating Hegemonic Masculinity"; Ocampo, "Making Masculinity"; Matthew H. Rafalow, Cynthia Feliciano, and Belinda Robnett, "Racialized Femininity and Masculinity in the Preferences of Online Same-Sex Daters," *Social Currents* 4, no. 4 (2017): 306–21.
46  Marcus Anthony Hunter, "All the Gays Are White and All the Blacks Are Straight: Black Gay Men, Identity, and Community," *Sexuality Research and Social Policy* 7, no. 2 (2010): 81–92.
47  Elizabeth Kiebel, Jennifer K. Bosson, and T. Andrew Caswell, "Essentialist Beliefs and Sexual Prejudice toward Feminine Gay Men," *Journal of Homosexuality* 67, no. 8 (2020): 1097–1117; Francisco J. Sánchez and Eric Vilain, "'Straight-Acting Gays': The Relationship between Masculine Consciousness, Anti-Effeminacy, and Negative Gay Identity," *Archives of Sexual Behavior* 41, no. 1 (2012): 111–19.
48  Schippers, "Recovering the Feminine Other."
49  Jeffrey M. Jones, "LGBT Identification Rises to 5.6% in Latest U.S. Estimate," Gallup, February 24, 2021, https://news.gallup.com.

## 17

## Radical Cheerbois

*Genderqueer Bodies Performing Queer Femininity*

ELROI J. WINDSOR

Boys are cute and girls are cool
But having to choose is a harsh cool
They think gender is binary
But what about the butches and fairies?
Don't know what I am?
Have no fear!
I'm whatcha call a genderqueer!
Na na na na na, you don't know what's in here!
Na na na na na, you don't know what's in here!
Got my friends to the left and my friends to the right
We don't give a damn, we'll fuckin' fuck all night!
Fuck your gender, fuck fuck your gender!
Fuck with gender, fuck fuck with gender!
Boys are cute and girls rule!
If I don't fit it, I feel uncool
Sometimes I just feel so bad
Binary gender is just a fad!
You see the world in zeros and ones?
Shit! You ain't havin' no fun!
Fuck your gender, fuck fuck your gender!
Fuck with gender, fuck fuck with gender!
–The Radical Cheerleaders


As a young radical queer punk, I admired radical cheerleaders from the sidelines. Then, as now, I was a fairly masculine genderqueer trans person. Radical cheerleading didn't feel like "my" space, and so I was not compelled to join any squads. But, in 2004, a friend invited me to participate in a radical cheerleading performance slated to open at a punk show. I was intrigued, and decided to explore the opportunity.

Cheerleading wasn't always the frilly, aesthetic performance that it is today. When it began in the mid-1800s, it was a practice reserved exclusively for gender normative, upper-class men. Through the early twentieth century, cheering was a way for young men to show off their athleticism and team spirit. But, by the 1960s, the activity transformed into a hyperfeminine, sideline performance and is currently dominated by cisgender girls and women.[1] Although mainstream cheerleading can be interpreted as a frivolous pastime aimed at appealing to the cisheterosexual male gaze, it can also be an empowering place for adolescent "girlie girls" "to revel and delight in the physicality of their bodies."[2] Despite the sport's masculine origins and potential for personal growth, cheerleading is most often cast as a place where conventionally attractive cisgender and heterosexual women bounce around in short skirts and tight tops for men's entertainment. As such, mainstream cheerleading has been a place where young women's youthful beauty and playful popularity flirts with stereotypes of sexual objectification. It often functions as a shallow substitute for the more important spectacle of men's football or basketball.[3]

## Rah! Rah! Radical Cheerleading

Radical cheerleaders weaponized mainstream cheer for creative political protest. Catalyzed by anarchist activism and queer politics, radical cheerleaders mobilized across the United States throughout the late 1990s and early 2000s. They shook pom-poms made from shredded plastic bags and happily shouted cheers against war and worker exploitation. They championed LGBTQ rights and sex-positivity. Their brash cheers infused playfulness within otherwise serious spaces like rallies and marches, as well as in everyday interactions. Their punk aesthetic blended the traditional short pleated skirts with ripped fishnets, colorful hair, and hairy armpits. Radical Cheerleader Mary Christmas described the project as

> a sensibility, like femme, it is more than just expression with a feminine twist. It's more than just girly-ness and more than just feminism. It's

trying to reclaim everything that's been taken away from you. Radical Cheerleading is like saying fuck what everybody has said to me, I'm going to take the good in everything I've been taught and fuck the rest. It's fun to have long hair and pigtails but I don't have to shave. It's about the best parts of being a woman, for me. . . . It's one of the only things that makes you feel okay to be girly and also makes you feel like you can defend yourself.[4]

With a loud-and-proud in-your-face attitude, radical cheerleading provided space for a fierce and feminist reclamation of femininity.[5]

Like their mainstream counterparts, radical cheerleaders were typically comprised of cisgender women. Reflecting the demographics of the anarchist punk scenes they came from, they were also predominantly young and white, but more visibly queer.[6] Occasionally, squads included cisgender men, often queer themselves, who embodied a feminine aesthetic similar to how the cis women presented. Cis men performers often donned wigs and dresses, but kept their beards, sneakers, and hairy legs. Radical cheerleaders' femme embodiment sometimes embraced a genderqueer identification, as in the cheer that started this chapter.[7] These performative tactics played with gender as an embodied practice.

## Let's Hear It for the Cheerboi

Since 1999, I had been performing as a drag king and having fun playing with gender onstage. I eschewed the conventional masculine characters often found in drag king performances. Instead, I enjoyed showcasing queerer masculinities. I performed my king debut as an eighties glam rocker, wearing a zebra-print Lycra suit and a long curly wig. Later, I joined a popular New York City drag king troupe, The BackDoor Boys, which parodied the boy band the Backstreet Boys, while simulating queer sex acts onstage onstage to the wild delight of our all-gender crowds. Given the fey boys I liked to perform onstage, I felt like I could bring another version of feyboy to radical cheerleading.

The friend who invited me to perform with the radical cheerleaders was a drag king known for his Atlanta performances as PeeWee Hymen. At the time, this friend was living as a masculine-of-center person and had not yet medically and socially transitioned to live as the trans man he is today. Back then, as female-assigned people who moved through the world with similar masculine gender presentations, neither of us felt particularly comfortable modeling our cheerleader roles after the feminine cis women who dominated the squads. But the man-in-a-dress expressions embodied by the cis men radical cheerleaders also didn't feel right. After some deliberation, we opted to participate as "cheerbois"—campy gay bois that channeled a look from white new age eighties pop stars. (Think Soft Cell and the Pet Shop Boys.) We coordinated our outfits, wearing black pants, red A-shirts, matching wristbands and sweatbands. We applied finely coiffed mustaches and elongated our sideburns. We harnessed cocks inside our boxers to affect a visible package. We added glitter and used exaggerated, flamboyant gestures. Ultimately, we took our pom-poms to the stage and cheered along with the other cheerleaders, most of whom embodied the femme aesthetic that define radical cheerleading squads.

## Queering the "Male" Body

As an editor of this volume, I have considered how the cheerboi expression relates to "male femininity" as an organizing concept. Is the cheerboi performance feminine, masculine, or some combination thereof? Is it drag or another form of gender performativity? It is a female or male or other-sex embodied performance? And what factors determine how to categorize the performance, if such categorization is desired?

When I originally wrote about the cheerboi performance for a presentation at the National Women's Studies Association in 2005, I argued that it was a performance of feminized masculinity. But, just as I wrote in the introduction to this book, I question the ways sex terms like "male" are assumed to refer only to the "natural" body into which one is born. Ultimately, cheerbois offer a queer interpretation of male femininity, which can mean more than what one might expect on the surface. As one radical cheer goes, "Gender fucks, you know you rock; anyone can have a cock!"[8]

NOTES

1 Natalie Adams and Pamela Bettis, "Commanding the Room in Short Skirts: Cheering as the Embodiment of Ideal Girlhood," *Gender & Society* 17, no. 1 (2004): 73–91.

2  Adams and Battis, "Commanding the Room," 83.
3  Mary Ellen Hanson, *Go! Fight! Win!: Cheerleading in American Culture* (Bowling Green, OH: Bowling Green State University Popular Press, 1995).
4  Jeanne Vacarro, "Give Me An F: Radical Cheerleading and Feminist Performance," Hemispheric Institute, https://hemisphericinstitute.org, 10.
5  Vacarro, "Give Me an F," 10.
6  Christine Ro, "Hey Hey! Ho Ho! Where Did Radical Cheerleaders Go?," Bitch Media, 2019, https://www.bitchmedia.org.
7  Radical Cheerleaders (Chicago), "Fuck with Gender," January 12, 2012, https://theradicalcheerleaders.wordpress.com.
8  Radical Cheerleaders, "Groove and Get Down," 2002, https://doremifaso.ca/archives/radicalcheers/cheers.html.

PART 5

# Male Femininities and Intimacies

An examination of the concept of "male femininities" is incomplete without an analysis of the way people who embody this gender expression relate to each other and to the broader society. In this section, we include four chapters that explore the intimacies of male femininities, including the sexualities of feminine men, their sociosexual relationships with each other within both queer and predominantly straight polyamorous communities, and their cultivation of relational space within queer spiritual communities. Much of the content focuses on the relationship to femininity among cisgender men, all of whom express some form of queer sexuality. The essays by Lester Eugene Mayers, Terrell J. A. Winder, and Rusty Barrett include perspectives from cisgender gay, bisexual, and queer-identified men, while Mimi Schippers's chapter examines the queer sexualities of cisgender heterosexual men in poly relationships. Like the other sections in this book, these perspectives are not intended as an exhaustive exploration of the intimacies of male femininities; indeed, there is much more to be studied on this topic. However, these chapters offer important insights into the ways men navigate femininity within their particular communities, all of which are subcultures of the broader heteronormative and monogamous society that classifies certain qualities of their beings as feminine.

A man who is feminine is often assumed to be gay. But sometimes he is not gay at all, as Travis Beaver explained in his chapter earlier in the book. Femininity embodied by cisgender men is difficult to uncouple from sexuality; recall how Beaver's interviewees bemoaned the ways they had to defend their straightness due to the fact that their gender expressions were so often assumed to signify a queer sexuality. Stereotypes about male femininity were so powerful that some people never fully believed these men were entirely heterosexual. The expectation that male femininity equates to same-sex sexuality suggests that feminine men who are gay might have an easier time negotiating their gender expressions, but this is not the case. Femininity among gay men is stigmatized, not only by people who are straight but also from within the LGBTQ community. Feminine gay men also report struggling to accept themselves. In addition, they often have difficulties finding satisfying sexual, romantic, and emotional relationships with other men due to the devaluing of femininity in gay men's communities.

The chapters in this section illustrate the ways that this devaluation is tied to the expectation that men strive toward hegemonic masculinity. Hegemonic masculinity requires that men uphold socially constructed and stratified standards of manliness. Currently, in the United States, men are expected to be strong, emotionally detached, independent, and competitive. To act like a man means to eliminate any trace of femininity. As part 6 of this volume details, the standards of hegemonic masculinity permeate social institutions. They are policed interpersonally, among men and between men and women. In upholding narrow boundaries of acceptable masculinity, alternative ways of expressing manhood are subordinated to the hegemonic model. Ultimately, hegemonic masculinity defines itself against women and femininity. To be a hegemonically masculine man means to be as unlike a feminine woman as possible.

A core feature of hegemonic masculinity is that it requires heterosexuality. To be a gay/bi/queer man in US society means that one will never fully benefit from the privileges associated with manhood. The story told by Lester Eugene Mayers in "Unloved" illuminates one man's life as a feminine Black gay man. Mayers describes enduring repeated rejection from partners as a feminine man, which left him lonely and confused about why his beauty made him so unworthy of romantic attention. Terrell Winder's chapter offers empirical insights into this dilemma. In his interviews with Black gay men, Winder explores how the act of bottoming during sex—being the receptive partner during anal penetration—is degraded within the gay community. His findings highlight the ways in which some sexual acts are feminized and associated with womanhood and consequently relegate men who participate in them to a lower status comparable to that of the overall status of women.

These accounts show how the intimate lives of Black gay men are shaped by negative associations with male femininity. They may feel internal shame about their gender expressions. They may feel ostracized or demeaned in their own communities. They may feel compelled to act more masculine, both to attract partners and to win the acceptance of heterosexual peers. In short, they may stifle a core part of who they are in order to gain acceptance. Yet, if they refuse to suppress their male femininities, they risk failing to find satisfying emotional, romantic, and sexual relationships with other men. While these chapters focus on Black gay men's communities, the same devaluation of male femininity has been documented in the communities of gay men of other races and ethnicities. The widespread disdain for femininity among men in gay communities illustrates the coercive and oppressive lure of hegemonic masculinity.

But life for feminine gay men is not without joy. As C. Winter Han argued in the previous section, femininity can be deployed strategically through drag queen performance culture. In drag contexts, gay men's male femininities are associated with situational power and can be a source of pleasure for both performers and audiences. Rusty Barrett's chapter, "Male Femininity as Spirituality among Radical Faeries," offers another context where feminine qualities are celebrated: the culture and community of radical faeries, which nurtures male femininity among its congregants. Radical faeries appreciate feminine qualities as worthy of spiritual admiration, honor, and festivity. In these spaces—subcultures of subcultures—there is a place for male femininities for gay men. Radical faeries may form deep bonds in their friendships with each other, communing and rejoicing in their feminine expressions. But, as many of the other readings in this section elucidate, much change is still needed to bring this acceptance into larger communities.

In straight contexts, characteristics of male femininities may have support within the context of polyamorous communities. However, Mimi Schippers argues that polyamorous men do not actually embody male femininity, because the qualities that are associated with femininity—being other-centered and communicative—are not gendered as feminine in this context. Schippers asserts that these qualities are instead ungendered: equally available to, and expected of, all women and men in poly scenes. While these qualities might be considered feminine in broader contexts, in that they defy the expectations of hegemonic masculinity, straight poly men do not necessarily experience them as exemplifying male femininities. Overall, Schippers's chapter explores the ways that some social and sexual contexts can make room for feminine expression that is valued, similar to gay men's drag and radical faerie spaces.

Taken together, the chapters in this section of the book offer a snapshot into the negotiation of male femininities in intimate spaces. But many questions remain. Future research might explore how feminine straight men navigate their gendered sexualities in their sociosexual relationships with women. Might they encounter similar situations as feminine gay men, in which their femininities are shamed and derided by prospective partners? Other studies might explore how feminine men form friendships and communities with each other, such as those that may exist in "emo" music scenes. What similarities and differences might exist in musical subcultures that are comparable to queer men's faerie sanctuaries? It is clear that much more scholarship is necessary to better understand the ways that male femininities can be nourished in intimate relationships. We hope that, by reading the chapters in this section, readers are inspired to explore other ways that male femininities and intimacies can flourish.

18

Unloved

*Lester Eugene Mayers*

What happens to the Black feminine male? Whose greatest pain comes from constant loneliness? The inability to be loved? To be in love? To give love? Simply because of his appearance, manners, and function? What happens to him?

Growing up in Brooklyn and Harlem between early 2009 and late 2015, I was fortunate enough to have a small group of friends who were like-minded and had a similar aesthetic. They were Black, openly gay, believed in no cages for fashion, and had strong "feminine" qualities. Most important, we all shared the burden of loneliness. Collectively, we couldn't figure out why people didn't find us attractive or wouldn't date us. Not to toot my own horn, but we were and are some sexy motherfuckers.

It wasn't long before we noticed that gay Black men in general were mostly interested in masculine, straight-acting gay men, no matter if they themselves were masculine or feminine. As time went on, my friends began to adhere to those masculine fashions, mannerisms, and ideologies that once made us feel lonely and unloved. They switched up everything feminine about them that made who they were. They changed not because they were in the midst of a personal revolution, but because they couldn't take the pain of loneliness. That switch came at the high price of becoming someone that they weren't. That's a price I'm never, ever willing to pay.

I've been on many dates that ended abruptly because, when I showed up in my glorious fashions, they would immediately tell me, "You're not my type" or "You remind me of my auntie"—like that's a goddamn compliment. In many ways they would suggest I am "craving for attention," and I am "too extra." At first, I used to deny my cravings for attention and the threat of my whole being—being *too extra*—but I realized I do *crave attention*, for a lot of reasons. I am extra, for a lot of reasons. Being able to admit that is the only reason I am able to survive in this lonely world.

The longest relationship that I've ever had was with a down-low Black man from the Carver Houses in Harlem. He was so fine. He was tall, caramel, and handsome, with waves in his hair. He played basketball in the gym with the other hetero guys in my high school. He had such a way with words that he could've convinced me that water wasn't wet and I would've believed him. He and I were emotionally involved and sexually committed for three years, yet, in order for our relationship to succeed, I had to follow his rules, which were:

1. Never come over to his house before 11 p.m..
2. When walking in the streets, I walk a block behind or in front of him.
3. When on a date to the movies (which always was in the less popular, far-out movie theaters at night), don't sit next to him until the lights go down.
4. And, most important, never tell *anyone* about us, not even my closest friends.

I was happy to oblige whatever he wanted and needed; it gave me a sense of belonging and cured my physical needs. I was his diary; I listened with intent and intensity as he spoke. Although I held every secret he shared, he never once inquired about my thoughts, feelings, and ideas. Our relationship revolved around him. I still haven't processed what the dynamics of our relationships did to me, mentally and emotionally. A month before I left for college, I found out that he had gotten a woman pregnant. I couldn't believe it! Years of playing background, being his secret, and this motherfucker could do this to me! I felt such rage, but never acted on it, because I never felt entitled to it. In the back of my mind I thought, "She is a woman and, naturally, she comes before me"—not to mention I still wanted to protect his image and his feelings. I waited for an apology from him, but it never came. Once again, I was back to the loneliness, and, dare I say, I've been there ever since.

From that day on, I've asked myself every day, "What is so unattractive and shameful about finding beauty in Black feminine gay men? What is it about me that makes me unlovable on a romantic level?" Still, I have no answer. I should mention that my friends have been in long-term relationships since they've switched up. I should also mention that they haven't smiled their familiar golden smile since.

I understand the basic need to feel loved and give love, but I will never understand changing yourself in hopes of someone liking or loving "the false you." I believe the standards of beauty must be erased entirely. I deserve to have the world notice my beauty. I don't have time to wait for the evolution of those standards to commence in order to find love.

\* \* \*

I myself believe that when it comes to matters of the heart,
the only sin is turning your back on love because of what
other people think.
—Cheryl West

All being considered, the question still remains: What happens to the Black feminine gay man whose greatest pain comes from constant loneliness and the inability to be loved, to be in love, and to give love simply because of his appearance, manners and function. What happens to him?" Worth examining. Worth correcting.

UNLOVED

*Lester Eugene Mayers*

When he appeared at the doors of love no signs welcomed Black
    femininity into there.
Into the loneliness, into the halting sounds of self-esteem.
Into the false smiles, into the silent cries.
However, the divine upon his right impels him to pull forever at the
    ladder of love gates.
Strangers calls ownership to the power of his Love.
Cynicism has bound him to his bed.
Still, he has the unmitigated gall to give love openly without receiv-
    ing it equally.

19

## Assume the Position

*Bottom-Shaming among Black Gay Men*

TERRELL J. A. WINDER

In the spring of 2014, Houston-based rapper Fly Young Red released the music video to his controversial song "Throw That Boy Pussy" to much discussion and debate among Black gay communities. The song unabashedly proclaims how the rapper wants to "see you clap that ass like a bitch. Yeah, I'm trying to get you back home. See if you can clap that ass on this dick!" Fly Young Red encourages his interest to dance "like a bitch," denoting the feminization of his male target. In this case, Red envisions his love interest as the bottom (the receptive partner during anal sex) and himself as the top (the penetrating partner. In the song, Fly Young Red's explicit desire for a feminine bottom stands in stark contrast to the idolization of straight-acting gay men espoused within many gay communities, across gay social platforms, and in social spaces.[1] More often, bottoms, particularly feminine gay men, are shamed for doing what should be considered the fundamental work of gay anal sex. Being a bottom, or bearing the marker of the penetrated partner, results in explicit bottom-shaming among gay men. Bottoms are often ridiculed for being too feminine, being too explicitly gay in public, or for subjugating their own masculinity to another man's through the act of anal sex.

For the purposes of this chapter, I define "bottom-shaming" as any practice that denigrates, humiliates, or embarrasses a man for engaging in receptive anal sex. I interrogate the way media, social media, and everyday conversations work to elevate masculine tops as superior to feminine bottoms. Through the examination of these occurrences, especially those of the seemingly harmless and mundane, I find that bottoming within gay sexual encounters is often explicitly denounced, and that this shaming can disrupt a sense of belonging for those who are ridiculed for identifying as bottoms. Much as we use other social cues to surmise a gender via expression, men who are considered too feminine are often subjected to bottom-shaming even without explicit confirmation of their sexual positioning preferences and behaviors.[2] Bottom-shaming operates primarily as a way to police the boundaries of masculinity and femininity, which, within gay communities, serves to support the oppression of women and to elevate patriarchal notions of masculinity and dominance.

Bottom-shaming relies on a hierarchical arrangement of sexual positions where bottoms literally occupy the bottom rung. While their existence is foundational to gay sexual relationships (i.e., someone must play the receptive role in anal sex), to hold the social position of "bottom" is often regarded as emasculating. Versatiles play the critical role of a middle-rung status in this social hierarchy, where they often avoid the negative stigmas associated with bottoming by maintaining a right to, and identity of, occasionally, "top." In this structure, tops are at the pinnacle and are viewed as rare unicorns in the gay world. Much like heteronormative stereotypes that women "catfight" over men, bottoms are often thought to fight over their tops. It is this parallelism of heteronormative relationships that undergirds the shaming of bottoms. Identifying as a bottom is socially undesirable for the assumed alignment with femininity; thus, bottoms are often explicitly called the "female" or "woman" in gay relationships. This view is not unique to Black queer communities; in a study of Latino gay men, researchers noted how the language of "activo" aligned with understandings of being a man, and "pasivo" was understood to mean acting as a woman.[3] The idolized gay bottom is the "unclockable" man, the masculine bottom, the man that doesn't give any indication of his gayness—in so many words, a "man's man." While the existence of feminine tops and masculine bottoms is a reality within gay social spaces, their presence only serves to reinforce this existing hierarchy: they operate as exceptions to its rules, but still work to confirm that they are not the norm. Yet their status within this hierarchy is varied, as masculinity always trumps one's actual sexual positioning preference or behaviors. Thus, masculine bottoms are celebrated as an exception to the excessive femininity of typical bottoms, and feminine tops are often met with disbelief, shock, or laughter from potential partners.

The idolization of masculine men as tops in gay relationships is often heightened through gay news outlets and memes on social media. Memes and headlines like "Are Tops Going Extinct in the Gay Community?," "Who's on Top?," and "Top Privilege?" reveal that this sexual hierarchy within gay communities is alive and well.[4] In my research with young Black gay men in Los Angeles, I found that they often rejected the idea that a feminine top could "climb their backs." Comments like "climb my back" to denote being the receptive anal sex partner add a sort of levity to a quintessentially heavy topic in gay communities. Men who act as bottoms often stated explicit desires for more masculine men to play the role of tops in sexual encounters. Others would also support these requirements by publically ridiculing those who had been suspected of letting a feminine man or "another bottom" act as the penetrative partner. These statements and limitations placed on sexual positions and acceptable levels of femininity draw clear lines within the community. Yet many acknowledge that the social expectations of being a top or bottom are often imperfect, and they undermine these distinctions by the gender expressions and narrative accounts of the men themselves.

In this chapter, I explore the way Black gay men use bottom-shaming to denigrate male femininity. To illustrate the impact and presence of this shaming, I draw from ethnographic and interview data collected between 2012 and 2016 among gay, bisexual, and pansexual men in Los Angeles. As part of a larger project, I conducted 50 in-depth interviews with Black gay, bisexual, and pansexual men, attended community meetings at a local nonprofit organization, attended local Black prides (e.g., West Hollywood Pride, Long Beach Pride), and spent time with many of these young men as they socialized in clubs and bars and at each other's homes. During my time as participant observer, I met over 250 Black gay men, some of whom I was able to later interview, whereas others I only encountered once or twice. As such, some of the interactions that I captured were comments, expressions, or conversations in passing. These ethnographic moments are reflective of the fluid and precarious spaces in which young people move in Los Angeles. In addition to this ethnographic research, I draw on everyday examples in the media of disparaging bottoms that circulate within gay communities. Through the analysis of discussions of bottom-shaming and male femininity, I reveal the prominence of anti-bottom rhetoric among this gay community, while simultaneously taking a closer look into the consequences of this shaming among young Black gay men in Los Angeles.

First, I explore the connection of Black womanhood to the treatment of bottoms within Black gay communities. I reveal that Black women and feminine gay bottoms have often been regarded as social problems. Then, I examine how male femininity is explicitly disparaged among Black gay communities. In so doing, I illuminate how the denigration of male femininity leads to internal stereotyping and discrimination within these communities. Taken together, these two sections underscore the strength of the connection between sexual positioning and gendered expressions of masculinity and femininity. The subsequent section shows the unreliability of using femininity as a proxy for "bottoms" and masculinity as proxy for "tops"; yet, even as these men acknowledge that these stereotypes don't always hold true, they continue to use gender expression as a viable method to assume the sexual positions of other gay men. Finally, I turn to the consequences of bottom-shaming and the implications of male femininities among Black gay men.

## Black (Gay) Bitches

Scholars have written about the Black bitch as a major trope in popular culture. In *Black Sexual Politics*, sociologist Patricia Hill Collins explores the "Black bitch" as an image used both to celebrate femininity and to deprecate womanhood.[5] Using the popular Missy Elliott song "Get Your Freak On," Collins details the impact of a long historical legacy of Black women—often portrayed as overly controlling, negatively independent, and stereotypically "angry Black women"—being cast as "freaks" and "bitches" who are relegated to lower-class existence in the public imagination.[6] However, in songs like Fly Young Red's "Throw That Boy Pussy," dancing like a bitch is encouraged for Black gay bottom men. This parallel relationship between heterosexual Black women and gay men is fraught with debate. Several think pieces, essays, and critiques have been written by Black women who find that gay men (often gay white men) espouse having "an inner Black woman" who comes out to be sassy in social interactions.[7] In some respects, we might consider this particular use of white patriarchy as a way to further oppress women, specifically Black women, by appropriating these negative Black stereotypes to further performances of white gay sexuality.

The tensions that exist between these two groups are important to consider, as they help to define the negativity toward bottoms who are frequently cast as "bitches" themselves, yet often still exercise a modicum of male privilege. Many scholars and activists have noted the negative social treatment and portrayal of Black women in the United States. From the 1965 *Moynihan Report* that blamed Black mothers for the social ills of the Black family to the enduring stereotype of the welfare queen, Black women have been subjected to scrutiny. Perhaps most famously proclaimed by Malcolm X during his address at the funeral of Ronald Stokes, a victim of police violence in Los Angeles in 1962, "The most disrespected woman in America is the Black woman. The most unprotected woman in America is the Black woman. The most neglected woman in America is the Black woman."[8] These words (used most recently during Beyoncé's 2018 Coachella performance) are a reminder of the precarious position of Black women as American citizens, calling into question the disrespectful language and messages used to categorize them. Subsequently, Black women have taken up and revised the idea of the "Black bitch" to one that establishes their agency over their bodies and minds. Collins discusses the transformation of the negative Black bitch to the "bad bitch," or a woman with complete autonomy and control of her own sexual desires and pleasures. Yet, as Collins notes, these conflicting tropes of "bitch" serve to render its usage as always contextual and forever shifting. In a similar fashion, a gay man who bottoms may identify as a "power bottom" to signal his ability to take over the dominant role in sexual encounters while still being the penetrated partner. The inherent contradiction of being penetrated and having power is not unlike the incongruous usages of "bitch" and "bottom" in that that they are consistently terms that can be used to connote strength or weakness.

Within LGBT communities, feminine gay men (often as perceived bottoms) and trans women bear the brunt of the pushback of heterosexual disdain for queer persons.[9] I am not arguing that these experiences are exactly the same, however; publically heterosexually identified men, among others, often rely on the familiar language of the "bitch" in order to compare feminine gay men and trans women to Black cis women, evoking the same social positionality of the bottom rung. Through disparaging language and controlling images, such as the negative connotations of the Black bitch, gay Black bottoms—or gay Black men perceived as overly feminine—are designated in gay communities as problematic for their agency in sexuality; in other words, the label of "bitch" disapproves of the choice to be a penetrated man. Thus, Black gay bottoms are cast as "bitches" who have given up their manliness by allowing another man to "top" him—in effect, voluntarily giving up their identity claims to manhood.

Consider one example that emerged in my interview with Ricky, a dancer and choreographer, who recounted a story about a trip to the mall with his boyfriend. Ricky was a twenty-eight-year-old native of Los Angeles's famed South Central neighborhood and a regular participant in the weekly leadership meetings at my nonprofit field site. Even as he complained about the negativity directed toward femininity, he still relied heavily on his position and identity as a man:

> I feel like . . . I've learned that when I was with my boyfriend one time and we were holding hands at the mall, and it was two, a set of gay boys behind us. And these hood niggas walked up to us, and we were just like, "Oh, shit, we gonna have to fight." 'Cause we were sitting here holding hands, and close and stuff, we were dating, so . . . And they went by saying, "We respect y'all." We was like, "What?" They were like, "We respect y'all because y'all not all like that," and he pointed to the gay boys and they were just laughing and kiking [gossiping] and I was like, "Oh, yeah, we understand that we're men. We're not trying to be women." So, it's not . . . There's a difference between a homosexual and a fag. And I don't consider myself a fag because I don't . . . it's not cool. I feel like I'm discriminating against my own type of sexual orientation, but I feel like it's those types of people that make it bad for normal people.

Ricky recognizes that his comments may be considered discriminatory by aligning himself with "normalcy," or conventional, heteronormative masculinity. His declaration that he and his boyfriend understand that they're men and not women—unlike the other, presumably more feminine gay men in this encounter—works to validate the lack of respect afforded to feminine gay men by the group of heterosexual men. Ricky deploys the language of the "fag" versus "homosexual" in an effort to justify why it is OK to look down on these *types* of gay men who "make it bad" for other more masculine gay men, who tend to be more palatable to heterosexuals—that is, it is OK to be gay, but be a gay *man*. Ricky, his boyfriend, and their heterosexual interlocutors look down on the other gay men for their proximity to womanhood through behavior such as laughing and gossiping in public. As such, this example underscores the ways that some gay men are ridiculed for their proximity to womanhood and femininity by both heterosexual and homosexual social actors. Much like C. J. Pascoe's findings among high school boys, the term "faggot" here is not used simply to denote sexuality, but as a way to highlight just how socially unacceptable it is for men, gay or straight, to be too feminine.[10] Additionally, the way that Ricky uses the label signals "non-normalcy" and draws out how male femininity is regarded as behavior that challenges social norms and conventional gender roles. In essence, men deemed too feminine are called "faggots" to reinforce the boundaries of man and woman. In other words, acting, dressing, or speaking the way women are expected to behave, not just being gay, can earn you the derogatory label "faggot."

## No Fats, No Fems: Disparaging Femininity in Black Gay Communities

Scholars have written about Black masculinity and the widespread social expectations for hypermasculine Black men among both Black and white Americans.[11] Specifically, sociologist David Pilgrim describes the "brute caricature" that undergirds the perception that Black men are particularly virile and pose a direct threat to the virtuousness of white women.[12] Gay men who are marked as feminine are considered too visible, too emotionally clingy, and, in many ways, a liability to gay men who are seeking to maintain a masculine façade to gain heterosexual acceptance, and characteristics such as strength, dominance, and emotional detachment are often used to discount and denigrate femininity among Black gay men. Within the community organization where I conducted many observations for this project, Black gay men would come together every week and discuss issues that they felt were specific to them. During one such weekly meeting, a local HIV advocate and community leader, Malachi, hoped to discuss what he felt was the current condition of the Black gay community.

A twenty-eight-year-old new member to the weekly group meetings, since he had recently relocated from Pennsylvania to Los Angeles. Malachi asked if he could bring up something that he had been thinking about. He said, "We have lost our identity . . . compared to the whites who have leather daddies, bears, twinks, etcetera." He went on state that the Black gay community is disparate, not as cohesive like the white gay community; he believed it only had "in/out," "DL" (down-low), "butch," and "femme" as identity categories. Quite a few of the young men seemed to agree with his assessment, while others seemed to crook their necks in bewilderment. He continued by saying that he also really wanted to discuss the issue around "no fats, no fems," and how it was affecting the Black gay community.

Malachi's comparison of Black gay community structure to the structure of the white gay community illuminated what he felt was unique to Black gay life: a limited number of options for categorization, and a lack of cohesion. His belief that the White gay community is more unified did not resonate with all members of the discussion. Nonetheless, he felt that this lack of cohesion was directly connected to how relationships are built among Black gay men. In other interactions, Malachi's affinity for a gay-first, Black-second identity support this elevation of white gay social life over that of Black gay life.[13] He offered that these limited labels are interrelated with the frequently seen "no fats, no fems" on many users' profiles on geospatial dating applications such as Grindr and Jack'd. Malachi's comments revealed his own struggles to find space within Black gay communities and his longing for the greater acceptance that he believes exists among white gay men. However, in no way is the expression "no fats, no fems" exclusive to Black gay communities; rather, it represents a larger perception within the gay community that it is best to be physically "in shape" and conventionally masculine. In several conversations, members of the group noted a form of discrimination in gay communities that rejects those who exhibit too much femininity and those who are seen as obese. According to Ricky, "[The gay community is] about [what] people make it out to be. 'Oh, gay marriage.' But as soon as you see two bottoms, and they wanna get married, you wanna talk about 'em. Or you see two trannies that wanna get married, you wanna talk about 'em. 'Transvest . . . That's disgusting.' But we're all gay! I don't say it's disgusting that you're a top. So, everyone discriminates within . . . We're discriminating against our own people, so to speak."

Ricky's perspective illustrates another way that bottoms can be subjected to shame when two men who are perceived as bottoms decide to couple. Colloquially, these relationships are often called "lesbian relationships"—a label that relies on negative attitudes toward women and femininity in order to disparage male femininity and shame specific types of gay men (i.e., bottoms) while simultaneously denigrating same-gender loving or queer women. The labeling of these partnerships as a "lesbian" couple reinforces a belief in the homonormativity of gay relationships; in o ther words, relationships should still have clearly defined roles—tops do masculinity, and bottoms do femininity.

Ricky's comments about transgender men and women also reflect their marginal acceptance within gay communities. While the term "LGBTQ" refers to a marginalized sexual community, the "T" is for "transgender," a gender term, and it is often just as contested among gay men as straight men. Yet, in direct conflict with Ricky's earlier admission of ridiculing gay men deemed "faggots," he attempted to discredit the type of boundary making that occurs while at the same time reinforcing his own negative behaviors and perspectives.

Finally, Ricky mentioned that he doesn't "say it's disgusting that you're a top." In this instance, he notes astutely that much of the disdain toward gay relationships relies on the belief that the truly inappropriate gay sexual position is the bottom. As such, comments of disgust are frequently aimed toward visibly feminine gay men who are perceived as bottoms. Online forum posters use their knowledge of bottom-shaming to create tongue-in-cheek campaigns with memes and slogans advocating for top-shaming. For example, one meme pictures a young boy cowering in a corner with a menacing finger pointed at him and comments such as "Ur just a penis!" or "Tops have no talent!" to poke fun at what is considered a nonissue (see fig. 1). Memes like these that highlight the disproportionate amount of shame and stigma directed toward bottoms drive home the existence and persistence of bottom-shaming.

## Feminine Tops and Masculine Bottoms

Frequently, femininity and masculinity are read as proxies for sexual position preference among gay men. Those men marked as feminine are assumed to be exclusive bottoms, due to their proximity to femininity and womanhood. For example, many gay men in the study recalled being asked if they were the man or woman in their relationships. Inherent in the question is the presumption that one person assumes not only a submissive role during sexual intercourse but also that they play a more feminine role in their relationship. We can view this question in its many forms as one way that heteronormative relationship structures and compulsory monogamy are overlaid on gay sexuality and relationships.[14]

While many of the gay men that I encountered in the course of this project acknowledged this perceived connection of bottoming with femininity, they also observed that male femininity could often be misleading when looking for a romantic partner. For example, two young men, Rahsaan and David, discussed how misreading femininity in gay social spaces could result in awkward sexual encounters:

> RAHSAAN: They [some men] look at these things in photos or how you look in the club.
> DAVID: They might hang with strippers and booty shakers in the club, but in the bedroom will make themselves look dumb because they're not bottoms.

In this conversation, Rahsaan and David illustrate how, in clubs or in pictures on social media, practices that are cast as typically feminine behaviors can lead to the presumption of a preference for bottoming. They elaborate further that people can "look dumb" when, during a sexually intimate encounter, they discover that feminine behavior doesn't necessarily mean that a gay man is a bottom. Although these types of conversations make it clear that these young Black gay men recognize the flaws in using femininity as a proxy for sexual positioning, they also reinforce the necessity of knowing someone's sexual position in order to pursue a sexual relationship. These experiences further support a commonly held belief in the inability to find a true top, especially given the discrediting of feminine tops in gay social spaces. Much like research on Black lesbians by sociologist Mignon Moore, the relationships between these young men are predicated on gendered presentations and sexual desire.[15] Yet, while both Black lesbians and Black gay men are concerned with levels of masculinity and femininity in gender expression, my respondents were much more openly expressive about the translation of these expressions into specific sexual roles.

The explicit connection of femininity with bottoms and masculinity with tops also created problems for men who were considered traditionally masculine, but were actually bottoms or versatiles. I discussed this tension with twenty-three-year-old Jawan, who was a transplant to the Los Angeles area from his native South Carolina. When I asked Jawan how he felt about his sense of belonging in the gay community of Los Angeles, he replied:

> JAWAN: Sometimes I feel . . . I don't feel like I belong sometimes, on a simple fact is 'cause the way I go about things, I carry myself, is that people automatically just assume that either I like trannies or I'm not gay, or I'm just here with a gay friend. And when they do find out I'm gay, it's strictly, "Oh, you're masculine." . . . You're looked upon as just strictly one thing . . . I mean, categorized, you know what I mean? Being labeled already because of how you carry yourself . . . "Labeled" as in the sexual preference as in top, bottom, versatile, versatile top and versatile bottoms.

Jawan's comments highlight the sort of social expectations and pressures that can exist within gay social spaces for bottoms to be feminine and tops to be explicitly masculine. His self-described level of masculinity created a sense of nonbelonging within the gay community because of assumptions people made about his preferred sexual positioning. In many ways, these sentiments reveal the tensions that exist for some gay men when they encounter the numerous categorizations and labels that are commonplace within gay communities. Jawan's comments illustrate that stereotypes and expectations around masculinity can have detrimental effects on the psychology of gay men.[16] The same disconnect was also espoused by a Los Angeles native named Kevin. At thirty-five, an older man than most of the group, Kevin, a noted drag queen in the community, often came to the group after Hollywood auditions for small roles in commercials or feature films. He once quipped that the group would be surprised how many men wanted "[his] titties on their back." In other words, he believed many would be shocked by the amount of people that prefer a feminine top, as that is something often scorned publicly. Much as women are not viewed as a penetrating partner in heterosexual relationship, feminine men are not considered as a penetrating partner in gay sex.

Just as gender roles exist for men and women, so, too, do those social roles exist for tops and bottoms. The societal expectations of bottoms and tops that have manifested as a hierarchy within gay communities along lines of masculinity and femininity often can create particular challenges within the dating world of gay men. In this sense, engaging in feminine behaviors undercuts your credibility as a man and as a potential top; this hierarchy suggests that some tops are better than others, and a feminine top is something you never want.

I discussed these expectations with Andrew, a twenty-four-year-old Los Angeles native. He spoke about the difficulties with dating given the belief that true tops should only be tops who had never previously bottomed: "It's crazy . . . you have bottoms who only date total tops, whatever that means? What the hell? I guess a total top is something . . . somebody whose, they have a virginal hole or something. I don't know. Can I say 'hole'?" Andrew's shock and disdain for bottoms who would only consider dating tops who have a "virginal hole" underscores the existing hierarchy of tops and bottoms. Yet, as prior research has shown, men who have sex with men often engage in some degree of both bottoming and topping, regardless of how they identify publically.[17] Andrew's reaction illustrates the extreme lengths that are drawn to ensure that someone is an actual "top" and in many ways reinforces the negativity associated with bottoming. In this particular case, bottom-shaming works to discredit anyone who may have previously engaged in bottoming and undermines one's position as "top" if he has ever bottomed. This attitude is not unique to my field site. Websites, blogs, and discussion boards frequently quip that tops are a rare find and disparage the idea that men who have bottomed in some sexual encounters can act as a top in another. For example, one meme illustrates a man vomiting at the idea that he has been topped by a bottom (fig. 2). Memes like this continue the narrative that bottoms should be in search of "true tops" who have not bottomed for others, and that it is disgusting for two men who have bottomed to be sexually intimate. Undoubtedly, this meme and others rely on the perceived connections between femininity and bottoming: in other words, if you are being penetrated by a bottom, you have allowed an even less masculine man to claim your manhood. The media suggestion and common myth that there exists a dearth of tops for bottoms across the many gayborhoods in the United States adds to the intensity of bottom-shaming by creating a desire to locate and identify "rare" total tops.

## Consequences of Bottom-Shaming

The role of bottom-shaming within gay communities creates unequal power positions in relationships and during interactions in gay social spaces. While it is unclear if bottom-shaming is more of an issue of tops belittling bottoms or intrabottom ridicule, the lack of attention to the negative and restrictive confines of gay sexuality have real consequences for the feelings of belonging and the self-image of Black gay men. One op-ed written for online news platform Elite Daily by Donny Meacham argues for the end of bottom-shaming. In his piece "Bottom Shaming: Yes, It's a Thing and It Needs to Stop," Meacham writes, "It's absolutely ludacris [sic] that a top would be the ones bottom shaming. If they're good enough to be in the bedroom with your dick inside of them, then why shame them in public?"[18] It is apt to consider the extent to which bottom-shaming works to further create divisions and a sense of inferiority among a population that already faces its fair share of denigration in media and from heterosexuals. The community cannot believe that it will ever shake the negative associations from outsiders who ask, "Who's the man in the relationship?" until gay men themselves disregard the question.

The Black gay men that I spoke with struggled to find a place within a gay community that often felt limited to superficial categorizations. As participants like Andrew and Jawan exemplify, these labels can be confining and inappropriate when using conventional notions of masculinity and femininity in order to classify various gay men into assumed preferred sexual positions. Not only are feminine men publically sub-

Figure 19.1. Stop top shaming meme. Source: https://bottommemes.tumblr.com.

Figure 19.2. Bottom disgust meme. Source: Latin_tony 69, www.instagram.com.

jected to bottom-shaming by other gay men, but often the stigmatizing shaming that they experience creates imbalances within relationships. Sentiments shared by Rahsaan, Andrew, and Jawan highlight the extent to which bottom-shaming and the disparaging of male femininity can create complications with potential sexual partners when sexual positioning preferences don't align with assumptions based on one's gender expression. Furthermore, through explicit bottom-shaming, Black gay men, like other gay men, reject male femininity as an ideal and in so doing reveal just how much the disdain for femininity relies on disparaging women in the process. While it is true that not all feminine men are bottoms, this fact does not change the reality that the practice of bottom-shaming is directed primarily toward feminine men. For Black gay men who express a more feminine gender presentation, the stakes can be very high. From social exclusion to social sanctions from family members and friends, Black gay men who are considered too feminine feel devalued and rejected by other Black gay men. The use of male femininity as a proxy for sexual roles has created a difficulty in social interactions between gay Black men that undermines their ability to challenge existing gendered norms and find acceptance.

Ultimately, the existence of bottom-shaming as a tactic to disparage male femininity does not negate the act of same-sex desire. In the words of Fly Young Red, "Man, I'm cool with his and hers, but I'm 'bout that his and his." In other words, whether gay men are bottoms, tops, or versatiles, they are engaged in relationships together. The shaming of bottoms and celebrating of tops in gay communities only serves to reinforce heteronormative understandings of the sexual social order. How can gay communities resist continual stigma when they rely on stigma-driven shame toward male femininity? Examining the reluctance of gay Black men to abandon the alignment of masculinity with tops and femininity with bottoms reveals the enduring strength of negativity toward femininity and womanhood more generally.

NOTES

1 C. S. Han, "They Don't Want to Cruise Your Type: Gay Men of Color and the Racial Politics of Exclusion," *Social Identities* 13 (2007): 51–67.
2 Judith Butler, "Performative Acts and Gender Constitution: An Essay in Phenomenology and Feminist Theory," in *The Routledgefalmer Reader in Gender and*

*Education* (New York: Routledge, 2006), 73–83; C. West and D. H. Zimmerman, "Doing Gender," *Gender & Society* 1, no. 2 (1987): 125–51.

3   Alex Carballo-Diéguez, Curtis Dolezal, Luis Nieves, Francisco Díaz, Carlos Decena, and Ivan Balan, "Looking for a Tall, Dark, Macho Man . . . Sexual-Role Behaviour Variations in Latino Gay and Bisexual Men," *Culture, Health & Sexuality* 6, no. 2 (2004): 159–71.

4   Blake Michaels, "'Are Tops Going Extinct in the Gay Community?' Love and Relationships," Gay Guys, July 7, 2015, www.gayguys.com/; Amy Sohn, "Who's on Top?," *New York Magazine*, May 22, 2003, http://nymag.com/; Zach Stafford, "Top Privilege?," Huffington Post, September 16, 2013, www.huffingtonpost.com/; Patricia Hill Collins, *Black Sexual Politics: African Americans, Gender, and the New Racism* (New York: Routledge, 2004).

5   Collins, *Black Sexual Politics*, 6.

6   Sierra Mannie, "Dear White Gays: Stop Stealing Black Female Culture," *Time*, July 9, 2014, http://time.com/; Alex Reaves, "No, You Don't Have an Inner Black Woman," *Affinity Magazine*, November 6, 2016, http://affinitymagazine.us.

7   H. A. Shugart, "Reinventing Privilege: The New (Gay) Man in Contemporary Popular Media," *Critical Studies in Media Communication* 20, no. 1 (2003): 67–91.

8   Malcolm X, speech at Ronald Stokes funeral, May 5, 1962, YouTube video, 39:56, June 13, 2020, https://www.youtube.com/.

9   Peter Glick, Candice Gangl, Samantha Gibb, Susan Klumpner, and Emily Weinberg, "Defensive Reactions to Masculinity Threat: More Negative Affect toward Effeminate (but Not Masculine) Gay Men," *Sex Roles* 57, nos. 1–2, (2007): 55–59.

10  C. J. Pascoe, *Dude, You're a Fag: Masculinity and Sexuality in High School* (Berkeley: University of California Press, 2011).

11  Patricia Hill Collins, *Black Sexual Politics: African Americans, Gender, and the New Racism* (New York: Routledge, 2004); Suzanne Marie Enck-Wanzer, "All's Fair in Love and Sport: Black Masculinity and Domestic Violence in the New," *Communication and Critical/Cultural Studies* 6, no. 1 (2009): 1–18; Archana Bodas LaPollo, Lisa Bond, and Jennifer L. Lauby, "Hypermasculinity and Sexual Risk among Black and White Men Who Have Sex with Men and Women," *American Journal of Men's Health* 8, no. 5 (2014): 362–72; Gregory Seaton, "Toward a Theoretical Understanding of Hypermasculine Coping among Urban Black Adolescent Males," *Journal of Human Behavior in the Social Environment* 15, nos. 2–3 (2007): 367–90; William A. Wolfe, "Overlooked Role of African-American Males' Hypermasculinity in the Epidemic of Unintended Pregnancies and HIV/AIDS Cases wth Young African-American Women," *Journal of the National Medical Association* 95, no. 9 (2003): 846.

12  David Pilgrim, "The Brute Caricature," Jim Crow Museum of Racist Memorabilia, November 2000, https://ferris.edu/JIMCROW/brute/.

13  Marcus A. Hunter, "All the Gays Are White and All the Blacks Are Straight: Black Gay Men, Identity, and Community," *Sexuality Research and Social Policy* 7, no. 2 (2010): 81–92.

14  Mimi Schippers, *Beyond Monogamy: Polyamory and the Future of Polyqueer Sexualities* (New York: New York University Press, 2016).
15  Mignon Moore, "Meanings of Gender Presentation in Black Lesbian Communities," *Signs: Journal of Women in Culture and Society* 32, no. 1, (2006): 113–39.
16  F. J. Sánchez, S. T. Greenberg, W. M. Liu, and E. Vilain, "Reported Effects of Masculine Ideals on Gay Men," *Psychology of Men & Masculinity* 10, no. 1 (2009): 73; F. J. Sánchez and E. Vilain, "'Straight-Acting Gays': The Relationship between Masculine Consciousness, Anti-Effeminacy, and Negative Gay Identity," *Archives of Sexual Behavior* 41, no. 1 (2012): 111–19.
17  Derek T. Dangerfield, Laramie R. Smith, Jeffrey Williams, Jennifer Unger, and Ricky Bluthenthal, "Sexual Positioning among Men Who Have Sex with Men: A Narrative Review," *Archives of Sexual Behavior* 46, no. 4, (2017): 869–84.
18  Donny Meacham, "Bottom Shaming: Yes, It's a Thing and It Needs to Stop," Elite Daily, January 19, 2016, www.elitedaily.com.

## 20

## Are Polyamorous Men Embodying Male Femininity?

MIMI SCHIPPERS

In an article published in the journal *Theory & Society*, I developed a conceptual framework for hegemonic masculinity and hegemonic femininity.[1] In that article, I asserted that what Raewyn Connell refers to as "subordinate masculinities" are not masculinities at all, but, instead, "male femininities."[2] I offered the following definition:

> Thus, what were identified by Connell as subordinate masculinities are ... simply hegemonic femininity embodied or enacted by men. Halberstam[3] and Messerschmidt[4] identify specific forms of female masculinity by looking at how women embody masculinity. Building on Halberstam and Messerschmidt, I propose that there are specific forms of male femininity. However, they are not simply femininity embodied by men, as Halberstam's and Messerschmidt's work would suggest. I argue that we limit male femininities to the characteristics and practices that are culturally ascribed to women, do the cultural work of situating the feminine in a complementary, hierarchical relationship with the masculine, and are embodied by men. Because male femininities threaten the hegemonic relationship between masculinity and femininity, they are both feminizing and stigmatizing to the men who embody them.[5]

According to this definition, then, male femininities are characteristics—not kinds of men—that any given culture, subculture, or group define as womanly or girlish and are embodied by people who identify as male or as men and, because they are embodying femininity, are stigmatized and cast out of the category of "normal" or "real" men. Because male femininities are labels attached to *culturally* defined feminine behaviors embodied by men, they are always contextual. What does a group, subculture, or society define as feminine? When men take up those feminine practices, what kind of social control and stigmatization is directed toward them? According to my initial definition, these were the questions a researcher might ask in order to identify male femininities in a particular context.

Since publishing that article, I have become increasingly uncomfortable with my original definition of "male femininities," for two reasons. First, unlike Jack Halberstam's "female masculinities," there was little room for the concept of "male femininities" as I defined it to be potentially transformative rather than reproductive of already established interpersonal or institutionalized gender relations.[6] According to my definition at the time, men who embody male femininities were social outcasts rather than social agents participating in and creating social life. Second, over the years of teaching the article and having conversations with my students and colleagues, I have grown uncomfortable with the lurking essentialism in the definition. The word "male" overstates the link between biological sex and the gender identity "man"; the label "male femininities" simply cannot help us to understand the social and cultural dynamics of genderqueer and trans individuals embodying socially prescribed norms of gender embodiment, especially when their gender displays or performances do not align with the gender identities of genderqueer and trans people. For instance, because masculinity and femininity are not identities, but a set of idealized practices and characteristics, any individual, regardless of gender identity, is capable of embodying hegemonic masculinity and hegemonic femininity. If a person who identifies as genderqueer embodies a contextually specific hegemonic femininity (i.e., characteristics or practices that are contextually defined as feminine and that establish a hierarchical relationship to masculinity as superior and dominant), I wouldn't want to call this "male femininities," because the individual embodying hegemonic femininity is neither "male" nor a "man." Additionally, the label "male femininities" implicitly presumes that everything once considered feminine remains feminine, even when embodied by people who do not identify as women or girls. Thus, my original definition begs the questions: When do male femininities become something other than femininity? When do individual, group, or subcultural endorsements and embodiments of male femininities transform the structure of gender relations or undo gender? According to Francine Deutsch, we must have ways to identify social processes by which individuals, practices, interpersonal relations, and institutionalized structures become less gendered as much as we must recognize the processes by which hegemonic gender relations are established and perpetuated.[7] My initial definition offered a conceptual apparatus to do the latter, but not the former.

These discomforts with my original definition of "male femininities" have become especially salient when I consider people who identify as male or as cisgender men and who are in polyamorous relationships. The word "polyamory" means multiple loves and refers to emotionally and sometimes sexually intimate relationships with more than one person. In previous work, I have focused on how poly relationships and poly sexual encounters challenge the hegemony of the monogamous couple as the only legitimate way to do emotionally and sexually intimate relationships. Because nondyadic relationships and sexual interactions disrupt monogamy as compulsory and "charmed,"[8] they also open up potential to transform gender, race, and class relations.[9]

In this chapter, I will explore if and how "male femininities" (men or male-identified people embodying characteristics or taking on practices that are, according to the dominant culture, feminine) take shape in poly subculture. I will then discuss how male femininities in poly subcultures might inform—and hopefully remedy—the problems in my original definition. Finally, I will offer an expanded and alternative sociological definition for "male femininities."

## Poly Men/Male Femininities?

Given the definition I provide above, and as I will describe below, cisgender, straight, polyamorous men could be perceived as embodying a form of male femininity. Despite this, other polyamorous people do not perceive polyamorous men as feminine. On the other hand, it is not uncommon for people unfamiliar with poly experiences, relationships, or subcultures to be curious about and question the masculinities of cisgender straight men who are in polyamorous relationships with partners who identify as women. This is especially the case if a woman partner has other lovers or partners who identify as men, in which case people outside of polyamorous communities may perceive poly men as not so much feminine, but as not especially manly or appropriately or exceptionally masculine. There is something here about suspicions that cisgender and straight poly men fail to be appropriately masculine, but they are *not* perceived as feminine due to being poly.

Offering an insightful critique of my concept of "male femininities," James Messerschmidt suggests that there are masculinities that are not perceived as feminine, but instead are stigmatized as threatening or toxic in order to establish hierarchies among groups of men.[10] For instance, he argues that Western leaders construct the Muslim Other as embodying a particularly dangerous masculinity in order to legitimate US policy in Iraq. In other words, not all stigmatized masculinities are feminized. In another critique,[11] Nancy Finley argues that my definition of "pariah femininities" (a label used when women or female-identified people embody hegemonic masculine characteristics) does not allow for the undoing of gender through the embodiment of pariah femininities within particular subcultural contexts.[12] Finley demonstrates quite convincingly that, within the subcultural context of women's roller derby, women embody pariah femininities as a strategy to collectively transform gender relations. These two important interventions in defining the social dynamics of masculinities, femininities, and gender relations—not all stigmatized masculinities are perceived as feminine and that stigmatized embodiments of gender can be transformative of gender relations—provide insight into the embodiment of femininity (according to dominant, mainstream culture) by poly men.

### Poly Men, Male Femininities, and Undoing Gender

Until recently, polyamory as a viable relationship option has remained outside mainstream culture. Because of its marginalization, a relatively coherent subculture of collective understandings and ethics for behavior has emerged among polyamorists through online blogs and forums, how-to books, podcasts, and localized community organizing. Significantly, unlike previous nonmonogamous subcultures, polyamory has emerged in the digital era. Not only does this make the subcultural norms and practices readily available to anyone who has access to a computer, it also allows for the development and cultivation of a relative consensus about poly ethics that stretch across time and space.[13] Included in these ethics are a set of ideas about how to be a good poly partner and new language for talking about relationships and emotions.[14] Because polyamory subcultures emerged in the wake of second- and third-wave feminism, and because many of the writers, bloggers, and community leaders identify as feminists,[15] gender egalitarianism is highly valued and central to the norms and ethics established in these digital, literary, and community subcultures.[16] These new ways of experiencing relationships in the context of a feminist ethics have created space for and encouraged men to shed certain features of hegemonic masculinity that manifest in interpersonal relationships. The expectations for being a good partner regardless of gender are more akin to the hegemonic expectations for what women are expected to do in heterosexual relationships.

For instance, polyamorists offer a collective understanding of sexual jealousy that acknowledges that jealousy is normal and perhaps likely, at least sometimes, but it is not inevitable.[17] More important for my purposes here, polyamorists encourage each other to do internal emotional work in order to understand the source of the jealousy and to contain it by cultivating other emotions. An alternative to feeling jealous in poly subcultures is feeling "compersion" in the American and "frubbly" in the British contexts: pleasure and joy rather than fear or anger when one's partner experiences pleasure with another person. Practicing compersion is offered as not just an alternative to, but also an antidote for, jealousy. According to the how-to literature and blogs, one of the best ways to cultivate compersion is to focus attention on the joy and pleasure a partner is experiencing with their other partner (referred to as a "metamour," which is a partner's other partner) rather than focus on one's self. Compersion, in other words, is about being other-centered and placing another person's emotional well-being ahead of one's own jealous feelings. Importantly, there is no gender structure to expectations for feeling compersion or frubbly. All genders are encouraged to work on understanding and eradicating jealousy and to cultivate other-centeredness.

We know from decades of research that being other-centered falls squarely on the feminine side of the gender binary. When a person who identifies as male or as a man cultivates compersion, is he embodying a form of male femininity? According to hegemonic assumptions about gender, being emotionally other-centered is considered feminine. With compersion being other-centered, we might presume men who cultivate feelings of compersion rather than jealous rage are embodying a male form of femininity.

Another example is poly subculture's emphasis on open dialogue; full disclosure; and honesty about feelings, desires, and expectations. In other words, polyamorous relationships require a lot of "processing" or talking things through. Like with compersion, all genders are expected to be open and willing to communicate. According to mainstream culture, being the "strong silent type" is a feature of hegemonic masculinity while listening and sharing is considered feminine. Polyamory subcultures overtly discourage being a "strong, silent type." In fact, research shows that people in polyamorous relationships tend to look down on men who feel or act possessive or controlling, or who are not willing to communicate.[18] When a male-identified person in a polyamorous relationship is willing to open up dialogue and disclose intimate details about his emotional life with others, is he embodying male femininity?

According to poly subcultural norms, these behaviors are neither feminine nor masculine. These are expectations for everyone, and so I would argue that, within poly subcultures, the men who are other-centered, willing to disclose and communicate, avoid jealousy and possessiveness, and cultivate compersion are *not* embodying male femininities. The subculture ungenders the norms of interpersonal relationships, which means that compersion and openness to communication are no longer perceived as gendered. This is not to say that there is no gender structure to the actual practices and experiences of people in polyamorous relationships (more empirical research is needed); rather, it is to say that the norms for being a good poly partner ungender the rules and roles, regardless of whether or not people actually follow them in their relationships.

However, as I stated above, people outside of poly subcultures sometimes perceive poly men as suspiciously masculine because they tolerate their partners' relationships with others, and they actively work to support their partners' other relationships through compersion, open communication, and accountability to the emotional well-being of others (including their metamours!). What kind of man would not experience jealous rage and accept this situation?

So, we have two very different ways of seeing poly men: one from the inside and one from the outside. On the one hand, poly people generally do not perceive poly men as embodying femininity for their partnering practices, but, on the other hand, outsiders are skeptical of their masculinities. This highlights how my original definition limited male femininities to a label usually imposed from outside in an effort to get hegemonic gender relations back on track. Certainly outsiders may perceive poly men as not living up to expectations for masculinity, but I would argue that those who are suspicious of the ways poly men do relationships, especially with women as partners and other men as metamours, are not embodying a male femininity. Instead—and, I think, quite interestingly—the men themselves are not seen as feminine people but as falling down on the job of being appropriately masculine in relationship to women or *as being exceptionally masculine.*

For instance, in my experience, outsiders do not deploy a stigmatizing male femininity to discourage poly men from adopting gender egalitarian relationship norms. Instead they construct narratives about polyamory as a flawed relationship style. One of those narratives is that polyamory does not work, is doomed to fail, and is thus impossible. Because men are inherently jealous, they argue, men might tolerate polyamory for a while, but eventually the relationships will fall apart, and everyone involved will be left in an emotional shambles. Instead of deploying a set of labels to stigmatize male femininities, many people, including outsiders who write about polyamory in the mainstream media, invoke essentialist and hegemonic ideas about masculinity to render polyamorous relationships as untenable, dangerous, or temporary. Rather than impugning the men as feminine, outsiders maintain hegemonic constructions of an essential masculinity—one where men are thought of as incapable of sharing lovers with other men—by denying the possibility or longevity of polyamory.

Another discursive tactic is for outsiders to emphasize that poly men have access to multiple women, and that access to sex with new and different women is why they tolerate other men as metamours. It takes an exceptionally strong and self-confident man, the narrative goes, to be able to bed many women and not be threatened by other men. In this case, again, hegemonic masculinity, not a male femininity, is deployed—not to get the men to fall back in line and embody hegemonic masculinity in their interpersonal relationships, but to construct polyamorous relationships in ways that reinscribe hegemonic gender relations. Notably, this is not an example of constructing threatening masculinities to establish hierarchies among masculinities, as Messershmidt demonstrated; instead, it positively renders poly men as exceptionally masculine in hegemonic ways.

I suspect that the deployment of both of these narratives (polyamory is impossible, or poly men are exceptionally masculine) rather than a stigmatizing male femininity have something to do with polyamory being a kind of relationship, not a kind of *person*. "Polyamorist" is not (yet) a sexual identity, but a social location in relationship to others. Poly men (unlike gay men or effeminate boys) are not seen as a qualitatively different kind of person compared to "real" or "normal" men and boys. And because "polyamorist" is not an identity label and thus not perceived as an expression of an internal, fixed self, stigmatizing discourses establishing a male femininity are neither readily available nor effective.

At the same time, the ethics and norms for being a good poly partner are potentially threatening to hegemonic gender relations. If poly men are not a different kind of man and are capable of overcoming jealousy or refusing to be controlling, being other-centered and communicative, then any man could do relationships according to poly subcultural norms and ethics. This makes polyamory as a viable relationship form particularly threatening to hegemonic gender relations and masculine dominant power dynamics in intimate relationships. Hence, outsiders don't construct male femininities to contain the threat; they contain polyamory by questioning the viability of polyamorous relationships or reconstructing polyamory as particularly beneficial to masculine men. In both cases, there is an insistence on hegemonic ideas about masculinity, men, and intimate relationships.

Given these dynamics, I propose we expand the definition of male femininities to include *discursive male femininities*, which refers to the labels imposed from outside in order to stigmatize men who embody femininity.[19] The definition must also include, however, *embodied male femininities*, which efers to the practices or norms that endorse and encourage people who identify as men to embody aspects of femininity and that, by doing so, challenge or transform gender relations. I believe both are important because 1) we do not want to lose sight of the ways people in mainstream culture deploy the mark of femininity in order to get men to tow the line and embody or value hegemonic masculinity (discursive male femininities); and 2) we don't want to miss the ways the embodiment of male femininities in interpersonal relationships, groups, or subcultures can be a conduit to undo gender (embodied male femininities).

Finally, it is important that we recognize and cultivate the ways the embodiment and endorsement of male femininities (and female masculinities) within a subcultural or institutional context can be one vehicle for reducing the significance and salience of gender difference in interpersonal interactions, ongoing relationships, group and subcultural norms, and institutionalized structures/systems. When a group, subculture, institution, or society accepts and normalizes men's embodiment of what was originally defined as feminine, those embodiments are no longer femininity within that context. This is important because, as long as we keep using the labels "feminine" or "femininity" to refer to practices that, in context, are normalized for men, we are constructing discursive male femininities and keeping the hierarchical gender binary in place.

## Conclusion

In conclusion, then, and to answer this essay's titular question—are poly men embodying male femininities?—my answer is no. Interpersonal expectations for men in poly relationships might be perceived as feminine from outside poly subculture, but, within, they are ungendered. Being other-centered, communicative, and capable of compersion do not constitute any kind of femininity, let alone a male femininity. Also, mainstream discourse and others outside of polyamory subculture do not stigmatize or feminize poly men. Because "polyamorist" is not an identity (and thus not a kind of person), men who do polyamory are not perceived as inferior or feminine compared to other men. In addition, because polyamory is a relationship style that is potentially threatening to heteromasculine dominance, polyamory is constructed as a doomed or dangerous way to do relationships.

Because—at least for now—polyamory is perceived in mainstream culture as a practice or relationship choice instead of a sexual orientation or identity, the construction of hegemonic male femininities is unavailable as a tactic to contain its potential to ungender certain aspects of intimate relationships. As some polyamorists work to normalize polyamory by claiming a fixed and inherent polyamorous identity, it might behoove them to consider how this would open up cultural opportunities to construct discursive femininities around polyamory, in which case polyamorous men could be construed as failed, dangerous, or feminine men in order to contain whatever changes in gender relations are happening in the subculture.[20] Moreover, because it is a relationship practice and subculture rather than an identity, there is room to encourage men to take on some characteristics that were originally considered feminine outside of the subculture, and to do so without stigmatization or feminization. As C. J. Pascoe suggests, social spaces in which embodied male femininities are encouraged, cultivated, and celebrated can facilitate the undoing of gender.[21] It seems that, at least in terms of subcultural norms and ethics, this is precisely the case with polyamory.

NOTES

1 Mimi Schippers, "Recovering the Feminine Other: Femininity, Masculinity, and Gender Hegemony," *Theory and Society* 36, no.1 (2007): 85–102.
2 R. W. Connell, *Masculinities* (Berkeley: University of California Press, 1995).
3 Connell, *Masculinities*, 2.
4 James Messerscmidt, *Flesh and Blood: Adolescent Gender Diversity and Violence* (New York: Rowman & Littlefield, 2004).
5 Schippers, "Recovering the Feminine Other," 96.
6 Halberstam, *Female Masculinity*.
7 Francine Deutsch, "Undoing Gender," *Gender & Society* 21, no. 1 (2007): 106–27.
8 Gayle Rubin, "Thinking Sex: Notes for a Radical Theory of the Politics of Sexuality," in *Pleasure and Danger: Exploring Female Sexuality*, ed. Carole S. Vance (London: Pandora, 1984), 267–319.
9 Mimi Schippers, *Beyond Monogamy: Polyamory and the Future of Polyqueer Sexualities* (New York: New York University Press, 2016).
10 James Messerschmidt, *Hegemonic Masculinities and Camouflaged Politics* (Boulder, CO: Paradigm, 2010).
11 Nancy Finley, "Skating Femininity: Gender Maneuvering in Women's Roller Derby," *Journal of Contemporary Ethnography* 39, no. 4 (2010): 359–87.
12 Deutsch, "Undoing Gender."
13 Elisabeth Sheff, *The Polyamorist Next Door: Inside Multiple-Partner Relationships and Families* (New York: Rowman & Littlefield, 2013).
14 Ani Ritchie and Meg Barker, "'There Aren't Words for What We Do or How We Feel So We Have To Make Them Up': Constructing Polyamorous Languages in a Culture of Compulsory Monogamy," *Sexualities* 9, no. 5 (2006): 584–601.

15 Christian Klesse, "Toward a Genealogy of a Discourse on Women's Erotic Autonomy: Feminist and Queer-Feminist Critiques of Monogamy," *Signs: A Journal of Women in Culture & Society*, forthcoming.
16 Elisabeth Sheff, "Polyamorous Women, Sexual Subjectivity and Power," *Journal of Conemporary Ethnography* 34, no. 3 (2005): 251–83; Elisabeth Sheff, "Poly-Hegemonic Masculinities," *Sexualities* 9, no. 5 (2006): 621–42.
17 Meg Barker, "'This Is My Partner, and This Is My ... Partner's Partner': Constructing a Polyamorous Identity in a Monogamous World," *Journal of Constructivist Psychology* 18, no. 1(2005): 75–88.
18 Sheff, "Poly-Hegemonic Masculinities."
19 For a discussion of discursive gender constructions, see James Messerschmidt, *Masculinities in the Making: From the Local to the Global* (New York: Rowman & Littlefield, 2016).
20 Christian Klesse, "Polyamory: Intimate Practice, Identity or Sexual Orientation?," *Sexualities* 17, nos. 1–2 (2014): 81–99.
21 C. J. Pascoe, *Dude, You're a Fag: Masculinity and Sexuality in High School* (Berkeley: University of California Press, 2007).

# 21

## Male Femininity as Spirituality among Radical Faeries

RUSTY BARRETT

The spiritual dimension of male femininity plays an important role across a wide range of religious traditions. Many religions have rituals that involve forms of gender crossing, androgyny, or male femininity as spiritual pathways. Among the Iatmul in Papua New Guinea, the *naven* ritual involves men adopting dress and behaviors typically associated with femininity as a way to gain higher spiritual consciousness.[1] Similar expressions of male femininity are found in the Tantric traditions in Hinduism and in Bahayana Buddhism, among Siberian shamans, and in Sufi Islamic traditions.[2] Androgyny was also central in early Christianity, as evidenced by Paul's claim that "there is neither . . . male or female, for you are all one in Christ."[3] Expressions of male femininity in religious contexts create a liminal, transitional ritual moment where an individual exists in the social spaces between normative expressions of gender as a binary system with clear delineations between "masculine" and "feminine."[4] These ritual unravelings of normative gendered behavior produce transcendent moments in which gender norms are temporarily suspended, allowing practitioners to escape from their mundane, everyday understandings of gender to reach a higher spiritual consciousness. Thus, religion and spirituality are often contexts where male femininity is valued and cultivated.

Throughout Western societies, women participate in various religious practices more frequently than men. Studies in the psychology of religion find that this pattern is not due to differences in biological sex or in expectations for men or women. Rather, they find repeatedly that participation in religious practices and expressions of spirituality are associated with higher levels of femininity among both men and women.[5] In other words, individuals who score higher on psychological measures of femininity are more likely to be involved in religious practices compared to more masculine-oriented individuals, regardless of biological sex or gender identity. More feminine or androgynous individuals, regardless of sex, also have a higher propensity for forms of mysticism.[6] While male femininity seems to correlate closely with experiences and expressions of religious spirituality, this may create conflicts for men in religious traditions with high expectations for gender normativity. A study of Catholic seminarians, for example, found that those with higher levels of femininity also experienced higher levels of stress.[7] Thus, while men who are more feminine might be drawn to religious practices and experiences, they are also likely to face negative evaluations of their femininity within many religious traditions. Male femininity is often understood as symptomatic of homosexuality, so that Christian denominations that view homosexuality as sinful have higher expectations for stereotypically masculine behavior. Within the ex-gay movement, for example, men trying to cure themselves of their homosexuality typically focus on altering their gender expression through participation in "masculine" activities like camping or playing sports.[8]

Faced with religious traditions that demand a rejection of male femininity, some men have turned to the creation of new traditions that embrace the feminine, such as the Male Goddess Movement, in which contemporary Pagan men reject Western constructions of masculinity as associated with negative social traits such as competitiveness or aggression.[9] Embracing male femininity typically also involves rejecting gender normative religious traditions like contemporary Christianity. This can be seen in the gay male traditions of the Sisters of Perpetual Indulgence and the radical faeries. The two groups have an overlapping history, as the founding members of the Sisters of Perpetual Indulgence were also participants in the very first radical faerie gathering in 1979.[10]

The Sisters of Perpetual Indulgence are a group of (primarily) gay men who dress in drag as nuns, participate in mock Catholic rituals, and do charity work for LGBTQI civil rights and health organizations. Novitiates in the order must demonstrate knowledge of LGBTQI history and social issues and do volunteer work for a period of time before they become full members of the order. It is not surprising that the relationship between the Sisters of Perpetual Indulgence and Christianity (particularly Catholicism) has been antagonistic. On Easter Sunday, for example, the sisters in San Francisco hold an annual "Stations of the Cross" gay bar hop and a "Hunky Jesus" contest where contestants compete to see who can produce the "hottest" portrayal of Christ.[11] Although the Sisters of Perpetual Indulgence are organized as a religious order, the actual religious beliefs of sisters vary widely. The order includes nuns who identify with a variety of religious traditions (including Christianity) as well as those who identify as atheists or agnostics.[12]

While the Sisters of Perpetual Indulgence convey an anti-Christian stance bt directly mocking Christian traditions and rituals, radical faeries position themselves in opposition to Christianity through the appropriation of elements from religious traditions with histories of antagonism with, or oppression by, Christian groups. This includes borrowings from pre-Christian European, Native American, Hindu, and Buddhist traditions, among others. The elements drawn from these various traditions are often those that also challenge typical Christian ideologies of gender normativity. While one might join the Sisters of Perpetual Indulgence without espousing any particular religious beliefs, the radical faerie movement centers on specific, shared understandings of spirituality.

The radical faeries directly link religious spirituality with male femininity, holding it to be an innate characteristic that endows gay men with specific spiritual gifts. Because the forces of heterosexism and modern urban culture dampen this gay male spirituality, radical faeries maintain *sanctuaries*: small rural communities where gay men can cultivate their natural gifts. There are currently eight radical faerie sanctuaries scattered across the United States, in addition to sanctuaries in France, Canada, and Australia. While a few faeries live and work at these sanctuaries, most live in more urban areas but participate in faerie gatherings, extended events where faeries meet in rural settings, often at one of the sanctuaries, to create safe environments to cultivate the natural spiritual gifts associated with male femininity.

The main leader of the radical faerie movement was Harry Hay, also an early leader in the Mattachine Society, one of the first gay rights organizations in the United States, and an open member of the Communist Party. Hay's Marxist beliefs contributed to the development of a distinct radical faerie ideology of gay male egalitarianism. Early faeries were are also influenced by 1970s radical feminism and drew ideas from feminist theology and forms of New Age feminist religious practice that incorporated forms of neo-paganism and goddess worship. The final influence in the development of radical faerie beliefs was the fascination with Native American culture typically associated with the hippie movement; radical faerie beliefs about gender and male femininity draw heavily on ethnohistorical studies of gender in Native American communities. In rejecting Christianity, radical faeries appropriate widely from religious traditions that celebrate femininity or androgyny, including Native American, Celtic, Norse, Greek, Sumerian, and Egyptian. Although the constellation of appropriated forms in radical faerie religious are themselves unique, they overlap with forms of appropriation found in other neo-pagan and New Age groups.

While often mistakenly assumed to be the same, neo-pagan and New Age movements have distinct theologies and involve different religious practices. Both movements have been accused of narcissism and participation in "the contemporary spiritual consumer market" appropriating "spiritual idioms from a range of other traditions."[13] Given an emphasis on individual spirituality among radical faeries, the movement clearly aligns with New Age traditions. However, radical faeries also share the neo-pagan belief that communing with the natural world can serve as a pathway to spiritual enlightenment. Faeries' sanctuaries are placed in rural settings (often without electricity or indoor plumbing) to aid in reaching higher spiritual consciousness by coming closer to nature. Faerie traditions, such as gatherings and sanctuaries, are ideologically linked to rurality and the combination of communion with nature and unity with fellow faeries creates the context in which higher consciousness becomes possible.[14] Rural or natural contexts are also understood as easier sites for realizing one's true male femininity because urban contexts are overrun by heterosexism and hetero-imitating gay men. Gendered meanings linking spirituality and rurality vary across contexts and social groups. The faerie view of the rural as essentially feminine directly contrasts with both trends of gay male migration to urban centers and the view of rurality as a space to find true primitive masculinity expressed by mythopoetic men's movements.[15]

## Radical Faeries

The first radical faerie gathering was held at the Sri Ram Ashram in Benson, Arizona, in 1979.[16] During it, 220 men participated in spontaneous rituals and discussions of spirituality and sexuality. In the "mud ritual"—the most widely discussed of the gathering—about 50 naked attendees began bringing water from the ashram to make mud from the desert dirt. After one of the men laid in the mud with an erection, the other men began packing mud around his penis until they had built a mound over the man. Other attendees circled them, chanting "om" and dancing.[17] Although playing naked in mud is common among faeries, the mud ritual is not repeated at other gatherings. Rather, it exemplifies the radical faerie ritual tradition where rituals emerge "in the moment" rather than repeating a prespecified structure. Although a few faerie rituals are repeated on specific occasions, such as dancing around the maypole on Beltane or taking turns sharing thoughts in a "heart circle," the faerie tradition privileges spontaneous ritual that follows individuals' whims.

Because the radical faerie approach to religious experience is highly individualistic, few rituals or common beliefs unite the range of faerie religious practices. Two primary core principles of faerie culture are central to an otherwise highly variable identity: an essentialist view of faerie male femininity (or androgyny) and the concept of subject-SUBJECT consciousness from the writings of Harry Hay.[18] Hay believed that gay men were not men, but actually belonged to a third gender that was male but naturally feminine. This "third gender" view of male femininity focused on healing one's "inner sissy kid" to recapture one's natural femininity. For example, in describing the first radical faerie gathering, Hay noted that

- We reached out to reunite ourselves with the cornered, frightened, rejected little Sissy-kids we all once were;
- We reached out to recapture and restore in full honors that magick of 'being a different species perceiving a different reality' (so beautifully projected almost a century ago by J. M. Barrie's *Peter Pan*) which may have encapsulated our boyhood and adolescence;
- We told that *different* boy that he was remembered. . . . loved . . . and deeply respected;
- We told him we now recognized that he, in true paradox, had always been the real source of our Dream, of our strength, again in true

paradox, that few Hetero Males can even begin to approach, let alone match;
- We told that beloved little Sissy that we had experienced a full paradigm shift and that he could now come home at last to be himself in full appreciation.[19]

Reuniting with one's inner sissy kid was necessary because, according to Hay, most gay men had lost touch with their natural male femininity and become obsessed with forms of masculinity typically associated with heterosexual men. For Hay, such "hetero-male imitation" was the result of life in a homophobic society, particularly when homophobia was supported by religions like Christianity. Hay called on his "Gay Brothers to tear off the ugly green frog-skin of Hetero-male imitation in which we had wrapped ourselves in order to get through school with a full set of teeth to reveal the beautiful Fairy Prince hidden beneath."[20] In order to come to recognize their own spiritual potential, faeries must reject forms of "hetero-male imitation" and embrace their natural male femininity.

## Two Spirit Traditions

In developing this essentialist view of faerie male femininity, Hay drew heavily on his own understandings of Native American Two-Spirit (or "third gender") traditions, specifically ethnohistorical studies of gender in Native American cultures. Hay moved to New Mexico in the 1970s, hoping to study the Tewa Two-Spirit (*kwidó*) tradition. He was particularly disappointed that contemporary Tewa gay men did not identify as *kwidó* and had little awareness of a Two-Spirit tradition within their community.[21] Given that he found little evidence of this tradition among the Tewa, Hay ultimately based his views of Native American gender and sexuality on ethnohistorical descriptions and discussions with non-Native anthropologists, in particular Sue Ellen Jacobs. Many contemporary anthropologists have raised questions about the accuracy of the depiction of Two-Spirit traditions by earlier ethnographers, so Hay's view of Native gender may be more founded on stereotypes than on actual Native traditions.[22]

The central aspects of Two-Spirit identity Hay used in developing radical faerie ideologies were the idea of a third androgynous gender that is neither male nor female but contains "two spirits," and the belief that members of this third gender category are born with spiritual gifts resulting from the presence of both gender spirits within one body. Will Roscoe describes Hay's use of Native American gender ideologies as an attempt to look past "Western history's blank pages" to find evidence of "queer social roles in which sexual and gender differences are not only expressed, but integral." The quest for such "social roles," Roscoe writes, led Hay to the Two Spirit tradition:

> The most well known examples are the Native North American two-spirits. Referred to as "berdaches" in the anthropological literature, two-spirits were males and females (and no doubt intersex individuals as well) who occupied an alternative gender role that was neither male nor female. Often, they served as religious leaders or shamans. For Harry, two-spirits were the premier example of how being queer could be the basis for a distinct social contribution. Now we know of many other alternative gender roles and identities, in Oceania, Asia, and Africa and in cultures that preceded or survived the rise of patriarchy in the Old World.[23]

It is important to note that while Roscoe attributes the Two Spirit tradition to Native American communities, he describes it entirely in the past tense, as if the tradition—or any actual Two-Spirit individuals—no longer exist. This perspective has, unsurprisingly, resulted in serious criticism of radical faeries from Native Americans who identify as Two-Spirit.[24] For Native Two-Spirit individuals, the specific meanings of the identity vary across tribes and include specific ritual roles or obligations. Given its local nature, Native Two-Spirits hold that one cannot claim the identity without first being Native American. Despite this, there are white radical faeries who identify as Two-Spirit.[25] The ability to appropriate and claim a stereotyped representation of Native identity is certainly an example of white privilege. Scott Morgensen describes this appropriation as a form of "queer settler colonialism" in which gay men appropriate Native traditions to link themselves to a precolonial moment in order to legitimize their position outside of normative colonial heteronormativity.[26] This appropriation also legitimizes both faerie opposition to Christianity and faerie understandings of male femininity.

Following his view of a third gender, Hay argued that gay men were not actually *men*, but rather were a distinct and separate "species" of *gay not-men* with identities rooted in male femininity.[27] Following Hay's belief that Native American Two-Spirits were spiritually gifted shamans and mystics, the essentialized understanding of male femininity among radical faeries is directly tied to religious spirituality: "The concept of Androgyny has been taken on by the Faeries and given a distinctly spiritual bent. Rather than referring to an asexual or omni-sexual state, Androgyny for the Faeries means radically juxtaposing elements of the masculine and feminine in psychological as well as physical formulations. The relationship of the archetype of the Androgyne to figures in myth and history has become a spiritual imperative for many radical faeries seeking a tradition to reclaim."[28] Although it may not be entirely accurate, Hay's interpretation of Native American gender and sexuality has become a central part of radical faerie identity. While faeries who actually identify as Two-Spirit have become less common, faeries continue to recognize the Native origins of the idea of a distinct and innate form of male femininity intimately linked to spirituality. Some have worked to create connections with actual Native Two-Spirit communities.[29]

## subject-SUBJECT Consciousness

At the center of the radical faerie view of male femininity as a form of spirituality is "subject- SUBJECT consciousness," an idea that comes directly from Hay's writings. Influenced by radical feminist views of the sexual objectification of women and by Marxist views of individuals as economic objects, Hay came to believe that many gay men had adopted the objectifying tendencies associated with heterosexual masculinity and, therefore, had lost their unique potential for escaping the tendency to objectify other individuals, particularly other gay men. As with his more general views of "hetero-male imitation," Hay felt that the dominant gay male culture of the 1970s (known as "clones") had adopted the hetero-masculine objectifying ideologies and treated one another as sexual objects for individual gratification.[30]

Part of radical faerie spiritual growth involves learning to escape the sexual and economic objectification of others as practiced by heterosexual men. Instead, faeries should seek to develop a subject-SUBJECT consciousness realized through recognition of one's innate male femininity. Part of the essentialized gender identity of gay not-men is the inherent ability to approach one another as *subjects*. Thus, Hay emphasizes and promotes the idea of monogomy in gay male relationships to avoid the tendency to perceive other men as sexual objects. Gay men are naturally able to approach one another as equals, although cultural dominance of heterosexual male masculinity makes it difficult to accept and recognize this ability. Monogamy allows faeries to cultivate this ability to perceive others as subjects rather than objects:

> The Hetero monogamous relationship is one in which the participants, through bio-cultural inheritance, traditionally perceive each other as OBJECT. To the Hetero male, woman is primarily perceived as sex-*object* and then, only with increasing sophistication as person-*object*. The Gay monogamous relationship is one in which the participants, through non-competitive instinctual inclinations *and contrary to cultural inheritances*, perceive each other as Equals and learn, usually through deeply painful trials-and-errors, to experience each other, to continuously to grow, and to develop *with* each other, *empathically*—as SUBJECT.[31]

This idea of subject-SUBJECT consciousness serves as the basis for beliefs regarding equality at radical faerie gatherings and sanctuaries. It is also directly tied to male femininity, for it is through rejection of heteronormative forms of masculinity that faeries come to recognize their natural potential to approach others as subjects rather than as economic and/or sexual objects. In his ethnography of radical faeries, Peter Hennen notes that the egalitarian ideals of subject-SUBJECT consciousness are not always met at radical faerie sanctuaries. There have been struggles over power and control between leaders of the movement throughout its history. Hennen is also critical of subject-SUBJECT consciousness because of its assumptions regarding the directionality of gay male objectification within clone culture that, Hennen suggests, could just as easily be an object-OBJECT consciousness that is inherently egalitarian.[32]

Although radical faerie culture is often difficult to define because of its individualistic approach to identity, ritual, and spirituality, both the ideal of subject-SUBJECT consciousness and the essentialist view of gay men as a type of third gender (naturally tied to spirituality) serve as fundamental tenets of radical faerie beliefs, which recur throughout various cultural practices that emphasize spirituality, egalitarianism, and, especially, male femininity.

Hay views Judeo-Christian religious traditions as mechanisms of domination over, and the oppression of, gay men. While the open persecution of gay men in many traditions played an important role, Western religions were seen as reproducing and enforcing the forms of gender inequality that led to the objectification of women. Through hetero-imitation of straight masculinity, this pattern of objectification spread to gay men, destroying the natural spirituality associated with gay male femininity. For Hay, Judeo-Christian theology was directly responsible for psychological and spiritual damage to the beloved "sissy boys" who may eventually come to identify as radical faeries.

### Expressions of Male Femininity

Building on Hay's view of gay men as a "third gender," radical faerie identity and spirituality are regularly described in terms of androgyny and male femininity in particular. This combination of opposing gender "energies" is the foundation of faerie spirituality: "We embody masculine and feminine energies in a unique way . . . the unconscious regenerative Earth Mother and the conscious constructive Sky Father. These seemingly opposite qualities often prove destructive when used in and for themselves. Our work as Faeries is to bring harmony between the two—to take the gifts of the Father back to the Mother."[33] As in other gender-crossing religious rituals, the harmony between genders realized at faerie gatherings may involve momentary experiences of heightened consciousness obtained through an embrace of male femininity. However, given faerie views of gay male femininity as innate, faerie spiritual experiences of gender crossing are framed in terms of gaining awareness of one's natural, androgynous identity. Embracing male femininity not only allows for spiritual transcendence but also allows for a return to the sissy that heterosexual society has tried to destroy. The experience of this recognition parallels other forms of spiritual awakening or conversion. One faerie describes this transformative moment of recognition:

> The day that the Queer Gods first touched my heart, awakening me to glimmers of what amazing adventures of spirit and flesh were still yet to come to me and my people, my old paradigms shattered. That day I saw visions of possibility, some magnificent, some horrific. The most important gift to come from this experience was the solid knowledge that the Divine was not limited to a heterosexual, bi-gendered, universalist worldview only, with no room for my own experiences springing from a newly formed understanding of the cosmos from multiverse view. The taste of this freedom touched me in all ways, transforming, once again, all previous possibilities of being queer in the world.[34]

Thus, while many religious traditions have rituals that involve forms of gender crossing to obtain momentary heightened consciousness, radical faeries see gender crossing as a means to a permanent change in consciousness. This change is a way of returning "home" to the spiritually gifted natural male femininity at the foundation of faerie beliefs.

Following Hay's view of faeries as not-men or a third gender, the question of whether or not faeries should actually be considered "men" is one that is regularly discussed in faerie communities. Indeed, given the goal of eliminating hetero-normative assumptions of masculinity, obtaining feminine spirituality is central to faerie spiritual experience. As one faerie described their experiences of goddess worship: "If I am, you know, the Goddess I am embodying what comes to me as this goddess energy, although I'm still holding on to the fact that I have a penis and I am a man . . . being gender variant is very important for me. It's not just about putting on women's clothes. It's about, you know . . . really getting in there and investigating what does it mean to be in this persona . . . how much of this is still me and how much of this is gay man . . . and how much is this what women are like?"[35] In seeking feminine spirituality, some faeries follow Hay in rejecting the label of "men" to describe faerie gender identity. However, the spiritual gift faeries possess is understood as unique to gay men, and male sexuality is central to faerie spirituality. Debates about the gender of radical faeries typically fall on the side of identification as men:

So, are Radical Faeries men? We rush to the shelter of we're all self-defining, the shapes, sizes and colors scattered through my stack of RFD [a popular radical faerie magazine], the chronicle of our tribe, and they look like men to me. Are looks deceiving? Am I just projecting? Is man a word we Faeries cannot own?

It's easy to forget we walk down different paths to Circle. To me, men are gravity. To me, men are nutrition. To me, men are passion. To me, Gatherings are forest rolls, stretching roots in the soil and weaving branches across the sun- and moonlit mountains of our lives. Pan, Cernunnos, Odin, Zeus, Apollo, Raven, Hermes, Thoth. Father of us all. To me.[36]

As the faerie movement grew, some sanctuaries and gatherings began to allow women to participate and the question of whether or not faeries must be "men" became a major issue. Despite the faerie focus on feminine spirituality and goddess worship, many faeries objected to the inclusion of women. One faerie reportedly complained about the presence of women by saying, "How am I supposed to worship the Goddess with all the feminine energy around?"[37]

Thus, for many faeries, faerie femininity is necessarily a male-embodied form of femininity. Given the essentialist views of queer spirituality at the foundation of faerie beliefs, it is not surprising that many faeries would adopt a similarly essentialist understanding of gender as founded in biology. Some faerie circles specifically allow transgender women to participate, while rejecting the participation of transgender men, because they were categorized as female at birth.[38] For some faeries, the inclusion of women or trans men went against the very foundations of faerie identity and spirituality:

> At the Nomenus Great Circle in Portland in 1997 I was blindsided by events and soon severed my relationship with them. Without consulting the Great Circle, a group had invited a heterosexual woman to take up residence on the land for five months, calling it "a visit." A week is a visit, not five months. It was a *fait accompli* not communicated in advance. I felt railroaded and disrespected by the subsequent decision, which I should have blocked, which essentially precluded gay male sacred space unless it was specifically asked for.

> The land became heterosexualized, desexualized generic residential hippie commune. Women living on the land, however, well intentioned, undermined and cut off at the root the sacred gay male space for which we had bought and developed the land—where we could do the hard work of integrating sex and spirit.[39]

For faeries like Artwit (quoted above), a specifically all-male community is required for the spiritual experience of awakening one's inner femininity and spirituality. The presence of women is felt to reproduce the heterosexist world outside of the sanctuary and thus destroy the safe space created by an exclusively gay male community. For faeries of this mindset, the spiritual gift of faerie femininity can only exist as a form of male-bodied femininity.

## Conclusion

Experiences of male femininity are associated with spiritual transformations across a wide range of religious traditions. Radical faeries appropriate elements from a variety of traditions and bring them together to develop a unique view of male femininity as an innate spiritual gift. Rather than accepting hegemonic norms that denigrate male femininity, radical faeries reframe their femininity in terms of spiritual transcendence. Thus, for radical faeries, queer spirituality and religious experiences emanate directly from male femininity. Rather than being viewed as insufficiently masculine, radical faeries view male femininity as a unique spiritual endowment that allows them to reach levels of consciousness beyond those available to hetero-cis-normative individuals.

For radical faeries, male femininity is an essential trait of all gay men. This innate femininity allows faeries to understand each other as equal subjects, free from the sexual objectification associated with heterosexual society. However, gay men are under extreme pressure to imitate heterosexual men—sometimes to diminish social stigma but, more often, to ensure their own safety. For radical faeries, this hetero-imitation leads gay men to treat one another as sexual objects similar to the way that straight men treat heterosexual women. Many forms of organized religion contribute to the social pressure to imitate heterosexual male forms of masculinity. In particular, Judeo-Christian traditions are seen as working to destroy the inner sissy that all gay men share. In promoting homophobic views, traditional religions attempt to destroy the spirituality that comes from possessing natural male femininity.

Radical faeries work to create spaces where individuals can cultivate the spiritual gift of femininity and gender nonconformity. The faerie path involves a return to the natural male femininity the heterosexual world has tried to destroy. For it is only by shedding the "ugly green frog-skin of heteroimitation" that gay men can realize the full potential of their precious spiritual gift: male femininity.

NOTES

1 Gregory Bateson, *Naven: A Survey of the Problems Suggested by a Composite Picture of the Culture of a New Guinea Tribe Drawn from Three Points of View* (Cambridge: Cambridge University Press, 1936).
2 Sabrina Petra Ramet, "Gender Reversals and Gender Cultures: An Introduction," in *Gender Reversals and Gender Cultures: Anthropological and Historical Perspectives*, ed. Sabrina Petra Ramet (New York: Routledge, 1996), 1–21; Marjorie Mandelstam Balzer, "Sacred Genders in Siberia: Shamans, Bear Festivals, and Androgyny," in Ramet, ed., *Gender Reversals*, 164–82; Tanvir Anjum, "Androgyny as a Metaphorical Practice in South Asian Sufi Culture," *Journal of Asian Civilizations* 38, no. 1 (2015): 91–112.
3 Johannes N. Vorster, "Androgyny and Early Christianity," *Religion and Theology* 15 (2008): 97–132; quote from Galatians 3:28.
4 See Anne Bolin, "Traversing Gender: Cultural Context and Gender Practices," in Ramet, ed., *Gender Reversals*, 22–51.
5 Annika Zemp and Ulf Liebe, "Exploring the Relationship between Holistic Spirituality and Gender Essentialism among Swiss University Students," *Social Compass* 66, no. 2 (2019): 238–55; Edward H. Thompson, "Beneath the Status Characteristic: Gender Variations in Religiousness," *Journal for the Scientific Study of Religion*, 30 (1991): 381–94; Edward H. Thompson and Kathryn R. Remmes, "Does Masculinity Thwart Being Religious? An Examination of Older Men's Religiousness," *Journal for the Scientific Study of Religion* 41, no. 3 (2002): 521–52; Leslie Francis and Carolyn Wilcox, "Religiosity and Femininity: Do Women Really Hold a More Positive Attitude towards Christianity?," *Journal for the Scientific Study of Religion* 37, no. 3 (1998): 462–69. See also David B. Simpson, Dinah S. Cloud, Jody L. Newman, and Dale R. Fuqua, "Sex and Gender Differences in Religiousness and Spirituality," *Journal of Psychology and Theology* 36, no. 1 (2008): 42–52.
6 Calvin Merce and Thomas W. Duram, "Religious Mysticism and Gender Orientation," *Journal for the Scientific Study of Religion* 38, no. 1 (1999): 175–82.
7 James R. Mahalik and Hugh D. Lagan, "Examining Masculine Gender Role Conflict and Stress in Relation to Religious Orientation and Spiritual Well-Being," *Psychology of Men and Masculinity* 2, no. 1 (2001): 24–33.

8   Amy Peebles, "Sexual and Spiritual Identity Transformation among Ex-Gays and Ex-Ex-Gays: Narrative a New Self" (PhD diss. University of Texas at Austin, 2004).
9   David Green, "What Men Want? Initial Thoughts on the Male Goddess Movement," *Religion and Gender* 2, no. 2 (2012): 305–27.
10  Jason Crawford, "'Go Forth and Sin Some More!' A Performance Geography of the San Francisco Sisters of Perpetual Indulgence" (PhD diss., Concordia University, 2011).
11  Christina L. Ivey, "'If We're Mocking Anything, It's Organized Religion': The Queer Holy Fool Style of the Sisters of Perpetual Indulgence" (PhD diss., University of Nebraska, 2016).
12  Melissa M. Wilcox, "'Spiritual Sluts': Uncovering Gender, Ethnicity, and Sexuality in the Post-Secular," *Women's Studies* 41 (2012): 639–59.
13  Michael York, "New Age Commodification and Appropriation of Spirituality," *Journal of Contemporary Religion* 16, no. 3 (2001): 361–72, 364.
14  See Scott Morgensen, "Arrival at Home: Radical Faerie configurations of Sexuality and Place," *GLQ: A Journal of Gay and Lesbian Studies* 15, no. 1 (2009): 67–96.
15  Robert Bly, *Iron John: A Book about Men* (Boston: Addison-Wesley, 1990).
16  Stuart Timmons, *The Trouble with Harry Hay: Founder of the Modern Gay Movement* (Boston: Alyson, 1990), 265ff.
17  Timmons, *Trouble with Harry Hay*, 267.
18  See Bill Rogers, "The Radical Faeries Movement: A Queer Spirit Pathway," *Social Alternatives* 14, no. 4 (1995): 34–37; Peter Hennen, *Faeries, Bears, and Leathermen: Men in Community Queering the Masculine* (Chicago: University of Chicago Press 2008); and Harry Hay, *Radically Gay: Gay Liberation in the Words of Its Founder*, ed. Will Roscoe (Boston: Beacon, 1996).
19  Hay, *Radically Gay*, 255.
20  Hay, 254.
21  Timmons, *Trouble with Harry Hay*.
22  See, for example, Lester B. Brown, *Two-Spirit People: American Indian, Lesbian Women, and Gay Men* (New York: Routledge, 1997); Jenny L. Davis, "'More than Just "Gay Indians"': Intersecting Articulations of Two-Spirit Gender, Sexuality, and Indigenousness," in *Queer Excursions: Retheorizing Binaries in Language, Gender, and Sexuality*, ed. Lal Zimman, Jenny L. Davis, and Joshua Raclaw (New York: Oxford University Press, 2014), 62–80; Carolyn Epple, "Coming to Terms with Navajo *nádleehí*: A Critique of Berdache, 'Gay,' 'Alternate Gender,' and 'Two-Spirit,'" *American Ethnologist* 25, no. 2: 267–90; Brian Joseph Giley, *Becoming Two-Spirit: Gay Identity and Social Acceptance in Indian Country* (Lincoln: University of Nebraska Press, 2006); and Lal Zimman and Kira Hall, "Language, Embodiment, and the 'Third Sex,'" in *Language and Identities*, ed. Dominic Watt and Carmen Llamas (Edinburgh: Edinburgh University Press, 2009), 166–78. See also Tatonetti, in this volume.
23  Will Roscoe, "Prelude—Welcome to Planet Faery," in *The Fire in Moonlight: Stories from the Radical Faeries, 1975–2010*, ed. Mark Thompson (Maple Shade NJ: White Crane, 2011, 19–26, 23.

24 Elizabeth Povinelli, *Empire of Love: Toward a Theory of Intimacy, Genealogy, and Carnality* (Durham, NC: Duke University Press, 2006); Kyle Andrew Pape, "Navigating Consciousness toward Liberation: Investigating a Contemporary Radical Faerie Manifestation through a Decolonial Lens" (master's thesis, Colorado State University, 2013); Scott Morgensen, *Spaces between Us: Queer Settler Colonialism and Indigenous Decolonization* (Minneapolis: University of Minnesota Press 2011).
25 See Pape, *Navigating Consciousness*.
26 Morgensen, *Spaces between Us*.
27 Hay, *Radically Gay*, 246.
28 Rodgers, "Radical Faeries Movement," 35.
29 See Morgensen, *Spaces between Us*.
30 On clones, see Martin Levine, *Gay Macho: The Life and Death of the Gay Clone*, ed. Michael Kimmel (New York: New York University Press, 1998).
31 Hay, *Radically Gay*, 210.
32 See Hennen, *Faeries, Bears, and Leathermen*; and Timmons, *Trouble with Harry Hay*.
33 Allen Page, "Army of Lovers," *RFD Magazine*, 1979, 38–39.
34 Donald L. Engstrom-Reese, "Queer Spirit Memories Grown in the Midwest," in Thompson, ed., *Fire in Moonlight*, 63–65.
35 Quoted in John Abraham Stover, "When Pan Met Wendy: The Negotiation and Contention of Gendered Spiritualities in the Radical Faeries" (master's thesis, Loyola University, 2005), 31.
36 Yusef Leo Schuman, "No Authority but Our Heart," in Thompson, ed., *Fire in Moonlight*, 247.
37 Stover, "When Pan met Wendy," 31
38 See Stover.
39 Artwit, "Impressions of an Improbable Faerie," in Thompson, ed., *Fire in Moonlight*, 193–202.

PART 6

# Male Femininities and Institutions

The final section of the book brings together a collection of perspectives about the ways in which male femininities are constructed and enacted in the social institutions of family and work. Just as with gender, institutions are socially constructed. Even though they might seem unwavering and immutable, institutions are malleable, flexible, and responsive to social change. All of the readings in this section show how institutions can both enable and constrain practices and expressions of male femininities, and each illustrates the possibility for social change and new gender imaginings.

All social institutions are gendered. This means that gender is used as an organizing principle in the ways that women, men, transgender, and nonbinary folks are channeled into different, and often unequally valued, social spaces. Gender—a persistent feature of work, family, education, sports, media, and our political and criminal justice systems—is present in the "processes, practices, images, and ideologies, and distributions of power in the various sectors of social life."[1] What is more, each of these institutions is also profoundly shaped by other intersecting inequalities that differentially influence the gendered choices available to social actors, as well as the consequences of these choices. The readings in this section show how social class, race, and sexuality intersect with gender to constitute different expressions of male femininities.

One way that the institutions of work and family are gendered is in the feminization of housework and childcare. Even though trends have changed over time, and we no longer expect the traditional man-as-breadwinner and woman-as-homemaker model, women continue to do more family labor than men. When women and men are both expected to remain in the labor force throughout their lives, the practice of sharing equally in childcare and housework is still very much more of an ideal than a reality. Yet cultural changes abound. Men who parent are now expected to be emotionally and physically present in the lives of their children and to partake in their care. Other cultural shifts such as the rise of single-father and gay, bisexual, and queer families are chipping away at age-old scripts and slowly transforming how we think about masculinities, femininities, and parenting.

Sociologist Barbara Risman's classic research on men who were forced into parenting without the help of a woman (ie., divorced and widowed heterosexual fathers) revealed that men described themselves as more nurturing and empathetic—or, in a word, more feminine—than did married fathers.[2] Her findings were transformative in exposing the ways that changes in social structure or circumstance can alter gendered personality traits. Likewise, scholars have shown that once gay men become fathers, some report a stronger desire to spend time with their children than to advance in their careers—a pattern that directly contradicts much of what we know about heterosexual fathers who commonly prioritize the role of breadwinner over the role of caregiver.[3]

Building on this body of scholarship, Jennifer Randles's chapter in this section demonstrates how programs that target low-income fathers of color accentuate the emotional and relational aspects of paternal involvement in ways that allow men to redefine femininized parenting practices as masculine. These programs provide men a mechanism to manage the tension between expectations of breadwinning and their inability to live up to those expectations in the face of systemic racism and economic inequities. Echoing other scholarship on fathering, Randles shows that, as parenting becomes increasingly central to men's family-based identities, men must appropriate femininity to cope with changing gender relations.[4] Her findings demonstrate the limits of subversion for these programs, as even though many men reject authoritarian understandings of fatherhood, they still struggle to meet new demands for caring and emotionality without feeling marginalized as feminine. Randles cautions that fatherhood initiatives that fall short of explicitly encouraging nongendered egalitarian parenting will ultimately pose little challenge to the existing gender order. However, her study still indicates the potential for imagining new configurations of parenting that creatively merge masculine expectations of breadwinning with feminine expectations of caregiving in novel ways.

Another cultural transformation in our contemporary family landscape is a small but notable trend of parents' growing acceptance, and even support, of their children's gender nonconformity. Reading Graciela Slesaransky-Poe's chapter alongside Joshua Adair's personal narrative is particularly telling of this shift. Adair's account of his own's family shame around his femininity in the late 1980s and 1990s stands in stark contrast to the way Slesaransky-Poe and her contemporaries grappled with their children's feminine and fluid gender expressions only a decade later. Slesaransky-Poe found that as the parents with whom she spoke grew to accept their kids' femininity, they became "radical translators" of the gender order, revealing the ways that a progressive gender consciousness can emerge through navigating mundane interactions with and for one's gender-nonconforming children. The fact that she and the parents in her small sample were also highly educated, mostly white, and middle- and upper-class allowed them to use their privilege to challenge the heteronormative gender binary and support their male children's childhood displays of femininity.

Regardless of social class or institutional context, femininity in men and boys incites discomfort in others, and many of the readings in this section spotlight the ways that male femininity is policed and disciplined. Slesaransky-Poe remembered that, "the happier our sons felt by freely expressing their femininity, the stronger the feeling of distress, discomfort, and confusion others around them felt." And, as Adair's traumatic memories of almost being murdered by his brother when forced to drink battery acid, demonstrate, these feelings of discomfort and confusion can quickly turn violent.

As we imagine new opportunities for social change and gender resistance, research on workplace culture provides support that such change is possible, even in the most hypermasculine of institutions characterized by risk, danger, fearlessness, and physicality. Studies of coal miners, deep sea oil riggers, and firefighters show that men's workplace discrimination against feminine men and women does not have to be inevitable.[5] Roscoe C. Scarborough's chapter explores how volunteer fighters with attributes or practices that depart from an institutional understanding of masculinity either strategically access the fire service brotherhood through careful impression management or subvert prevailing gender norms by challenging deeply institutionalized conceptions of masculinity. Scarborough's findings provide support for the ways that workplace discrimination can be interrupted by the actions of defiant actors.

Taken together, the readings in this section show that even though institutions resist change, they are not unchangeable. When even a small number of defiant actors begin to question the existing order, institutionalized norms can unravel, opening up emergent opportunities for generations of folks who can then do gender differently.

NOTES

1 J. Acker, "From Sex Roles to Gendered Institutions," *Contemporary Sociology* 21, no. 5 (1992): 565–69.
2 B., Risman, "Can Men 'Mother'? Life as a Single Father," *Family Relations* 35, no. 1 (1986): 95–102.
3 Tina Miller, *Making Sense of Fatherhood* (Cambridge: Cambridge University Press, 2010); Nicholas W. Townsend, *The Package Deal: Marriage, Work, and Fatherhood in Men's Lives* (Philadelphia, PA: Temple University Press, 2002); Dana Berkowitz, "Maternal Instincts, Biological Clocks, and Soccer Moms: Gay Men's Parenting and Family Narratives," *Symbolic Interaction* 34, no. 4 (2011); Abbie Goldberg, *Gay Dads: Transitions to Adoptive Fatherhood* (New York: New York University Press, 2012).
4 Berkowitz, "Maternal Instincts"; Goldberg, *Gay Dads*.
5 Angus Chen, "Invisibilia: How Learning to Be Vulnerable Can Make Life Safer," NPR, June 17, 2016, https://npr.org; Jessica Smith Rolston, *Mining Coal and Undermining Gender: Rhythms of Work and Family in the American West* (New Brunswick, NJ: Rutgers University Press, 2014).

## 22

## Funeral Rights

JOSHUA G. ADAIR

As a feminine kid growing up in rural west central Illinois in the late eighties and early nineties, I learned quickly to disguise and to obscure my femininity as much as I could. Everything about me—my gestures, voice, movements—proved insufficiently boyish, according to everyone from my paternal grandmother to my third grade teacher. My older brother, three years my senior, took an especially strong dislike to my femininity, which embarrassed him in front of his friends and made him a target for harassment, too. My femininity, it seems, was transferable; my brother proved guilty by association. In retaliation, he tried to murder me on multiple occasions, including by encouraging me to drink battery acid. Much to his disappointment, following Gloria Gaynor's lead, I survived.

Fearful of and traumatized by the terrible ways my femininity caused many people to treat me, I began devoting enormous amounts of energy to downplaying and disguising it. I wanted to obliterate it entirely, but it always came bubbling back up. To this day, even though I understand it as a construct and a performance, I also know that femininity is not a dress that can simply be taken off and hidden in a closet. Even when carefully controlled, mine always emerges at awkward moments, surprising even me. I see myself move a certain way or blurt out something in excitement and know before the moment has passed, usually from the look on my audience's faces, that I have broken some rule that I neither understand nor know how to follow.

Never was this clearer to me than on the morning of my partner's funeral on August 16, 2002. He had struggled with severe mental illness his entire life and, after several failed attempts, succeeded at committing suicide three days earlier. I was heartbroken and inconsolable. My grief was compounded considerably by the fact that his mother—a woman who disapproved of our relationship and me—took control of his funeral arrangements and only grudgingly invited me to attend if I would serve as a pallbearer. As those were premarriage days, I had no rights or say-so in what happened, so I agreed to her terms, as not going would have been unbearable.

As she expressly forbade me from bringing anyone else to the funeral, I showed up alone, anxious and distraught. I was placed in the front row with the other pallbearers—five machinists from the local arsenal with whom Aaron had worked—who were all wearing khaki pants and plaid shirts. Dressed in a sleek black suit, I stuck out like the proverbial sore thumb. The other pallbearers looked stunned and uncomfortable, uncertain why they had been asked to carry someone they had barely known to his final rest. Like the guys with whom I attended high school, my presence raised their hackles right off. They had not suspected anything about Aaron until I appeared; it took only seconds to recognize me for what I am. They did not speak or even look my way as we torturously waited for the services to start.

After they concluded, the pallbearers were asked to line up in the lobby of the funeral home to wait for the casket to be rolled out so that we could load it into the hearse. A receiving line had formed, so our wait was long. As I stood there, hanging my head, I began to weep uncontrollably. I cried so hard that my tears splattered on the floor and polka-dotted my shoes. I was in such a state that I did not even care that my behavior was unmanly. My casket compatriots, however, cared considerably. "She's hysterical," one whispered to his friend and then chuckled softly.

After the casket had been loaded, Aaron's stepfather, a machinist for John Deere and the manliest of men, recognized that I was in no shape to drive myself to the cemetery. He gruffly offered me in a place in their backseat, and I accepted in an embarrassingly cracking voice. I actually squeaked, and his wince made clear that I needed to adjust my actions or incur the consequences. This, of course, suggests that it was all an act—a performance—that could be halted whenever I chose. Femininity is often regarded in this manner, as an artifice adopted to irritate or beguile, depending on the circumstances. I never experienced it as such, but my actions were critiqued frequently enough to teach me that others see it that way.

I cried softly all the way to the cemetery and avoided answering questions to avoid another verbal violation of his masculine mores. Sitting in the stifling sun at the cemetery, I continued to cry. I attracted a great deal of unwanted attention as I prayed for the entire affair to end. At one point Aaron's uncle approached me. "Would you like a rose from the casket spray to keep?" he asked. It seemed such a kind gesture for him to acknowledge our attachment and my probable desire for some memento. For a split second I thought, "That's something my grandmother would do." And it is, but it's also something I would do, so I squeaked out a "Yes." "Well, then, go get one!" he barked, seemingly annoyed at my presumption that he meant to collect one for me. Who did I think I was, a damsel in distress?

There's not much to tell after my rose rebuke. No matter how hard I studied and practiced, my femininity always managed to seep out. Over time, I became more comfortable with it and fought it less. That's the privilege of achieving some age and of surviving in a world that is frequently hostile to femininities. It still, on occasion, invites trouble—especially in moments of extreme emotion. I always return to that morning of August 16, 2002, when I was frustrated with femininity and the way our culture tends to feel about it, especially since I love it. I had tried to change not because I wanted to, but because my behavior elicited so many negative responses. I also resented that behaviors I had worked so hard to quell could suddenly rear up and demand expression despite the fact that they only complicated the situation further. In hindsight, however, for all that those moments caused others to characterize me as overwrought or ingenuine, I regard the sincerity and anguish in my response to the sudden, violent death of a loved one as authentic and deeply representative of who I understand myself to be. I had every right to express my sorrow, even if it struck them as unnatural.

# 23

## When Our Boys Wished to Be Girls

### *A Retrospective Look at Parenting Gender-Nonconforming Young Boys*

GRACIELA SLESARANSKY-POE

My eighteen-year-old son was three when he began to express his gender in ways that defied society's expectations of boyhood. Back then, families with children like ours did not have a lot of guidance in navigating what, at that time, felt like very scary and unfamiliar territory. In those early days, we lacked the confidence and conviction we now have that there was no harm in allowing our boys to nourish their feminine sides, that the best we could do was to love them, to embrace them, to listen to them, and to follow their leads. We did not realize that by partnering with their schools, learning to make our way through the legal system, and surrounding them—and us—with supportive and welcoming communities, our children would not only be OK, but would thrive and grow into well-adjusted, self-confident, and healthy young adults.

In those days, the few available resources were neither affirming nor helpful. Some attempted to cast blame on allegedly overprotective mothers or absent fathers while others promoted conversion therapy that included banning some colors and forbidding dress-up play, approaches that can lead to physical, mental, and psychological distress that could result in self-harm and even suicide. Psychological treatments were allegedly designed to bring gender expression in line with social norms and to alleviate children's distress, discomfort, or confusion.[1] It was clear to us, however, that it was not our children who were distressed, uncomfortable, or confused.

The happier our sons felt by freely expressing their femininity, the stronger the feeling of distress, discomfort, and confusion others around them seemed to feel. We worried about our sons' futures, worried that they—and their siblings—would be teased, bullied, excluded, and isolated. We experienced deep angst and fear for our their lives and safety. We endured stigma and judgment by people who had never walked in our shoes. We felt a great sense of aloneness. As parents, we silently asked: Had we done something wrong?

I clearly remember that, back then, we wondered if our young sons would grow up to be gay. Many families, including ours, would welcome that possibility. Yet, even though we initially interpreted our children's "signals as incipient homosexuality . . . something, often something [we] could not articulate, [led us] to search for a construct outside sexuality to which to attach it."[2] We did not know, at that time, the proper terminology. Over the years, we learned about what is now known as the social construction of gender, the distinction between gender identity and expression, and sexual identity/orientation. Looking back, I wish we could have spared our kids—and ourselves—from the stress and suffering caused by our fears, our ignorance, and our lack of understanding, our not knowing how to disrupt the "gender truth regime."[3] It has taken, and continues to take, time, purpose, education, advocacy, and community to create room for our children, and to allow children like ours to be who they are and to create safe spaces for them to thrive.

## Our Online Community

In 2004, after multiple and extensive online searches, I found a brochure titled *If You Are Concerned about Your Child's Gender Behaviors: A Guide for Parents*, published by the Children's National Medical Center in Washington (CNMC), that helped me begin to understand my son better.[4] It not only explained what, at that time, was labeled "gender variance" but it also mentioned a listserv for families run by psychiatrist Edgardo Menvielle and social worker and psychotherapist Catherine Tuerk, who were also the codirectors of the CNMC Gender Development Program.[5] They shared a similar professional orientation toward supporting gender-nonconforming children and their families. And, for Catherine, this was personal: she is the mother of a now adult man in his forties who was gender-nonconforming as a young child. Catherine and her son were subjected to intensive reparative therapy to help her son become more "boyish." She shared that the pain of those early years was intolerable; the feeling of being seen as a bad mother was unbearable. She was determined to help other families raise and embrace their feminine boys, masculine girls, and gender diverse kids in the most loving, compassionate, and supportive ways.

The very next day, I called Dr. Menvielle, who, after a thorough screening process, gave us access to the listserv. We soon discovered that we were not alone. I spent nights reading email archives and daily posts, many times in tears. Everyone's trepidation, confusion, anxiety, and was so raw and familiar. This community of judgment-free parents and professionals was exactly what we needed. As families, we helped each other support our own children and learn how to deal with the hostile outside world. We learned to become "facilitative parents" who follow our children's lead, strive to allow them to express themselves in their own unique gendered ways, and help them adapt to a world that is hostile to their gender expressions and identities.[6] To quote one of the fathers who shared his story, "The listserv saved my life, my child's life. It saved my marriage. It saved our family."

## The Stories

For the purpose of this chapter, I reached out to a small group of listserv families whose gender-nonconforming boys had grown into teenagers or young adults and now identify as cisgender men.[7] Generally, it is the mothers' voices that we hear the most, so I expressly asked fathers to participate. When the listserv was active, families shared that dads in particular felt discomfort, shame, and even judgment for not being able to help their sons accomplish hegemonic masculinity.[8] I was particularly interested in learning how, over time, mothers' and fathers' early thoughts and feelings might have shifted.

The voices in this chapter come from the parents of four children, mine included. First are Jess and Brian, a white Mormon couple from the Midwest, who had originally struggled to accept their son's feminine interests and expressions, particularly given their religious beliefs and conservative political ideologies.[9] Jess started a support group for Mormon mothers of LGBTQ+ children, and, after seeing the positive impact it had, Brian started one for dads. Next is Erik, a Black man from the Mid-Atlantic, whose parenting experience was shaped by growing up with an older gay brother who died of AIDS and his desire to ensure that his son would live a happy, healthy, productive life. The group also includes Cole, an introverted, soft-spoken, mild-mannered white scientist who works at a university in the Northeast and shared that he felt responsible for his son's gender nonconformity because of not being manly enough himself. And lastly are Lori and Matt, a white couple from California who are very public about their experiences raising their gender-nonconforming son.[10] Lori started the blog Raising my Rainbow and later wrote a book with the same title. Matt, a police officer, also speaks openly about their son's experiences, in particular about how the blog's readership, especially men, "blame" him for his son's gender nonconformity.

All four families have some commonalities that are similar to many of the listerv participants: we are all cis heterosexual biological parents, middle-class, and college educated. Each couple started the process of understanding and acceptance at different stages. Within each couple, the mother arrived at a supportive place first. But, through intense negotiation, all couples were able to find some alignment in the ways our children's gender expressions were "allowed." Not all couples (in and outside our online community) were so fortunate. Many marriages ended in divorces and custody battles, generally centered around the father not being able to come to terms with having a feminine son, blaming the mother for giving into—or accusing her of encouraging—their son's gender nonconformity.

Of the four boys whose parents' experiences are included in this study, three continue to perform in gender-nonconforming ways; one of them is a drag queen. The fourth boy no longer identifies as gender-nonconforming. As stated earlier, gender nonconformity, especially in boys, often appears to signal homosexuality. Two of these boys are openly gay, including the drag queen. The sexual identities of the other two are unknown to the parents.

What follows are the narratives of how these families learned about their sons' gender nonconformity, the different roles that mothers and fathers play in their children's acceptance and advocacy, and the ways parents negotiate and set boundaries to allow their children be who they are while at the same protect them outside their homes. These seemingly individual and personal stories mirror much of the emerging research on the collective experiences of families raising gender-nonconforming children.

### "I Am a Girl! I Have Long Hair!" How Did This All Start?

Our first clear indication of our son's interest in everything feminine was when, at three years of age, he put a blanket on his head and said that he was a girl. He spent a significant amount of time playing dress-up with some of his sister's hand-me-down Disney princess costumes. Looking back, there were multiple signals we previously missed. Between twelve and eighteen months, our son always carried around and even slept with his sister's D.W. stuffed doll (the sister in the animated PBS show *Arthur*), even though he had a stuffed Arthur doll. Arthur and D.W. looked very similar, except D.W. had hair and wore a pink dress. Since preschool, most of his friends had been girls, and the types of activities he engaged in would be classified as feminine. At that time, we thought it was cute. It was not until his insistence on dressing up in girls' clothing became constant that it created some struggles. He wore his princess costumes in the house, and, when we had family and friends over, they would make judgmental comments, making us feel very conflicted about how to respond to our son.

Similarly, Erik shared with me that his son's first expressions of femininity were when "[he] would use his clothing or his sister's clothing to effect stereotypically feminine outfits and appearance . . . He also showed preference for more feminine activities such as ballet dancing (specifically the ballerina's role) and was much more interested in performances and activities that are typically feminine (dance performances, figure skating, etc.)." Our boys were fascinated and almost obsessed with what sociologist Emily Kane calls "icons of femininity," wearing pink or frilly clothing–skirts, dresses, or tights–and playing dress up in the most feminine attire possible.[11] They enjoyed having their fingernails or toenails polished, played with Barbie dolls, and loved to dance, especially ballet.

For some of our children, their desire to dress up was so strong that if they did not have what they needed, they improvised and accessorized with what was available to them. Jess and Brian, who only have boys, recalled how their son, at age two, would "take beads off the Christmas tree" to make necklaces or try on a neighbor's shoes. "He wanted to be pretty," said Brian.

For those of us who also had daughters, it became evident that we had different standards for our children. We accepted practices of girlhood masculinity and yet we struggled with boyhood femininity, a pattern that reinforced a "form of cultural sexism," or the disproportionate value placed on normative masculinity that allows girls far more latitude to display gender nonconformity than it does for boys.[12] Our disparate and asymmetrical reactions also mirror other studies of parents of gender-nonconforming children.[13]

Kane also found that parents, particularly fathers, accept or encourage some tendencies considered atypical for boys, but that this acceptance is balanced by efforts to approximate the hegemonic ideals of masculinity. The following narrative from Erik mirrors Kane's findings:

> In a male-centric society, people holding roles typically held by "dads" would probably have more difficulty accepting [nonconformity] to expectations of how a son should be "male." . . . In the case of dads with a gender-nonconforming son, the dad may feel a sense of failure about not "teaching" the son how to be masculine, or possibly even an inadequacy in their own masculinity. Taking these to heart could lead to potentially destructive behaviors exhibited by the parent. That's not to say that the mom could not equally be affected, but I expect that in our society today, it's biased towards the dads.

Those feelings of failure and inadequacy may translate to fathers censoring their children's expressions, which in turn places an even larger burden on mothers, who may find themselves attempting to mitigate both their son's and husband's (or other male partner's) feelings and emotions.[14]

### It's a Phase: "He's Gonna Grow Out of It"

At the beginning, some parents thought the gender nonconformity was an experimental phase our kids would outgrow. Jess remembered talking to the pediatrician when her son was three: "The pediatrician basically just said, 'Oh, he'll grow out of it. This is like, this is not a thing. He's gonna grow out of it.' But he never did, of course. He never did."

When relatives kept telling Cole and his wife that it was probably a phase, they both would say to each other, "I don't think this is a phase." Erik said that he also thought this at first, or that it was his son's attempt to mirror his older sister or mother. "But it became clear that it was more than that," he said, "as his attraction to feminine expression seemed to exceed theirs."

Once we realized that it was not a phase, we felt the need to make meaning out of our own and the world's different, often conflicting, explanations for our sons' gender nonconformity. We were subjected to scrutiny, disapproval, unsolicited advice, and lectures about our parenting practices and philosophies. Dealing with our own feelings of confusion and guilt was difficult and painful. For many of us, there was a pull between the rational and the emotional. Many of us consider ourselves to be open-minded, progressive people. But, very early on, seeing our own sons in these situations generated significant cognitive dissonance. We had many conflicted emotions and feelings, including hypocrisy. One dad reflected on those early feelings in a listserv post,

> The reason I joined [the listserv] was not so much to gain insight into how to advocate on behalf of my gender-variant son, but to better come to terms with my own feelings . . . I will be honest, daily seeing my son in a dress, and accessorizing with a pom pom symbolizing "girl" hair and gaudy bead necklaces has been, and is, heartbreaking for me. Yes, I'll admit it, I am disappointed. [My wife] has been in pain as well—breaking into sobs two or three times a week. But her experience has not been exactly the same as mine so I'm mostly speaking for myself here. I have had a very difficult time relating to [my son]—playing Barbies, throwing him up in the air as he fantasizes being a ballerina, etc. I was prepared for our son to not have the same interests as I have. But in no way was I prepared for this. I'm not a super-macho guy. I have a lot of "feminine" qualities. Added to the feelings of loss and guilt are feelings of hypocrisy. I believe in full respect for every gender variation and sexual orientation. I even teach a class on gender, race, class, and sexual orientation in the media from a liberal perspective (I am a professor). Yet when your own son is outside the gender norm, it truly challenges whether you can walk the walk.[15]

Interestingly, when I reached out to this dad to discuss this post a few years later, his reaction was one of great surprise. He did not recall having written it. He was both shocked and relieved that, in just a few years, he did not identify with those negative feelings anymore. Despite this father's change in perspective, his narrative reveals how even self-proclaimed open-minded parents can feel tremendous amounts of social and cultural pressures towrd gender conformity.

### Doing the Work: Mothers Researching, Advocating, and Accepting Children's Gender Diversity

A common theme on our listserv was that mothers, or those in the mother role, took the lead in researching children's gender nonconformity, a pattern which led to accepting, embracing, and advocating for our child's gender nonconformity before our male partners did. Our sons' "consistent, insistent, and persistent" expression of gender nonconformity resulted in the mothers' "consistent, insistent, and persistent" search for answers and explanations. And it was we who facilitated our husbands' journeys to understanding and acceptance. For example, consider Lori's experience: she explained that she spent her days "finding the research." When Matt came home from work, Lori would say, "This is what I'm finding out today." Matt understood that Lori was processing the information and giving it back to him in ways he would be able to access. He welcomed it, and her labor: "I'm game for that but just highlight the text I need to read," he said.

Mothers' quests for ensuring children's well-being enabled many of us to rethink gender altogether.[16] Mothers play a critical role in teaching alternate beliefs, making gender diversity visible, limiting heteronormative influence, and challenging hegemonic beliefs as we make space for our children's gender diversity in and out of our homes. That process, which is "taken on almost exclusively by mothers, invokes competing maternal mandates of raising 'proper' children versus modeling selfless devotion to children's happiness and well-being."[17] Paradoxically, as we play a central role as advocates for our children, by becoming experts in issues of gender diversity and advocating for gender equity, we reinforce gender stereotypes of women as the primary nurturers and caretakers of their children.[18]

While all parents experience transformation from and with their children, what we experienced with our own children felt unprecedented. We did not set out to practice gender-progressive politics from the outset; we came to a new gender consciousness and understanding by virtue of our children's assertions as expressed in the daily unfolding of family life.[19]

## Fathers and the Blame Game: "It's Not That I'm a Weak Father!"

In many cases, fathers feel pressure to comply with some form of normative masculinity. In her study on parents of gender-nonconforming children, Kane found that heterosexual fathers typically seek to "accomplish their son's gender by their own personal endorsement of hegemonic masculinity, while heterosexual mothers and gay parents are more likely to be motivated by accountability to others in relation to those ideals."[20] In short, heterosexual fathers invoked a sense of accountability to their own moral or normative framework and felt uniquely responsible for not having crafted appropriately masculine sons.

Lori, the mother with the blog Raising My Rainbow told me that she gets hate mail from men who, in her words, "seem to be hypermasculine." They tell her she is "messing up her child and that her child is horrible," that this is "'all her husband's fault." She elaborated: "Either they think that I wanted a daughter so I'm forcing my son to become a daughter, or it's his fault [and could have been prevented], if he were around more, if he were a better dad, if he were more manly, and if his sperm wasn't messed up." Her husband, Matt, laughed and added:

> That's what's funny. They obviously don't know about our family dynamic. A lot of them say, "Oh the dad's not around, that's why he's like that." Well they don't know anything. . . . They don't know that I'm here all the time. They'll say, "Where's this dad? Where's the dad that . . ." And I'm like, if they met me and sat down and had a beer with me they'd be like, "Holy shit! This guy is here, he is involved. He is, you know, what's considered a man's man." You know? But it's really easy for them to attack her and be like, "The reason your kid is like this is because there's no father, there's no dad in the picture."

In his explanation, Matt defends his role as a father who is both present and involved and reaffirms his normative masculinity as a "man's man," someone with whom his critics could sit down and have a beer. Invoking normative masculine tropes of beer drinking is one of the ways Matt can manage the (mis)conception that his own failed masculinity is the reason he is unable to craft his son's normative gender identity.

Historically, causes of gender nonconformity were attributed to some parental deficit. Indeed, parents themselves were the targets of correction along with their children. Early clinical interventions were designed to phase out parental approval of nonconformity as well as parents' roles in perpetuating their child's "problem."[21] Jake Pyne states that clinicians taught parents behavior modification techniques and "corrective treatment" that encouraged gender normative activities and discouraged gender-nonconforming expression.[22]

For Cole, the early days of his son's gender nonconformity created a lot of tension with his wife, mostly because his child's grandparents blamed him. According to Cole, "[My wife] and I never really fought, honestly, which is a miracle. It was mostly dealing with the tension. Only one grandparent basically said, 'I think you guys are doing the right thing.' But three of the four were unhappy; and two of them were very unhappy. That created a lot of tension. But it never put a wedge between me and [my wife]. It was more like, 'Okay, how are we going to deal with this?'" Cole took comfort in theories of gender nonconformity that pointed to genetic and biological explanations, and eschewed environmental and psychological factors:

> I felt relief because now I had research I could follow and a resource that said very clearly that this has nothing to do with the way you parent. Two of the grandparents were basically saying that this was an effect of me being a weak father. So, to be able to say, "No, there's been some research around this stuff, and it has nothing to do with that. It's genetic." ... It was such a relief. I was so emotional about that aspect of things.

Families use different narratives to make sense of their children's gender nonconformity. Some resort to biomedical discourses that locate gender diversity within the larger area of normal human variation.[23] Others resort to spirituality. Cole found solace in the existence of research that excluded parenting style but faulted genetics in explaining his son's gender nonconformity.

### There Are Many Ways of Being a Boy! But Not Everyone Knows That Yet

Like their parents, children constructed a variety of stories to explain why they felt different from other children. Catherine, the listserv cofacilitator, told me that some children may say, "I am half girl and half boy," or "I think I swallowed a girl," or "I am a girl on the inside and a boy on the outside," or "I am a girl." One afternoon, after picking up my son from preschool, he surprised me with a deep metaphysical question: "Mom, do you know that when we die, we are born again?" He went on to say, "Mom, I was a girl before, and now I am a boy, but I will be a girl again. And you were a boy before, now you are a girl, and you will be a boy again." My son was probably only four years old, and already he was searching profoundly for ways to make sense of himself.

Catherine taught us to say that there are different ways of being a boy, and that these are all acceptable. Consider this email she sent to the listserv in 2007: "It is critical to tell them over and over that there are different kinds of boys. Keep it simple. There are boys who like boy things, boys who like boy and girl things, and boys who like mostly girl things. They also need to know that unfortunately most people do not know that there are different kinds of boys. This is why they can't always play dress up or with their favorite toys whenever and wherever they want." Looking back, knowing what I know now, I can see how this explanation is problematic for the ways that it reifies the gender binary and excludes the possibility of gender transition for children. However, when our children were very young, it offered a simple and concrete response that helped them, their siblings, family, friends, and others understand their gender interests and expressions. It was also helpful to offer a rationale for why, sometimes, it was not OK to play dress up. I vividly recall a time when my son was in first grade: he arranged to go to a female classmate's home for an after-school playdate. Because I knew the family and was concerned about the potential for the girl's older brothers to tease my son, I asked him not to play dress-up. Showing clear signs of disappointment, he asked why. I explained that the family did not know yet that there were many different ways to be a boy, to which he replied, "But you will teach them, right?" And I said, "Yes, I will!"

The intense gender monitoring of where, when, and with whom it was safe to be himself demanded a great deal of effort. As parents, we engaged in perpetual emotional labor,[24] as "the primary conduits of expert knowledge, in ways that were culturally assimilable" to others.[25] One such way was to talk about the different ways of being a boy. It was also a means of affirming our boys' experiences, of not judging them for not being able to fully embrace their feminine sides outside of our homes. When they could not, we were careful to indicate that the reason why was not because there was something "wrong" with them, but because there were those who did not have that insight yet. We were very intentional about avoiding "faulting" our children for their gender interests and expressions or making them responsible for other people's discomfort.

## "It's Just Easier to Leave the Barbie in the Car!" On Negotiations and Boundaries

Even at our homes, after initial acceptance, families went through difficult negotiations about where and when our children could express their gender fluidity. We had to consider many factors. What could they wear? When could they wear it? What toys could they bring to a playdate, the park, or a store? These are difficult negotiations, especially if one of the parents is at a different comfort level than the other. We all engaged in what Tey Meadow refers to as gender editing, efforts to minimize visible public expression of nonconformity to avoid difficult situations and scrutiny.[26] For example, Matt explained, "It's just easier to leave the Barbie in the car. We don't have to take it to the supermarket because I don't wanna deal.... I know there's not going to be a confrontation or anything. But it's just like, uncomfortable stares and looks and like, 'Is that a boy or a girl?' Or calling him 'she.' It's uncomfortable and you're just like, 'Why do I have to deal with this person I'm never gonna see again?'"

Editing or hedging children's gender expression requires parents to find clarity about their own comfort levels, and to negotiate with one another as they compromise to offer a united message about what is acceptable and what is not. I recall dreading shopping for clothes with my kids. We were all well aware of the hypocrisy that our daughter could buy clothes in the boys' athletic section, but our son could not buy clothes from the girls' section. I knew that for my husband, dress-up costumes were permissible, but "real" girls' clothes were off-limits. I remember how happy I was when I found a pink shirt in the boys' department that said "Strong Boys Wear Pink," a shirt that my son eningded up wear often. But we all knew that this was just a temporary compromise.

Parents like us often engage in different types of boundary work, the creation of arbitrary rules regarding where, how, and with whom it was OK to transgress gender boundaries.[27] Our son had an understanding that he could wear "princess costumes" at preschool and at home, but not elsewhere. I knew that this was one boundary my husband needed and that I respected. Though some boundaries were clear in our mind, occasions presented themselves when we had to make impromptu decisions, such as when our kids had friends over and they wanted to play on the swingset in our backyard, a yard we shared with many of our neighbors. Was it considered in or out of our house? Could he swing on the swing in his princess costume? Thus, while we as parents tried to create boundaries around acceptable and unacceptable spaces for gender-nonconforming expressions, the practical realities of our children's play spaces were not as easily categorized.

## From Family Acceptance to "Radical Translation"

Parenting our kids has become an act of empowerment, activism, resistance, and expansion of our own boundaries. Our sons may not have been able to do it without us, and we could not have done it without them. They have taught us important lessons and opened doors we did not even know existed. Looking back, we, individually and collectively, have made so much progress, and at the same time, we still have much work to do. Our young sons invited us on a journey we did not expect to take. We transformed our families and communities "into gendering sites of innovation."[28]

Instinctively, we understood that we had no choice but to accept our boys' feminine and fluid gender expressions—that it was not them who needed to be changed, but the rest of us. Given proper support, community, and opportunities, many families across cultural categories of race, ethnicity, social class, religion, and political views have learned to respond positively to their children.[29] And we now have the research to support what our hearts knew all along: that family acceptance of our children's gender-expansive behavior is the key to mental, physical, and emotional health and well-being for both children and parents.[30]

Over time, our male partners learned to accept their feminine boys. They were able to differentiate and put some distance between their own masculinity and that of their sons. Some dads were strong advocates for their children and for others. Many parents, mostly moms, became "radical translators" of the gender order to make our experiences and lessons understood by those in positions of power.[31] We worked to create safe, affirming, and welcoming spaces for our children in our schools, places of worship, camps, athletic facilities, dorms, and community organizations, sometimes personally, on behalf of our children, sometimes professionally, on behalf of other children and families. In my case, I became a radical translator, a vocal advocate for gender diversity, equity, and justice work, which now informs my teaching, scholarship, and service. I have shared our experiences raising our son in writing and through public speaking, professional presentations, and organizational consulting work.[32]

Our collective activism expanded beyond our own children. Many of us took—and continue to take—risks, making ourselves and our children vulnerable, sharing our private lives in an effort to bring awareness and education. We strive to help others avoid our mistakes and learn from our successes, just like Catherine did with us. As we pay it forward, we are intentional about breaking the ingrained, pervasive, invisible, and hegemonic gender systems that oppress, exclude, erase, and punish gender diversity. We use our highly educated, mostly white, middle- and upper-class privilege and our identities as mothers to open hearts and minds. As we try to convey a message of love and understanding, we also want to chip away at our heteronormative gender binary. And, in doing this work, we empower and transform ourselves.

NOTES

1 Jake Pyne, "The Governance of Gender Non-Conforming Children: A Dangerous Enclosure," *Annual Review of Critical Psychology* 11 (2014): 79–96.
2 Tey Meadow, *Trans Kids: Being Gendered in the Twenty-First Century* (Berkeley: University of California Press, 2018), 53.

3 Elizabeth P. Rahilly, "The Gender Binary Meets the Gender-Variant Child: Parents' Negotiations with Childhood Gender Variance," *Gender & Society* 29 (June 2015): 338–61.
4 Children's National Medical Center, *If You Are Concerned about Your Child's Gender Behaviors: A Guide for Parents* (Washington, DC: CNMC, 2003).
5 Formerly the Outreach Program for Children with Gender-Variant Behaviors and Their Families.
6 Diane Ehrensaft, "Raising Girlyboys: A Parent's Perspective," *Studies in Gender and Sexuality* 8 (2007): 269–302.
7 The original listserv no longer exists. As technology evolved, email-based listservs like ours became obsolete. Several attempts were made to maintain the original membership from the past two decades. Fortunately, there is so much more information available and so many new sources of online communities of strength and support for families that the listserv has ceased to exist. By 2012, the listserv's membership was approximately 350 families.
8 Emily W. Kane, "'NO WAY MY BOYS ARE GOING TO BE LIKE THAT!' Parents' Responses to Children's Gender Nonconformity," *Gender & Society* 20 (April 2006): 149–76.
9 Names have been changed to protect confidentiality.
10 Lori and Matt Duron requested that their real names be used, for they speak and write openly about their experiences raising heir son.
11 Kane, *NO WAY MY BOYS*, 149–76.
12 Meadow, *Trans Kids*.
13 Kane, *NO WAY MY BOYS*, 149–76.
14 Meadow, *Trans Kids*.
15 CNMC listserv email, December 2006.
16 Krysti N. Ryan, "'My Mom Says Some Girls Have Penises': How Mothers of Gender Diverse Youth Are Pushing Gender Ideology Forward (And How They Are Not)," *Social Sciences* 5 (November 2016): 73–94.
17 Ryan, "My Mom Says," 68.
18 Ryan, 68.
19 Rahilly, *Gender Binary*, 338–61.
20 Kane, *NO WAY MY BOYS*, 150.
21 Jake Pyne, "'Parenting Is Not a Job . . . It's a Relationship': Recognition and Relational Knowledge among Parents of Gender Nonconforming Children," *Journal of Progressive Human Services* 27 (January 2016): 21–48.
22 Pyne, "Parenting Is Not a Job."
23 Meadow, *Trans Kids*.
24 Arlie R. Hochschild, *The Managed Heart: Commercialization of Human Feeling* (Berkeley: University of California Press, 1983), cited in Meadow, *Trans Kids*, 97.
25 Meadow.
26 Meadow.
27 Meadow, *Trans Kids*.

28  Cecelia L. Ridgeway, *Framed by Gender: How Gender Inequality Persists in the Modern World* (New York: Oxford University Press, 2011), cited in Krysti Ryan, "Examining the Family Transition: How Parents of Gender Diverse Youth Develop Trans-Affirming Attitudes," *Sociological Studies of Children and Youth* 23 (November 2017): 67–96.
29  Edgardo Menvielle, "A Comprehensive Program for Children with Gender Variant Behaviors and Gender Identity Disorders," *Journal of Homosexuality* 59 (March 2012): 357–68.
30  Caitlin Ryan, Stephen T. Russell, David Huebner, Rafael Diaz, and Jorge Sanchez, "Family Acceptance in Adolescence and The Health of LGBT Young Adults," *Journal of Child and Adolescent Psychiatric Nursing* 23 (November 2012): 205–13.
31  Brendan Hart, "Autism Parents and Neurodiversity: Radical Translation, Joint Embodiment, and the Prosthetic Environment," *BioSocieties* 9 (June 2014): 284–303, cited in Meadow, *TransKids*, 97.
32  See, for example, Ana María García and Graciela Slesaransky-Poe, "The Heteronormative Classroom: Questioning and Liberating Practices," *Teacher Educator* 45 (October 2010): 244–56; Graciela Slesaransky-Poe and Ana María García, "Boys with Gender Variant Behaviors and Interests: From Theory to Practice," *Sex Education* 9 (May 2009): 77–86; Graciela Slesaransky-Poe and Ana María García ,"Marginalized Differences Are Socially Constructed," in *Condition Critical: Key Principles for Equitable and Inclusive Education*, ed D. Lawrence-Brown and M. Sapon-Shevin (New York: Teachers College Press, 2013), 66–86; and Graciela Slesaransky-Poe, Lisa Ruzzi, Conie DiMedio, and Jeanne L. Stanley, "Is This the Right School for My Gender Non-Conforming Child?," *LGBT Youth Journal*, 10 (February 2013): 29–44.

# 24

## Negotiating Masculinity in the Fire Service

*Accessing Brotherhood or Subverting Gender Norms*

ROSCOE C. SCARBOROUGH

Conjure up a mental image of a firefighter.[1] Your firefighter might be rescuing a victim from a window with smoke billowing out of it, manning a nozzle on a house fire with fire spreading overhead, or responding to the September 11 attacks on the World Trade Center. The character who came to mind is probably a male, possibly with a mesomorph build and a mustache. The vast majority of career and volunteer firefighters in the United States and internationally are male.[2] In addition to being a demographic majority, a masculine aura pervades, and is valorized in, firefighting culture.[3]

Masculinity is sacred in the fire service, yet contested. Drawing on three years of participant observation as a firefighter, I examine the on-the-ground gender politics at the Monacan Volunteer Fire Department.[4] On the fireground, the inability to manhandle a large diameter hoseline by oneself earns the label "pussy," "bitch," or the current in-house synonym of the week. Around the firehouse, eating a salad for dinner or adopting a liberal political stance results in one "losing their man card" or being challenged to "man up." Firefighters with attributes or behaviors that depart from an institutional understanding of masculinity are ostracized as feminine.[5] Participation in shared group rituals and conforming to institutional gender norms offers access to a fraternal community—the firefighting brotherhood. Firefighters who express traits others perceive as insufficiently masculine enact three strategies to access the brotherhood: passing, compensating, and condoning. Conversely, firefighters employ questioning and soapboxing to subvert prevailing gender norms. Collectively, these five interactional strategies show how firefighters with traits that others perceive as feminine negotiate masculinity on the fireground and around the firehouse.

## Masculinity in the Fire Service Brotherhood

Firefighting is a masculine career or volunteer service that involves risk, danger, heroism, fearlessness, and physicality.[6] Many American firefighters grow up in rural, working-class households where a "country boy" habitus preconditions men for the rigors of firefighting.[7] Militaristic characteristics are central to firefighting masculinities, including a public service ethos, strong role commitment, firm discipline, and inclusive team affiliations.[8] Occupational identities are based upon masculine notions of emotional fortitude, physical strength, technical competence, and collective understandings of risk and responsibility.[9] These characteristics are central to the "hegemonic" firefighter masculinity,[10] which is performed for and judged by other men.[11] This homosocial celebration of masculine attributes serves as the foundation of a close-knit brotherhood.[12]

Masculinity is not the same in every firehouse. Firefighter masculinity is complex, manifold, contradictory, continually negotiated, and embedded within particular institutions.[13] In hierarchy of gendered identities that are defined in relation to each other, masculinity and femininity are mutually constituted.[14] Insofar as it is organized around heroism and blue-collar skills and attributes, hegemonic firefighter masculinity is constructed in opposition to white-collar work and feminized characteristics.[15] Thus, masculinity is a central fixture of firefighter culture, functioning as a basis for inclusion and exclusion.

The experiences of female firefighters offer insight into the impact of gender nonconformity on the male-dominated fire service. Female firefighters experience difficulty receiving recognition for their skills.[16] Female bodies are problematized, and women must prove their competence in order to confirm their professional identities.[17] Female firefighters encounter insufficient instruction, hostility, silence, hyper-supervision, lack of support, strained relationships with coworkers, and stereotyping.[18] In male-dominated organizations, women often feel as if they do not belong; as a result, their self-concepts suffer, and reactionary professional identities develop.[19] Additionally, recognition of nonphysical traits is resisted because it shifts understandings of gender appropriate work, disrupts male sociality, and signals potential erosion of discipline, professionalism, and skill.[20] The politics surrounding masculinity are high stakes because masculinity is the basis of membership.

Progressive institutional reforms, operating guidelines, and administrative actions are diversifying departmental demographics and masculinities in firehouses across America.[21] Yet an institutional focus neglects the gender politics that are present in everyday interactions. As "microsituational encounters are the ground zero of sociological action and evidence," it is necessary to study how gender boundary work occurs in face-to-face encounters.[22] This research examines how gender norms are bolstered and subverted in routine interactions both in the firehouse and on the fireground.

## Context and Method

As part of a larger project on solidarity and inequality in the fire service, the data for this study are drawn from three years of participant observation and thirty interviews with firefighters at the Monacan Volunteer Fire Department. I mapped how firefighters who exhibit traits that other firefighters perceive as insufficiently masculine access the fire service brotherhood or challenge the dominant conception of masculinity.

I became a firefighter, completed the requisite training, and served for three years as a member of a fire crew. My primary data are detailed field notes on face-to-face encounters in the firehouse, during training, and on the fireground. Additionally, I interviewed thirty firefighters about their experiences at Monacan and their views on masculinity. These interviews offered a window into the individual perspectives of Monacan firefighters and their thoughts on gender relations in the fire service. Working inductively, I utilized my insider status as an active member of the department to examine how firefighters who display characteristics that other firefighters view as feminine or insufficiently masculine navigate a hypermasculine organizational culture.

Monacan is an ideal context to study contested masculinity in the fire service. Located in the American South, it is a busy volunteer department that runs more than two thousand calls a year. The department has a distinct working-class white male culture at its core.[23] A majority of its leaders and members are working-class, white, politically and socially conservative men. These firefighters tend to display traditional masculinities, which emphasize physical strength and emotional fortitude. Conversely, almost half of the membership has ties to a local university. These student-firefighters are younger, mainly come from middle-class backgrounds, are more diverse racially and ethnically, and are more likely to be women; they also tend to be politically and socially liberal and display a broad range of masculinities. Shorter tenures limit opportunities for these student-firefighters to be promote to leadership positions and implement progressive institutional reforms. The ever-present tension between these factions provides a fertile environment for analyzing the on-the-ground politics of masculinity.

### Negotiating Perceived Feminine Attributes in a Hypermasculine Context

Masculinity is *the* foundation of community in the fire service, a sacred, "collective representation" of the group.[24] Yet many firefighters have attributes or practices that do not align with the hegemonic firefighter masculinity and that they negotiate using one or more approaches. The social composition or dynamics of a specific encounter may determine the strategy a firefighter utilizes.

Passing, compensating, and condoning allow firefighters with embodiments or practices that are perceived to be insufficiently masculine to access the firefighting brotherhood. Passing is suppressing individual opinions, preferences, dispositions, or characteristics that can be considered feminine. Compensating is making up for a deficiency in a masculine characteristic by emphasizing another masculine attribute. Condoning employs self-criticism or justifications to manage attributes that others label as feminine or excuse the gender policing behavior of others.

Questioning and soapboxing challenge gender norms to realize a more inclusive firefighting brotherhood. Questioning consists of initiating a dialogue about an individual's behavior or institutional conventions. Soapboxing involves an active, sometimes militant, critique of a behavior or prevailing institutional norms. Though these approaches can lead to conflict, they also subvert the dominant fire service masculinity.

## Passing

Firefighters possessing characteristics that do not align with the dominant fire service masculinity often try to blend in as one of the guys. This might involve strategic management of one's self-presentation or passive acceptance of prevailing gender norms.

Firefighter Joyner, who also serves as an officer in the navy, passes by suppressing his liberal political beliefs to fit in among conservative firefighters at Monacan, both at work and around the firehouse, to avoid conflict and social marginalization: "Just like in the navy, you don't share how you really feel. You hide a big part of your beliefs on politics, religion, whatever. Don't ask, don't tell, right? In both places, I've got more education than the guys I'm working with and that can be intimidating to them, you know, so I try to bury that cause it makes things easier. Whether it's talk about George Bush or gay jokes, I've got an opinion, but I don't share it. It makes it easier to blend in as one of the guys." A conservative worldview is a central aspect of the firefighter masculinity. Liberal beliefs are considered effeminate and symptomatic of a soft, empathetic, feminine orientation. Firefighter Joyner hides a conviction that does not fit the mold of masculinity at Monacan, allowing him to pass.

Passing allows firefighters to suppress emotions and appear impervious to death, trauma, and violence. For example, one morning at 5:50 a.m., Monacan receives an alarm for a cardiac arrest. A crew of six firefighters, police, and an ambulance all rush to the scene. When our crew enters the residence, a police officer is performing CPR on the victim, while the victim's wife screams in the hallway. The victim is a man in his sixties, unresponsive, without a pulse or respiration. Several of us take turns performing CPR, while the AED and an IV are set up. After multiple rounds of CPR, administering drugs intravenously, and receiving a few shocks from the defibrillator, the patient regains a heartbeat and starts to breathe again. The man is lifted onto a gurney, wheeled out to the ambulance, and rushed to a local hospital for cardiac care.

Upon returning to the station, the crew begins packing up their gear, making jokes about doing CPR to the rhythm of "Another One Bites the Dust," and critiquing the poor leadership of the emergency medical technician (EMT) orchestrating the resuscitation. Everyone maintains an emotionally impervious front. As the others disperse, Firefighter

Hart, who has acted as an informal mentor during my first few months at Monacan, asks me, "Was that your first time doing CPR?" Attempting to maintain an unflappable emotional front, I reply, "Yeah, it was about what I expected." Hart, in a paternalistic manner, comments, "Well, if you feel like it's something that you need to talk about, just let me know, 'cause everybody deals with stuff like this differently." In mixed company, firefighters bury emotions to pass as one of the guys. In confidence, Hart invites me to discuss feelings in a mentorship capacity.

Passing often consists of little more than keeping one's mouth shut—an effective approach for concealing opinions, beliefs, insufficient knowledge, or sexuality. However, it is less effective at mitigating characteristics that can't be hidden, including a diminutive physical build, veganism on steak night, or the inability to raise a twenty-eight-foot extension ladder.

## Compensating

Though it is possible to conceal many attributes or practices that may be judged as insufficiently masculine, other traits and behaviors cannot be suppressed. Once an insufficiently masculine attribute is exhibited, compensating allows a firefighter to accentuate a characteristic or practice that aligns with the hegemonic firefighter masculinity.

In the absence of a structure fire to display one's masculine prowess, a central proving ground is the dinner table. Firefighters who are vegetarian, advocate for healthy options, avoid junk foods, or eat modest portions are ridiculed as feminine. The all-you-can-eat buffet serves as an arena for performing and policing gender.

CiCi's pizza buffet is a favorite destination for C-Crew's Saturday night dinners. After a lengthy coughing fit after inhaling a flake of crushed red pepper, Lieutenant Gordon finds himself on the receiving end of jokes. Juvenile insults are hurled across the table as Gordon turns red and continues coughing. Firefighter Woods jokes, "You need some water to cool down your vagina?" Firefighter Miller replies, "I think the hot pepper is a little too spicy for him. How about we get some ice cream?" After a long coughing fit, Lieutenant Gordon slaps the red pepper shaker across the table and declares, "Fuck y'all. I'm allergic to that shit, I swear. I'm going to get a plate of gluttonous goodness." Gordon returns with a plate of macaroni and cheese, pizza, breadsticks, and other buffet favorites. Everyone eats one or two plates of food, but Gordon forces down three plates of pizza and a plate of desserts. While everyone is waiting for him to finish his dessert, Gordon compensates for his embarrassing episode: "I just wanted to say 'Fuck y'all' one more time. And that I declare myself the CiCi's pizza buffet champion for my one-man effort to eat this place out of business." Everyone laughs. Gordon adds a disclaimer: "Don't judge me, 'cause if we get a fire call, y'all will see me puking in the front yard before I mask up." Gordon compensates for his inability to eat spicy foods by consuming more food than anyone else.

Compensating allows a firefighter to substitute one masculine characteristic for another that is lacking, but not all characteristics exchange equitably. For example, Firefighter Yang, who Lieutenant Gordon describes as "some little brown Asian kid who weighs like a hundred pounds and has that fucked up lisp," struggles to operate a hose line or deploy an extension ladder. Finding an essential skill that does not rely on physical ability, Yang trains and becomes proficient at pump operations. Similarly, many firefighters who lack fireground skills elect to pursue certification as EMTS. Pump operators and EMTs are essential to the functions of a fire department, but many view investments in these competencies as cop-outs to avoid physical trials on the fireground.

While firefighters who express traits others perceive as feminine or insufficiently masculine often compensate, this strategy is not always effective because many firefighters resist the recognition of nonphysical traits.[25] Attempts to compensate for a lack of strength, technical skill, or other embodied capacities frequently fail because physicality is a sacred pillar of the hegemonic fire service masculinity.

### Condoning

Many firefighters who express traits that do not align with hypermasculine norms employ jokes, self-criticism, or justifications to manage perceived femininities or excuse the gender policing behavior of peers or supervisors. In the fire service, this often involves rationalizing the aggressive maintenance of gender norms in the name of tradition or attributing deviation from these norms to the failings of an individual.

During fire academy, probationary firefighters spend six months building a foundation of knowledge, learning practical skills, and integrating into fire service culture. On the first day of practical exercises for fire academy, Probationary Firefighter Martin misses a carpool with the rest of the cadets from Monacan. Around 8:20 a.m., at the county training center, Instructor Rogan is briefing the new cadets on the logistics of the day when his lecture is interrupted by the whine of a small gas engine outside. This causes everyone to look out the window, but a blanket of dense January fog obscures the perpetrator. Eventually, Probationary Firefighter Martin, in full turnout gear, drives a Vespa-type scooter up to the window in front of the classroom, looks through the window at the class, and then circles the building to park. In disbelief, Instructor Rogan declares: "Holy Mother of God, I thought I'd seen it all. I was wrong. There's a firefighter in full PPE [personal protective equipment] riding a 49cc scooter." Minutes later, Martin walks in teary-eyed from the cold and dripping wet. Rogan questions Martin: "Did you just ride up on a scooter, late to academy, on our first practical, wearing your PPE?" In a self-deprecating tone, Martin attempts to justify his late arrival: "Yeah, I thought we were supposed to meet at the station at 7:30, not 7:00. I missed it in the email." Instructor Rogan makes an example out of Martin in front of all the cadets and instructors: "Well, you can't wear your turnout gear on your scooter, or whatever that little thing is. If it was a Harley, at least it *might* look cool. I admire your effort to get here, though. I hope you realize that we're going to have to call you Scooter from here on out. It can't be avoided." Instructor Rogan disparages Martin for owning a scooter, which departs from the masculine norm of lifted pickup trucks, which are pervasive in Southern firefighter culture. Rogan also criticizes Martin for his unprofessional late arrival, which threatens the proud male exceptionalism of fire service culture. Martin fails to rationalize behavior that is incongruent with the punctuality, reliability, and responsibility demanded of first responders. The nickname "Scooter" follows him until he drops out of the academy—an enduring stigma for conduct that is out of sync with institutional expectations.

Firefighters condone the aggressive policing of feminine behaviors. As part of a personnel swap to accommodate new volunteers and attrition, Probationary Firefighter Thompson, who is a vegetarian, joins C-Crew. On Thompson's first shift, Firefighter Davidson announces:

"Tonight for dinner, we've got grilled chicken and grilled squash for the boys and we've got salad for the girls." Davidson correlates grilled foods with masculinity, while denigrating the salad as feminine. Afterward, I ask Firefighter Thompson about his thoughts on this sort of banter. He dismisses the jab: "It doesn't get to me. That's just how he is. He's always joking about everything." Thompson dismisses this comment as derivative of Davidson's personality, rather than a critique of fire service culture.

Firefighters condone harassment of peers with attributes perceived as insufficiently masculine under the banner of upholding fire service traditions and a "boys will be boys" patriarchal culture. This strategy is central to excusing the aggressive policing of gender norms in the fire service. Individuals who fail to conform or criticize the fire service's patriarchal culture are marginalized as flawed cultural heretics.

Questioning

While passing, compensating, and condoning allow firefighters with traits others view as feminine or insufficiently masculine to gain access to the fire service brotherhood, many firefighters with perceived feminine traits challenge the status quo. Questioning consists of initiating a dialogue about institutional conventions or an individual's behavior. Many firefighters possessing characteristics that depart from the hegemonic fire service masculinity ask questions in hopes of altering the behavior of a fellow firefighter or the gender politics of the department.

While the fireground is a place of action where orders go unquestioned, the training ground is a space where dialogue is encouraged. During training on aerial operations with the ladder truck, the one-hundred-foot aerial ladder is extended to the most vertical angle possible. Three probationary firefighters are awaiting a command behind the truck in full turnout gear. One of the longer-serving members, Firefighter Evans, barks: "Are y'all gonna climb the tower [ladder] or are you gonna be a bunch of faggots?" The probationary firefighters exchange glances, no doubt pondering the best response to stay in the good graces of their superior. After a few seconds of silence, Probationary Firefighter Hussein, an Iraqi American known for vocalizing liberal views, asks a question: "What does climbing the ladder have to do with being gay?"

Evans's reply does not answer Hussein's question: "That's just firehouse talk. Listen, if you want to get released [promoted to firefighter], you gotta be ready to assist with aerial operations. That means climbing the aerial. Now quit being a bunch of pussies and let's get it over with." Hussein does not further pursue the issue, and the probationary firefighters take turns scaling and descending the aerial ladder.

When Probationary Firefighter Hussein questions why sexuality is linked to professional competence, his query breaches the interactional flow, creating a momentary interlude for critical dialogue about homophobic language. Firefighter Evans sidesteps Hussein's question because discussing the symbolic violence of language or making a concession to a liberal worldview threatens hegemonic firefighter masculinity. Evans justifies his comment as "firehouse talk," emphasizing a tradition of vulgar homosocial banter in the fire service. Comparable to the "fag discourse" of middle and high school–aged boys, Evans uses the term "faggot" as a proxy for one who lacks the emotional and physical fortitude to perform fireground work. In this case, a faggot is understood to be the inverse of a firefighter.[26]

Questioning provides an interactional breach or pause that allows for discussion of word choice, behavior, or institutional culture. This strategy is often used to prompt a dialogue about gender norms and puts the onus on others to justify their actions or beliefs. Though questioning only sometimes challenges gender norms explicitly, the goal of this dialogue is to facilitate critical reflection. This strategy plants a seed that can initiate changes to everyday behaviors or institutional practices.

## Soapboxing

While asking questions invites a dialogue, direct and forceful confrontation forces one's voice to be heard. Soapboxing involves an active, sometimes militant, engagement with an individual or prevailing institutional norms, which, when discriminatory behavior goes unchecked or the cultural status quo becomes untenable, one may choose to subvert. For firefighters with traits that others perceive as feminine, this may include sustaining critical inquiry, lecturing others, expressing one's feelings, or making formal demands for institutional reform. Firefighter Jones's evolution from being a quiet guy on the social periphery of Monacan to a vocal, progressive critic of policing and racial injustice in contemporary America is an example of soapboxing.

Among the conservative majority of firefighters, holding liberal political views is seen as a sign of emotional fragility and feminine sensitivity. Any breach from a dogmatic commitment to an ideology of America as a post-racist meritocracy is blasphemy. In his views, Jones falls into the minority of firefighters. In addition, he is one of only two African Americans and the only openly gay member of Monacan.

Jones becomes more vocal about communicating his concerns over time. Early in his tenure, Jones would sit silently as other firefighters discussed social issues, even when race was used as a scapegoat to explain a range of problems associated with poverty. In the wake of the deaths of Trayvon Martin and Michael Brown at the hands of police, Firefighter Jones adopts the cause of educating his fellow firefighters about racial profiling and police violence impacting African American men. Jones recalls a one-on-one conversation with Firefighter Smith:

> We would talk about police brutality and I would say how I've been followed by police multiple times when I was doing absolutely nothing. He was like, "You continue to repeat yourself. Well, you must have been doing something." I was like, "I was walking my dog. I swear. I don't think all police are racist but some of them are; it's the way it is." He would refuse to believe it. He would always say, "I'm sure you were doing something." I would say, "I wasn't," and it came to a head where we couldn't talk about it anymore because it wasn't going to go anywhere.

Among the conservative core of Monacan's membership, a belief in the integrity of law enforcement inhibits acknowledgment of racial profiling. As Jones continues to give voice to people of color, he describes the social rifts that formed between him and others on his crew: "Certain people, certain white people, would feel like I was attacking them, like I was attacking the idea of whiteness or something, whereas I was just talking about my life, just like white people and black people experience things differently." These rifts between Jones and others intensify as time goes on, and Jones is marginalized for expressing a progressive worldview that does not align with hegemonic firefighter masculinity. These debates become heated. Jones describes the ongoing conflict:

One member from Monacan commented, saying how we shouldn't make this all about race and that we should be upset that people die. I, at last, just said to her, "Well, yeah, it's horrible people die, but this is clearly about race. The guy said racist things." Then Chief commented, "You're not being fair to her." That was a last point when I said, "Oh, I don't feel like I belong here," because for weeks Taft, Smith, Lawrence, and Gordon had been saying mean stuff to me and then Taft had been saying stuff on Facebook and not once did Chief talk to me, which I figured, "Oh, he doesn't want to get involved. That's fine. I get it. He wants to stay above the whole thing." Then this one girl says one thing that was, I don't know, incorrect, and I corrected her, I feel like in a polite way, and then he got involved. It felt like a huge double standard and completely unfair.

On a metaphorical soapbox, Jones is committed to educating his peers about police violence and social justice. Yet, when a superior intervenes in a biased manner, Jones feels too alienated to continue his affiliation:

I actually asked to have a meeting with Chief . . . and he asked a representative from the county to be there, too. I basically explained how I felt like I was being treated, how I felt. Honestly, not through malice, but I think, they weren't going to listen to me at all. They weren't going to try to listen. I really think it was like, you hit a certain age, you live your life a certain way, they're not going to take the time to listen to that gay guy talk about his life experiences, it's just not going to happen.

In the end, Jones attributes the root cause of his conflict at Monacan to his race and sexual orientation. However, the perception of his liberal politics as a deficiency in his masculinity plays a significant role in his social marginalization. He does not give up proselytizing for his cause, but he does resign from the department.

Soapboxing is an effective strategy for voicing one's concerns about existing cultural norms. Jones's case highlights the collateral damage that can result from challenging the hegemonic fire service masculinity. Other forms of soapboxing, such as an educational approach or an emotional plea, might result in less overt conflict.

## Gender Politics in the Firefighting Brotherhood

This research details how firefighters with attributes or practices that depart from an institutional understanding of masculinity access the firefighting brotherhood or subvert the prevailing norms of masculinity. Passing, compensating, and condoning do not challenge traditional conceptions of masculinity; these approaches allow firefighters with traits that others perceive as feminine or insufficiently masculine to participate in the brotherhood. Conversely, questioning and soapboxing are strategies of active resistance that challenge deeply institutionalized conceptions of masculinity.

Masculinity is the traditional basis of solidarity among firefighters.[27] Policing gender norms in the firehouse is not understood as toxic bullying or victimization of the marginalized. Rather, defending masculinity and policing femininities are seen as moral acts that pay tribute to tradition and a shared understanding of what it means to be a firefighter.

The introduction of feminine embodiments and practices into a hypermasculine social context has implications for individuals and institutions. An individual who conforms to existing gender norms is rewarded with an affirmation of his identity and solidarity in the brotherhood. On the other hand, one who subverts these norms may suffer exclusion, ridicule, and conflict and be denied opportunities for promotion. These are the individual costs of resisting and subverting gender conventions, in addition to the implications for fire departments and the fire service as a whole. While the fire service is becoming more inclusive for women, nonbinary individuals, and firefighters with attributes that are perceived to be feminine, these shifts also have negative consequences for fire service institutions. If masculinity atrophies as the primary basis of belonging in the fire service, other traditions and cultural practices must fill this void. In response, many volunteer fire departments have not found a substitute for homosocial community, resulting in declining membership across the United States. Many volunteer departments are developing recruitment and retention plans with economic incentives, such as free training and certification, tuition reimbursement, and live-in programs. Meanwhile, career departments offer competitive salaries and other benefits to ensure sufficient staffing.

Masculinity has been discussed as if it is monolithic and settled, yet this negates the variable and evolving character of gender politics across the fire service. This research classifies all firefighters into binary categories: conforming insiders and nonconforming outsiders, a dichotomy that illustrates the role of gender in inclusion and exclusion. However, there may be tiers of inclusion, situational marginalization, or alienation, and each department has its own idiosyncratic culture; many departments are further subdivided into crews, shifts, or platoons, which have their own fractal, distinctive idiocultures.[28] There are significant differences in institutional regulation of behavior across departments. In many, the formal organizational structure, human resource policies, and standard operating guidelines curtail some of the most toxic interpersonal behaviors. Volunteer organizations often lack this elaborate regulatory apparatus. Instead of incentivizing involvement through payment for services, volunteer fire departments rely on shared group culture to engender feelings of affiliation and belonging among members. Hazing, bullying, and other nefarious behaviors are often valorized as rites of passage to achieve social status. Additional strategies for navigating rigid gender norms may be identified in other fire departments or social contexts where masculinity is the basis for community.

The types of services provided by fire departments are changing across America, which may shift the role of masculinity as a basis for camaraderie. Call volume is increasing, especially for emergency medical services. This is paired with a decline in community need for fire suppression. As professional competence shifts from operating a hoseline to interpreting an electrocardiogram, it is unclear if traditional masculinity will remain a centerpiece of firefighter culture.

Around the firehouse and on the fireground, Monacan firefighters conflate gender and sexuality. In practice, firefighters do not draw distinctions between these terms. It is not that they lack the education or vocabulary to articulate the differences; rather, acknowledging nonbinary gender identities and normalizing a range of sexualities threatens to erode the conservative, homosocial brotherhood of the fire service. Future research must analyze the complex intersections of gender, gender identity, and sexuality and their roles in solidarity and exclusion processes of an evolving fire service.

An extension of this research could examine what motivates firefighters to uphold or subvert gender norms. An expanded project could mine the emotional experience of firefighters to understand the role that gender plays in feelings of belonging or being excluded. It would also be valuable to identify cultural processes that allow for feelings of belonging to develop around gendered identities. If a strong institutional culture can alter deeply engrained behaviors, it is necessary to identify the organizational practices or standard operating guidelines that create inclusive institutions.[29]

NOTES

1. I thank Dana Berkowitz, Michele Darling, Chong-suk Han, Molly Petry, Russell Scarborough, Elroi J. Windsor, and my spring 2018 Social Psychology students for providing thoughtful feedback on this manuscript. Earlier versions of this paper were presented at the 2018 meetings of the Eastern Sociological Society in Baltimore, Maryland, and the 2018 Roots and Branches of Interpretive Sociology conference in Philadelphia, Pennsylvania.
2. Dave Baigent, "One More Last Working-Class Hero: A Cultural Audit of the UK Fire Service" (PhD diss., Anglia Ruskin University, 2001); Carol Chetkovich, *Real Heat: Gender and Race in the Urban Fire Service* (New Brunswick, NJ: Rutgers University Press, 1997).
3. Amy S. Greenberg, *Cause for Alarm: The Volunteer Fire Department in the Nineteenth-Century City* (Princeton, NJ: Princeton University Press, 1998).
4. Pseudonyms are used to protect the identity of all individuals and organizations.
5. Susan L. Miller, Kay B. Forest, and Nancy C. Jurik, "Diversity in Blue: Lesbian and Gay Police Officers in a Masculine Occupation," *Men and Masculinities* 5, no. 4 (2003): 360.
6. Matthew Desmond, *On the Fireline: Living and Dying with Wildland Firefighters* (Chicago: University of Chicago Press, 2007); Thomas Thurnell-Read and Andrew Parker, "Men, Masculinities, and Firefighting: Occupational Identity, Shop-Floor Culture, and Organisational Change," *Emotion, Space, and Society* 1, no. 2 (2008): 127.
7. Matthew Desmond, "Becoming a Firefighter," *Ethnography* 7, no. 4 (2006): 387.
8. Baigent, "One More Last Working-Class Hero," 21.
9. Greenberg, *Cause for Alarm*; Thurnell-Read and Parker, "Men, Masculinities, and Firefighting," 127.
10. R. W. Connell, *Gender and Power: Society, the Person, and Sexual Politics* (Stanford, CA: Stanford University Press, 1987).
11. Michael Kimmel, *Guyland: The Perilous World Where Boys Become Men—Understanding the Critical Years Between 16 and 26* (New York: Harper Collins, 2008), 47.

12  Matthew Desmond, *On the Fireline: Living and Dying with Wildland Firefighters* (Chicago: University of Chicago Press, 2007); Greenberg, *Cause for Alarm*.
13  Susan Ainsworth, Alex Batty, and Rosaria Burchielli, "Women Constructing Masculinity in Voluntary Firefighting," *Gender, Work, and Organization* 21, no. 1 (2014): 37; Careen Mackay Yarnal, Lorraine Dowler, and Susan Hutchinson, "Don't Let the Bastards See You Sweat: Masculinity, Public and Private Space, and the Volunteer Firehouse," *Environment and Planning A: Economy and Space* 36, no. 4 (2004): 685.
14  Ainsworth et al., "Women Constructing Masculinity," 37.
15  Baigent, "One More Last Working-Class Hero," 101.
16  Ruth Woodfield, "Gender and the Achievement of Skilled Status in the Workplace: The Case of Women Leaders in the UK Fire and Rescue Service," *Work, Employment, and Society* 30, no. 2 (2016): 237.
17  Tamika Perrot, "Beyond 'Token' Firefighters: Exploring Women's Experiences of Gender and Identity at Work," *Sociological Research Online* 21, no. 1 (2016): 1.
18  Janice D. Yoder and Patricia Aniakudo, "'Outsider Within' the Firehouse: Subordination and Difference in the Social Interactions of African American Women Firefighters," *Gender and Society* 11, no. 3 (1997): 324.
19  Deneen M. Hatmaker, "Engineering Identity: Gender and Professional Identity Negotiation among Women Engineers," *Gender, Work, and Organization* 20, no. 4 (2013): 382.
20  Alex Hall, Jenny Hockey, and Victoria Robinson, "Occupational Cultures and the Embodiment of Masculinity: Hairdressing, Estate Agency and Firefighting," *Gender, Work, and Organization* 14, no. 6 (2007): 541.
21  Chetkovich, *Real Heat*.
22  Randall Collins, "Situational Stratification: A Micro-Macro Theory of Inequality," *Sociological Theory* 18, no. 1 (2000): 18.
23  Roscoe C. Scarborough, "Risk a Lot to Save a Lot: How Firefighters Decide Whose Life Matters," *Sociological Forum* 32, no. S1 (2017): 1079.
24  Emile Durkheim, *The Elementary Forms of Religious Life* (New York: Free Press, [1912] 1995). Collective representations are symbols that have a common intellectual and emotional meaning to members of a group. These symbols help constituents make sense of the world and provide a basis for solidarity.
25  Hall et al., "Occupational Cultures," 541.
26  C. J. Pascoe, *Dude, You're a Fag: Masculinity and Sexuality in High School* (Berkeley: University of California Press, 2007).
27  Durkheim, *Elementary Forms of Religious Life*.
28  Gary Alan Fine, "Small Groups and Cultural Creation: The Idioculture of Little League Baseball Teams," *American Sociological Review* 44, no. 5 (1979): 733.
29  Scarborough, "Risk a Lot to Save a Lot," 1073.

## 25

## Resisting Femininity in Responsible Fathering

*Men and the Gendering of Care in US Fatherhood Policy*

JENNIFER RANDLES

No, I don't [change diapers.] There's a lot of women out there that demand that the husband act like the wife, and you know there's a lot of husbands that listen to that.... I won't do anything to take care of [my kids]. I'll supply funds, and she'll take care of the kids.
—Donald Trump, 2005

We need fathers to realize that responsibility does not end at conception. We need them to realize that what makes you a man is not the ability to have a child—it's the courage to raise one.
—Barack Obama, 2008

These statements from two eventual US presidents point to distinct ideas of men's parenting that reflect changing views of fathering as a gendered practice. Trump's reference to women who expect men to "act like the wife" by changing diapers signaled that men who "take care" of kids are feminized. Obama's remark flipped this logic by noting that raising a child is what "makes [a father] a man." For Trump, parental caregiving is emasculating; for Obama, it is masculinizing. This tension is central to US fatherhood policy.

As part of welfare reform in 1996, Congress included provisions to promote *responsible* fatherhood, defined as "taking responsibility for a child's intellectual, emotional, and financial well-being" by making a "choice to be an active, engaged parent."[1] The federal government has since funded hundreds of programs focused on increasing men's economic stability and paternal involvement through vocational training and parenting classes. Many programs target parents who identify as men, mostly low-income fathers of color.

In the groundbreaking *Female Masculinity*, Jack Halberstam discusses the way patriarchy rests on a taken-for-granted notion that masculinity inheres in men.[2] Masculinity is particularly visible, Halberstam argues, when it leaves the sphere of white, middle-class male bodies and is produced by and for women. Gender relations, especially as they are legitimated and maintained, become legible by dislocating masculinity outside of male practices and experiences. This questioning of how masculinity can be performed by women-identified female bodies—and the implication that men can subvert gender norms through practices and embodiments deemed feminine—are key for understanding the gender implications of policy that encourages fathers' greater involvement in family life. Fatherhood programs characterize responsible fathering as something that emerges through the expression of caring masculinity as part of "real" manhood. But what happens when men try to craft care-focused paternal identities that depend on behaviors typically associated with mothering and women? Does this support or undermine gender equality in families?

To answer these questions, I draw on data I collected as part of a qualitative study of a US federally funded responsible fatherhood program I call "DADS." The program encouraged men's parenting by teaching fathers that they are uniquely valuable for children as role models of masculine nurturance. Based on in-depth interviews and focus groups with sixty-four low-income fathers of color, in this chapter I show how men in DADS grappled with and embraced messages that engaged fathering entails caregiving and emotional expressiveness in addition to breadwinning—in other words, in their gendered abilities to model nurturance and parental love *as men*.

## (Re)Defining Fatherhood around Femininity

Concerns over "fatherlessness," its connection to poverty and other social problems, and the sense that "troubled masculinities" cause men to reject patriarchal responsibilities motivate responsible fatherhood policy.[3] In her research, Anna Gavanas finds that the US fatherhood responsibility movement mobilized around the assumption that parenting has become feminized and synonymous with mothering.[4] In response, it sought to masculinize domesticity while "carving out specifically 'male' notions of parenting."[5] This required challenging conventional models of fatherhood rooted in biology, marriage, and breadwinning that have been critiqued as emotionally distant and insufficiently caring, while ensuring that men who are caregivers are not deemed feminine.

Normative understandings of the family responsibilities of fathers have varied considerably throughout the past three centuries. While fathers were tasked with being moral teachers during the preindustrial era and distant breadwinners in the nineteenth and early twentieth century, they are now expected to be masculine role models as well as nurturing "new" fathers.[6] This social construct of the "new" or "involved" father—one who is emotionally attuned to his children and present in their lives and helps with childcare responsibilities—has gained social and political traction in recent decades.[7] However, the norms and values comprising the culture of new nurturant fatherhood have outpaced the actual conduct of fathering,[8] as men overall still interact with and care for their children less than mothers do.[9]

New fatherhood highlighting men's caregiving and emotionality in families is not actually new, nor has it made parenting egalitarian. As Michael A. Messner argues, the new fathering movement of the last century that focused on increasing men's emotional engagement and time spent with children was less about gender inequality than promoting a particular style of male parenting.[10] By endorsing a "culture of daddyhood" that framed fathers as children's pals, playmates, and role models,[11] new fatherhood allowed men to anchor successful masculine identities in the father role.[12] It also gave privileged men cultural license to enjoy the emotional aspects of parenting without participating equally in the work of childcare.[13] This movement has served as a powerful ideological mechanism for ensuring that many of the feminized aspects of parenting—such as housework and emotional labor—remain peripheral to normative constructions of involved fathering. Cultural representations of the new father"belie how, for many men, paternal involvement still occurs within a gendered division of parenting labor in which fathers are part-time, secondary "helpers."[14]

New fatherhood discourses focused on the relational aspects of parenting have historical precedent in fathering programs of the early twentieth century that valorized fathers' nonfinancial contributions by making domestic work, especially childcare, seem manly.[15] Defining nurturance as central to successful manhood and fatherhood is one strategy fathers have used to overcome the emasculating effects of race and class inequalities that typecast marginalized men as failed providers.[16] Nevertheless, being a primary family breadwinner is still central to notions of middle-class white masculinity, which is predicated on the exclusion of low-income and poor men, especially men of color, who are frequently stereotyped as irresponsible, "absent" fathers who produce sons with compromised masculinity.[17] New fatherhood has redefined patriarchy at critical historical junctures, especially during downturns in men's economic standing, but not necessarily in ways that have challenged race, class, and gender inequalities.[18] On the contrary, by masculinizing nurturance as a way of resisting the feminization of parenting, new fatherhood has actually reinforced these inequalities in novel and covert ways.

Pierette Hondagneu-Sotelo and Michael A. Messner argue that cultural images of the new father—presumed to be a white, highly educated professional who is nurturant and in touch with his feelings—reinforce patriarchal privileges that conceal the subordination of women and marginalized men.[19] Much of the day-to-day care of children is still performed by women, either their mother or hired low-income women, mostly women of color. Moreover, the softer form of masculinity associated with the new father exists only in contrast to qualities associated with traditional masculinity, such as domination and stoicism, now projected onto less privileged men.[20] New father discourses allow men to embrace what Melanie Heath calls "soft-boiled masculinity" that "empowers them to be more sensitive and caring husbands and fathers . . . by ignoring the structural conditions that empower men and provide payoffs based on claims to manhood."[21] That is, privileged men can capitalize on new father ideas that sustain patriarchy without fundamentally challenging hegemonic understandings of masculinity, parenting, and the gendered division of family labor.

Unlike the new fatherhood ideal, social and political discourses that attach significance to men's roles as parents, rather than as workers or husbands, is relatively new. The state now actively constructs fatherhood through government-sponsored social service programs that seek to influence fathers' identities as men and parents—and specifically as *manly* parents.[22] Whereas welfare programs have historically framed fathering exclusively in terms of male wage earning, responsible fatherhood programs address men as both breadwinners and family caregivers.[23] Government-funded marriage promotion programs, for example, strategically emphasizes men's nurturance with the goal of encouraging a greater commitment to a breadwinner identity.[24] As fathers—and, notably, *fathering*—receive more attention in welfare state policies, there is a greater emphasis on how men should provide their children with both money and care, and on how male parenting provides unique benefits for children and families.

Responsible fatherhood programming rationalizes the importance of fathers' parenting by teaching that children need male parents who demonstrate essential masculine qualities—*essential* both in the sense that they are indispensable and a reflection of innate features of manliness. Many commentators argue that, without fathers, boys fail to develop a stable sense of masculinity, and girls lack a sense of physical and emotional security that support heterosexual trust and intimacy.[25] Others contend that fathers uniquely promote children's cognitive and social capacities, self-control, moral sensitivity, and physical development by giving children "an opportunity to explore and interact with the essence of maleness itself and to explore male-female differences."[26] Maggie Gallagher claims that children without fathers never cultivate "an image of maleness that is not at odds with love."[27] Fathers are valuable, these authors presume, because they teach children they are worthy of recognition and love from men.

The research on "father absence" has found that, on average, children who live apart from their biological fathers do have worse outcomes, including lower high school graduation rates, lower levels of childhood social-emotional adjustment, and poorer adult mental health.[28] Yet few studies have directly examined whether the gender of the missing parent in single-parent families is responsible for the different outcomes between one- and two-parent families.[29] There are no overall differences in the psychological adjustment or gender traits of adolescents raised with and without male role models.[30] This suggests that fathers are important as parents, not because they are male, men, or masculine, but because they provide the resources, attention, and care children need to thrive.

Yet men still struggle to create care-focused paternal identities that allow them to nurture without feeling stigmatized as feminine, especially when their earning abilities are compromised. Based on her research with Portuguese fathers, Sobia Aboim finds that men do identity work to create a hybrid masculine sense of self that weaves together the more expressive, seemingly feminine aspects of parenting with contrasting masculine elements such as the image of the responsible family provider.[31] Andrea Doucet finds similar themes in her study of Canadian fathers who distanced themselves from femininity by distinguishing the care they provided from "mothering" and emphasizing masculine forms of care focused on encouraging children's autonomy and physical play.[32] This discrediting of women and femininity is a way of maintaining and legitimating the gender dominance of men and masculinity.[33] As long as fathers experience tension in embracing caregiving when it is not secondary to breadwinning—as it still often is for privileged men—even nurturance will be conceptualized in terms of gendered hierarchies.

Attempts to masculinize caregiving take on a unique resonance for marginalized men. Redefining responsible fatherhood to highlight the emotional and relational aspects of paternal involvement allows low-income men to manage a different tension between expectations of financial provisioning and their inability to live up to those expectations in the context of severe economic and social constraints.[34] As family complexity has increased, low-income fathers have redefined paternal provision to include providing emotional support for, spending quality time with, and physically doing things on behalf of their children.[35] Emphasizing stereotypically feminine aspects of parenting allows low-income men to manage more flexible expectations of successful fathering. Elaine A. Anderson and Bethany Letiecq find that fatherhood programming shapes men's perceptions of fathering as a masculine practice by encouraging them to explore more expressive parenting styles.[36] In their research, Kevin Roy and Omari Dyson similarly discover that fatherhood programs enable marginalized men to construct alternative versions of masculinity focused on male caregiving that allow them to manage race and class stigma.[37]

As with gender, most people understand parenting as an essential binary. Just as masculinity normatively refers to the practices of male bodies or those who identify as men, "fathering" typically refers to what male parents do. These socially constructed binaries—man/woman, masculinity/femininity, father/mother—all assume and rely on opposition as a way of rationalizing, interpreting, and judging social relationships.[38] Utilizing new fatherhood discourses, fatherhood programs allow men to redefine parenting practices and traits formerly associated with femininity and mothering as masculine, but not in ways that fundamentally challenge patriarchy or promote truly egalitarian parenting. Gender scholars have theorized cases of men co-opting femininity to strategically maintain patriarchal privileges as processes of "loose essentialism,"[39] "masculine rescripting,"[40] the "flexibility of patriarchy,"[41] and "hybrid masculinities."[42] I similarly show in what follows how men's attempts to define care as a masculine activity within the context of a responsible fatherhood program do not necessarily transform patriarchal culture when that redefinition involves drawing hierarchical distinctions between masculine and feminine forms of care.

## Masculinizing Care to Promote Responsible Fatherhood

From August 2014 to November 2015, I conducted in-depth interviews with fifty fathers and focus groups with twenty-one fathers (seven of whom were prior interviewees) who participated in DADS, which received a 2012 federal grant to provide fatherhood programming for men between the ages of sixteen and forty-five. Participants could complete their high school diplomas through an on-site charter school; earn money through paid vocational training in landscaping, recycling, and janitorial services; and take voluntary fathering and relationship skills classes. Fathering classes used the "24/7 Dad" curriculum, which addressed manhood and fathering, the demonstration and management of feelings, and communication, among other topics. I asked these sixty-four men about their experiences in the program—what they learned, and how these experiences shaped their views of parenting.

In many ways, DADS challenged hegemonic understandings of masculinity, especially the idea that responsible fathers must be successful breadwinners. This was crucial given that poor fathers of color are often denied status as good fathers due to the way inequalities undermine their abilities to earn and provide. Still, staff explained that education and employment services were primary components of the DADS program because men had the natural drive to provide and needed jobs and earnings to feel "manly" enough and deserving of being in their children's lives. Staff and participants also frequently mentioned the need for fathers to "man up" as good, caring parents. As a trope of hegemonic masculinity, this directive to "man up" revealed the continuing articulation between program messages about proper manhood and fatherhood.

Fathers described learning how to think of care as a masculine activity and specifically as a way to *provide* for their children. Low-income men of color especially struggle to meet gendered expectations of breadwinners. Overall, the men I studied were significantly disadvantaged. All fathers identified as cisgender men of color, most lived well below the poverty line, and few had graduated from high school. Those who were employed earned between $200 and $600 per month. Conceptualizing care as a form of provision allowed fathers to claim statuses as masculine caregivers and good providers who offered children unique benefits as *male* parents who modeled nurturance and healthy emotional expression.

Men incorporated stereotypically feminine aspects of parenting into their paternal identities by weaving together archetypes of the traditional masculine provider and the new, caring father who is manly enough to show his feelings, especially for his children. Orlando, a thirty-five-year-old Latino father of five, defined a good father as "someone always there, caring, emotionally, physically involved, financially. I'm more involved.... The way it used to be, my dad was the provider. It has to be more than that. They need my time, more being there, more listening, more love." Hank, a forty-four-year-old Latino father of four, similarly described how he learned from the program that responsible fathers provide for their children "in any way you can. Listen to what they have to say, consider their feelings. Be attentive to them." He regretted that his own father, a good financial provider, was not an "emotional provider." Like Orlando and Hank, most fathers I interviewed used the language of provision to describe caregiving and role modeling. Tanner, a thirty-seven-year-old mixed-race father of two, defined responsible fathering as "being a provider in the means of emotional support, guidance, living up to the whole statement of the difference between right and wrong, having honor in all that you do." Describing himself as a good father and "real man" because of his ability to nurture, Tanner elaborated:

> I care for them, whether it's tying my daughter's shoes or doing her hair, taking and finding that pleasure in doing those things and holding on to them. That's basically what fatherhood is all about. . . . If they need to talk, I listen. Anyone can be a dad by producing that offspring, but it takes a real man to be a father. . . . It takes a real man, in this class, learning how to communicate and be in touch with your feelings. I provide for them because I take care of them.

Through DADS, men learned to think of themselves as providers of masculine care and role models of healthy masculinity based on physical presence and emotional connection rather than on money.

Fathers distinguished this type of masculine care from the feminine care mothers give children. Monty, a thirty-four-year-old Latino father of six, explained:

> Mom is more for the loving. For fathers, there's a different kind of love. Dads do the sports thing, and moms do the "Come here, and I'll make everything better for you" thing. But both are love. That's another thing they taught in the [DADS] classes. Two different parents are two different parts. The dads are there to do certain things with the kids, and a boy needs his father in his life just like the girl needs her father in life. They both need a manly type of love.

This was a primary topic of discussion in the focus groups. Fathers passionately described how upsetting it was when a man fathered a child in the biological sense—a mere "sperm donor," one noted—and left others to take responsibility by caring for that child. Children specifically need love from fathers, the group agreed, because children are more confident when men care for them and teach them they are worthy of male love. The following conversation, excerpted without interruption from the third focus group, highlighted how fathers thought male parents provide children with a unique and indispensable form of affection:

XAVIER (TWENTY-ONE, BLACK, FATHER OF ONE): Fathers play a direct role in taking care of a child, in being present with the kids.

JAMES (NINETEEN, MIXED-RACE, FATHER OF TWO): Yes, a good dad is a person who's there to provide, protect, and love their family. Everything the child needs, not just money, and especially love. A dad is there to provide for them and to be there through everything, playtime, bath time, all that with your kids.

RODRIGO (NINETEEN, MIXED-RACE, EXPECTANT FATHER): Right, it's money, but more important, a father, he balances that with the ability to show them affection, too. To show them love specifically from their father, it's not the same as love from the mother. Once you have a baby, you realize the baby's going to learn from its father what it doesn't learn from its mother. They need their dad, the male, to be there. . . . It makes them a better person. Growing up feeling that love and affection from both parents, they're not going to miss something.

Though most fathers described caring for their children as a central component of responsible fatherhood and manhood, very few spoke about accepting responsibility for performing equitable care labor within their families. Men frequently used phrases such as "being there," "being around," and "providing my time" to describe the importance of paternal presence, and many stressed how men should nurture children through communicating and playing with and listening to them. However, very few noted that parenting could be a gender-neutral activity, or that men should fully assume equal responsibility for meeting children's financial, emotional, and practical needs. Rather than conceptualizing parenting outside the bounds of gender, men learned that caregiving by male parents is uniquely valuable for children.

Participants specifically described how fathers are not feminized, and are actually more masculine "real" men, when they emphasize the emotional components of paternal involvement. Distinguishing "fathering" from "mothering," as the program emphasized, allowed men to stake a masculine space in what they perceived to be a feminized social sphere. Redefining paternal provision to emphasize love, care, and time also allowed men to circumvent definitions of providing focused on money that discount poor men of color.

### Redefining Emotional Expression as a Masculine Strength

Men also learned through DADS that tenderness, toward oneself and others, could be a core component of a masculine paternal identity. Fathers frequently cried during interviews and described how they cried in front of their children. Many described the program as a "support group" for men who had little access to venues for developing a nurturant paternal masculinity in a society that often typecasts marginalized men as "deadbeats" who refuse to financially support their children, much less care for them. Nicholas, a nineteen-year-old Latino father of one, explained how the program reinforced for him that

> it's OK to cry and have feelings. I was raised by my mom, who taught me how to feel. I was never like, "Oh, you're weak if you cry." No, if I've got to cry, I'm going to cry, and the program said that's OK. Sometimes a lot of guys have a hard time doing it because they don't really have anyone to talk to about how to be a father or a man. But here, if they hear somebody else talk about it, they really look at it differently.

As it did for Nicholas, the program helped many respondents embrace emotionality as part of their masculinity and fatherhood, especially if they had been taught to believe that "real men" did not cry. Notably, Nicholas and many other fathers had learned this particular lesson from their mothers and other women who raised them, not necessarily their fathers. Hank explained:

> My dad don't hug. He won't allow himself to feel. I love my kids, and I'm not embarrassed to hug them or tell them I love them. Even my sons, I'll give them a little peck on the cheek. I don't do it if I know it's going to embarrass them, but I'll give them a strong hug, not a buddy hug, a lovable hug. . . . I just don't think it's healthy for anybody, whether you're male or female, to try raising a child, whether it's a boy or a girl, and have too much toughness there. I tell my son it's OK to cry.

Men in the first focus group also noted that the program encouraged them to share their feelings, a behavior they believed was not acceptable in other social contexts. The following exchange between fathers illuminated how DADS taught them that children benefited from seeing men express their emotions:

> SAUL (TWENTY-TWO YEARS OLD, LATINO, FATHER OF ONE):
> We don't know what women know because women don't know what men know. They don't know how we feel. Our side really doesn't ever get seen because it's not talked about. For men, like your feelings, we don't really share that stuff. That's something that we're able to do here.
> KEEGAN (TWENTY-ONE YEARS OLD, BLACK, FATHER OF THREE): With this class, it makes dads feel like we're needed and that it does make a difference in the kid's life with the daddies in the house.... Just because we don't show emotions like the girls do don't mean we don't worry about a whole bunch of stuff.
> CAYDEN (TWENTY-FOUR YEARS OLD, BLACK, FATHER OF TWO):
> We have to put our feelings under our shoes.
> JESSE (TWENTY YEARS OLD, BLACK, FATHER OF TWO): Yeah, Black guys especially are supposed to be strong and manly.
> CAYDEN: Being a father is not something that you can do just because you're a man. It's a skill you got to master. I used to feel like money made me a father, and that just because I'm a man and you're a woman, I'm a father. [DADS] changed me. Money doesn't make the father, love does.

Fathers also told me that they considered their fellow participants role models of caring fatherhood who helped them overcome "natural" male predispositions to be distant and less affectionate toward their children. Aaron, a twenty-one-year-old Black father of three, explained how DADS enabled him to challenge his male tendency to pull back from his family: "I think it's just something about being a man. It's just in our DNA. [DADS] changes minds because some men have been raised in environments where they didn't see any other fathers around their kids, just dads leaving all the time. Here they get that experience from other dads telling them, 'It's OK, I've been there for my son or daughter.'" Emmett, a twenty-four-year-old Black father of one deceased child, explained how becoming a father and participating in the program opened him up to being more vulnerable and expressive—for instance, to be able to cry in public. Our interview focused on the trauma of losing his four-week-old daughter to Sudden Infant Death Syndrome (SIDS) and how DADS staff and fellow participants were invaluable support as he grieved her passing. His peers empathized the stigmatization of men who expressed their emotions in public as effeminate. Collectively they helped him reframe emotionality, especially in relation to parenting, as a manly behavior. Emmett explained:

> I was taught a man doesn't cry. "Shut up, why are you crying? Are you girly? Are you a little girl?" I was picked on, after a while it worked, and I stopped. I've held back crying for so many years, so it just breaks out. . . . But I've learned that a dad is a man, the provider, protector, the nourisher, and he's aware of his child's well-being. He knows when to cry, when not to cry, and, yeah, that it's OK to cry. What makes a man is that he's aware of his emotions, he's self-aware, and he's in control, which can mean crying.

Many fathers admitted that defining these traits as masculine, rather than feminine, was difficult. But other men in the program validated their efforts to embrace sensitivity and emotional expressivity as part of their "manly" parenting practices.

### Conclusion: Fathering Is a Feminine Issue

As parenting becomes increasingly central to men's family-based identities, men must appropriate femininity to cope with changing gender relations.[43] Though many men reject authoritarian understandings of fatherhood, they often struggle to meet new demands for caring and emotionality without feeling marginalized as feminine. As this chapter has shown, they devise creative strategies to negotiate the gender tensions that emerge between masculine expectations of breadwinning and feminine expectations of caregiving, such as by redefining paternal provision to focus on nurturance. These strategies have paradoxical implications for family inequality. On one hand, they underscore men's abilities to nurture and express a full range of emotions. On the other, they rely on "soft essentialist" ideologies that fortify ideas that parental roles are gendered and distinct.[44] Ironically, legitimizing men's caregiving—especially as male role models, playmates, and sources of male love—creates a masculine space in a traditionally feminized social sphere without reframing parenting as more gender-neutral or even demanding men's equal participation in care labor.

The interview context itself was a window into the way fathers thought about parenting as a gendered practice. There was significant social distance between me— a white, highly educated, middle-class, feminine, cisgender woman—and the low-income fathers of color I studied. Visibly pregnant during interviews, I followed Michael L. Schwalbe and Michelle Wolkomir's advice in interviewing men by positioning fathers as experts and acknowledging them first and foremost *as parents* who were qualified to give me suggestions about how to cope with the upcoming arrival of my first child.[45] I embodied meanings that men attached to parental responsibility, especially differences between "mothering" and "fathering." Fathers' remarks about my pregnancy revealed assumptions that I would adopt a feminized parenting style wholly different from theirs because I was a woman. Yet the qualities they ascribed to me as a feminine female parent—caring, affectionate, concerned for my child's future well-being—were not distinct from those they saw as masculine qualities for themselves. Yet there was a sense that these same attributes benefited children differently when expressed by men, through the masculine influence of fathering on childrearing.

This case has significant implications for understandings of male femininities. Co-opting the language of care when describing men's unique value as parents reinforces the taken-for-granted notion that masculinity is an essential quality of maleness. This tendency to assume that something is masculine merely because men do it—and that its worth derives from this gendered quality—is a core ideology of patriarchy, one of the many mechanisms by which privileges accrue to men, males, and masculinity. Jack Halberstam describes how gender relations become legible by dislocating masculinity outside male bodies, practices, and experiences.[46] Yet, as this case has shown, they also become visible through attempts to masculinize elements deemed feminine when the goal is to make these elements seem more legitimate for men. Gender hierarchies depend on ascribing less social and economic value to stereotypically feminine practices, even when men perform them. One reason these hierarchies persist despite apparent challenges to the gender order is because, rather than embracing male femininities, there is a much greater tendency to masculinize behaviors with prior feminine associations.

In an essay entitled "Fathering is a Feminist Issue," Louise B. Silverstein argued that redefining fatherhood to make nurturance, attachment, and care central to gender socialization for men is an essential step in changing the cultural construction of masculinity into something less oppressive for both men and women and for the transformation of patriarchal culture.[47] In recognizing that males and men have the same capacity for nurturance and caregiving as females and women, we must also reject the gendered assumption that care is an essentially feminine activity that risks undermining the gender identities of fathers. DADS allowed men to challenge stereotypes that fathers should be emotionally inexpressive breadwinners and to rationalize their involvement based on the idea that responsible fathering is a gendered practice distinct from mothering. The former is a huge step forward in making parenting more egalitarian, but the latter merely entrenches ideology that fathering must somehow deny feminine characterizations. R. W. Connell once wrote: "When pictures of men with guns are rare, and pictures of men with [strollers] are common, we will really be getting somewhere."[48] This research suggests that, even when we reach this day, we will still have far to go if men feel they need to account for how caregiving can be manly and masculine caregiving uniquely benefits children. Fathering will realize its full feminist potential only when male parents are valued *as caregivers*, not as men. Beyond being common, fathers with strollers must not fear being feminized.

NOTES

1 US White House, "Promoting Responsible Fatherhood," Washington, DC, 2012, https://obamawhitehouse.archives.gov, 1, 3.
2 Jack Halberstam, *Female Masculinity* (Durham, NC: Duke University Press, 1998).
3 Fiona Williams, "Troubled Masculinities in Social Policy Discourses," in *Men, Gender Division, and Welfare*, ed. Jennie Popay, Jeff Hearn, and Jeanette Edwards (New York: Routledge, 1998), 63–97.
4 Anna Gavanas, *Fatherhood Politics in the United States: Masculinity, Sexuality, Race, and Marriage* (Urbana: University of Illinois Press, 2004).
5 Gavanas, *Fatherhood Politics*, 99.
6 Joseph H. Pleck, "American Fathering in Historical Perspective," in *Changing Men: New Directions in Research on Men and Masculinities*, ed. Michael S. Kimmel (Beverly Hills, CA: Sage, 1987), 83–97.

7 Gavanas, *Fatherhood Politics*; Maureen Waller, *My Baby's Father: Unmarried Parents and Paternal Responsibility* (Ithaca, NY: Cornell University Press, 2002).
8 Ralph LaRossa, "Fatherhood and Social Change," *Family Relations* 37, no. 4 (1988): 451–57.
9 Claire M. Kamp Dush, Jill E. Yavorsky, and Sarah J. Schoppe-Sullivan, "What Are Men Doing While Women Perform Extra Unpaid Labor? Leisure and Specialization at the Transitions to Parenthood," *Sex Roles* 78, nos. 11–12 (2018): 715–30.
10 Michael A. Messner, "'Changing Men' and Feminist Politics in the United States," *Theory and Society* 22, no. 5 (1993): 723–37.
11 Ralph LaRossa, *The Modernization of Fatherhood: A Social and Political History* (Chicago: University of Chicago Press, 1997).
12 Michael Kimmel, "Masculinity as Homophobia: Fear, Shame, and Silence in the Construction of Gender Identity," in *Theorizing Masculinities*, ed. Harry Brod and Michael Kauffman (Thousand Oaks, CA: Sage, 1994), 58–70.
13 Michael A. Messner, *Politics of Masculinities: Men in Movements* (Walnut Creek, CA: AltaMira, 2000).
14 Glenda Wall and Stephanie Arnold, "How Involved Is Involved Fathering? An Exploration of the Contemporary Culture of Fatherhood," *Gender & Society* 21, no. 4 (2007): 508–27.
15 LaRossa, *Modernization of Fatherhood*.
16 Kimmel, "Masculinity as Homophobia."
17 Allen Kim and Karen Pyke, "Taming Tiger Dads: Hegemonic American Masculinity and South Korea's Father School," *Gender & Society* 29, no. 4 (2015): 509–33; Kimmel, "Masculinity as Homophobia"; Nicholas Townsend, *The Package Deal: Marriage, Work, and Fatherhood in Men's Lives* (Philadelphia, PA: Temple University Press, 2002).
18 Robert Griswold, *Fatherhood in America* (New York: Basic Books, 1993).
19 Pierette Hondagneu-Sotelo and Michael A. Messner, "Gender Displays and Men's Power: The 'New Man' and the Mexican Immigrant Man," in *Theorizing Masculinities*, ed. Harry Brod and Michael Kauffman (Thousand Oaks, CA: Sage, 1994), 200–218.
20 Hondagneu-Sotelo and Messner, "Gender Displays and Men's Power."
21 Melanie Heath, "Soft-Boiled Masculinity: Renegotiating Gender and Racial Ideologies in the Promise Keepers Movement," *Gender & Society* 17, no. 3 (2003): 423–44, 441.
22 Laura Curran and Laura Abrams, "Making Men into Dads: Fatherhood, the State, and Welfare Reform," *Gender & Society* 14, no. 5 (2000): 662–78; Jennifer M. Randles, "Repackaging the 'Package Deal': Promoting Marriage for Low-Income Families by Targeting Paternal Identity and Reframing Marital Masculinity," *Gender & Society* 27, no. 6 (2013): 864–88.
23 Ann Shola Orloff and Renee Monson, "Citizens, Workers, or Fathers? Men in the History of US Social Policy," in *Making Men into Fathers: Men, Masculinities and the Social Politics of Fatherhood*, ed. Barbara Hobson (New York: Cambridge University Press, 2002), 61–91.

24 Randles, "Repackaging the 'Package Deal.'"
25 David Blankenhorn, *Fatherless America: Confronting Our Most Urgent Social Problem* (New York: Harper Perennial, 1996); David Popenoe, *Life without Father: Compelling New Evidence That Fatherhood and Marriage Are Indispensable for the Good of Children and Society* (New York: Free Press, 1996).
26 Kyle D. Pruett, *Fatherneed: Why Father Care Is as Essential as Mother Care for Your Child* (New York: Broadway, 2000): 57.
27 Maggie Gallagher, "Father Hunger," in *Lost Fathers: The Politics of Fatherlessness in America*, ed. Cynthia R. Daniels (New York: St. Martin's, 1998), 163–82, 165.
28 Sara McLanahan, Laura Tach, and Daniel Schneider, "The Causal Effects of Father Absence," *Annual Review of Sociology* 39 (2013): 399–427.
29 Timothy J. Biblarz and Judith Stacey, "How Does the Gender of Parents Matter?," *Journal of Marriage and Family* 72, no. 1 (2010): 3–22.
30 Henry Bos, Naomi Goldberg, Loes Van Gelderen, and Nanette Gartrell, "Adolescents of the U.S. National Longitudinal Family Study: Male Role Models, Gender Role Traits, and Psychological Adjustment," *Gender & Society* 26, no. 4 (2012): 603–38.
31 Sofia Aboim, *Plural Masculinities: The Remaking of the Self in Private Life* (Burlington, VT: Ashgate, 2010).
32 Andrea Doucet, *Do Men Mother?* (Toronto, Canada: University of Toronto Press, 2006).
33 R. W. Connell and James Messerschmidt, "Hegemonic Masculinity: Rethinking the Concept," *Gender & Society* 19, no. 6 (2005): 829–59; Mimi Schippers, "Recovering the Feminine Other: Masculinity, Femininity, and Gender Hegemony," *Theory and Society* 36, no. 1 (2007): 85–102.
34 Kathryn Edin and Timothy J. Nelson, *Doing the Best I Can: Fatherhood in the Inner City* (Berkeley: University of California Press, 2013); Renata Forste, John Bartkowski, and Rebecca Allen Jackson, "'Just Be There for Them': Perceptions of Fathering among Single, Low-Income Men," *Fathering* 7, no. (2009): 49–69; Waller, *My Baby's Father*.
35 Edin and Nelson, *Doing the Best I Can*; Forste et al., "Just Be There for Them."
36 Elaine A. Anderson and Bethany Letiecq, "Situating Fatherhood in Responsible Fatherhood Programs: A Place to Explore Father Identity," in *Situated Fathering: A Focus on Physical and Social Spaces*, ed. William Marsiglio, Kevin Roy, and Greer L. Fox (Lanham, MD: Rowman & Littlefield, 2005), 187–208.
37 Kevin Roy and Omari Dyson, "Making Daddies into Fathers: Community-Based Fatherhood Programs and the Construction of Masculinities for Low-Income African American Men," *American Journal of Community Psychology* 45, nos. 1–2 (2010): 139–54.
38 Connell and Messerschmidt, "Hegemonic Masculinity"; Schippers, "Recovering the Feminine Other."
39 Michael L. Schwalbe, *Unlocking the Iron Cage: The Men's Movement, Gender Politics, and American Culture* (New York: Oxford University Press, 1996).

40  Brian Donovan, "Political Consequences of Private Authority: Promise Keepers and the Transformation of Hegemonic Masculinity," *Theory and Society* 27 no. 6 (1998): 817–43.
41  Allan G. Johnson, *The Gender Knot: Unraveling Our Patriarchal Legacy* (Philadelphia, PA: Temple University Press, 2005).
42  Tristan Bridges and C. J. Pascoe, "Hybrid Masculinities: New Directions in the Sociology of Men and Masculinities," *Sociology Compass* 8 no. 3 (2014): 246–58.
43  Aboim, *Plural Masculinities*; Doucet, *Do Men Mother?*; Randles, "Repackaging the 'Package Deal.'"
44  Tristan Bridges and Michael Kimmel, "Engaging Men in the United States: Soft Essentialism and the Obstacles to Coherent Initiatives in Education and Family Policy," in *Men and Masculinities around the World: Transforming Men's Practices*, ed. Elisabetta Ruspini, Jeff Hearn, Bob Pease, and Keith Pringle (New York: Palgrave Macmillan, 2011), 160–73.
45  Michael L. Schwalbe and Michelle Wolkomir, "Interviewing Men," in *Handbook of Interview Research: Context and Method*, ed. Jaber F. Gubrium and James A. Holstein (Thousand Oaks, CA: Sage, 2002), 203–21.
46  Halberstam, *Female Masculinity*.
47  Louise B. Silverstein, "Fathering is a Feminist Issue," *Psychology of Women Quarterly* 20 (1996): 3–37.
48  R. W. Connell, "Politics of Changing Men," *Australian Humanities Review* (1995), accessed March 27, 2018, http://www.australianhumanitiesreview.org.

# Conclusion

## Male Femininities and Dismantling the Binaries and Boundaries of Gender

DANA BERKOWITZ, ELROI J. WINDSOR, C. WINTER HAN

Our primary goal for this collection was to bring together a mix of first-person narratives, essays, and empirical studies that would help readers understand the complexities and configurations of male femininities. Through our own exploration of gender nonconformity, creativity, and resistance, we, as editors, wanted to bring together both innovative and accessible writings that capture what it means to transgress gender norms and binaries at this historical moment, when gender binaries are actively being challenged and confronted and alternative ways of identifying are being explored. Another goal for this book was to provide a way for our students to see their own experiences mirrored in its pages. We hope we have succeeded in these objectives, and that these readings launch lively and engaging debate and discussion, both in and out of the classroom, that critically interrogates the boundaries and binaries of gender and sexuality and provides students with the opportunity to explore what it means for men to engage, embrace, and perform male femininities in all its potential forms.

In their collection *Imagining Masculinities*, C. J. Pascoe and Tristan Bridges write that "scholars have never been so interested in femininity or femininities as masculinity scholars have been in masculinity."[1] Like those authors, we hope that this text prompts scholars to theorize about masculinities in ways more in line with feminist theorizing, and to incite feminist scholars to engage more with femininity in ways that are not dismissive or reductionist. Reading these selections alongside one another provides a chance to think seriously about what it means to use male femininities as sites of knowledge production for feminism.

However, in order to think about how male femininities can act as such, we first need to consider the historically ambivalent and conflicted relationship of feminism to femininity. Demarcated by women who grew up in a society that enforced their participation in feminine activities and deprived them of access to the masculine, women of the second-wave feminist movement shunned and repressed all things coded as feminine. Within that social context, to succeed as a feminist meant rejecting femininity. In their quest to empower women and girls to be strong, bold, and powerful, second-wave feminists paradoxically cast the message that having any sort of affection for femininity meant that you were not a "true" feminist.

However, with the advent of third-wave feminist and queer scholarship, we now know that feminisms and femininity are not necessarily mutually exclusive: the road to gender inequality is not paved with rejecting all things feminine, and donning feminine accoutrements does not disqualify one from being and identifying as a feminist. Consonant with this historical shift, many of the authors in this text consider the ways that valuing the feminine is within the scope of a feminist future and ask us to consider the messages we are sending to women and men, girls and boys, and to transgender and nonbinary folks about the value of femininity.

We realize that "doing femininity" is not political in and of itself, nor are all performances of femininity radical acts. But celebrating femininity by socially rewarding reproductive labor, care work, and emotional support can open up opportunities for resistance among folks of all genders and sexes. Validating the sexual and intimate pleasures that come with the work of creating performative genders and sexualities in the antinormative bodies inhabited by male femininities opens up new spaces for feminist praxis, and knowledge production.

However, at the same time as we may begin to celebrate the pleasures of femininity in men, and among trans and nonbinary folks, femininity among women and girls continues to be perceived as indicative of vulnerability, fragility, and frivolity, in order to justify structural gendered inequities in wage labor and physical and sexual violence. Thus, we should seriously question what it means to be more inclined to celebrate the pleasures of femininity in everyone except women and girls, and what this accomplishes for feminism. How does valuing configurations of femininity in boys, men, and trans folks, but not in women and girls, continue to serve men's interests as men and reaffirm male dominance? Finally, how might scholars of gender, particularly of male femininities, engage more deeply with "feminism" as opposed to simply "femininity?"

Resistance is an everyday act, and the embodied practices of male femininities can and do chip away at the gender system. When men perform, embrace, and embody femininity, we see that what is deemed "feminine" is not mutually exclusive for men and women. Rather, qualities of femininity can be redeployed by otherwise masculine actors, changing the nature of what we mean by "femininity" all together. Rather than performing femininity as the absence of masculinity, men in the readings that we have provided often engage in femininity alongside masculinity, thereby embracing both and, in so doing, challenging the gender binary as not only fluid, but non–mutually exclusive. Individuals can, and often do, perform masculinity and femininity simultaneously; thus, femininity is not a trait found in some people while masculinity is found in others. Instead, all of those characteristics that we've come to label as "feminine" or "masculine" can be taken on by all people, regardless of their gender identity.

Yet we cannot emphasize more strongly that there is more at stake to bringing these readings into conversation with one another than simply their theoretical contributions. In much the same way that the rejection for all things feminine does not lead to structural equality, the quest for masculinity, in all its forms, for all, is not an ideal to celebrate. Indeed, one can argue that masculinity in its most exaggerated forms is responsible for interpersonal and sexual violence, war and the fetishization of militarism and weaponry, and callous responses to public health and climate disasters. Men performing and practicing femininity is good for humankind. Embracing and valuing femininity has serious implications that extend far beyond gender theory, and we do not claim to have all the answers. In fact, this book may raise more questions than it answers. And it should come as no surprise that we still have a long way to go in fully theorizing what is meant by "male femininities." No doubt there are many more types of male femininity being practiced by men all over the world. Likewise, if male femininity is different from female femininity, is it possible for individuals who do not identify as men to engage in male femininities? We suspect that it is. Future projects will take on these nonmale male femininities and may conceive of masculinity and femininity in diverse and more robust ways than the contents of this book currently capture. In addition, youth are actively changing the landscape of gender in exciting ways, and, as we write, essays on the limitlessness of gender abound. Femme-identified people write about embracing they/them pronouns.[2] The pronoun "it" is being reclaimed in some nonbinary/trans communities. People who may appear aligned in their sex/gender/gender expression are identifying as nonbinary and insisting they be recognized as such. These assertions are sometimes met with resistance; indeed, some critics balk at the idea that identity equals analysis and instead emphasize the need for understanding the ways in which gender oppression is embedded structurally. This critique calls for a feminist perspective that acknowledges how people can experience pleasure and joy in identifying with binary gender while simultaneously working to dismantle the supremacy of this system. In addition to needing more intersectional analyses of gender that account for these discordant positions, we also should challenge the structurally embedded hierarchies that privilege male/man/masculinity over female/woman/femininity while relying on their binary configurations.

Given the rapid pace of change around gender performativity and expression during the past decade, we anticipate that many of these readings will soon be outdated. Nonetheless, they will hopefully provide a framework for future scholars and writers to explore the multitude of ways that male femininities have always been, and continue to be, a part of the lives of men. We encourage scholars of the next generation to keep thinking and writing about the challenges male femininities present to the gender binary, not simply by blurring the boundaries but by demonstrating whether those boundaries have ever existed at all.

NOTES
1 C. J. Pascoe and Tristan Bridges, *Exploring Masculinities: Identity, Inequality, Continuity and Change* (Oxford: Oxford University Press, 2015), 429.
2 Tre'vell Anderson, "Nonbinary Femmes Must Be Included in the Feminist Movement," *Out*, February 15, 2019, https://www.out.com; S. E. Smith, "Beyond the Binary: Yes, Nonbinary Femmes Exist," http://meloukhia.net.

## ACKNOWLEDGMENTS

We owe a debt of gratitude to the many smart, thoughtful, creative, and generous people who helped bring this volume into fruition. First and foremost, we want to thank our authors, who provided the chapters that grace these pages and worked with us patiently over the course of the five years it took to complete this book.

Many thanks to Ilene Kalish, our editor at NYU Press, who was excited about this project from the beginning, who kept us on target, and who never gave up on us. We deeply appreciate the two anonymous reviewers who provided tremendously generative feedback that strengthened our book. Our gratitude also goes out to B. Ethan Coston, who, early on in this book's inception, pointed out flaws in our call for papers and provided critical feedback that shaped how the book evolved.

Dana would like to thank Michael Kimmel, who imagined this book. Thanks to Elroi and Chong-suk, who stepped up when she needed them and helped push this book into new directions that she is immensely proud of. Dana is also grateful for her parents and sister, Daryl, for their steadfast support of her work. Finally, to Casey, Levi, and baby Lula, who make life so much better every day.

Elroi would like to thank graduate students Lindy Moore and Aaliyah Carter for their research assistance, and Dana and Chong-suk for their sustained patience, insights, and comradery. Elroi is also grateful for Avie and Izzy for keeping life light and wild, and for Moki for her fierce femme love and support.

Chong-suk would like to thank Scott for his steadfast support and Dana and Elroi for making this journey more enjoyable than it might have been otherwise. Chong-suk would also like to thank his family, particularly his siblings Sophia, Helen, and Alex. Finally, his nephew Caleb and his niece Caetlyn for all the love they shower on him.

ABOUT THE CONTRIBUTORS

JOSHUA G. ADAIR is Professor of English at Murray State University, where he also serves as coordinator of Gender and Diversity Studies. Adair's work and teaching, whether in literary, historical, or museum studies, examines the ways we narrate—and silence—gender and sexuality; it has appeared in over fifty scholarly and creative nonfiction journals. His recent publications include *Defining Memory: Local Museums and the Construction of History in America's Changing Communities*, 2nd ed., edited with Amy K. Levin (Rowman & Littlefield, 2017); "O [Queer] Pioneers: Narrating Queer Lives in Virtual Museums" (*Museum & Society* 2017); "The Art of Shrinking: Minority Stress, Coping, and Camp in Beverley Nichols's *Merry Hall* Trilogy," coauthored with Rebekah Goemaat, (*Interdisciplinary Literary Studies*, 2016); and *Museums, Sexuality, and Gender Activism*, edited with Amy K. Levin (Routledge, 2019).

RUSTY BARRETT is Associate Professor in the Linguistics Department at the University of Kentucky. His research focuses on language and discrimination, highland Mayan languages, language revitalization, and language and gender/sexuality. He is author of *From Drag Queens to Leathermen: Language, Gender, and Gay Male Subcultures* (Oxford University Press, 2017) and coeditor of the *Oxford Handbook of Language and Sexuality* (forthcoming) with Kira Hall.

KATELYNN BISHOP is an interdisciplinary feminist sociologist with a PhD in Sociology from the University of California, Santa Barbara. Her research and teaching interests include gender, sexuality, race, embodiment, and consumer culture. She is currently working on a book project entitled "Imperfect Fit: Bras, Embodied Difference, and the Limits of Consumerism." Her writing appears in *Body & Society*, *Gender & Society*, and *Teaching Sociology*. She currently teaches at Sacramento City College

TRAVIS BEAVER is Associate Professor of Sociology at Massachusetts College of Liberal Arts. He earned his PhD in Sociology from the University of Texas at Austin. His current research explores how heterosexual masculinities have been transformed by feminist and LGBTQ activism.

STEPHANIE BONVISSUTO is a PhD candidate in the Department of Women's, Gender, and Sexuality Studies at Stony Brook University. Her doctoral research examines the constitutive relationship between the social subject, all-gender spaces, and available queer praxes in the construction of gender and sexual identities. Stephanie received a joint master's degree in Women's Studies and Sociology from Brandeis University and degrees in Women's Studies and Sociology from the University of Massachusetts Boston. As an undergraduate, she also worked as the university's student coordinator of its queer student center, which built on her experience as a sitting board member and peer trained facilitator at the LOFT: the LGBT Community Center of Westchester, NY.

KC COUNCILOR is Assistant Professor of Communication, Media, and Screen Studies at Southern Connecticut State University. He earned his PhD in Communication Arts at the University of Wisconsin-Madison. You can see more of his work at www.kccouncilor.com.

STEVEN F. DANSKY has been an activist, a writer, and a photographer for more than fifty years. He is the publisher of Christopher Street Press and the executive director of Outspoken Films and *Outspoken: Oral History from LGBTQ Pioneers*. He was in the civil rights and anti-war movements; a community organizer on New York's Lower Eastside; and, in 1969, he was an influential member of Gay Liberation Front (GLF). He is referenced in most books on the formative years of the LGBT movement from 1971 to the present. He published the literary journal *Faggotry*; a founder of effeminism, he was a copublisher of *Double-F: A Magazine of Effeminism*; and was in the *Come Out!* newspaper collective. He is the author of several books including *Now Dare Everything: Tales of HIV-Related Psychotherapy* (Routledge, 1994) and *Nobody's Children: Orphans of the HIV Epidemic* (Routledge, 1997). As an essayist, he is frequent contributor to the *Gay and Lesbian Review*. His essays have been anthologized in several collections, including the essay "Hey Man," in *The Stonewall Reader* (Penguin, 2019) and "The Look of Gay Liberation," *Gay and Lesbian Review* (2019). Dansky's photography and art have been both published including *LensWork* (2012); *Art and Queer Culture* (Phaidon, 2019); and in solo and group exhibitions. His documentary *From Trauma to Activism* was screened in several major cities (Las Vegas, New York, and San Francisco), and included in the Pride of the Ocean Film Festival. *On Performing Identity* was shown at the Leslie-Lohman of Gay and Lesbian Art, New York.

DIANE EHRENSAFT is Associate Professor of Pediatrics at University of California San Francisco, and Director of Mental Health of the Child and Adolescent Gender Center, UCSF Benioff Children's Hospital. She is a developmental and clinical psychologist who specializes in research, clinical work, training, and consultation related to gender-expansive children, and publishes and lectures both nationally and internationally on this topic. She is presently coinvestigator in a four-site NIH grant studying the effects of puberty blockers and gender-affirming hormones in gender-expansive and transgender youth. She is coeditor with Dr. Colt Keo-Meier of *The Gender Affirmative Model* (American Psychological Association, 2018), and author of *The Gender Creative Child* (Experiment, 2016); *Gender Born, Gender Made* (Experiment, 2011); *Mommies, Daddies, Donors, Surrogates* (Guilford, 2005); *Building a Home Within* (coedited with Toni Heineman, Brookes, 2005); *Spoiling Childhood* (Guilford, 1999); *Parenting Together* (University of Illinois Press, 1990). She received her PhD from the University of Michigan and has served on the faculty of the University of San Francisco; University of California, Berkeley; Wright Institute (Berkeley), Psychoanalytic Institute of Northern California; and Access Institute (San Francisco). She is a member of WPATH and a chapter work group member for the WPATH Standards of Care Version 8 and also on the Board of Directors of Gender Spectrum, an organization providing education, advocacy, and support to families, schools, and community to build gender inclusivity. She is also a founding member, board member, and senior clinician of A Home Within, a national organization that offers pro bono psychotherapy and serves the emotional needs of children and youth in foster care.

PATRICK R. GRZANKA is Professor of Psychology and core faculty in the interdisciplinary program in Women, Gender, and Sexuality at the University of Tennessee. His transdisciplinary research on complex inequalities at the nexus of race, gender, and sexualities has been funded by the National Science Foundation and published in various academic journals, including *Journal of Counseling Psychology, Sexualities, WSQ: Women's Studies Quarterly, Sexuality Research and Social Policy*, and *American Journal of Bioethics*. He is the 2018 recipient of the Michele Alexander Early Career Award from the Society for the Psychological Study of Social Issues. His first book, *Intersectionality: Foundations and Frontiers* (Routledge, 2019), is now in its second edition, and he is working on a new book (under contract with Cambridge University Press) that traces scientific, legal, and cultural debates about the etiology of sexuality orientation and their implications for civil rights and social justice.

PETER HENNEN is an Associate Professor Emeritus at Ohio State University Newark. His research is interested in how gender and sexuality are constructed and deployed in varying social, cultural, and historical formations. He is the author *of Faeries, Bears, and Leathermen: Men in Community Queering the Masculine* (University of Chicago Press, 2008). He has produced extensive ethnographic data and historical/comparative analyses of gay and queer masculinities.

MARY INGRAM-WATERS is Assistant Dean, Honors Faculty Fellow, and Principal Lecturer at Barrett, the Honors College, Arizona State University, where she teaches courses on social media, fan cultures, and gender and sexualities. Drawing on her training as a sociologist from the University of California, Santa Barbara, Ingram-Waters directs a group of talented undergraduate honors students in overlapping research projects on social media platforms, electronic games, fandoms, gender and sexualities. With her students, she has published on subjects that include revenge porn, queer readings of electronic games, and African American women fans' use of Twitter. She has also spoken to local and national media about football fans, including their gendered experiences of fantasy football.

JOHN KNOEBEL was a high-profile member of New York City's pioneering Gay Liberation Front (1969–1972). He participated in the first

Gay Pride March in June 1970 and was a member of GLF's 95th Street Men's Living Collective. He was a proponent of consciousness-raising groups for gay men and coauthored two foundational guides to C-R. He participated in many major GLF demonstrations, including the five-day protest occupation of NYU's Weinstein Hall, the August 1970 Times Square protest, and the subsequent second Greenwich Village gay riot. In 1970, he represented GLF in meeting with Black Panther leader Huey Newton and attended both sessions of the Panthers' Revolutionary People's Constitutional Convention in Philadelphia and Washington, DC—meetings that also served as the first national conferences of radical gay male activists. After GLF disbanded, he joined other former GLF men in helping define a politics of gay men in support of feminism. He coauthored the widely reprinted "Effeminist Manifesto" and was an editor of the Effeminist magazine, *Double-F*, from 1972 to 1976. Subsequently, he pursued a thirty-three-year career in LGBTQ publishing as a senior executive of the *Advocate* and *OUT* magazines. After retiring from the *Advocate*, he joined Steven Dansky in creating the LGBTQ oral history site www.outspoken-lgbtq.org and coedited the book *The Come Out! Reader*. He organized the June 2019 fifty-year reunion of GLF members. He continues to write and speak on LGBTQ history.

RAY LEBLANC is a PhD candidate in Cultural Studies at George Mason University. They previously obtained a master's degree in Anthropology from Louisiana State University in 2017. LeBlanc's research explores cultural practices, media representations, and the political economy of contemporary drag queening.

LESTER EUGENE MAYERS is a published writer, poet, director, commencement speaker and Black vernacular master persevere. A Brooklyn native and graduate of the Department of Theatre Arts at SUNY New Paltz, he won the 2017 SUNY Chancellors Award for Artistic Excellence. He is a current MFA candidate at the Jack Kerouac School of Disembodied Poetics. Gay-Black-feminine and a feminist, he tackles issues that have historically been ignored by the public. After self-publishing his first book, *100 Poems for 100 Voices*, he successfully completed a sold-out poetry tour. In June 2019 he released a poetry album on iTunes, Spotify, and Tidal. He was then honored and awarded by the National

Association of Colored Women, the oldest black women's organization in America. He has been published by the Huffington Post, Arsenal Pulp Press, Sojourner Truth Library, and I Am from DriftwoodLGBTQ archive. He has performed at many universities, including SUNY Oswego, Pace University, University at Buffalo, and Delta University. He completed a poetry book entitled *African Booty Scratcha (lovin da ashy-blaq fat chall wit yellow teef, peasy head & a broken smile.)*, dealing with dark-skinned children finding self-beauty and confidence in the world (independently published, 2019).

NIKOLA C. OSTMAN is a linguistics undergraduate student set to graduate from Lawrence University in the summer of 2022. His main focuses of study are East Asian languages, particularly Chinese and Japanese, and history.

KENNETH PITCHFORD is a poet, novelist, and writer whose poetry has been set to music by Lockrem Johnson and Ned Rorem. His books of poetry include *The Blizzard Ape* (Scribners, 1958); *A Suite of Angels* (University of North Carolina Press, 1967); *Color Photos of the Atrocities* (Little, Brown, 1973); *The Contraband Poems* (Templar, 1976); and *Dedications* (Derringer, 1987). He is also the translator of *The Sonnets to Orpheus of Rainer Maria Rilke* (Purchase, 1981) and the author of a play, *The Wheel of the Murder*, which was produced by Joseph Papp. His work has appeared in more than eighty-five magazines, including the *New Yorker*, *Poetry*, *Ms. Magazine*, *American Poetry Review*, the *Village Voice*, the *Nation*, the *New Republic*, *Rat*, and the *Liberation News Service*. His most recent appearance in print was a sonnet published in the *Gay & Lesbian Review*. His writing has appeared in nineteen anthologies, including *Gay and Lesbian Poetry in Our Time* (St. Martin's, 1988); *The Columbia Anthology of Gay Literature* (Columbia University Press, 1998); and *The Gay Rights Movement* (Greenhaven, 2003). He has taught writing workshops at the New School, New York University, and Columbia University.

JENNIFER RANDLES is Professor and Chair of Sociology at California State University, where she specializes in family, gender, poverty, and social policy. She is the author of *Proposing Prosperity: Marriage*

*Education Policy and Inequality in America* (Columbia University Press, 2017) and is currently writing a book on responsible fatherhood policy entitled "Essential Dads: Inequality and the Politics of Fathering in the United States."

ROSCOE C. SCARBOROUGH is Associate Professor of Sociology at the College of Coastal Georgia. In addition to ethnographic research on firefighters, his research interests include culture, inequality, media, music, qualitative research methods, and theory.

MIMI SCHIPPERS is Professor of Sociology and Gender and Sexuality Studies at Tulane University. Her research focuses on empirically documenting and theorizing masculinities, femininities, sexualities, and culture. She is author of the following books: *Polyamory, Monogamy, and American Dreams: The Stories We Tell About Poly Lives and the Cultural Production of Inequality* (Routledge, 2019); *Beyond Monogamy: Polyamory and the Future of Polyqueer Sexualities* (New York University Press, 2016); and *Rockin' Out of the Box: Gender Maneuvering in Alternative Hard Rock* (Rutgers University Press, 2002). Schippers received her PhD from the University of Wisconsin-Madison.

GRACIELA SLESARANSKY-POE, PhD, (she/her/hers), is a professor and the former founding dean of the School of Education at Arcadia University, where she cochairs the President's Commission on Justice, Equity, Diversity, and Inclusion. Her teaching, scholarship, and service are informed by her commitment to equity, access, and anti-oppressive education. She supports multiple educational institutions and has authored several publications on creating safe, welcoming, affirming, and gender inclusive schools. She is the recipient of several awards and recognitions, including the 2017 Champion of Social Justice, given by the Parent Education and Advocacy Leadership (PEAL) Center for "her work in creating welcoming, inclusive, and safe schools and organizations for gender non-binary and transgender children, youth and adults." She is the parent of two amazing kids, her true teachers.

JESÚS GREGORIO SMITH is Assistant Professor of Ethnic Studies at Lawrence University of Appleton, an Associated Colleges of the Midwest

(ACM) Andrew W. Mellon Fellow, as well as a 2020 Woodrow Wilson National Fellow. He received his PhD in Sociology in 2017 from Texas A&M University, where he studied systemic racism, gender, class, and sexuality as well as mental and sexual health. He has published several articles in such venues as *AIDS & Behavior, Issues in Race and Society,* and *Humanity & Society*. Jesús coedited a collection of essays *Home and Community for Queer Men of Color: The Intersection of Race and Sexuality* (Lexington, 2019) where he also contributed a chapter on HIV criminalization and Black gay men. His work has appeared in *Rolling Stone, Vice,* and the *Washington Post*, and on the BBC and NPR, among others. His current book manuscript, "Fat, Fem, and Fabulous: Sexual Racism and Resistance in Virtual Communities," is under contract with New York University Press.

AMY L. STONE is Professor of Sociology and Anthropology at Trinity University and author of *Queer Carnival* (New York University Press, 2022); *Gay Rights at the Ballot Box* (University of Minnesota Press, 2012); and *Cornyation: San Antonio's Outrageous Fiesta Tradition* (Maverick, 2017), along with being coeditor of *Out of the Closet, Into the Archives: Researching Sexual Histories* (State University of New York Press, 2015). They study lesbian, gay, bisexual, and transgender (LGBT) politics, urban life, and health.

LISA TATONETTI is Professor of English at Kansas State University where she studies, teaches, and publishes on queer Indigenous literatures. She is coeditor of *Sovereign Erotics* (University of Arizona Press, 2011), an award-winning collection of Two-Spirit creative work, and author of *The Queerness of Native American Literature* (University of Minnesota Press, 2014), which won the 2015 Thomas J. Lyons Book Award and is on the ALA 2016 Over the Rainbow Recommended Reading List. She is completing her current book manuscript, "Indigenous Knowledges Written by the Body: Female, Two-Spirit, and Trans Masculinities," while on a Rockefeller Fellowship at the National Humanities Center.

SAMANTHA LIZBETH TORRES is a Master's-Level Graduate Student at Fordham University's Graduate School of Social Service. Through the Posse Foundation, she received her Bachelor of Arts in Psychology and Theatre Arts from Lawrence University in 2020. As a human rights defender and change-maker in the making, she strives to bridge the gaps in our society and ensure a better tomorrow for all.

TERRELL J. A. WINDER is Assistant Professor of Sociology at the University of California, Santa Barbara. His research interests are racial and sexual stigma, sexual health, and identity development. In previous projects, he has assessed the role of mobile technology for the prevention and treatment of HIV, the impact of community organizations in religious and racial identity development, and the barriers to PrEP use among Black men who have sex with men. Winder's current book project investigates the impacts that chosen family, community organizations, and media have on the gender expression, racial identification, sexual identity, and life trajectories of young Black gay men.

ABOUT THE EDITORS

DANA BERKOWITZ is Associate Professor of Sociology and Women's and Gender Studies at Louisiana State University. She received her PhD in Sociology with a certificate in Women's and Gender Studies from the University of Florida in 2007. She is the author of *Botox Nation: Changing the Face of America* (New York University Press, 2017). Her scholarship has also appeared in journals such as *Journal of Marriage and Family*, *Qualitative Health Research*, *Journal of Contemporary Ethnography*, *Qualitative Sociology*, and *Symbolic Interaction*.

ELROI J. WINDSOR is Professor of Sociology at the University of West Georgia. While working on a doctoral degree at Georgia State University, Windsor specialized in gender and sexuality, studying trans men's health care experiences and the surgical body modification practices of cisgender and transgender consumers. Windsor is coeditor, with Mindy Stombler, Dawn M. Baunach, Elisabeth O. Burgess, and Wendy Simonds, of *Sex Matters: The Sexuality and Society Reader* (W. W. Norton, 2014, 2019; Allyn & Bacon, 2009). Currently, Windsor is focusing on the sociology of the body and embodiment and is working on a book based on ethnographic research with health care body workers who deal with parts of people and deceased bodies.

C. WINTER HAN is Professor of Sociology at Middlebury College. His work explores the intersection of race and sexuality. He is the author of Racial Erotics (University of Washington Press, 2021), *Geisha of a Different Kind: Race and Sexuality in Gaysian America* (New York University Press, 2015) and coeditor of *Home and Community For Queer Men of Color: The Intersection of Race and Sexuality* (Lexington, 2020). Prior to becoming an academic, he was an award-winning journalist and served as the editor in chief of the *International Examiner*, the oldest continuously publishing pan-Asian Pacific American newspaper in the United States.

# INDEX

Page numbers in *italics* indicate Figures.

Aboim, Sobia, 351
Acosta, Katie L., 228
activo/pasivo sex positioning, 229, 233, 237
affective exchange, in Indigenous writing, 97
aging: ageism and, 159, 162; in Botox advertisements for men, 149, 150, 159, 162; men's bodies and, 128
all-inclusive krewes, 195
Almaguer, Tomas, 24
alternative masculinity, 212, 222
amateur/professional drag performance boundaries, 204–6
*American Anthropologist*, 18
Anderson, Elaine A., 351
Anderson, Kim (Cree/Métis), 99
androgyny: Christianity and, 290; radical faeries and, 297, 299
Apollo, Krewe of, 195, 197–201, 204
appended effeminacy, 28
aristocratic effeminacy, 28–30
art installations, male pregnancy in, 166, 172–78, *173*, *175*, 181–82
Asian drag queens. *See* gay Asian drag queens; race
athleticism: cheerleading and, 250; heteronormativity and, 51–54; masculinity and, 152, 156
Atkinson, Jim, 146

BackDoor Boys, 251
Bahayana Buddhism, 290
Barber, Kristen, 128

barre, 51
Beatie, Thomas, 178–79
beaus, 23
beauty salons, men's, 128
*Becoming Two Spirit* (Gilley), 93
"Before He Cheats" (Underwood), 190
Belcourt, Billy-Ray (Driftpile Cree Nation), 92
belonging, Black gay men and, 272, 274, 276
Benton, Nick, 41
"berdache" terminology, 2SQ and, 90–93
Beyoncé, 266
bisexuality/bisexuals: antagonism towards, 124; increasing rates of, 246; in krewes, 195, 198–202; Latinx queer men and, 233–34
"bitch" trope, Black women and, 266–67
Black gay men: belonging and, 272, 274, 276; Black women tensions with, 265–66; bottom-shaming and, 14, 262–76; "brute caricature" and, 268; community cohesion of, 269–70; femininity and, 256–57, 259–61, 268–70; loneliness and, 259–61; masculinity idolization and, 264; sex positioning hierarchy and, 263–64, 270, 273; sexual positioning presumptions and, 271–73; "true tops" and, 273–74
*Black Sexual Politics* (Collins), 265
Black women: "bitch" trope and, 266–67; Black gay men tensions with, 265–66; bottom-shaming and, 265; lesbians, 239–40, 272; stereotypes of, 265–66

383

blame game, parents of gender-nonconforming boys and, 323–24

bodies: aging and men's, 128; breasted men enhancing, 136–38; breasted men reimagining, 138–40; culture and, 107; cyborg, 110; embodying male femininities, 107–11, 286–87; gender and, 107–8, 145; gender inequality and, 108; gender transition and, 13, 107, 109, *112–14*, 119; gynecomastia and, 126–27, 131, 140n11; masculinity and, 145–46; meaning assigned to, 108–9; men's self-care for, 143; objectification and, 109; objectification of men's, 127–28; objectification of women's, 139; pseudogynecomastia and, 126; technology and, 110. *See also* breasted men; male pregnancy

Botox, 13; branding and, 143–44; masculinity and, 147; number of users of, 144. *See also* Brotox

Botox advertisements for men: aging in, 149, 150, 159, 162; Botox advertisements for women compared to, 150–51; for career security/advancement, 156–59, *158*; class and, 153, 156, 162–63; for family man/fathers, 159–61, *160*; generic, 148–52, *149–51*; with hypermasculine tropes and images, 152–56, *154–56*; naturalness and, 151–52; race in, 148–49, 153, 156, *156*, 157, 163; study methods for, 147–48; women rewarded in, 153; women's suggestions in, 161

bottoming. *See* sex positioning

bottom-shaming: "bitch" trope and, 267; Black gay men and, 14, 262–76; Black women and, 265; consequences of, 274, 276; defining, 262; "fag" slur and, 267–68, 270; femininity and, 262, 276; heteronormativity and, 276; "lesbian relationships" and, 270; male femininities and, 264–65; memes, 273–74, *275*; patriarchy and, 263; sex position hierarchy and, 263–64, 270, 273; top-shaming in response to, 270

"Bottom Shaming" (Meacham), 274

boundary work, of parents of gender-nonconforming boys, 325–26

boutique fitness, 13, 47, 51–54

Brannon, Robert, 22

Brant, Beth, 105n44

bras: breasted men and, 125–26, 129–38; crossdressing compared to breasted men with, 134–35; femininity and, 133; masculinity and, 135; self-expression and, 133–34; sexual pleasure from, 135–36; tactile aspects of, 136

breasted men, 13, 107, 108; bodies reimagined by, 138–40; bras and, 125–26, 129–38; breast development awareness in, 130–31; causes of, 125; concealment techniques and, 131–32; cosmetic surgery and, 131; crossdressing compared to bras on, 134–35; feminism and, 139–40; gender experimentation and, 132–36, 138–39; gender identity and, 129; gynecomastia and, 126–27, 131, 140n11; interview methodology for, 129–30; masculinity and, 135, 138; pseudogynecomastia and, 126; self-expression of, 133–34; sexual pleasure from bras on, 135–36; social expectations of, 127; supplements and enhancements for, 136–38; transgender men compared to, 139

Bridges, Tristan, 196, 365

"bro privilege," 83

Brotox: advertisements for, 147–63; branding of, 143–44; male femininity repudiation and, 162–63; number of users of, 144; rise of, 144. *See also* Botox advertisements for men

"Brotox" (Taylor, P. L.), 143

Brown, Michael, 340

"brute caricature," Black gay men and, 268

Buddhism, Bahayana, 290

bullying: effeminate straight men and, 78; among firefighters, 342–43; of gender-expansive children, 66. See also violence
*The Butch Manual*, 31–32
Butler, Judith, 43, 226

camp: drag performance and, 196, 215; "The Effeminist Manifesto" on, 36–37; "straight," 28
Carballo-Dieguez, Alex, 230, 242
career security/advancement, Botox advertisements for men for, 156–59, 158
Carnival, 196–207. See also Mardi Gras; masque balls
Carolla, Adam, 32
"casual" masculinity, effeminate straight men compared to, 77–78
celebrity drag queens, 191–92
cheerbois, 9, 187–88; drag kings compared to, 10; female masculinity and, 10; male femininities and, 10, 252; radical cheerleading and, 251–52
cheerleading. See radical cheerleading
Cher, 214
"Chicano Men" (Almaguer), 24
childcare: "The Effeminist Manifesto" on, 39; fatherhood and, 346, 348–49; femininity and, 307; masculinity and, 351–55; from mothers compared to fathers, 354–55
Children's National Medical Center in Washington (CNMC), 315–16
Christianity: androgyny and, 290; homophobia and, 295; homosexuality in, 291; radical faeries and oppressiveness of, 299, 302–3; Sisters of Perpetual Indulgence and, 291–92
Christmas, Mary, 250–51
cisgender heterosexual men: cisgender heterosexual boys incorporating femininity, 66–68; femininity and, 74–75, 255–56; gay Asian drag queens using white, 220–21; hybrid masculinities and, 74; male femininities and, 7, 47; male femininities in transgender men compared to, 121; male pregnancy in movies and television and, 168–72; metrosexuals and, 145–46; polyamorous, 14, 255, 257–58, 279–88. See also effeminate straight men; polyamorous men
cisgender women: "faux queens" and, 216–17; pregnancy and, 167; radical cheerleading and, 251
cisnormativity, "single exception" theories and, 123–24
citizenship, drag performance and cultural, 197, 206–7
Clarke, Adele, 147
class: Botox advertisements for men and, 153, 156, 162–63; boutique fitness and, 51; effeminate straight men and, 75; fatherhood and, 349, 351; firefighters and, 332–33; Latinx queer men and, 231; men's beauty salons and, 128; metrosexuals and, 145, 146; molly houses and, 30; parents of gender-nonconforming boys and, 309, 317, 327
Clinton, Hillary, 3
CNMC (Children's National Medical Center in Washington), 315–16
Collette, Toni, 217
Collins, Patricia Hill, 265, 266
colonialism, queer settler, 296–97
colonial masculinity, 99
communication, polyamory and, 284
compensating, firefighters and, 335–36
"compersion," 283
condoning, firefighters and, 336–38
Connell, Raewyn W., 145, 227–28, 279, 360
*Connie and Carla*, 216–17
context: drag performance in, 194–96, 204–7; gay Asian drag queens in, 217–21; gender performativity of Latinx queer men and, 236–37, 241–42
Corbett, Ken, 64

"corrective treatment," parents of gender-nonconforming boys and, 323
cosmetic effeminacy, 27
cosmetics. *See* Botox; Brotox; makeup
cosmetic surgery: breasted men and, 131; men and, 128; penile implants, 146; reconstructive surgery, 146
Coxx, Sharon, 189–90
Craig, Larry, 84
Cree, 92
"crisis" of masculinity, 146, 157
crossdressing: breasted men with bras compared to, 134–35; "male crossdressers" and, 116
crying, masculinity and, 356, 358
Crystal, Billy, 170
C-sections, male pregnancy and, 168, 171, 181
cultural citizenship, drag performance and, 197, 206–7
cultural studies, effeminacy in, 21
culture: bodies and, 107; of Indigenous people, 293; transgender children and, 60. *See also* Latin culture
cyborg bodies, 110

DADS program, 352–58
dandies, 23, 76
Dansky, Seven F., 12, 18–19, 35–44. *See also* "The Effeminist Manifesto" (Dansky, Knoebel, Pitchford)
Davis, Jenny L., 94
*Dear Masculinity* (Councilor), 112–14
decolonization, 2SQ and, 103
Deutsch, Francine, 280–81
DeVito, Danny, 168, *169*
discursive male femininities, 286–87
Dole, Bob, 213
Doucet, Andrea, 351
drag performance, 14, 186–87; amateur/professional boundaries with, 204–6; camp and, 196, 215; Carnival, 196; in context, 194–96, 204–7; cultural citizenship and, 197, 206–7; "The Effeminist Manifesto" on, 43; fathers and, 193, 202–4; "faux queens" and, 216–17; first time, 189–92; as "gaystreaming," 197; joy and, 257; in Krewe of Apollo's ball, 199–201; krewes and, 204; LGBTQ krewes and, 199–202; makeup and, 98, 190, 200; names for, 190; in Order of Osiris' masque ball, 201–2; payment for, 190, 191; as protest, 195–96; race and, 194; raids against, 196; research methods for, 197–98; respect for, 197, 206–7; royalty in masque balls and, 200; security for, 189. *See also* masque balls
drag kings: cheerbois compared to, 10; drag queens compared to, 215; "fag drag" and, 10; "male" bodies and, 9–10; masculinity and, 251
drag queens, 9; celebrity, 191–92; drag kings compared to, 215; femininity and, 191, 192; first time, 189–92; gay Asian, 14, 187; gender exploration by, 216; gender notions reinforced by, 214–15; Humphrey on, 17; male femininities and, 193–94; names for, 190; Newton on, 17–18; payment for, 190, 191; violence against, 189, 192
*Drag Queens at the 801 Cabaret* (Rupp and Taylor, V.), 195
dreaming, Indigenous people and, 101–3
Driskill, Qwo-Li, 105n44
Duchovny, David, 217
Duran, Lori, 68
Dyson, Omari, 351

ectopic pregnancy, 174
effeminacy: in ancient Greece, 22–23, 26–27; appended, 28; aristocratic, 28–30; cosmetic, 27; in cultural studies, 21; defining, 21–26; "The Effeminist Manifesto" on oppression of men and, 36–39; female masculinities and, 32–33; hegemonic masculinity and, 12, 22, 26; homosexuality and, 21, 23–25, 28–33,

82; London molly houses and, 29–30; male femininities and, 75; misogyny in terminology of, 21; moral, 27, 28; "pansy craze" and, 24; political, 26–27; somatic, 27–28; typologies of, 18, 26–28; of Wilde, 23–24; women and, 32

effeminate straight men: attributes of, 76–79; bullying and, 78; "casual" masculinity compared to, 77–78; class and, 75; emotions and, 78–79; femininity embraced by, 80; gay men's advances rejected by, 85; gender normativity politics and, 87; glass closet and, 75, 84–86; heteronormativity and, 83, 87–88; heterosexuality signaling of, 82–83; homophobia disavowals by, 85; as homophobia targets, 87; makeup and, 76–77; as metrosexuals, 71, 76, 79, 87; mistaken for gay, 71–75, 80–82, 86; repressed homosexuality and, 83–86; sexuality and gender expression of, 80–84; uptalk and, 76

"The Effeminist Manifesto" (Dansky, Knoebel, Pitchford), 12, 18–19; on camp, 36–37; on childcare, 39; cultural revolution of, 40; on drag performance, 43; on gynarchism, 35; impact of, 44; language and terms in, 41; on lifestyle, 38; on Male Principle, 37; on male supremacy, 35; on masculinity, 36–38, 43; on masoch-eonism, 37, 43; on oppression of effeminate men, 36–39; on patriarchy, 35–36, 39, 43; reactions to, 42; second-wave feminism influencing, 41; on sexism, 35; on tactics, 38–39; on transgender people, 43–44; on women's leadership, 35–36

Eguchi, Shinsuki, 228

Elite Daily, 274

Elliott, Missy, 265

embodied male femininities, 107–11, 286–87. *See also* bodies

emotions: effeminate straight men and, 78–79; fathers engaging with, 348, 356–58; femininity and, 79; firefighters and, 335; in male pregnancy, 179; masculinity and fathers' expression of, 356–58; of parents of gender-nonconforming boys, 325

erotic sovereignty, 105n44

estrogen, 61, 137

*Excluded* (Serano), 115, 117–18

"fag drag," 9, 10

"fag" slur: bottom-shaming and, 267–68, 270; firefighters and, 338–39

families: funerals, male femininities and, 311–13; gender and, 307–8; in Mardi Gras, 202–4; violence within, 311. *See also* fathers/fatherhood; parents; parents of gender-nonconforming boys

family man, Botox advertisements for, 159–61, *160*

"Fathering is a Feminist Issue" (Silverstein), 360

fathers/fatherhood: absence of, 350–51; Botox advertisements for, 159–61, *160*; childcare and, 346, 348–49; childcare from mothers compared to, 354–55; class and, 349, 351; drag performance and, 193, 202–4; emotional engagement of, 348, 356–58; as experts, 359; femininity and, 308, 347–52, 358–60; grief and, 358; hegemonic masculinity and, 319, 320; hybrid masculinities and, 352; interviewing strategies for, 359; masculinity in childcare by, 351–55; masculinity in emotional expression of, 356–58; need for, 350; normative masculinity reinforced by, 322–23; normative understandings of, 348; nurturance and, 349, 354; Obama on, 346; as providers, 353–54; redefining, 347–52; responsibility of, 346–48, 352–55; as skill, 357; "soft-boiled" masculinity and, 349; sperm donors compared to, 354; Trump on, 346; "24/7 Dad" curriculum for, 352; welfare programs and, 350

"faux queens," 216–17

"Felt Theory" (Million), 97
female masculinities: assumptions of, 8; cheerbois and, 10; effeminacy and, 32–33; Halberstam on, 9; lesbians and, 6; male femininities compared to, 3–4; Serano on, 120–21; tomboys and, 87
*Female Masculinity* (Halberstam), 1, 9, 347
femininity: Black gay men and, 256–57, 259–61, 268–70; bottom-shaming and, 262, 276; bras and, 133; childcare and, 307; cisgender heterosexual boys incorporating, 66–68; cisgender heterosexual men and, 74–75, 255–56; defining, 6; devaluation of, 3; drag queens and, 191, 192; effeminate straight men embracing, 80; emotions and, 79; fatherhood and, 308, 347–52, 358–60; feminism and, 117; firefighters and, 333; gay Asian drag queens and, 218, 219, 221–23; gay men and, 3, 213–14, 255–57; hegemonic, 228, 245; intersectionality and stereotypes of, 48–49; intersex people and, 10; Latinx queer men and, 232, 235–36, 238–42, 245; as liberating, 238–40; makeup and, 48; male pregnancy and, 180–81; masculinity embodied alongside, 7, 367; metrosexuals and, 145–46; mysticism and, 291; other-centeredness and, 283–84; parents of gender-nonconforming boys on play and dress and, 318–19; pariah, 282; performing, 186; polyamorous men and, 257–58; radical faeries and, 257; Serano on, 117–19, 123; sex positioning and, 236, 237–38, 271–74; transgender boys and, 62; transgender girls and, 63–65; transgender men and, 109; women decoupled from, 4, 6, 11, 110. *See also* male femininities
femininity for self-actualization, 240–42
feminism: breasted men and, 139–40; femininity and, 117; male femininities and, 365–67; second-wave, 41, 66, 283; third-wave, 283, 366; transgender women and, 65
"femmephobia," 119
Field, Dawon, 175
Finley, Nancy, 282
firefighters, 15, 309; backgrounds of, 331; changing demands of, 343; class and, 332–33; compensating and, 335–36; condoning and, 336–38; emotions and, 335; "fag" slur and, 338–39; femininity and, 333; future research on, 344; hazing and bullying among, 342–43; inclusivity of, 342; masculinity in brotherhood of, 330–32, 342–44; passing and, 334–35; politics and, 333, 334, 340; PPE and, 337; probationary, 337–39; questioning and, 338–39; race and, 338, 340–41; soapboxing and, 339–41; study methods for, 332–33; women as, 331
fitness, 13, 47, 51–54
*Flawless*, 212–13
Fly Young Red, 262, 265, 276
fops, 23
*Forbes*, 143, 159
"For Men" branding, 143–44
Foshey, Sadie A., 176, 177
Foucault, Michel, 22
fraternity hazing, 207
"frubbly," 283
*Full-Metal Indigiqueer* (Whitehead), 90
funerals, male femininities and, 311–13

Galindo, Rudy, 51
Gallagher, Maggie, 350
Gavanas, Anna, 347–48
gay Asian drag queens, 14, 187; alternative masculinity and, 212, 222; in context, 217–21; femininity and, 218, 219, 221–23; limitations of, 219; male femininities and, 212; Orientalist tropes and, 220; race and, 219–20; racism against, 211, 217; stereotypes and, 218–19, 222;

white cisgender heterosexual men as punchlines for, 220–21
gay Black men. *See* Black gay men
gay Latinx men. *See* Latinx queer men
gay male femininity, 212–14, 222–23
gay men: effeminate straight men mistaken for, 71–75, 80–82, 86; effeminate straight men rejecting advances from, 85; femininity and, 3, 213–14, 255–57; gender normativity politics and, 87; hegemonic masculinity and, 228–29; in krewes, 195, 198–202; masculinity and, 3, 32, 210–11; race and, 211, 217–18, 221; sex positioning hierarchy and, 263–64, 270, 273; "straight-acting," 213, 221; traits associated with, 72–73. *See also* Black gay men; bottom-shaming; gay Asian drag queens; Latinx queer men; sex positioning
"gaystreaming," drag performance as, 197
gender: bodies and, 107–8, 145; breasted men experimenting with, 132–36, 138–39; Butler on, 226; drag queens exploring, 216; drag queens reinforcing notions of, 214–15; effeminate straight men's expression of, 80–84; egalitarianism, 283; family and, 307–8; fluidity, 1, 2; gender identity and expression of, 117; heteronormativity and, 226–27; Indigenous categories of, 90, 93; Latinx queer men moving beyond binary of, 242–44; as learned, 185–86; malleability of, 110; nature and nurture views of, 117–18; normativity politics, 87; poststructuralist challenges to essentialism of, 31–32; queer theory and, 6; radical faeries debating, 300–301; religion and expectations of, 290–91; scholarship on, 3; "single exception" theories and, 123–24; social constructionist approach to, 6; social institutions and, 307; toys and, 2; 2SQ and, 94; untethering sex from, 2; work and, 307–8. *See also* men; women

*Gender as Soft Assembly* (Harris, A.), 55
gender crossing rituals, in religion, 299–300
Gender Development Program, CNMC, 315–16
gender editing, 325–26
gender-expansive children, 13, 47, 49–50; bullying of, 66; cisgender heterosexual boys incorporating femininity, 66–68; femininity and transgender boys, 62; femininity and transgender girls, 63–65; future of, 68–69; gender resilience and, 67; harassment of, 65; identifying, 60–61; male femininities and, 56–58; masculinity and transgender boys, 59–62; nurture/culture and, 60; pronouns and, 55–56, 59; second-wave feminism and, 66; social transition and, 58–59; transgender children and, 57–65; violence against, 63–64. *See also* parents of gender-nonconforming boys
gender identity: breasted men and, 129; *Dear Masculinity* comic exploring, 112–14; gender expression and, 117; non-binary, 1, 121–23; Serano on, 116–17, 119–20
gender inequality: bodies and, 108; complexities of systemic, 15; modern, 3; religion reinforcing, 299; "stalled revolution" and, 2
gender inversion model of homosexuality, 86
gender performativity, 185–86; context of Latinx queer men and, 236–37, 241–42; expectations and, 235–36; Latinx queer men and, 229–30, 232–36
gender resilience, 67
gender studies, changing landscape of, 1–2
gender transition, 13, 107, 109; *Dear Masculinity* comic exploring, 112–14; male femininities in, 119; parents of gender-nonconforming boys and, 324
*Gender Trouble* (Butler), 43

generic ads marketing Botox for men, 148–52, *149–51*. *See also* Botox advertisements for men
*The Gentrification of the Mind* (Schulman), 40
"Get Your Freak On," 265
Gilley, Brian, 93
Gilman, Sander, 146
"girlboys," 67–68
glass closet, effeminate straight men and, 75, 84–86
goddess worship, of radical faeries, 292, 300–301
"Goodbye to All That" (Morgan), 41
goths, 76
Greece, effeminacy in ancient, 22–23, 26–27
Greene, Richard, 66
grief: fathers and, 358; funerals, male femininities and, 311–13; heteronormativity and, 14
Grindr, 269
gynarchism, "The Effeminist Manifesto" on, 35
gynecomastia, 126–27, 131, 140n11

Haiken, Elizabeth, 128, 146, 152
hair maintenance, Latinx queer men and, 239
Halberstam, J. Jack, 1, 9, 10, 32, 120, 280, 347, 359
Hale, Sadie E., 222
Halperin, David, 4, 212, 214, 218, 222
Halstead, Ara, 68
Haraway, Donna, 110
Harris, Adrienne, 55
Harris, Kamala, 3
Hart, Molly, 190
Hay, Harry, 292, 294–300. *See also* radical faeries
hazing: among firefighters, 342–43; fraternity, 207. *See also* violence
Heath, Melanie, 349

hegemonic femininity, 228, 245
hegemonic masculinity: defining, 228; effeminacy and, 12, 22, 26; fathers and, 319, 320; gay men and, 228–29; heterosexuality and, 256; Latinx queer men and, 229–30, 234, 243–44; polyamorous men and, 285–86; sex positioning and, 229; societal expectations of, 256; unattainability of, 244
Hennen, Peter, 298
"hetero-male imitation," radical faeries and, 295, 297
heteronormativity: athleticism and, 51–54; bottom-shaming and, 276; effeminate straight men and, 83, 87–88; gender and, 226–27; grief and, 14; latent homosexuality and, 87; Latinx queer men and expectations of race and, 233–34; sex positioning and, 227; "single exception" theories and, 123–24; 2SQ and, 98–99
heterosexuality: assumptions of, 227; effeminate straight men signaling, 82–83; hegemonic masculinity and, 256; privilege of, 83–84, 86. *See also* cisgender heterosexual men; polyamorous men
"Hey Man" (Dansky), 41
Hinduism, 290
*The History of Sexuality, Volume 2* (Foucault), 22
Hochschild, Arlie Russel, 2
Hoffman, Philip Seymour, 212–13
Hokowhitu, Brendan (Ngāti Pūkenga), 99
homophobia: Christianity and, 295; conceptual development of, 84; declining significance of, 74; effeminate straight men as targets of, 87; effeminate straight men disavowing, 85; as homosexuality indicator, 83–85; internalized, 84–86; 2SQ and, 95

homosexuality: in Christianity, 291; effeminacy and, 21, 23–25, 28–33, 82; effeminate straight men and repressed, 83–86; Effeminists on, 19; gender inversion model of, 86; gender normativity politics and, 87; homophobia as indicator of, 83–85; latent, 87; in Latin culture, 24; McCarthyism on "security risk" of, 25; parents of gender-nonconforming boys and, 315
Hondagneu-Sotelo, Pierette, 349
hormones, transgender people and, 61, 123
hybrid masculinities: cisgender heterosexual men and, 74; fathers and, 352

Iatmul, 290
*Imagining Masculinities* (Pascoe and Bridges), 365
Immergut, Matthew, 128
inclusive masculinity theory, 74
*Indigenous Men and Masculinities* (Innes and Anderson, K.), 99
Indigenous people: affective exchange in writing by, 97; "berdache" terminology and, 90–93; colonial masculinity and, 99; dreaming and, 101–3; gender categories of, 90, 93; radical faeries and culture of, 293. *See also* Two-Spirit, queer Indigenous
Innes, Robert Alexander (Plains Cree, Cowessess First Nation), 99
institutions, male femininities and social, 307–10
internalized homophobia, 84–86
intersectionality: femininity stereotypes and, 48–49; male femininities and, 12
Intersections of Race and Sexuality project, 230–31
intersex people: femininity, masculinity and, 10; gynecomastia and, 126–27; interviewing, 129–30

intimacies, of male femininities, 255–58
"it" pronoun, 368

Jack'd, 269
Jacobs, Sue Ellen, 295
jealousy, polyamory and, 283
Jenner, Caitlyn, 3
Joe's Bar, 189–92
*Johnny Appleseed* (Whitehead), 95–103
Johns, Michelle Marie, 231
Johnson, Marsha P., 41
joy, drag performance and, 257
*Junior*, 168, 169, 171

Khanyezi, Amanda, 176
Kim Chi, 220
Kimmel, Jimmy, 32
Kimmel, Michael, 24, 146
King, Larry (Latisha), 63–64
Klinefelter syndrome, 127, 129, 135
Knoebel, John, 12, 18–19, 35–44. *See also* "The Effeminist Manifesto" (Dansky, Knoebel, Pitchford)
Krewe of Apollo, 195, 197–201, 204
Krewe of Divas, 204
Krewe of Yuga, 196
krewes: all-inclusive, 195; amateur/professional drag performance boundaries among, 204–6; drag performance and, 199–202, 204; LGBTQ, 195, 198–202; in masque balls, 194; parents and, 202–4; royalty among, 200. *See also* Mardi Gras; masque balls
Krieger, Nick, 55, 61, 68
*kwidó* (Tewa Two-Spirit) tradition, 295

Lafait, Capucine, 173
Lambda Literary Awards, 90–92
Lamont, Michèle, 197
Lancaster, Roger N., 24
Langendoerfer, Kaitlyn Barnes, 128
latent homosexuality, 87

Latin culture: homosexuality in, 24; machismo and, 239, 245
Latinx queer men, 14, 187; activo/pasivo sex positioning and, 229, 233, 237; bisexuality and, 233–34; class and, 231; contextual gender performativity and, 236–37, 241–42; contradictory behavior among, 232–35; femininity and, 232, 235–36, 238–42, 245; gender binary and, 242–44; gender performativity and, 229–30, 232–36; hair maintenance and, 239; hegemonic masculinity and, 229–30, 234, 243–44; on ideal men, 232–33; on liberation from masculinity, 238–40; machismo and, 239, 245; male femininities and, 226; race and heteronormativity expectations of, 233–34; on self-actualization through femininity, 240–42; sex positioning and, 229–30, 233, 237–38, 243, 246; study methods for, 230–31. *See also* race
laws, on pregnancy, 167
Lee, Erica Violet (Cree), 92
Lee Mingwei, 166, 167, 172–78, *173, 175,* 181–82
Lepault, Sofie, 173
"lesbian relationships," bottom-shaming and, 270
lesbians, 115; Black, 239–40, 272; female masculinities and, 6; gender normativity politics and, 87; in krewes, 195, 198–202; in masque balls, 201–2; Radicalesbians, 41, 42
Letiecq, Bethany, 351
Levine, Martin P., 25
LGBTQ krewes, 195, 198–202. *See also* krewes
lifestyle, "The Effeminist Manifesto" on, 38
Loe, Meika, 128, 146–47
Log Cabin Republicans, 213
London molly houses, 29–30
loneliness, Black gay men and, 259–61

Longhurst, Robyn, 127
Lorde, Audre, 105n44

machismo, Latin culture and, 239, 245
Madonna, 214
makeup: cosmetic effeminacy and, 27; drag performance and, 98, 190, 200; effeminate straight men and, 76–77; femininity and, 48; 2SQ and, 96–98, 101
Malcolm X, 266
"male" bodies, drag kings and, 9–10
"male crossdressers," 116
male femininities: assumptions of, 8; attributes of, 76–79; benefits of, 367; bottom-shaming and, 264–65; Brotox and repudiation of, 162–63; cheerbois and, 10, 252; cisgender heterosexual boys incorporating femininity and, 66–68; cisgender heterosexual men and, 7, 47; concept of, 4–7; conceptual problems with, 280–81; configuring, 47–50; deconstructing, 7–11; defining, 75, 279–80; discursive, 286–87; drag queens and, 193–94; effeminacy and, 75; embodied, 107–11, 286–87; female masculinities compared to, 3–4; feminism and, 365–67; funerals and, 311–13; future projects on, 367–68; gay, 212–14, 222–23; gay Asian drag queens and, 212; gender-expansive children and, 56–58; in gender transition, 119; hiding and suppressing, 311; historicizing, 17–19; intersectionality and, 12; intimacies of, 255–58; Latinx queer men and, 226; male pregnancy and, 165–66, 171, 172, 177–78, 181; in masque balls, 200–201; metrosexuals and, 145–46; non-binary gender identity and, 121–23; performing, 185–88; pleasures of, 366; polyamorous men and, 281–87; queer theory approach to, 7–8; race and, 7, 245; radical faeries recognizing, 298; Serano on, 118–19; social constructionist approach to, 5–6, 8; social institutions and, 307–10; as

spirituality among radical faeries, 290–93, 301–2; survival and, 61; testosterone and, 61; time and place forming concept of, 48; transcending, 68–69; transgender children and, 57–58; in transgender men compared to cisgender men, 121; 2SQ and, 95–97; violence targeting, 64; women practicing, 4
Male Goddess Movement, 291
male pregnancy, 13, 107, 108; in art installations, 166, 172–78, *173*, *175*, 181–82; backlash to, 178–80; case study of, 172–78, *173*, *175*; C-sections and, 168, 171, 181; definition of, 167; ectopic pregnancy compared to, 174; emotions in, 179; femininity and, 180–81; male femininities and, 165–66, 171, 172, 177–78, 181; in movies and television, 166, 168–72, *169*, 181; mpreg and, 166, 170–71; race and, 176–78; social media and, 180; as surrogacy, 179–80; transgender men and, 178–80; on YouTube, 175–78
Male Principle, "The Effeminist Manifesto" on, 37
male supremacy, "The Effeminist Manifesto" on, 35
"man boobs," 125. *See also* breasted men
*Manhood in America* (Kimmel, M.), 24
*The Man Show*, 32
Mardi Gras, 187; amateur/professional drag performance boundaries at, 204–6; background of, 194–95; Carnival drag performance at, 196; family participation in, 202–4; in Mobile, 195; raids during, 196; research methods for, 197–98; respect for drag performance at, 197, 206–7; social relations of, 202–4. *See also* masque balls
Martin, Trayvon, 340
Marxism, 292
*Masculindians* (McKegney), 99–100
masculinity: alternative, 212, 222; athleticism and, 152, 156; Black gay men and idolization of, 264; bodies and, 145–46; Botox ads for men with hypermasculine tropes and images, 152–56, *154–56*; Botox and, 147; breasted men and, 135, 138; "casual," 77–78; childcare and, 351–55; colonial, 99; compensating and firefighter, 335–36; condoning and firefighter, 336–38; "crisis" of, 146, 157; crying and, 356, 358; drag kings and, 251; "The Effeminist Manifesto" on, 36–38, 43; emotional expression of fathers and, 356–58; eroticized, 211; fathers reinforcing normative, 322–23; femininity embodied alongside, 7, 367; in firefighter brotherhood, 330–32, 342–44; fitness and, 51–54; gay men and, 3, 32, 210–11; hybrid, 74, 352; increasing patterns of, 2–3; intersex people and, 10; Latinx queer men on liberation from, 238–40; men decoupled from, 6, 9; men rejecting, 4–5; metrosexuals and, 145–46; Muslim Other and, 282; as normal, 18; passing and firefighter, 334–35; penile implants and, 146; performing, 186; questioning and firefighter, 338–39; Serano on, 117; sex positioning and, 271–74; soapboxing and firefighter, 339–41; "soft-boiled," 349; subordinate, 279; testosterone and, 108; toxic, 12; transgender boys and, 59–62; Viagra and, 146. *See also* female masculinities; hegemonic masculinity
masoch-eonism, "The Effeminist Manifesto" on, 37, 43
Mason, Troy, 176
masque balls: amateur/professional drag performance boundaries and, 204–6; audience at, 202–4; definition of, 194; of Krewe of Apollo, 199–201; krewes in, 194; lesbians in, 201–2; male femininity in, 200–201; of Order of Osiris, 201–2; parents at, 202–4; race and, 201; royalty in, 200; social relations of, 202–4. *See also* Mardi Gras

Mastroianni, Marcello, 169–70
Mattachine Society, 292
Mayers, Lester Eugene, 256, 259–61
McCarthyism, on homosexuality as "security risk," 25
McInerney, Brandon, 64
McKegney, Sam (settler), 99–100
Meacham, Donny, 274
Meadow, Tey, 325
memes, bottom-shaming, 273–74, 275
men: aging and bodies of, 128; beauty practices of, 128; body self-care of, 143; breasted, 13; cosmetic surgery and, 128; defining, 49; "The Effeminist Manifesto" on oppression of effeminate, 36–39; masculinity decoupled from, 6, 9; masculinity rejected by, 4–5; objectification of bodies of, 127–28. *See also* Botox advertisements for men; cisgender heterosexual men; fathers/fatherhood; gender; Latinx queer men; male femininities; male pregnancy; polyamorous men
men's beauty salons, 128
Menvielle, Edgardo, 315–16
Messerschmidt, James, 282
Messner, Michael A., 348–49
metrosexuals, 71, 79, 87, 145–46
Million, Dian, 97
Misaki, Adam, 175
misogyny: of effeminacy terminology, 21; gay male femininity resisting, 222; trans-, 13, 119
"mistaken for gay" incidents, 71–75, 80–82, 86
Mobile, Mardi Gras in, 195
mollies, 23, 29
molly houses, London, 29–30
Monacan Volunteer Fire Department, 330–44
monogamy, radical faeries and, 298
Moore, Mignon, 239–40, 272
moral effeminacy, 27, 28
Morgan, Robin, 41

Morgensen, Scott, 90–91, 296–97
*Mother Camp* (Newton), 17–18
mothers: childcare from fathers compared to, 354–55; of gender-nonconforming boys doing research, 321. *See also* families; parents; parents of gender-nonconforming boys
movies and television, male pregnancy in, 166, 168–72, *169*, 181
*Moynihan Report*, 266
mpreg, 166, 170–71
Muñoz, José Esteban, 218
"Muriel Rukeyser" (Rich), 42
Muslim Other, masculinity and, 282
*My Daughter He* (Waldron), 62
mysticism, femininity and, 291

*National Geographic*, 55
National Women's Studies Association, 252
naturalness, Botox advertisements for men and, 151–52
nature, gender and sexuality and, 117–18
*naven* ritual, 290
negotiations, of parents of gender-nonconforming boys, 325–26
neo-paganism, 293
New Age movements, 293
*Newsweek*, 165, 179–80
Newton, Esther, 17–19, 196, 214–15
*New York Times*, 42, 68, 83
Ngo, Thao, 175
*Nina Here Nor There* (Krieger), 55, 68
Nixon, Lindsay (Cree-Métis-Saulteaux), 92
non-binary gender identity, 1, 121–23
Núñez de Balboa, Vasco, 93
nurture: fathers and, 349, 354; gender and sexuality and, 117–18; transgender children and, 60

Obama, Barack, 346
objectification: bodies and, 109; of men's bodies, 127–28; of women's bodies, 139
object-OBJECT consciousness, 298

Ojeda, Tomas, 222
openness, polyamory and, 284
oppositional sexism, 118–19
Order of Osiris, 195, 197–98, 201–2
Orientalist tropes, gay Asian drag queens and, 220
other-centeredness, 283–84

"pansy craze," 24
parents, 14–15; amateur/professional drag performance boundaries and, 204–6; at masque balls, 202–4. See also families; fathers/fatherhood; mothers
parents of gender-nonconforming boys: acceptance of, 321–22, 326–27; activism of, 327; blame game and, 323–24; class and, 309, 317, 327; concerns of, 314–15; "corrective treatment" and, 323; on different kinds of boys, 324–25; emotional labor of, 325; on femininity in play and dress, 318–19; gender editing and, 325–26; gender transition and, 324; homosexuality and, 315; negative initial reactions of, 320–21; negotiations and boundary work of, 325–26; normative masculinity reinforced by, 322–23; online community for, 315–16; on "phase" expectations, 319–20; as radical translators, 327; research by, 321; stories from, 316–17; terminology for, 315
pariah femininities, 282
Pascoe, C. J., 268, 288, 365
passing, firefighters and, 334–35
patriarchy: bottom-shaming and, 263; "The Effeminist Manifesto" on, 35–36, 39, 43; flexibility of, 352; harms caused by, 56; new fatherhood redefining, 349
PeeWee Hymen, 251–52
Pelosi, Nancy, 3
penile implants, 146

performing male femininities, 185–88. See also drag performance; gender performativity
personal protective equipment (PPE), 337
Pilgrim, David, 268
"pink boys," 68
Pitchford, Kenneth, 12, 18–19, 35–44. See also "The Effeminist Manifesto" (Dansky, Knoebel, Pitchford)
place, in social constructionism, 48, 74
police brutality, 340
political effeminacy, 26–27
politics: firefighters and, 333, 334, 340; gender normativity, 87; of radical faeries, 292
"polyamorist" identity, 286
polyamorous men, 255; acceptance of, 287; digital subcultures of, 282–83; femininity and, 257–58; hegemonic masculinity and, 285–86; jealousy and, 283; judgment of, 285; male femininities and, 281–87; masculinity and, 284–85; other-centeredness and, 284; perceptions of, 284–85; "polyamorist" identity and, 286
polyamory, 14; acceptance of, 287; communication, openness and, 284; concept of, 281; digital subcultures of, 282–83; jealousy and, 283; judgment of, 285; marginalization of, 282; other-centeredness, 283–84; second-wave feminism and, 283
*POP! The First Human Male Pregnancy* (art installation), 166, 172–78, *173*, *175*
poststructuralism, gender essentialism challenged by, 31–32
"powder puff football," 196, 207
PPE (personal protective equipment), 337
pregnancy: cisgender women and, 167; definition of, 166; ectopic, 174; laws on, 167. See also male pregnancy
*Priscilla, Queen of the Desert*, 199
privilege, of heterosexuality, 83–84, 86

probationary firefighters, 337–39
pronouns: gender-expansive children and, 55–56, 59; "it," 368; they/them, 1, 368; transgender children and, 59
prostitution, 30
protest, drag performance as, 195–96
providers, fathers as, 353–54
pseudogynecomastia, breasted men and, 126
Pyne, Jake, 323

queer settler colonialism, 296–97
queer theory, 1; binaries destabilized by, 10–11; fluidity and, 49, 50; on gay men and masculinity, 210–11; gender and, 6; on male femininities, 7–8; sexual relations and, 6
questioning, firefighters and, 338–39

*Rabbit Test*, 169–71
race: in Botox advertisements for men, 148–49, 153, 156, *156*, 157, 163; drag performance and, 194; firefighters and, 338, 340–41; gay Asian drag queens and, 219–20; gay men and, 211, 217–18, 221; Latinx queer men and expectations of heteronormativity and, 233–34; male femininities and, 7, 245; male pregnancy and, 176–78; masque balls and, 201; police brutality and, 340. *See also* Asian drag queens; Black gay men; Latinx queer men
racism, against gay Asian drag queens, 211, 217
radical cheerleading, 14; admiration for, 249; cheerbois and, 251–52; cisgender women and, 251; concept and aims of, 250–51; mainstream cheerleading compared to, 250
Radicalesbians, 41, 42
radical faeries, 14; androgyny and, 297, 299; Christianity's oppressiveness and, 299, 302–3; femininity and, 257; gender crossing rituals of, 299–300; gender debates of, 300–301; goddess worship of, 292, 300–301; "hetero-male imitation" and, 295, 297; history of, 293–94; Indigenous culture and, 293; male femininities as spirituality among, 290–93, 301–2; male femininities recognized by, 298; monogamy and, 298; politics of, 292; queer settler colonialism and, 296–97; rituals of, 294; sanctuaries of, 292, 301; sissy kids and, 294–95, 303; spiritual awakenings of, 299–300; subject-SUBJECT consciousness and, 297–99; transgender women in, 301; 2SQ traditions and, 295–97
radical translators, parents of gender-nonconforming boys as, 327
"Raising Girlboys" (Ehrensaft), 67–68
*Raising My Rainbow* (Duran), 68
Raising My Rainbow blog, 322
*Real Men Don't Eat Quiche*, 31
reconstructive surgery, 146
*Redstockings Manifesto*, 41
Reilly, Andrew, 229, 236
religion: gender crossing rituals in, 299–300; gender expectations in, 290–91; gender inequality reinforced by, 299; Sisters of Perpetual Indulgence and, 291–92. *See also* Christianity; radical faeries
respect, for drag performance, 197, 206–7
responsibility, of fathers, 346–48, 352–55
Rich, Adrienne, 42
Riggs, Damien W., 179
Rippon, Adam, 51
Risman, Barbara, 308
Rivera, Sylvia, 41
*The Rocky Horror Picture Show*, 202
Rogers, Robbie, 51
Roscoe, Will, 296
Roy, Kevin, 351
royalty, in masque balls, 200

*Ru Paul's Drag Race,* 197, 220
Rupp, Leila, 195

Salcedo, Veronica B., 228
Sam, Michael, 51
sanctuaries, radical faerie, 292, 301
Sanders, Deion, 156, *156,* 157
Schacht, Steven, 215
Schippers, Mimi, 226, 228, 230–31, 237, 245
Schulman, Sarah, 40
Schumacher, Joel, 212–13
Schwalbe, Michael L., 359
Schwarzenegger, Arnold, 168–71, *169*
second-wave feminism: "The Effeminist Manifesto" influenced by, 41; gender-expansive children and, 66; polyamory and, 283
self-actualization, femininity for, 240–42
sentimental movement, 30–31
Serano, Julia, 107; on female masculinity, 120–21; on femininity, 117–19, 123; on gender identity, 116–17, 119–20; on hormones and transgender people, 123; on male femininities, 118–19; on male femininities as part of gender transition, 119; on male femininities in cisgender and transgender men, 121; on masculinity, 117; on nature and nurture views of gender and sexuality, 117–18; on non-binary gender identity and male femininities, 121–23; on "single exception" theories, 123–24; writings of, 115–16
sex: assumptions of, 8; malleability of, 110; physical traits and, 8; untethering gender from, 2
sexism: "The Effeminist Manifesto" on, 35; Effeminists on, 19; femininity of transgender girls and, 63; oppositional and traditional, 118–19
sex positioning: activo/pasivo, 229, 233, 237; Black gay men and bottom-shaming, 14, 262–76; femininity and, 236, 237–38, 271–74; hegemonic masculinity and, 229; heteronormativity and, 227; hierarchy of, 263–64, 270, 273; Latinx queer men and, 229–30, 233, 237–38, 243, 246; masculinity and, 271–74; presumptions with, 271–73; terminology in, 231; top-shaming and, 270; "true tops" and, 273–74; versatiles in, 263; "verse" men and, 227, 230, 238. *See also* bottom-shaming
sexuality: of effeminate straight men, 80–84; malleability of, 110; nature and nurture views of, 117–18; "single exception" theories and, 123–24; 2SQ and, 94. *See also specific types*
sexual jealousy, polyamory and, 283
sexual pleasure, from breasted men wearing bras, 135–36
sexual relations, queer theory and, 6
Shah, Nayan, 211
SIDS (Sudden Infant Death Syndrome), 358
Silverstein, Louise B., 360
Sinfield, Alan, 23–24
"single exception" theories, 123–24
sissy kids, radical faeries and, 294–95, 303
Sisters of Perpetual Indulgence, 291–92
"slash," 171
*A Slightly Pregnant Man,* 169–70
"small ts," 57–58
"snap judgments," 72
soapboxing, firefighters and, 339–41
social constructionism: on gender, 6; on male femininities, 5–6, 8; time and place in, 48, 74
social institutions, male femininities and, 307–10
social media, male pregnancy and, 180
social transition, transgender children and, 58–59
"soft-boiled" masculinity, 349
somatic effeminacy, 27–28
*Spaces between Us* (Morgensen), 90–91

sperm donors, fathers compared to, 354
spin class, 51–54
spirituality: mysticism, femininity and, 291; neo-paganism and, 293; New Age movements and, 293; radical faeries and awakenings of, 299–300; radical faeries and male femininities as, 290–93, 301–2; Sisters of Perpetual Indulgence and, 291–92. *See also* radical faeries; religion
"stalled revolution," gender inequality and, 2
STAR (Street Transvestite Action Revolutionaries), 41
*Star Trek: Enterprise*, 169–70
stereotypes: of Black women, 265–66; gay Asian drag queens and, 218–19, 222; oppression of, 72
Stokes, Ronald, 266
Stonewall rebellion, 25
StraightActing.com, 32
"straight-acting gays," 213, 221
"straight camp," 28
Street Transvestite Action Revolutionaries (STAR), 41
subject-SUBJECT consciousness, 297–99
subordinate masculinities, 279
Sudden Infant Death Syndrome (SIDS), 358
Sufi Islam, 290
suicide, 311
surrogacy, male pregnancy as, 179–80
survival, male femininities and, 61

tantra, 290
Taylor, Peter Lane, 143
Taylor, Verta, 195
*Tearoom Trade* (Humphrey), 17
technology, bodies and, 110
television and movies, male pregnancy in, 166, 168–72, *169*
Tengan, Ty P. Kāwika (Kanaka Maoli), 99

testosterone, 8, 9, 49; male femininities and, 61; masculinity and, 108
Tewa Two-Spirit *(kwidó)* tradition, 295
Thatcher, Margaret, 3
*Theory & Society*, 279
"theybies," 69
"they/them" pronouns, 1, 368
third-wave feminism, 283, 366
Thompson, Edward H., 128
Thompson, Emma, 168, *169*
"Throw That Boy Pussy," 262, 265
time, in social constructionism, 48, 74
tomboys, female masculinities and, 87
topping. *See* sex positioning
top-shaming, 270
toxic masculinity, 12
toys, gender and, 2
traditional sexism, 118–19
transgender people: "The Effeminist Manifesto" on, 43–44; gender transition and, 13, 107, 109, 112–14, 119; hormones and, 61, 123; increasing rates of, 246; 2SQ compared to, 100
transgender children: femininity and transgender boys, 62; femininity and transgender girls, 63–65; identifying, 60–61; male femininities and, 57–58; masculinity and transgender boys, 59–62; nurture/culture and, 60; pronouns and, 59; social transition and, 58–59; violence against, 63–64
transgender men: breasted men compared to, 139; femininity and, 109; male femininities in cisgender men compared to, 121; male pregnancy and, 178–80. *See also* male pregnancy
transgender women: feminism and, 65; in radical faeries, 301
transmisogyny, 13, 119
"transsexual," 116
"Trans-Woman's Manifesto" (Serano), 115
Trinneer, Connor, 170
"true tops," 273–74

Trumbach, Randolph, 23–24, 28–30
Trump, Donald, 346
Tuerk, Catherine, 315–16
TurboSpin, 51–54
"24/7 Dad" curriculum, 352
Two-Spirit, queer Indigenous (2SQ), 13, 50; "berdache" terminology and, 90–93; colonial masculinity and, 99; decolonization and, 103; dreaming and, 101–3; erotic sovereignty and, 105n44; gender and, 94; heteronormativity and, 98–99; history of, 92–94; homophobia and, 95; in *Johnny Appleseed*, 95–103; *kwidó* (Tewa) tradition, 295; makeup and, 96–98, 101; male femininities and, 95–97; as medicine, 102–3; queer settler colonialism and, 296–97; radical faeries and traditions of, 295–97; sexuality and, 94; transgender people compared to, 100; violence against, 93, 96; Whitehead on, 91–92, 94, 100

Underwood, Carrie, 190
"Unloved" (Mayers), 256, 259–61
uptalk, 76

VanDerWerff, Todd, 212
Vardalos, Nia, 216–17
versatiles, in sex positioning, 263
"verse" men, 227, 230, 238
Viagra, 128, 138, 146
*Village Voice*, 42
violence: against drag queens, 189, 192; in families, 311; hazing and, 207, 342–43; male femininity as target of, 64; police brutality and, 340; suicide and, 311; against transgender children, 63–64; against 2SQ, 93, 96. *See also* bullying

Wakefield, Danny, 165, 178–80
Waldron, Candace, 62, 64–65

welfare programs, fathers and, 350
West, Candice, 185
West, Cheryl, 261
*When Men Are Pregnant*, 172–75, 178, 181
*Whipping Girl* (Serano), 115–16, 118–20
White, Edmund, 210
Whitehead, Joshua (Oji-Cree): decolonization and, 103; *Johnny Appleseed* by, 95–103; Lambda Literary Awards turned down by, 90–92; on 2SQ, 91–92, 94, 100
Wilde, Oscar, 23–24
*The Wilde Century* (Sinfield), 23–24
Williams, Shawna, 43–44
*William's Doll* (Zolotow), 66
Wolkomir, Michelle, 359
"Woman-Identified Woman" (Radicalesbians), 41
women: Botox advertisements for men compared to, 150–51; Botox advertisements for men rewarding, 153; Botox advertisements for men using suggestions from, 161; effeminacy and, 32; "The Effeminist Manifesto" on leadership of, 35–36; femininity decoupled from, 4, 6, 11, 110; as firefighters, 331; male femininity practiced by, 4; objectification of bodies of, 139. *See also* cisgender women; female masculinities; gender; lesbians; mothers
"women-less weddings," 196
Wong, Virgil, 166, 172–78, *173*, *175*, 181

*Xena: Warrior Princess*, 202

Yoshino, Kenji, 197
YouTube, male pregnancy on, 175–78

Zhang, Enrique, 220
Zimmerman, Don H., 185
Zolotow, Charlotte, 66

www.ingramcontent.com/pod-product-compliance
Lightning Source LLC
Chambersburg PA
CBHW020239030426
42336CB00010B/540